Conciliation – Compulsion – Conversion

British Attitudes Towards Indigenous Peoples 1763–1814

Readings in the Post / Colonial Literatures in English

72

Conciliation – Compulsion – Conversion

British Attitudes Towards Indigenous Peoples 1763–1814

Merete Falck Borch

Amsterdam - New York, NY 2004

The paper on which this book is printed meets the requirements of "ISO 9706:1994, Information and documentation - Paper for documents - Requirements for permanence".

ISBN: 90-420-1942-5 (Bound)

Printed in The Netherlands

Contents

Maps (after Chapter 4)

☙

Acknowledgements

For their inspiration, encouragement and constructive criticism in connection with the writing of this book, I would like to express my gratitude to Associate Professors Bruce Clunies Ross, Jørgen Sevaldsen and the late Niels Thorsen, all of the English Department at the University of Copenhagen. I would also like to thank Emeritus Professor Glyn Williams of Queen Mary and Westfield College, London, and Professor Henry Reynolds, formerly of James Cook University, Townsville, for their very helpful comments and suggestions for improvement, as well as Ann Langwadt for her invaluable editorial assistance. In addition, I would like to thank the Technical Editor of the Cross/Cultures Series, Dr. Gordon Collier, for his efforts and help, as well as Henning Serritslev for his expertise in drawing the maps.

Acknowledgements are also due to the Danish Research Agency for their publication grant and to the Royal Library for their reprographic assistance.

Introduction

THE STUDY OF THE HISTORY of the British Empire underwent considerable development in the course of the twentieth century. In the early decades, much research was focused on the role played by Britain in the shaping of the Empire and on the impact of British influence and British institutions in the colonies. After mid-century, a reaction against this anglocentric perception of imperial history set in, one that has sustained a long succession of revisionist studies. Ronald Robinson and John Gallagher, for example, repeatedly pointed to developments in the colonies as the cause of significant events in the history of the Empire.[1] Historians from the former colonies have strengthened this trend by exploring the history of their country or region from a local perspective. In conjunction with this, postcolonial theories have underscored the need to re-examine the impact of encounters with 'the Other' on European self-perception as well as on perceptions of other peoples and have thus contributed to questioning basic assumptions about the writing of European-based history.[2]

Now, at the turn of the millennium, this has been supplemented by accounts of British action and attitudes in relation to the Empire which have drawn on the insights gained from re-thinking imperial history but which have also re-directed attention to developments in Britain as significant factors in that history. Thus P.J. Cain and Anthony Hopkins, in their influential study, have

---

[1] For example, Ronald Robinson & John Gallagher with Alic Denny, *Africa and the Victorians: the Official Mind of Imperialism* (London: Macmillan & New York: St Martin's, 1961).

[2] See Bill Schwartz, "Conquerors of Truth: Reflections on Postcolonial Theory," in *The Expansion of England: Race, Ethnicity, and Cultural History*, ed. Schwartz (London & New York: Routledge, 1996): 9–31.

proposed to put "the metropolitan economy back at the centre of analysis," although they also acknowledge the significance of "peripheral interpretations" of the history of the Empire.[3] Similarly, C.A. Bayly's study of the Empire at the turn of the eighteenth to the nineteenth century, while placing far greater weight on developments outside Britain than does the work of Cain and Hopkins, also shows the importance of social and political factors within Britain.[4]

The present study, which centres on imperial relations with indigenous peoples, has a similar orientation. It is inspired by the history of the exploitation and dispossession of the original inhabitants of the settler colonies, a history that has received much attention in recent decades. What has more immediately prompted me to undertake this study has been the impression I have gained that such works show a tendency to merge the governments in the colonies with the government in London under the single label of "the British," although the preeminent focus has in fact been placed on the actions of the colonial governments. While it may, indeed, be difficult to distinguish between the two in terms of the policies pursued, this nevertheless obscures the fact that there were differences between them – that they worked under different conditions and were subject to differing influences. It thus seemed worth examining in detail the attitudes and policies of the imperial government in London in relation to indigenous peoples. Needless to say, this has not been prompted by any desire to accuse either colonial or imperial governments of the wrongs attached to the history of treatment of colonized peoples, or to exonerate them. Rather, the aim is to extend the understanding of one particular area of that history as a contribution to a better understanding of the whole issue of relations between colonizers and colonized. The focus on the actions and reactions of the British government means that relatively little is said about the role of the indigenous peoples in the formation of policies; it is important to stress, however, that this is due to the particular focus of the study and not to a lack of recognition of the equal significance of indigenous actions in shaping events.[5]

---

[3] P.J. Cain & Anthony G. Hopkins, *British Imperialism;* vol. 1: *Innovation and Expansion 1688–1914* (London & New York: Longman, 1993): 5–10.

[4] C.A. Bayly, *Imperial Meridian: the British Empire and the World 1780–1830* (London: Longman, 1989).

[5] The term 'indigenous' is used throughout this work to denote the peoples who lived in North America, Australia and Africa before the beginning of colonization. In the former two areas most of these peoples were hunters and gatherers; in the latter many were pastoralists. While there were – and are – a great many differences between these peoples, they all had in common the fact that they were firmly established on their land

My aim, then, is to study the development of attitudes among ministers and government officials in London towards the peoples who already inhabited the land on which British colonists settled. Particular attention is paid to the perception of the rights enjoyed by these peoples, how they should be protected, and how the colonial governments were perceived to handle relations with them. The area of study includes the colonies of North America, New South Wales and the Cape of Good Hope, the settler colonies possessed or acquired between the 1760s and the 1820s;[6] their different backgrounds and circumstances notwithstanding, they provide an opportunity for comparing attitudes towards different groups of people as well as for examining the development of attitudes over time.

The temporal scope of this study is somewhat wider than suggested by the title. The Royal Proclamation of 1763 marks the intensification of official interest in Indian affairs in North America, and the cession of the Cape Colony to Britain in 1814 signifies the end of the second British occupation of the Cape. However, in order fully to understand the developments occurring within that period of time, it has been necessary to go back to the effectual beginning of imperial involvement in Indian affairs in the 1750s as well as to include the climax of humanitarian influence in the Colonial Office in the 1830s. However, neither 1814 nor the 1830s constitutes a logical end-point for a study of official attitudes to indigenous peoples that continued to receive expression for as long as the imperial government was involved in the formation of policy towards them (usually until the colonies in question received some measure of self-government). Practical considerations have set the present limitations; it must remain for the future to bring the study to its logical conclusion.

'Attitudes' are an intangible object of study; in this case, the object of interest is an abstract concept of 'official attitudes' which can, I believe, be extracted from the documents produced at the Colonial Office and which can be seen as the foundation on which policy measures were based. For this reason

---

when the first Europeans arrived. The peoples of the various areas are referred to by the names which seem to be most commonly used (Indian, Aborigine/Aboriginal, Khoisan, Nguni), although it is recognized that in many cases these names are controversial. In some instances, names of distinct groups are used (Iroquois, Xhosa).

[6] Settler colonies are taken to refer to those territories in which large numbers of Europeans settled. Although many British also settled in the West Indies, they have been excluded, because the number of indigenous peoples had become so very small by the time the imperial government became seriously involved in the administration of the islands.

the attitudes of individuals as revealed in private papers and letters, although often very interesting, are not included. Despatches sent from London to the colonies form the basic source-material for the discussion presented in this study; while it is recognized that motives and intentions underlying the letters varied according to author and circumstances, I nevertheless believe that a detailed reading of a wide range of documents reveals basic assumptions about indigenous peoples and the policy adopted towards them. Manuscript records, chiefly from the Public Record Office, form the basis of the primary material, supplemented by printed records. Numerous quotations are included in the discussion in order to provide the reader with a sense of the language and style of the despatches and to give the full context of important statements.

Each of the areas examined here has been subjected to detailed study in the past. A large number of older works deal with British imperial policy towards the colonies as well as with the history of imperial administration; as indicated above, many recent studies focus on colonial history, including policy towards the indigenous peoples. Needless to say, it has been impossible to include all the secondary material that might be relevant to the present study, but an attempt has been made to select recent as well as older works so as to achieve a balanced view of the scholarship conducted within each geographical area.

Attitudes, even 'official' ones, are not shaped in isolation. For this reason, the development of government attitudes needs to be seen in the context of the general ideas and theories about indigenous people current during the period under examination. A large number of thinkers in Britain and beyond expressed their views on the peoples in the newly discovered parts of the world; these ideas are represented here in selection. While it is next to impossible to prove a connection between 'official' and more general attitudes, the developmental drift suggests such a connection.

In the first of the chapters that follow, an overview is presented of British expansion, especially in North America, before the 1750s, as well as of the governmental and administrative apparatus connected with the running of the colonies. The picture that emerges takes on clearer contours in keeping with the subject of the succeeding chapters; no claim is made to exhaustive treatment of British expansion or the domestic situation in Britain. Likewise, little attempt is made to enter into the controversies often surrounding these topics. The aim of the opening chapter is to establish a framework within which the details of government attitudes and policy can be discussed.

Chapters 2 to 4 examine the material relating to each of the geographical areas. Chapter 2 is concerned with government attitudes towards the Indians in the North American colonies between the 1760s and the 1780s, when the ending of the American War of Independence severed connections with a large number of the Indian tribes. Chapter 3 traces official attitudes to the Aboriginal peoples in what was to become New South Wales, beginning with the early planning of the colony and continuing through the first decade or so of its existence. Chapter 4 discusses government attitudes towards the various groups of indigenous peoples at the Cape during the British occupation around the turn of the century, though, as I mentioned above, cognizance is also taken of later developments. There is a certain incongruity in the fact that Chapter 2 deals with several distinct though geographically connected colonies, whereas the next two chapters examine in detail only one colony each. It has seemed reasonable to adopt this approach because Indian affairs during this period were conducted through two Crown officials and were thus viewed in London as a supra-colonial matter subject to unified consideration.

Chapters 5 and 6 discuss the development of legal and intellectual ideas concerning indigenous peoples, based on a selection of writings by legal and philosophical authors. Developments within each of the two fields are outlined and connections with government attitudes are suggested.

The discussion of imperial attitudes and policies over more than half a century and in three different contexts arguably offers a broader insight into the formation of such attitudes and policies than geographically and temporally more confined studies, because it reveals aspects which only become visible with time and distance. Furthermore, by placing this discussion in the context of contemporary intellectual thinking and theorizing, broader perspectives are suggested that encourage a more profound understanding of developments.

It is unquestionable that the creation of the British Empire brought suffering, loss and death to those who were colonized; and there is equally no doubt that colonization was to a large extent motivated and dominated by economic and strategic considerations whose primary aim was to encourage profitable trade and financial benefit for Britain. Yet discussions of the development of the British Empire that focus solely on such factors often seem to lack a dimension; the aim of the present study is to suggest further perspectives that may contribute usefully to our general understanding of how the Empire was shaped.

1 Colonial and Administrative Background

English expansion

ENGLISH OVERSEAS ACTIVITY in the modern era was spurred by a desire to partake in the rich trade with other parts of the world that was pioneered by the Portuguese and the Spanish in the fifteenth and sixteenth centuries. By the second half of the sixteenth century, the English, along with the Dutch and the French, were beginning to explore these possibilities, with English merchant companies (such as the Muscovy Company of 1553, the Levant Company of 1581, and the East India Company of 1600) establishing profitable contacts with the Near and Far East. Enterprising individuals were breaking the Portuguese monopoly on the slave trade between Africa and the Americas, and trading posts or factories were gradually established on the west coast of Africa, in India, and elsewhere.

In the western hemisphere, the Spanish were engaged in creating an empire for themselves, mainly in order to get hold of the vast amounts of precious metals found there, which they extracted by means of the forced labour of the indigenous inhabitants. Rumours of Spanish exploits and profits gradually aroused the interest of the English in that part of the world also. Apart from attempts by such men as Martin Frobisher and John Davis to find a northwest passage to Asia in the late sixteenth century, voyages of discovery were undertaken in the west, beginning with John Cabot in 1497, followed by John Rut in 1527 and Richard Hore in 1536, and culminating in the circumnavigation of the world by Francis Drake in 1577–80. Based on rights of discovery supposed to have been acquired by the English monarchs through such voyages, patents were granted towards the end of the century by Queen Elizabeth to the adventurous half-brothers Humphrey Gilbert and Walter Raleigh, with a view to establishing colonies in Newfoundland and Virginia respectively.[1]

Although unsuccessful, these ventures were in reality the beginning of English territorial expansion beyond the British Isles. Dreaming of gold and of valuable trade with local commodities or, failing that, with goods produced by settlers, merchants and others looking for profitable investments continued to make attempts at colonization until finally, in 1607, the first permanent settlement was established at Jamestown in Virginia by the Virginia Company. Slightly later, colonies were founded at St Kitts and Barbados – the beginnings of English settlement in the Caribbean, which was to play a significant role in the shaping of the British Empire. Thus, while expansion based on trading relations was beginning in the east, English domination through settlement was the pattern taking shape in the west. This duality, though not the geographical division, would continue to characterize the Empire throughout its existence.

Life in Virginia was precarious for many years; conflict with the original inhabitants of the area was a serious problem, as was the incompetence of the settlers, who had little experience of farming or other manual labour and little inclination towards hard work. Frequent disagreements among the leadership contributed to creating an unstable situation. On the other hand, the New England colonies, beginning in 1620, were marked by the religious determination of a small group of sectarians. The Puritans, many of them from exile in Holland, were hardworking and their settlements usually flourished quickly. In the course of the seventeenth century, other colonies were established along the east coast. Some were settled mainly by religious groups (Pennsylvania by Quakers; Maryland by Catholics); in others, such as Carolina, the economic motive was the most prominent one.[2] New York was ceded by the Dutch, joining the list of colonies in 1664.[3]

---

[1] Anthony McFarlane, *The British in the Americas 1480-1815* (London: Longman, 1994): ch. 1.

[2] See, for example, McFarlane, *The British in the Americas*, for an overview of developments in the colonies in America.

[3] Nothing further is said here of the Dutch in North America or of their relations to the Indians, as their presence was of brief duration and did not extend into the period under consideration in this study; but see, for example, Allen W. Trelease, "Dutch Treatment of the American Indian, with Particular Reference to New Netherland," in Howard

By the early eighteenth century, the British colonies in North America had become consolidated settlements along the coast and the immediate hinterland and were fast developing their own values and objectives. The goods produced, which were in high demand in Europe, became the basis of a vigorous trade which brought considerable wealth to the colonies; gradually merchants and government in Britain came to see the importance of the colonies to economic growth in Britain and tried through legislation such as the Navigation Acts to ensure that the American trade did not fall into other European hands.

Thanks mainly to economic success, favourable living conditions, and accelerated immigration, the colonies also experienced a high rate of population growth – by the middle of the century approximately one million Britons had settled in the Americas[4] – and adventurous colonists gradually began to spread further inland, where they came into contact with new and in some cases very strong Indian groups.

Relations with the American Indians

The encounter with the indigenous peoples of North America was of immense importance, right from the earliest settlements.[5] Initial relations with the Indians varied; at Jamestown two Englishmen were wounded in the first encounter, but the English were generally treated with hospitality by the Indians as they reconnoitered the shore, and the landing of the colonists at the site chosen for the settlement apparently went unopposed. However, within a month the Indians had attacked the settlement, and the early efforts of the colonists were concentrated on fortification.

Though it would thus seem that the Indians began to resist the presence of the settlers once their intention to stay became clear, the main chief of the area, Powhatan (or Wahunsonacock), initially tolerated the English, perhaps because, as Harry Porter suggests, he believed that they could be used as allies against groups threatening his hegemony.[6] Despite worsening relations and the in-

---

Peckham & Charles Gibson, ed. *Attitudes of Colonial Powers Toward the American Indian* (Salt Lake City: U of Utah P, 1969): 47–60.

[4] McFarlane, *The British in the Americas*, 154.

[5] See Map 1 for the approximate distribution of Indian groups at this time.

[6] Harry Culverwell Porter, *The Inconstant Savage: England and the North American Indian 1500–1660* (London: Duckworth, 1979): 286.

creasingly ruthless behaviour of the English, the Indians continued to supply the settlers with corn even beyond their capacity.[7]

Eventually even Powhatan lost faith in the English; in his account of the settlement from 1610–11, William Strachey related that Powhatan was worried that the English would take his land.[8] In 1622 and again in 1644 the Indians attacked and killed many of the settlers under the leadership of Powhatan's brother, Opechancanough. Both attacks were followed by large-scale acts of revenge by the settlers.

In New England, initial relations were marked by mutual suspicion, with an armed struggle on one of the first days after the landing. It would seem that the settlers from the *Mayflower* who settled at what became Plymouth, by accident chose the area of a group of people who had been wiped out by disease (introduced by visiting European ships), so that their initial settlement offered no immediate threat to anyone.[9] The entire Indian population of New England seems to have fallen victim to disease in the previous years. Eventually, friendly relations developed with some of the neighbouring tribes and open hostilities with others, leading to war with the Pequot in 1636.[10]

Early policy towards the Indians was usually laid down by the colonial assemblies, though occasionally the Virginia Company, for example, would issue directions to be pursued in this field. In Jamestown the assembly ordered in 1620 that everyone trading with the Indians were to deal fairly with them; it was also specified that no settler was to steal from them (on penalty of a fine or whipping). Hanging was the punishment for providing the Indians with wea-

---

[7] Edmund Sears Morgan, *American Slavery, American Freedom: the Ordeal of Colonial Virginia* (New York: W.W. Norton, 1975): ch. 4. See also, generally, Wilcomb Edward Washburn, *Red Man's Land/White Man's Law* (Norman & London: U of Oklahoma P, 1995), part 2.

[8] Porter, *The Inconstant Savage*, 330.

[9] *The Inconstant Savage*, 428.

[10] The account presented by Alden T. Vaughan, *New England Frontier, Puritans and Indians 1620–1675* (Boston MA & Toronto: Little, Brown, 1965), of relations between Puritans and Indians has been much criticized. Thus Wilbur Jacobs sees Vaughan as "an apologist for the Puritans" in his "British-Colonial Attitudes and Policies toward the Indian in the American Colonies," in Peckham & Gibson, ed. *Attitudes of Colonial Powers*, 102, n14; Jacobs himself presents a more uniformly negative picture of Puritan attitudes towards the Indians (85), as does Francis Jennings, *The Invasion of America: Indians, Colonialism and the Cant of Conquest* (Chapel Hill: U of North Carolina P, 1976).

pons.[11] Thus a fine balance was aimed at between not antagonizing the Indians and protecting the settlement.

The 1622 attack changed this. Some at least claimed that now the settlers could justly wage war against the Indians and drive them off the land because the latter had shown their true colours. The Virginia Company swore revenge: "we must advise you to root out from being any longer a people, so cursed a nation, ungrateful to all benefits and uncapable of all goodness."[12]

A peace treaty was signed in 1646 when the bloodshed following the second attack had subsided. In this treaty, the successor of Opechancanough, Necotowance, ceded the area in which the colony was situated to the English; on the other hand, it was recognized that north of the colony was Indian land in which the English had no rights or powers.[13] Gradually, in subsequent years, relations with the Indians were brought under greater regulation, which included rules for the buying of Indian land, but as the settlers grew stronger the rights of the Indians were also increasingly ignored by individual colonists.

In New England, land was purchased on a systematic basis, although there is some debate about whether this was caused by expediency or principle.[14] As in Jamestown, purchases had to be validated by an official stamp. The New Englanders went further than the Virginians in incorporating groups of Indians in their communities; in the second half of the seventeenth century, villages were established for christianized Indians, although in general missionary efforts by the English were not overwhelming. Relations between Indians and Puritans were, however, seriously damaged by King Philip's War in 1675.[15]

It is commonly maintained that the most positive policy towards the Indians was formulated in Pennsylvania, granted as a proprietary colony to William Penn by Charles II in 1680. The Quakers' belief in the inherent equality of all men guided Penn's directives for dealing with the local Indians. He purchased land from them and kept records of these purchases, which were read again to the Indians at regular intervals in accordance with oral tradition.

---

[11] Porter, *The Inconstant Savage*, 413.

[12] *The Inconstant Savage*, 463–65.

[13] *The Inconstant Savage*, 516–17. Cf, however, Robert A. Williams Jr., *The American Indian in Western Legal Thought* (Oxford & New York: Oxford UP, 1990): 219, who mentions that Necotowance had to acknowledge that "his people held this reservation from the 'King's Majesty of England'."

[14] *The Inconstant Savage*, 489–91, and Jennings, *The Invasion of America*, 134–38.

[15] *The Inconstant Savage*, 528–30, and *The Invasion of America*, passim.

Settlers were prohibited from giving or selling alcohol to the Indians and the Indians were encouraged to bring their disagreements with the settlers directly before the governor. According to Urs Bitterli, the sincerity of the administrators explains why the first sixty years of the colony's existence met with no serious disturbances.[16]

Though variations were great, in most colonies there was the same pattern of relations with the Indians, from the first uncertain beginnings where efforts (not always successful) were made to avoid offending the Indians yet provide for the security of the settlement, through a period of mounting hostility and actual warfare, to the final phase in which the colonists had secured their position and were able to dictate the terms of coexistence with the Indians in the immediate vicinity of the settlements, a process that was made easier by the fact that these Indians were usually weakened by introduced diseases and cultural dispossession.[17]

Even at this stage, though, the Indians, especially those further inland, were not wholly without bargaining power, thanks to two factors of great significance in shaping the relationship between Indians and settlers in North America.

The first of these was the fur trade, which constituted an important means of profit for both parties. It was also recognized that trade was an important means of keeping the peace with the Indians in the frontier districts, where the encroachment of the settlers on new areas of Indian land continually endangered relations. The tendency of traders to cheat the Indians, however, in some cases countered the positive effects of the trade.

The second factor which ensured a certain balance in the relationship between Indians and settlers was the need among the English to maintain the

---

[16] Urs Bitterli, *Cultures in Conflict: Encounters between European and Non-European Cultures 1492–1800,* tr. Ritchie Robertson (*Alte Welt – neue Welt: Formen des europäisch–überseeischen Kulturkontakts vom 15. Bis zum 18. Jahrhundert*, 1986; Cambridge: Polity, 1989): 109–32. Cf, however, Francis Parkman, *The Conspiracy of Pontiac* (1870; London: Macmillan, 1899), vol. 1: 85–86, who somewhat deflates the reputation of the Quakers on this point. McFarlane, *The British in the Americas*, 76–83, generally presents a very negative picture of relations between settlers in the colonies and the Indians.

[17] See, for example, James H. Merrell, "'The Customes of Our Countrey': Indians and Colonists in Early America," in Bernard Bailyn & Philip D. Morgan, ed. *Strangers within the Realm: Cultural Margins of the First British Empire* (Chapel Hill & London: U of North Carolina P, 1991): 117–56.

friendship of at least some of the Indian groups so that they would fight as allies with them against that perpetual enemy, the French.

French interest in North America began with voyages of exploration in the early sixteenth century, which eventually resulted in the establishment of Quebec in 1608. The primary aim of this was to establish a trading post for the fur-trade, which was just then beginning to grow. A few years later, Jesuits and other missionary groups started to arrive, establishing missions which exerted a considerable influence among the large Indian population of the area.

The French settlement grew very slowly, but after 1663 when it came directly under royal control the French population started to increase at a greater rate.[18] By the second half of the seventeenth century regroupings among the Indians caused the fur-trade to move further west, and the French followed. Eventually they reached the Gulf of Mexico along the river systems of the Ohio and the Mississippi, west of the British colonies (see Map 2).

Whereas English relations with the Indians from the beginning were marked by the fact that they created relatively large settlements and thus wanted Indian land, French relations were shaped by the fact that trade was and remained their primary goal. As William Eccles and many other scholars have pointed out,[19] this necessitated friendly relations based on equality, since the French were wholly dependent on the Indians to provide the furs they required. As the fur-trade developed, the Indians also became dependent on it, especially as European firearms were used as payment and quickly became indispensable to their warfare. Missionary activity has also been identified as instrumental in shaping relations with the Indians.[20]

Due to their close involvement in the fur-trade, the French, especially the so-called *coureurs de bois*, came to know their Indian trading-partners well (perhaps to a larger extent than the English) and eventually adopted many Indian traits such as hardiness, ability to live off the land and, to the dismay of the missionaries, liberal attitudes towards sexual relations. Certain Indian practices (food and to some extent clothing) were readily adopted almost universally by the colonists.[21]

---

[18] William John Eccles, *The Canadian Frontier* (New York: Holt, Rinehart & Winston, 1969): 38.

[19] Eccles, *The Canadian Frontier*, 24.

[20] For example, Mason Wade, "The French and the Indians," in Peckham & Gibson, ed. *Attitudes of Colonial Powers*, 61–80.

[21] Eccles, *The Canadian Frontier*, 90–92.

The impact of the interdependence between settlers and Indians on French policy towards the latter was significant. Although it is often said that the French claimed sovereignty over, and ownership of the land in, their colonies, Eccles points out that in fact the French made claims to sovereignty against the other European nations but were careful to leave the matter open with the Indians. French expansion west- and southward spread the French very thinly and laid them open to attack from the Iroquois, so they had to be very cautious in their dealings with the Indians.

Nor, according to Eccles, did they try to maintain that the Indians in or around New France were French subjects; they were not even successful in subjecting the Indians to French law within the French colonies, a matter which was recognized as "extremely delicate" by the French Crown. Any attempt to force the Indians would most likely have jeopardized their friendship.[22]

It has become a commonplace that French relations with the Indians were better than those of the other colonizing powers. Thus Francis Parkman, for example, wrote in 1912: "Spanish civilization crushed the Indian; English civilization scorned and neglected him; French civilization embraced and cherished him."[23] Cornelius Jaenen is strongly opposed to this tradition, claiming that French attitudes towards and relations with the Indians were no different from or better than those of the other colonizing nations;[24] in any case, this kind of generalization would seem very easily to lead to a superficial understanding of actual relations. Yet the tradition is important because it reflects perceptions at the time. It was often observed by English colonists that the French appeared to have a better understanding of the Indians than they

---

[22] *The Canadian Frontier*, xiii, 77–78. Cornelius Jaenen paints a somewhat bleaker picture, stating that French practice in Canada was one of widespread legal and ecclesiastical discrimination against the Indians, Cornelius John Jaenen, "The Meeting of the French and Amerindians in the Seventeenth Century," in *Interpreting Canada's Past*, 2 vols., ed. J.M. Bumsted (Toronto: Oxford UP, 1986), vol. 1: 31–32.

[23] Quoted in John Harold Kennedy, *Jesuit and Savage in New France* (New Haven CT: Yale UP, 1950): 21. The quotation is repeated approvingly by Wade, "The French and the Indians," 61.

[24] Jaenen, "The Meeting of the French and Amerindians in the Seventeenth Century," 28. Cf John Richard Alden, *John Stuart and the Southern Colonial Frontier: A Study of Indian Relations, War, Trade and Land Problems in the Southern Wilderness 1754–1775* (1944; New York: Gordian, 1966): ch. 1, and J.A. Dickinson, "French and British Attitudes to Native Peoples in Colonial North America," *Storia Nordamericana* 4 (1987): 41–45, both of whom support the view that French attitudes and Indian relations were essentially no different from those of the British.

themselves did, and consequently that the Indians would rather trade with the French than with the English (or the Dutch).

Although the character of the relationship between the French and the Indians need not be further discussed here, it is important to note that military alliances between the two groups developed from the very beginning of contact. The main Indian allies of the French were the Huron and, after they were practically wiped out in the 1640s by the Iroquois, the Ottawa, the Algonkins and others.

The Iroquois formed a formidable barrier to the south and also prevented the English and Dutch traders in New England from moving further west in their search for furs; in order to maintain this position, it was vital for the Iroquois to keep up the supply of firearms on which they had become dependent to control the neighbouring tribes. The French and to a lesser extent the English and the Dutch were thus involved in, and partly the cause of, a complex power-struggle between the northern Indian tribes. The Indians, for their part, used the colonists to their own advantage, playing one nation against another and maintaining alliances only so long as these were to their advantage.[25]

By the beginning of the eighteenth century it was becoming clear to the British that the Indians were increasingly turning to the French as allies and trading partners. As pointed out by John Alden, this tendency was further strengthened by the fact that the British colonies were guided in their dealings with the Indians by conflicting aims and interests, whereas the French acted with greater unity under the control of royal governors (of whom there were only two: one in Louisiana and the other in Quebec).[26]

In the south, where white settlements had not developed very far inland by the 1750s, the British ability to offer goods at lower prices than the French maintained a certain balance of foreign influence among the Indians, if the trade was not mishandled. In the older colonies to the north, where settlers were beginning to move across the great mountain ranges of the Alleghenies and Appalachians and where relations with the Iroquois were not handled with sufficient care, the colonists had few friends among the Indians. In the far north, the longstanding trading relations between the Indians and the French determined the direction of Indian alliances. As a consequence of this situation, the French in North America were becoming stronger and were increasingly seen as a potential threat to the British possessions there.

[25] Eccles, *The Canadian Frontier*, xiii.

[26] Alden, *John Stuart and the Southern Colonial Frontier*, 4.

Britain in the eighteenth century[27]

The French presence in North America (as well as elsewhere around the world) became very important to the British in the eighteenth century. During the previous century the English had been preoccupied with internal political problems, but wars were conducted against Spain (in which Jamaica was acquired) and especially against the Dutch, who were seen as interfering in the profitable trade with the colonies. It was in the course of the three wars fought with the Dutch between 1652 and 1674 that New York was acquired. However, with the accession of William of Orange in 1688 to the English and Scottish thrones, the Dutch became allies of the British. William was engaged in constant war against the French and could count on British solidarity, since the French court had given refuge to the ousted King James II and his family. French royal absolutism came to represent everything the English had fought against in the revolutions of the seventeenth century; through continental alliances, Britain became deeply involved in the struggle against French expansionism in Europe.

This hostility came to dominate foreign policy throughout the eighteenth century, which, apart from a brief period of alliance in the 1720s, was punctuated by major wars with the French: the War of the League of Augsburg (fought as King William's War in North America) at the end of the seventeenth century; the War of the Spanish Succession 1702–13; the War of the Austrian Succession 1743–48; the Seven Years War 1756–63 (in North America, the French and Indian War 1755–60); the American War of Independence, which France entered in 1778 (Spain in 1779, Holland in 1780), and which ended in 1783; and, finally, the exhausting Revolutionary and Napoleonic Wars 1793–15.

British relations with the Spanish were also marked by tension. Because of their close alliance with France, the Spanish were involved in most of the hostilities mentioned above; but disputes about trade in the Caribbean and elsewhere also caused conflicts between the two nations alone, such as the War of Jenkins' Ear in 1739–44 and the Nootka Sound Crisis in 1790.

While Britain was not triumphant in all these wars, significant victories meant that Britain in the course of this century emerged as a considerable

---

[27] See Earl A. Reitan, *Politics, War and Empire: the Rise of Britain to a World Power* (Arlington Heights IL: Harlan Davidson, 1994) and Linda Colley, *Britons: Forging the Nation 1707–1837* (New Haven CT & London: Yale UP, 1992), for discussions of this period.

power in European affairs. The British also gained a dominant position in world affairs as the possession of overseas trading posts and colonies came to be seen as increasingly important and these were incorporated into British war strategies through the growing emphasis on and development of naval power as Britain's particular source of strength.

The transatlantic colonies were involved in all the wars of the eighteenth century but most particularly (apart from the War of Independence) in the Seven Years War, as its nickname "The Great War for Empire" indicates. The conquest of Quebec and gains in the Caribbean left Britain at its most powerful in North America at the end of the war, but in turn created a number of problems in relation to the British colonists there.

The almost complete removal of the French presence meant that the threat of attack from that quarter no longer served as a check on settler ambitions to move westward, thus greatly increasing the possibility of clashes with the Indians (as evidenced by Pontiac's War in 1763); it also increased the risk of the costly extension of British rule if the settlers were successful.

Disagreement between the mother country and the colonies about settler contributions to their own defence both during and after the war created a climate of tension. The British government was primarily concerned with repairing the economy after a long and expensive war which had caused considerable hardship at home. Determination that the colonies should contribute to this, combined with the desire to control trade and prevent smuggling, gave birth to the various Duty Acts which caused such violent reactions in the colonies, where ideas about political and personal liberty differed dramatically from views in government circles; eventually, open fighting erupted.

The controversy concerning the thirteen colonies and their loss in the ensuing war caused considerable political upheaval in Britain; as C.A. Bayly points out, other matters both overseas and in Britain in the decades before and after the war contributed to a general economic depression.[28] However, the impression created by numerous historians in the past that the British "lost interest" in overseas expansion and that there was a more or less complete break between the "first empire" of the American colonies and the "second one" emerging at the turn of the century has been rejected by many. Nor is it universally accepted that a reaction set in that prompted greater interest in expanding British trading

[28] C.A. Bayly, *Imperial Meridian: The British Empire and the World 1780–1830* (London: Longman, 1989): 2, 78–79.

power in Asia, as suggested by Vincent Harlow's famous hypothesis of a "swing to the east."[29]

It is rather more convincing to view the development of the Empire in the second half of the eighteenth century (as, indeed, in the first half) in the light of continuity and gradual development rather than sharp breaks, and policy concerning it as guided by pragmatism rather than in terms of a coherent plan for expansion.[30] Immediately after the War of Independence, the major imperial concern was the growing demand in Ireland for legislative independence; the situation of the East India Company repeatedly attracted attention, as did the need to find a viable solution to the government of the French and English population in Quebec. These large issues from opposite corners of the empire were addressed in the course of the 1780s and '90s, along with many lesser questions such as the dispatch of a fleet of convict-ships to New South Wales, disputes with Spain over the Falkland Islands and the northwest coast of America, the slave trade between Africa and the West Indies, attempts to establish trading posts in the East Indies, and the sending of a trade mission to China.

These problems, large as well as small, were dealt with as they arose, often on the basis of information supplied by interested parties, with little reference to theoretical considerations about the aim of overseas involvement; the general impression of the way in which governments dealt with the Empire is that a comprehensive, fully formulated policy did not exist. As David Mackay points out, neither "a capacity for long-term planning" nor a "philosophy of empire" existed at this time in Britain, where most administrative problems

[29] Vincent Todd Harlow, *The Founding of the Second British Empire 1763—1793*, 2 vols. (London: Longmans & New York: Green, 1952–64): esp. vol. 1. Harlow believed that the turn towards the east had already begun before the loss of the American colonies. Criticism of these traditional views can be found in, for example, Ronald Hyam, "British Imperial Expansion in the late Eighteenth Century," *Historical Journal* 10.1 (1967): 113–31, Ronald Hyam & Ged Martin, *Reappraisals in British Imperial History* (London: Macmillan, 1970), David L. Mackay, "Direction and Purpose in British Imperial Policy, 1783-1801," *Historical Journal* 17.3 (1974): 487–501, and Peter Marshall, "The First and Second British Empires: A Question of Demarcation," *History* 49.165 (February 1964): 14–23 .

[30] See Hyam & Martin, *Reappraisals in British Imperial History*, and Mackay, "Direction and Purpose in British Imperial Policy." See also J.P. Cain & Anthony G. Hopkins, *British Imperialism*, vol. 1: *Innovation and Expansion 1688–1914* (London & New York: Longmans, 1993): 54–58.

were solved with reference to precedent rather than through innovation.[31] The common denominator of most projects around the world was profitable trade of one kind or another, and when difficulties arose the means best suited to securing that aim were usually adopted, though always with one eye on the potential consequences for relations with other powerful European nations. The British Empire developed largely in response to the immediate needs and views of a long series of changing governments.

At the end of the century, the wars with the French made the acquisition of strategic posts imperative and for this reason tended to lend more coherence to imperial policy and planning. This coincides with what Bayly calls "Britain's new imperial age," which he sees as taking shape in the last decades of the century, attended by an upsurge in royalism and nationalism and by improvements in administrative and governmental practices. Though Bayly's emphasis on the concept of "the second British Empire" may call for some modification under the impression of continuity just referred to, the emergence of the factors he mentions as well as the impact of the war may still have given rise to a greater sense of imperial purpose, as he maintains.[32]

Britain emerged from the Napoleonic wars with considerable colonial possessions; the growth in British trade, stimulated by emerging industrialization as well as other economic investments overseas, further strengthened Britain's position as a world power. Although a large part of trade and investments was directed towards Europe and the USA, a significant section of it was carried on in various parts of the Empire and even beyond it, encouraging a more coherent view of British interests in the world and, in practical terms, eventually the adoption of the laissez-faire principle of free trade. The expansion of British economic and territorial influence was followed by the gradual emergence of policies for the Empire, exemplified by schemes for emigration and the extension of political institutions for self-government in the colonies of settlement which came into existence in the 1840s and '50s.

---

[31] Mackay, "Direction and Purpose in British Imperial Policy," 492. Mackay's interpretation is accepted by Peter James Marshall, "The Eighteenth-Century Empire," in *British Politics and Society from Walpole to Pitt 1742–1789*, ed. Jeremy Black (Basingstoke: Macmillan, 1990): 194–97. Mackay also maintains that the colonies were regarded with little interest most of the time during the eighteenth century; see also Trevor Richard Reese, "The Origins of Colonial America and New South Wales: An Essay on British Imperial Policy in the Eighteenth Century," *Australian Journal of Politics and History* 7.2 (November 1961): 186.

[32] Bayly, *Imperial Meridian*, ch. 4 and 5.

The structure of government

The domestic political situation in Britain naturally had an important bearing on imperial developments. The eighteenth and early nineteenth centuries were characterized by the remarkably long political tenures of Robert Walpole, the Duke of Newcastle, Lord North, William Pitt the Younger, and Lord Liverpool, interspersed with periods of political chaos where governments replaced each other with startling frequency.

To some extent this was a reflection of the changing relationship between Crown and Parliament, where the monarchs alternately insisted on the right to choose their ministers and had to recognize the power of Parliament to determine the make-up of government; the conflict between the Tory and Whig traditions continued to exert its influence on political developments.[33] It was also a reflection of the intense political factionalism of this period, where strong leaders who dominated their followers were at times replaced by weaker ones who failed to impose order within the ranks.

Positions in Parliament and government were usually perceived as service to the king rather than to a particular political line of thinking, at least until the latter part of the eighteenth century, and much of the political life of members was taken up with securing favourable places for themselves and their friends.[34] The role of the king in politics has been the subject of much debate among scholars; the traditional belief that George III, as opposed to his predecessor, dominated his ministers and largely governed the country himself has been replaced by a more balanced view which recognizes the desire of the king (as in the case of his grandfather) to be informed about and to have a say in important matters but which also shows the developing institutionalization of ministerial decision-making and the evolving importance of the Cabinet.[35]

The political unrest which marked the turn of the century, with demands for greater popular participation, was countered by a consolidation of power

---

[33] See Reitan, *Politics, War and Empire.*

[34] Lewis B. Namier, *The Structure of Politics at the Accession of George III*, 2 vols. (London: Macmillan, 1928) and *England in the Age of the American Revolution* (London: Macmillan, 1930), provides still-valid detailed accounts of mid-eighteenth century political life. For more recent work, see, for example, Black, ed. *British Politics and Society from Walpole to Pitt 1742–1789*, and Jonathan Charles Douglas Clark, *English Society 1688–1832: Ideology, Social Structure and Political Practice during the Ancient Regime* (Cambridge: Cambridge UP , 1985).

[35] See, for example, Ian R. Christie, *Myth and Realities in Late Eighteenth Century British Politics* (Berkeley: U of California P, 1970): ch. 2 and 7.

among the ruling classes combined with cautious reforms in the political system to ensure greater efficiency and cut down on waste. This "constructive conservatism" (together with some repressive measures) ensured a great degree of continuity in the political leadership of the country in the early nineteenth century, in which political control was adapted to the changing conditions brought by industrialization and urbanization.[36] Although the Reform Act of 1832 opened up the political system to the emerging middle class and other reforms in the 1830s and '40s ameliorated the conditions of labourers, this movement did not challenge the basic structure of the British political system. Nevertheless, it did introduce the influence of new forces which would eventually cause more profound changes in the way in which both Britain and the colonies were ruled.

The power-struggle between the king and his ministers and between various political groups or movements is an important element in the context of colonial policy; equally important for an understanding of the issues involved in this study, however, are the development of departmental organization and the practices adopted at different times for administering the colonies. The remainder of the present chapter will be devoted to presenting an outline of this.

By the beginning of the eighteenth century, a regular system of Crown control over the government of the colonies was only beginning to come into existence. Originally the colonies were founded on the basis of charters which gave the company or proprietor receiving them broad powers in establishing local government, although it had to conform to English law and was subject to directions from the Crown. In the course of the seventeenth century, most of the colonies acquired a form of government which was based on an appointed governor and council on the one hand and an elected assembly on the other. Essentially, self-government based to a large extent on a kind of representative forum laid the foundations for a colonial tradition of independence in governmental matters which became a dominant element in relations between mother country and colonies by the mid-eighteenth century.

During the seventeenth century, the king or, during the Interregnum, the Protector, sometimes attempted to assert his power over the colonies, and after the Restoration a number of the charters were revoked, thus bringing those colonies directly under royal rule with a governor appointed by the king. This was also the case with the colonies acquired by conquest from Spain and Holland. At various points, committees were established in England by the

---

[36] Bayly, *Imperial Meridian*, 193–95.

Crown to oversee trade and colonial matters; most significant was the establishment in 1675 of the committee known variously as the Lords of the Committee of Trade and Plantation ("the Lords of Trade") or the Committee of Council for Trade and Plantations. Although this body attempted to impose some kind of uniformity on the rule of the colonies, especially with regard to those of New England, by the time of the accession of King William, and partly helped by the political changes at the time, American colonial government remained to a large extent uncontrolled by Britain.[37]

However, by the end of the century this began to change with the establishment by William III in 1696 of a more enduring Board of Trade and Plantations. The creation of this board was no doubt a reflection of the increasing importance of the colonies to Britain in terms both of trade and of war-time strategy; King William was concerned to avoid a similar board from being created by Parliament, thus ensuring the continuation of royal power over the colonies.[38]

The lords commissioners were to supervise the development of trade as well as conditions and government in the colonies based on correspondence with colonial officials, to make representations to the Privy Council on these matters, and to issue reports when ordered to do so by one of the Secretaries of State or the Privy Council. They were also empowered to suggest suitable candidates for colonial offices to the Privy Council, which made the formal appointment.

The Board in general had little power to initiate action or to draw up policy, except in an indirect way through its communication with colonial officials interpreting orders from the government.[39] Executive power lay with the Privy

---

[37] For developments in the seventeenth century, see Oliver Morton Dickerson, *American Colonial Government 1696—1765: A Study of the British Board of Trade in its Relation to the American Colonies, Political, Industrial, Administrative* (Cleveland OH: Arthur H. Clarke, 1912): ch. 1, Hubert Llewellyn Smith, *The Board of Trade* (New York & London: G.P. Putnam's Sons, 1928): ch. 1, and McFarlane, *The British in the Americas*, ch. 7.

[38] See Dickerson, *American Colonial Government*, 20–22, and A.H. Basye, *The Lords Commissioners of Trade and Plantations, commonly known as the Board of Trade 1748–1782* (New Haven CT: Yale UP, 1925): 1. Much of the following is based on Basye, whose work remains one of the most thorough studies of the Board of Trade. See also Jack Marvin Sosin, *English America and the Revolution of 1688: Royal Administration and the structure of Provincial Government* (Lincoln: U of Nebraska P, 1982): ch. 16–17. Among other things, Sosin emphasizes the sense of insignificance experienced by the early commissioners of trade.

[39] Llewellyn Smith, *The Board of Trade*, 34.

Council, the committee of the Council hearing the reports of the board, and especially the two Secretaries of State, who had personal access to the king.

The office of the Secretary of State was an old institution; in earlier times the person filling it had had the function of a private secretary to the king, but gradually the position developed into an advisory and executive office concerned with both domestic and foreign policy. At some point, possibly in the sixteenth century,[40] the secretaryship was divided between two (sometimes three) men, one in charge of the Northern Department (dealing with northern Europe), the other of the Southern Department (southern Europe, Ireland and, from the turn of the century, the colonies[41]). Both dealt with domestic matters and each could do the other's business.[42] They were two of the most significant ministerial posts in the country, and the chief minister was usually either one of the Secretaries of State or the First Lord of the Treasury.

In relation to the colonies, the Southern Secretary was empowered to give orders to governors and commanders-in-chief and in this way controlled an important domain of colonial government. Thus, from the very beginning of the existence of the Board of Trade, the foundations were laid for a struggle between Board and Secretaries. The privilege of nominating governors and other major officials and the right to correspond directly with these were jealously fought over throughout the Board's existence. The division between two bodies gave the administrative work a somewhat unsystematic character which was frequently criticized by contemporaries involved in the work[43] and which was further exacerbated by the frequent changes of presidents of the Board as well as Secretaries of State.

The history of the Board is marked by alternate periods of declining and increasing significance, to a large extent determined by the personality and political standing of the president. The long presidency of the Earl of Halifax

---

[40] Margaret Marion Spector, *The American Department of the British Government 1768–1782* (1940; New York: Octagon, 1976): 12.

[41] Basye, *The Lords Commissioners of Trade and Plantations*, 24.

[42] For the early history of the office of secretary of state, see Mark Alméras Thomson, *The Secretaries of State 1681–1782* (London: Frank Cass, 1968): ch. 1.

[43] See Gerald Sandford Graham, *British Policy and Canada 1774–1791: A Study in Eighteenth Century Trade Policy* (London: Longmans, 1930), who quotes Thomas Pownall (former governor of Massachusetts) and William Knox (under-secretary) to this effect (11–12).

from 1748 to 1761 was one such period of growing importance.[44] Halifax showed considerable interest in colonial affairs as well as a certain degree of personal ambition and was for both reasons determined to ensure that the Board's work did not go unrecognized.[45]

After ministerial rearrangements in 1751, in which Halifax felt slighted, an order-in-council was issued in 1752 which, as a form of compensation to Halifax, consolidated the orders under which the Board worked. It was specified that the Board was to nominate all colonial civil officials and that all correspondence (except that concerned with foreign affairs) with these was to be conducted by the board. Finally, in 1757, Halifax was admitted to Cabinet; it is significant, however, that he became a member in his own right, not as the president of the Board, and his successor, Lord Sandys, did not obtain the same privilege.

At the accession of Sandys, the power of nomination was again removed from the Board by a new order-in-council of 1761; it was restored to the Secretary of State for the Southern Department, at this time William Pitt the Elder, who had complained of the encroachment of the Board on what he felt to be his area of business and whom the leaders of government wanted to mollify. Although the channels of correspondence remained the same, contemporary observers clearly felt that the importance of the board had been diminished, Horace Walpole stating that it had been "reduced to its old insignificance."[46]

Similar dealings took place in 1763 when Charles Townshend became president (for a month); his support was required by Bute in connection with the peace treaty with France, and in return he, like Halifax, received a place in the Cabinet, although the division of powers between the Board and the Secretary of State was not altered.[47]

In 1766 another order-in-council again changed the working basis of the board, removing the right to make original representations to the king, permit-

---

[44] No attempt will be made here to discuss all the holders of office concerned with the government of the colonies. Only a small number may be mentioned here as illustrations of developments in the offices. A list of the relevant presidents and Secretaries of State is provided in Appendix I at the end of this study.

[45] See, for example, Clarence Walworth Alvord, *The Mississippi Valley in British Politics: A Study of the Trade, Land Speculation, and Experiments in Imperialism culminating tin the American Revolution* (1917; New York: Russell & Russell, 1959), vol. 1: 114–24, for details of Halifax's tenure.

[46] Quoted in Basye, *The Lords Commissioners of Trade and Plantations*, 107.

[47] Basye, *The Lords Commissioners of Trade and Plantations*, 120.

ting it to make reports only when ordered to do so, and transferring the right of correspondence with the colonies to the Secretary of State. Apparently this change was initiated by Hillsborough as a condition for accepting the presidency in that year, based on his experience from an earlier period of presidency (1763–65). He had recognized the fact that dividing colonial affairs between two bodies created an untenable situation. Since Hillsborough realized that it was entirely unlikely that he would be given greater powers, he opted for the alternative, hoping thereby to decrease the burden of work falling on the Board.[48]

It is interesting that in spite of the many changes in the relationship between the Board of Trade and the Secretary of State the distribution of the actual work (apart from nominations for offices) was relatively stable, the Board dealing with routine matters and the Secretary carrying out policy measures.[49] It appears from A.H. Basye's study that the volume of work conducted by the board was less affected by the degree of significance attributed to it than by external forces such as wars with the French or the War of Independence, which tended to put a stop to ordinary correspondence.[50]

The greatest change in the division of powers over colonial affairs took place in January 1768 when a third secretaryship was created for the purpose of dealing with colonial matters. Such a step had been contemplated before (especially in 1757, when Halifax attempted to satisfy his desire for distinction, and in 1766 during the Rockingham ministry) and was now finally achieved as part of yet another political crisis, in which the opposition, headed by Lord Bedford (and possibly supported by the de facto leader of the Chatham ministry, Lord Grafton), tried to squeeze out Shelburne, Secretary of State for the Southern Department, by depriving him of an important section of his office.[51] This plan was unsuccessful, and Hillsborough was appointed Third Secretary instead. It was widely claimed later that the creation of another Secretary of State had the king's approval because it was perceived to strengthen his hold over colonial affairs.[52]

---

[48] See letter from Hillsborough to Grenville, August 1766, quoted in Basye, *The Lords Commissioners of Trade and Plantations*, 157.

[49] For information on the day to day work of the Board, see, for example, Mary Patterson Clarke, "The Board of Trade at Work," *American Historical Review* 17 (1911–12): 17–43.

[50] Basye, *The Lords Commissioners of Trade and Plantations*, eg, 103, 190.

[51] *The Lords Commissioners of Trade and Plantations*, 166–68.

[52] Spector, *The American Department of the British Government*, 20.

This move obviously transferred all responsibility for the colonies from the Southern Secretary to the new Secretary, and in July of the same year the Board of Trade was in effect appended to his office, when the Third Secretary was ordered to attend all meetings of the board and was from then on regarded as both president and Secretary of State.

The appointment of the third Secretary of State caused some controversy; although it does not seem to have been the intention of the king, some believed that the Third Secretary's powers were more limited than that of the other Secretaries because his office was specifically to deal with the colonies (thus preventing him from taking part in the business of the other two departments).[53] This interpretation was supported by the fact that the Third Secretary was commonly referred to as "Secretary of State for the colonies" and the office as "the American Department" (although colonies other than the American ones came within its orbit). The other Secretaries continued to attempt to limit his powers and regain control over colonial patronage and the disposition of troops.[54]

It is clear that most of the changes mentioned above were to a very large extent caused by internal political considerations and intrigue rather than consideration of what might enhance the conduct of colonial affairs, although Basye argues, with reference to the final creation of a secretaryship for the colonies, that "back of all the political manoeuvres there must have been a feeling that this long-contemplated step could be delayed no longer."[55]

This should not prompt one to conclude that colonial matters were not regarded as important enough to warrant serious political planning; on the contrary, the area was clearly regarded as important enough to fight over, a conclusion which is of course borne out by the increasingly vital interest with which American affairs were followed by government as well as Parliament as rebellion loomed and eventually broke out.

The "American Department" was subjected to great criticism in 1780 by Edmund Burke, spokesman for the opposition to Lord North's government. His Bill for Economical Reform would among other things abolish the third secretaryship, which was treated with great contempt in Burke's speech; it was

---

[53] *The American Department of the British Government*, ch. 2.

[54] See A.H. Basye, "The Secretary of State for the Colonies," *American Historical Review* 28 (1923): 13–23, and Spector, *The American Department of the British Government*, ch. 5. Hillsborough was apparently not entirely satisfied with the powers of his office: see Alvord, *The Mississippi Valley in British Politics*, vol. 2, 42.

[55] Basye, *The Lords Commissioners of Trade and Plantations*, 169.

also represented as a means of extending the power of the Crown. The bill was defeated by a mere seven votes, an indication of the weak position of the government at this time. In March 1782, with the fall of North, the third secretaryship was finally abolished when the new ministry headed by Rockingham divided business between two Secretaries of State as earlier; one headed the Foreign Department and the other the Home Department, including colonial affairs. At the same time, the Board of Trade was abolished.

The power-struggles in relation to colonial affairs naturally subsided after this. After the end of the war and the loss of the thirteen American colonies, the quantity of relevant affairs diminished for a while, although both the remaining parts of British North America and the West Indies continued to demand attention. The new Home Department was headed for a short while by Shelburne, who tried to establish a "Plantation Branch" in the office. Three of the clerks from the Colonial Department and Grey Elliott, the clerk of reports from the Board of Trade, were transferred to the new office, but although Elliott was made under-secretary the following year, the idea of a colonial branch of the department did not catch on; successive Secretaries of State showed little interest in this idea (Elliott left the department two years later ; he seems not to have had a successor).[56]

In 1784 a standing Committee of the Council for Trade and Plantations was established; two years later this was abolished and re-established on a slightly different footing.[57] As opposed to the earlier Board, the main business of this committee was trade, the colonies being considered almost entirely by the Board in this connection, although all colonial legislation continued to be transmitted to the Board. It could, however, still be asked by the Privy Council to review other aspects of colonial affairs.

From this time onwards, the main body of colonial matters – routine correspondence, nomination of officials, regulation of their work, and the framing of new policy measures – rested largely with the Secretary of State (although other sections of government such as the Treasury and the Admiralty also continued to have dealings with the colonies). Occasionally, special committees would be established to consider issues connected with or touching on the

---

[56] For the changes in this period, see Spector, *The American Department of the British Government*, ch. 10, J.C. Beaglehole, "The Colonial Office, 1782–1854," *Historical Studies: Australia and New Zealand* 1 (1940–41): 170–89, and Helen Taft Manning, *British Colonial Government after the American Revolution 1782–1820* (New Haven CT: Yale UP & London: Oxford UP, 1933): ch. 3.

[57] See Llewellyn Smith, *The Board of Trade*, ch. 3.

colonial situation, such as the committees created in the 1770s and '80s to solve the problem of overfilled prisons.

Little active interest was taken during this period by the Secretaries of State in improving the apparatus for controlling colonial affairs; there was no staff especially devoted to looking after this part of business. Much depended on the attention devoted by the Secretary of State and his under-secretary to this particular section of the department. During the later years of Pitt's first term of office, two of his most able and trusted ministers, Lord Grenville and Henry Dundas, were in charge of colonial matters. Yet it may well be the case that the consistency of colonial administration suffered from the abolition of the old Board of Trade, which, though perhaps a weak body, at least devoted practically all its time to colonial matters.[58]

In 1801 colonial affairs were turned over to the Secretary of State for War, a third secretaryship created in 1794 as a consequence of the war with the French. It was intended that responsibility for the colonies go to this Secretary from the start, but various political considerations meant that this did not occur until seven years later, when Pitt's ministry was replaced by that of Henry Addington.[59] The peace with France would seem to have given the then minister, Lord Hobart, plenty of time to deal with the colonies but, as it turned out, the peace was only temporary and the Secretary of War soon had his hands full again, with the result that there would have been little time for the colonies except with respect to their strategic significance. Perhaps for this reason, one Secretary of War, Windham, decided in 1806 to have two under-secretaries, one for war and one for the colonies.

At the end of the war, the under-secretaryship for war was abolished but concern with colonial matters increased. During the long period of Lord Liverpool's ministry, the Secretary of State, Lord Bathurst, and his under-secretary, Goulburn, devoted considerable attention to the problems connected with governing the colonies; the two are credited with inaugurating a new period in colonial administration.[60] The fact that the Napoleonic Wars were

---

[58] Manning, *British Colonial Government after the American Revolution*, 474. Mackay, "Direction and Purpose in British Imperial Policy," 494–97, also finds that colonial government in this period was particularly marked by lack of effectual measures and power to implement new policy directions.

[59] For details about these changes, see Douglas MacMurray Young, *The Colonial Office in the Early Nineteenth Century* (London: Longmans, 1961): 8–11.

[60] See Manning, *British Colonial Government after the American Revolution*, ch. 15, and Beaglehole, "The Colonial Office," for a description of developments during this

then drawing to a close no doubt explains in part the increasing attention which the colonies received. The dramatic increase in the number of colonies after the peace, which ensured Britain many of the territories held during the wars (among them the Cape), also made greater administrative demands. Simultaneously, interest by Parliament in the government of the colonies also grew, inspired initially by the issue of the slave trade and later by the constitutional situation in Australia and Canada. It was at this time that it became common to refer the office as "the Colonial Office,"[61] although a department separate from the War Office was in fact not created until 1854.

As a consequence of these developments, the administration of the colonies was gradually enlarged. In 1825 the first permanent under-secretary, R.W. Hay, was appointed; in the same year, James Stephen, Jr. was appointed joint legal counsel to the Colonial Office and the Board of Trade (he had been advisory counsel since 1813). Hay retired in 1836 and was succeeded by Stephen, who remained in office until 1847. Such permanent and fairly long tenures doubtless contributed in large measure to the continuity and extension of the work of the Colonial Office, which had hitherto been dependent on Secretaries and under-secretaries who came and went with relative frequency (though some of the under-secretaries had held office under succeeding ministers). This became particularly relevant in the years after Bathurst's term in office; in the period between 1827 and 1835 no fewer than nine men held the position of Secretary for War (in 1834 alone, three different Secretaries of State were appointed).

By the 1830s, the Colonial Office had acquired a character very different from that of the late eighteenth century. The staff had been greatly increased (from no clerks or secretaries devoted entirely to colonial matters in the 1790s to twenty-five permanently employed persons in 1833[62]), the volume of correspondence had grown tremendously (13,000 incoming and outgoing despatches in 1830[63]), and work in the office had been organized and regularized. The legal and financial conditions of the individual colonies were subjected to scrutiny (by sending out commissions and through the annual "Blue" Books),

---

period. Isobel Eirlys Edwards, *The 1820 Settlers in South Africa: A Study in British colonial Policy* (London: Longmans, Green & Company, 1934): 1–3, paints a much more negative picture of the efforts of the Bathurst–Goulburn team.

[61] Beaglehole, "The Colonial Office," 178.

[62] "The Colonial Office," 182.

[63] "The Colonial Office," 184. See John S. Galbraith, *Reluctant Empire: British Policy on the South African Frontier 1834–1854* (Berkeley: U of California P, 1963): ch. 2, on the Colonial Office in the 1830s and 1840s.

incoming and outgoing correspondence was registered, and the whole process of dealing with the letters was systematized, one aspect being the under-secretary's habit of minuting every incoming letter for the convenience of the Secretary of State, an innovation made by Stephen, who enjoys a degree of fame (perhaps somewhat exaggerated by his hagiographers[64]) for his thorough and highly influential work at the Office.

The outline presented here of the administrative organization involved in dealing with colonial matters shows quite clearly that it had its ups and downs. There was definitely a peak in the 1760s and '70s, after which a period of less concern followed, lasting until the end of the Napoleonic Wars, when interest in the administration of the colonies again began to increase. This is certainly reflected in the quantity of documents produced on the colonies. The final decades of the thirteen American colonies are marked by an overwhelming amount of material, whereas the early years of New South Wales and the Cape are represented by a much more modest number of documents. Later, as the nineteenth century wore on, the amount again increased dramatically.

The significance of individuals in formulating attitudes and carrying out policies is also a matter of considerable interest. One aspect of this is the role of the governor in formulating policy and the way in which this official was perceived by the administration. The distance between the colonies and Britain and the slowness of communication meant that the governor very often had to act on his own initiative before receiving instructions from the government in London. As the governor was the Crown's representative in the colony and was, as such, an extension of the imperial policy-making body, the policies he pursued in such situations would ideally be identical to those the government would wish to lay down. However, the situation was usually rather more complicated than that.

As Helen Taft Manning has shown, the position of the governor was difficult; he was expected to carry out without fail all instructions received from London and in other ways govern the colony according to the views ruling there – but his situation did not always enable him to do so.[65] For one thing, he

[64] This point is also made by A.G.L. Shaw, "James Stephen and Colonial Policy: The Australian Experience," *Journal of Imperial and Commonwealth History* 20 (1992): xxx. For an example of the eulogy on James Stephen, see Paul Knaplund, *James Stephen and the British Colonial System 1813–1847* (Westport CT: Greenwood, 1974): 35 and elsewhere.

[65] See Manning, *British Colonial Government after the American Revolution*, ch. 4, for details about the governor's situation. See also A.G.L. Shaw, "London and the

had little power over the filling of important jobs in the colony, which meant that he could not select the ablest men, nor did he have the power of patronage at his disposal to help him achieve what he wanted. Secondly, at least in the colonies with an elected assembly, he was to a certain extent dependent on that body for money, even for part of his own salary. This created an untenable situation, since the governor often had to disallow measures enacted by the assembly. Thirdly, since the filling of governorships was an important part of patronage in England, rewarding government supporters, it meant that the men who got these important jobs were not always very well qualified for them.

Circumstances such as these significantly influenced the power and ability of the governor to follow the expected line of government. Furthermore, local elites with strong and often diverging views about their own situation often tried to influence the governor or obstruct his work. Even governors who were entirely loyal to the imperial government might find it impossible to lay down the desired policy, and in the worst of cases a governor with little personal integrity might allow himself to be persuaded by the colonists and rule contrary to his own orders.

Consequently, the views on policy expressed by the governors cannot be regarded as wholly representative of the imperial point of view, as is also shown by the fact that decisions made by the governors were sometimes reversed by the Secretary of State. In other cases, however, officials in Britain were happy to accept the governor's view on a given matter, even when it conflicted with their own, because they saw that he would have better information about local affairs.

The situation may well have been somewhat different in newly established colonies where no elite had yet come into being or in conquered colonies where such an elite may have been hostile or at least reserved towards the new government. In these cases, extra care may also have been exerted in the choice of governor, as seems to have been the case in both New South Wales and the Cape.[66] In such situations, the governor would often have extended powers and would rule without having to take a local assembly into account. It is possible

---

Governors: Relations in Eastern Australia 1825–45," in *Australia and Britain: Studies in a Changing Relationship*, ed. A.F. Madden & Wyndraeth Humphries Morris–Jones (London: Frank Cass, 1980): 1–20.

[66] For the former, see Alan Frost, *Convicts and Empire: A Naval Question 1776–1811* (Melbourne: Oxford UP, 1980): 133, and, for the latter, Manning, *British Colonial Government after the American Revolution*, 91.

that in the early years of rule the governor there may have come closer to the ideal of representing the home government.

With regard to the bureaucracy in London, the question of who formulated policy in relation to the colonies is of similar interest. While the Secretaries of State and, for the early period, the presidents of the Board of Trade were ultimately responsible for the work done in their departments, some scholars have maintained that a large part of that work was in fact carried out by the under-secretaries.

Franklin Wickwire, for example, attributes great importance to under-secretarial influence in the period up to the American revolution. He claims that the under-secretaries often had a decisive hand in the formulation of correspondence and even in turning policy decisions into practice. Especially John Pownall, for many years secretary to the Board of Trade and afterwards under-secretary to the Secretary of State for the colonies, is regarded as a central influence in carrying out and perhaps even shaping policy towards the American colonies.[67] Likewise, Alan Frost considers the under-secretary of the Home Department in the 1780s, Evan Nepean, to have been extremely influential in directing and carrying out the measures of the department, and Beaglehole points to the great importance of the permanent under-secretaries in the nineteenth century.[68] Others, such as Marion Spector, place somewhat greater weight on the directives which the under-secretaries must have received from the Secretaries of State,[69] and Manning rejects any significant role for these officials in the last two decades of the eighteenth century.[70]

As Wickwire shows, the basis for any under-secretarial influence was the trust and often friendship which existed between the Secretary of State and his second-in-command.[71] Yet the corollary of the idea of influential under-secretaries is often the belief that their superiors, the Secretaries of State, were weak or inefficient (or both). Thus Frost, for example, is eloquent on the failings of Lord Sydney, Secretary of State for the Home Department 1782–83 and again

---

[67] Franklin Bacon Wickwire, *British Subministers and Colonial America 1763–1783* (Princeton NJ: Princeton UP, 1966).

[68] Frost, *Convicts and Empire*, 130–33; Beaglehole, "The Colonial Office," 186–87.

[69] Spector, *The American Department of the British Government*, ch. 8, although (ch. 9) she recognizes the potential of the under-secretaries for giving advice and influencing the secretaries of state.

[70] Manning, *British Colonial Government after the American Revolution*, 89.

[71] Wickwire, *British Subministers and Colonial America*, 64–85.

1783–89, and believes that Pitt himself gave the final approval for much of Nepean's work, at least towards the end of Sydney's second period in office.[72]

Individual Secretaries of State and their impact on their office have been frequently discussed by scholars in this field; some ministers, such as Sydney, have been represented as mediocrities, others as highly capable and active men.[73] There is no doubt that the personality, talent and ambition of these men influenced the way in which they conducted their work and the amount of personal effort they put into it. Nevertheless, it was the Secretaries of State who had to answer for their work before the Cabinet and the monarch; though there is plenty of evidence to show that the under-secretaries had a large share in formulating correspondence, especially in routine matters; as Spector points out, many of them also corresponded in their own name with colonial governors and other officials,[74] although their actions had to be approved by the Secretary of State, who would have to defend them if need be.[75]

Ultimately, when viewed over half a century or more, considerable importance can be attached to the fact that colonial administration was divided among several bodies, as well as to the rapid turnover in Secretaries of State, presidents of the Board and, perhaps less often, under-secretaries. It suggests that individual attitudes to such an issue as the indigenous peoples of the colonies may well be less significant than the general tendencies that emerge. When most of the officials at a particular time appear to hold similar views, a pattern of what might be called 'official thinking' becomes visible which sheds much more light on the attitudes of a period than do the contributions of individuals. Although a certain focus on individual opinions is inevitable and legitimate, the emphasis in the following chapters will be on tracing the more general views.

---

[72] Frost, *Convicts and Empire*, 17, 45. Alan Atkinson, "The First Plans for Governing New South Wales, 1786–1787," *Australian Historical Studies* 24 (1990–1991): 39–40, seems to hold a different view about Sydney.

[73] See, for example, Beaglehole, "The Colonial Office," 175, Manning, *British Colonial Government after the American Revolution*, 90–91, or Thomson, *The Secretaries of State*, 18–20.

[74] Spector, *The American Department of the British Government*, 116.

[75] See Galbraith, *Reluctant Empire*, 17–19.

Towards consolidation of control

By the middle of the eighteenth century, then, Britain was in possession of a large number of colonies and trading posts around the world. The largest of the settler colonies were in North America, where vast tracts of land continually lured colonists to push on further west. The land, however, was not uninhabited, and relations with the Indians, which were from the outset of critical importance to the settlements, were causing ever greater concern in government circles. Indian alliances with the French pointed up the fact that the latter constituted a considerable threat to the British settlements. The colonies in North America, as elsewhere, were becoming increasingly involved in the European struggle between the two nations, and this cost much energy throughout the eighteenth century.

The North American colonies also came under closer scrutiny by the mother country in the course of the eighteenth century. Previously, the colonies had largely been left to their own devices, but this began to change with the attempts of the Board of Trade and the Secretaries of State to direct both the internal and the external affairs of the settlements. As the century wore on, the interest and intensity with which this control was exercised varied, but at no time did it cease completely; after the turn of the century, indeed, it increased considerably. The share of this administration devoted to relations with indigenous peoples is the concern of the following chapters.

❧

2 North America c. 1760–83

The beginnings of imperial control – the superintendents

IMPERIAL INVOLVEMENT in relations with the Indians in the North American colonies began in earnest around the middle of the eighteenth century. Indian resentment of intrusions on their land by the settlers as well as of the dishonesty of the people engaged in the fur trade led to frequent skirmishes between settlers and Indians and predisposed the Indians in favour of the French, as was mentioned in the previous chapter. The government in Britain increasingly felt the need to improve relations in order to prevent these effects.

At various times in the first half of the century (especially at times of war with the French), the British government had considered plans for uniting some or all of the colonies, one of the effects of which would have been unified action towards the Indians. At other times, they tried to influence relations with the Indians through instructions to the colonies concerning trade or the distribution of presents.[1] However, none of these measures resulted in more stable or united management of Indian affairs.

From the late 1740s, various influential people in America began to agitate for centralized control, with Indian affairs under somebody appointed by the Crown, and in 1753 the Board of Trade ordered a congress to be held at Albany to consider the whole issue. The congress was held in June 1754 and the pro-

---

[1] John Richard Alden, *John Stuart and the Southern Colonial Frontier: A Study of Indian relations, War, Trade and Land Problems in the Southern Wilderness 1754–1775* (1944; New York: Gordian, 1966): ch. 1.

ceedings from it were received in London in October. These contained a number of papers supporting the idea of centralized Crown control.

Already in April of the same year, Lord Halifax as president of the Board of Trade had authored two reports on frontier defence in America, in one of which he had suggested a similar solution to the problems marring relations with the Indians. The two "commissaries-general" proposed by Halifax were envisaged to deal with the issues of land purchase and the conduct of trade, the latter to be managed through the issuing of licences for use at selected posts only.[2]

At the request of the Secretary of State, the Board wrote a report on the whole issue of defence in America, in which they recommended the appointment of a commander-in-chief who was also to be made commissary-general for Indian affairs; however, in October this was again changed, probably under the influence of the papers from the Albany Congress,[3] so that the superintendency became a separate office (albeit under the command of the commander-in-chief).[4] There is little doubt that the signs of impending hostilities were largely responsible for the decision finally to do something radical about a situation which had been a matter of concern for a number of years.[5]

As a consequence of these reports, it was decided in 1755 to appoint two superintendents, one for the Northern Department and one for the Southern Department (with the Ohio as the dividing line). The superintendents quickly made themselves useful, especially in the north, where William Johnson's

---

[2] Proposal for Building Forts etc.: upon the Ohio and other Rivers in North America, April 30, 1754, CO 5/6.

[3] John Richard Alden, "The Albany Congress and the Creation of the Indian Superintendencies," *Mississippi Valley Historical Review* 27 (1940–41): 193–210. Alden argues in detail that the Albany Congress was the determining influence in the decision to establish the superintendencies.

[4] Clarence Edwin Carter, ed. "The Office of Commander in Chief: A Phase of Imperial Unity on the Eve of the Revolution" in *The Era of the American Revolution*, ed. Richard Brandon Morris (1939; Gloucester MA: Peter Smith, 1971): 190–91. Alden, *John Stuart and the Southern Colonial Frontier*, 141–47, takes great pains to show that ultimately the superintendents were subject to instructions from London. This is also clear from the correspondence between the superintendents and London. The superintendents were, however, dependent on the commander-in-chief to cover their expenses. In general, see Alden, *John Stuart and the Southern Colonial Frontier*, ch. 9 for a detailed description of the development of the superintendencies.

[5] Report of the Board of Trade on the Plan of general Concert for Defence in America, August 8, 1754, CO 5/6: 125–29 and Report of the Board of Trade on the Proceedings of the Albany Congress, October 29, 1754, CO 5/6: 138–46.

longstanding close relations with the Iroquois Confederacy of the Six Nations meant that these Indians soon became the close and faithful allies of the English. In the south, the appointment of John Atkin was apparently less fortunate, although in some cases he managed to improve trade relations.[6] At his death in 1761, John Stuart was appointed to fill the office, which he did with success.

The decision to appoint Crown officials to handle relations with the Indians involved the government in London directly in the conduct of these affairs. As a consequence of this, there is a relatively large amount of material with a bearing on the question of official attitudes towards the Indians compared to other areas. The correspondence between the superintendents of Indian affairs in America and the officials in London, especially the Secretary of State for the Southern Department and the Board of Trade, constitutes the most significant source of information; occasionally, important information is also gained from the letters to the various governors and the commanders-in-chief. This material forms the basis of the discussion in the present chapter.

The question of land

The reports of the superintendents made it clearer than ever that one of the major causes of Indian dissatisfaction and the reason why the Indians were more friendly towards the French was the encroachment of the British settlers on their land. In the letters from the Board of Trade and the Secretary of State, this dissatisfaction was widely accepted as reasonable, with reference being frequently made to the "just complaints" of the Indians.[7] Concern was expressed about, and emphasis placed on, the need to redress this situation and to uphold the treaties signed with the Indians ("solemn engagements," "just and faithful observance of treaties and compacts").[8]

---

[6] Alden, *John Stuart and the Southern Colonial Frontier*, ch. 4–8.

[7] For example, Fox to Johnson, March 13, 1756, in *Documents Relative to the Colonial History of the State of New York* (hereafter *New York Colonial Documents*), 18 vols., ed. Edmund Bailey O'Callaghan & Berthold Fernow (Albany NY: Weed & Parsons, 1856–83), vol. 7: 76; Lords of Trade to Governor Hardy, March 19, 1756, in *New York Colonial Documents*, vol. 7: 77; Report of the Lords of Trade, November 18, 1761, in *New York Colonial Documents*, vol. 7: 471.

[8] For example, Board of Trade to Fauquier, June 13, 1760, CO 5/1367: 205; Lords of Trade to Pitt, February 21, 1760, in O'Callaghan & Fernow, ed. *New York Colonial Documents*, vol. 7, 429; Instructions to Governors, December 2, 1761, CO 324/17: 83.

This at once brings to the forefront the most basic question involved in determining the attitude of the British government towards the Indians – the view of the legal position of the Indians in relation to land. As the documents contain some important indications of how the rights of the Indians to their land were perceived by British government officials at this time, this provides a suitable starting-point for a discussion of the developing attitudes and policies towards the Indians.

The Board of Trade made at least three significant statements on this issue. In a letter to Governor Fauquier of Virginia in June 1760, the Board referred to a proposal to form a settlement on the Ohio. In explaining their opposition to this, they described the land in terms of two kinds of possession: first, "dominion" over the whole area; second, the "lands claimed as hunting grounds" by the Indians. The dominion or sovereignty over the land, which was the cause of the struggle with France, was referred to later in the letter as "the Dominion and possession."[9] This indicates that the Indians were perceived to have something less than full ownership over their "hunting grounds." While this right of occupancy needed to be respected, it would be insufficient to render the Indians full legal owners of the land.

Several things suggest that this was not the general view of the British officials. In the context of the Ohio in 1760, the question is complicated by the presence of the French, who may have been considered to have acquired both sovereignty and property rights from the Indians, who would only have retained rights of occupancy. The situation was thus more complex than at the beginning, when the British were the first to encounter an Indian nation.[10]

A letter, also from 1760, from the Board of Trade to the Secretary of State, William Pitt, shows that when the Indians were the sole inhabitants the matter was regarded differently. A proposal had been made to form certain new settlements within the colony of New York, and the members of the Board approved of this, "provided it be done with a proper regard to our engagements with the Indians." It was envisaged that the Indians

> may possibly claim part of them [the lands] as their hunting grounds reserved to them by the most solemn treaties, upon an exact observance of which, not

[9] Board of Trade to Fauquier, June 13, 1760, CO 5/1367: 204–205.

[10] See also the Royal Proclamation of 1763, discussed and quoted below, which establishes the fact that sovereignty over the west belonged to the British king, but seems to recognize the property rights of the Indians.

> only our interests, but our rights in regard to the claims of other foreign powers do greatly depend.[11]

"Our interests" probably refers at least in part to peace with the Indians, whereas "our rights" would seem to mean that the sovereignty over the area covered by the treaties was perceived to have been obtained from the Indians – a clear indication that in this case the Indians were regarded as the original owners of the land in terms both of sovereignty and of property rights. It also shows that the Indians were considered to retain full property rights in the land which they had reserved to themselves as a condition of the treaties.

This interpretation is further supported by a statement made in a report from 1761 by the Board of Trade concerning settlements on the Mohawk River; reference was again made to

> the Cruelty and Injustice with which they [the Indians] had been treated with respect to their hunting grounds, in open violation of those solemn compacts by which they had yielded to us the Dominion, but not the property of those lands.[12]

– again an unambiguous statement to the effect that the Indians were seen as the original owners and that they retained property rights in the areas reserved to them. These observations are supported by the general employment of "their land" or "their property" when referring to areas inhabited by Indians, often in conjunction with "right." There is little doubt that in the early 1760s the Indians were regarded as owning all unceded land, not only because this was the most expedient approach or the most morally compelling one but also because this was perceived to be the actual legal situation.

While this basic and very important point is fairly clear, the view in itself did not preclude a positive attitude towards the western expansion of white settlement among British government officials, as the excerpt from the letter to Pitt above shows. White settlement was perceived to be morally and legally valid when the Crown had acquired sovereignty over the area and the land had been purchased fairly from the Indians (and other regulations had been observed). Indeed, it was usually claimed that British settlement in North America was legitimized by purchase from the Indians (fair or otherwise).

---

[11] Lords of Trade to Pitt, February 21, 1760, in O'Callaghan & Fernow, ed. *New York Colonial Documents*, vol. 7, 428–29.

[12] Order of the King in Council on a Report of the Lords of Trade, November 23, 1761, in O'Callaghan & Fernow, ed. *New York Colonial Documents*, vol. 7, 472.

The American colonists and their wealthy sponsors in England were very much interested in pushing into the uncolonized regions, as Clarence Alvord has shown in great detail.[13] However, Alvord also claims that, from the time of the War of the Austrian Succession, western expansion was an acknowledged goal of successive British governments. He mentions, as evidence of this, the grant to the Ohio Company of land on the Ohio in 1748 and the Royal Instructions to Virginia in 1754 to grant land on the western side of the Alleghenies. He also maintains that after the beginning of the war in 1756 the Board of Trade, while making general recommendations to protect Indian land, continued to be in favour of expansion until Lord Egremont became Secretary of State for the Southern Department in 1761, when a temporary change of policy took place.[14]

This interpretation is contradicted by several things. In 1756, when Sir William Johnson received his commission as superintendent he was directed to

---

[13] Clarence Walworth Alvord, *The Mississippi Valley in British Politics: A Study of the Trade, Land Speculation, and Experiments in Imperialism culminating in the American Revolution* (1971; New York: Russell & Russell, 1959), vol. 1: ch. 3.

[14] Alvord, *The Mississippi Valley in British Politics*, vol. 1, 115–26. It needs to be mentioned that Alvord wrote *The Mississippi Valley in British Politics* primarily with the intention of exploring the developing relationship between the British and the American colonists with respect to western expansion in the period 1763–1774 (with an obvious bias towards the colonists); relations with the Indians were thus not his main concern, but rather were dealt with as part of the general picture. His starting point was the view that those British politicians who argued in favour of retaining Canada rather than Guadaloupe at the peace negotiations with France had thereby bound themselves to a policy favourable to exploiting the western acquisitions and he therefore basically found that most British governments favoured expansion. He also found, as the present point shows, that this had roots back to the time before the war. While a pioneer study at the time of its original publication in 1916, Alvord's work has been seriously criticized on various points (not all of them relevant to the topic of this study): see, for example, Philip Lawson's criticism of Alvord's discussion of the debate on Canada in connection with the peace treaty (*The Imperial Challenge: Quebec and Britain in the Age of the American Revolution* (Montreal & London: McGill–Queen's UP, 1989): 9) and Jack Marvin Sosin's attack on the general framework of Alvord's analysis (*Whitehall and the Wilderness: the Middle West in British Colonial Policy 1760–1775* (Lincoln: U of Nebraska P, 1961)); nevertheless, it remains one of the most thorough and detailed studies of the questions discussed in this chapter and is therefore frequently referred to here, though reservations are sometimes expressed regarding Alvord's interpretations.

> communicate to the Indians all the orders the King has given for prohibiting settlements upon their land; for redressing their just complaints with regard to the patented lands, and for preventing the like abuses for the future.[15]

At the same time, the governor of New York received orders to introduce legislation in the assembly for "vacating and annulling these exhorbitant and fraudulent patents."[16] While this measure does not seem to have been carried out, the letters suggest a sincere wish to halt encroachments on Indian land. Pennsylvania showed a greater inclination to adopt this approach than New York when, in 1758, in the treaty of Easton, it promised not to extend its settlement west of the Allegheny Mountains. In October 1761 the commander of Fort Pitt, Colonel Bouquet, similarly prohibited further settlement to the west.

The Board's perception of policy development is set out in the letter to Governor Fauquier in June 1760, mentioned above. Fauquier had argued in favour of allowing the settlement on the Ohio, requested by certain army officers in fulfilment of a promise made in 1754 to encourage enrolment in the army. The cause of the Board's negative attitude to this petition was the outbreak of war, which had changed the situation with regard to the expansion of settlement. Before the war, they wrote,

> no Contest […] existed with any foreign power in reference to the Dominion of the country, nor was it then understood to be parts of Lands claimed by the Indians as their hunting grounds.[17]

At the time of writing, however, a different interpretation had developed. For one thing, the struggle with the French had yet to be determined ; secondly, the Board of Trade maintained that peace and alliance with the Indians had been obtained only by promising not to encroach on their land. Therefore, they concluded,

> it appears to us, that the attempting to make any Settlement upon those Lands, would be a measure of the most dangerous Tendency; That it would be an open violation of our late solemn Engagements with the Indians […]; That [...] the Impropriety of encouraging Settlements upon Lands, the Dominion and

---

[15] Secretary Fox to William Johnson, March 13, 1756, in O'Callaghan & Fernow, ed. *New York Colonial Documents*, vol. 7, 76.

[16] Lords of Trade to Governor Hardy, March 19, 1756, in O'Callaghan & Fernow, ed. *New York Colonial Documents*, vol. 7, 77.

[17] Board of Trade to Fauquier, June 13, 1760, CO 5/1367: 204.

> Possession of which remain yet to be decided by the Sword, is so obvious, that we are at a loss to guess at the Motive which could induce you to encourage such a proposition.[18]

The Board was squarely opposed to any settlement on the Ohio "until His Majesty's further pleasure be known." While concern for Indian reactions was only part of the reason for this position, it is clear that the expansionist policy identified by Alvord, if it ever existed, had been stopped by the war.[19]

Egremont was thus continuing rather than changing Board of Trade policy when, in December 1761, he issued instructions to the governors of the seven royal colonies "forbidding them to grant Lands or make Settlements which may interfere with the Indians bordering on those colonies."[20] The governors were ordered in the future to pass all requests for land grants on to the Board of Trade for approval.

Alvord claims that the government saw these directions as "merely tentative in character; and it was fully understood in political circles that they would remain in force only until the end of the war."[21] This policy, however, was confirmed and extended by the Royal Proclamation issued after the peace in 1763. In it, the Allegheny Mountains were established as a boundary between Indians and colonists and all the land west of it was reserved for the use of the Indians while the general power of buying land from the Indians was reserved to the Crown (see Map 3).

The exchange of letters surrounding the creation of the Proclamation reveals a number of things about Indian policy. Traditionally, historians have concentrated on the role of particular politicians in formulating the policy; Shel-

---

[18] Board of Trade to Fauquier, June 13, 1760, CO 5/1367: 205.

[19] This also seems to be the conclusion reached by Oliver Morton Dickerson, *American Colonial Government 1696–1765: A Study of the British Board of Trade in its Relation to the American Colonies, Political, Industrial, Administrative* (Cleveland OH: Arthur H. Clarke, 1912): 336–56.

[20] Draught for an Instruction, December 2, 1761, CO 324/17: 82. Further evidence that this policy was established before Egremont became secretary of state in October of that year is provided by the Instructions to Amherst, May 15, 1761, CO 5/23: 130, which contain a similar order not to grant land, along with a specific reference to a change of policy. A.H. Basye reaches the same conclusion, stating further that the Board "was simply carrying out a policy already vaguely determined"; *The Lords Commissioners of Trade and Plantations, commonly known as the Board of Trade 1748–1782* (New Haven CT: Yale UP, 1925): 115, note 32.

[21] Alvord, *The Mississippi Valley in British Politics*, vol.1, 127.

burne's significance as President of the Board, especially, has been hotly disputed.[22] It is now fairly certain that he played a minor part in the deliberations and that the Secretary of State bore the main responsibility for the work conducted in the spring and summer of 1763.

In fact, rather than discussing individual contributions to the bureaucratic procedure, it is worth laying emphasis on the conclusions drawn by such scholars as H.R. Humphreys and Jack Sosin: first, that the principles contained in the proclamation were the consistent result of the deliberations preceding it (and not of some last minute changes made by men unacquainted with the thoughts underlying it as claimed by Alvord);[23] and, secondly, that the policy thus formulated was not based on the ideas of any one person but, rather, the result of the experience gained during the war and the regulations laid down at that time, which simply received the stamp of official approval in the Proclamation.[24] Sosin emphasizes the view that what counted in shaping policy was "practical experience" rather than any considerations of theory among the politicians.[25]

The policy adopted was basically formulated in two documents: a letter written by Egremont on May 5 (with a large number of enclosures) directing the Board of Trade to consider the issues connected with Britain's new acquisitions following the peace with France, and the report, dated June 8, written by the Board in response to this. A draft drawn up by John Pownall, secretary of the Board, preceded the final report.

There is considerable difference between Pownall's draft and the final report on the question of expansion and Indian land. The sections of the draft

---

[22] Alvord, for example, strongly advocated the role of Shelburne and his potential divergence from the others in the Grenville ministry (*The Mississippi Valley in British Politics*, vol.1, ch. 5–7). R.A. Humphreys rejects both the emphasis on Shelburne and the idea that the final proclamation deviated from the agreed policy; Humphreys, "Lord Shelburne and the Royal Proclamation of 1763," *English Historical Review* 49 (1934): 241–65. See also Sosin, *Whitehall and the Wilderness*, ch. 3.

[23] Humphreys, "Lord Shelburne and the Royal Proclamation of 1763", 258 (though Lawson objects to this in relation to the provisions concerning Quebec; see *The Imperial Challenge*, 9).

[24] Sosin, *Whitehall and the Wilderness*, ch. 2–3. Francis Paul Prucha, on the other hand, sees the Proclamation and especially the boundary line as "a great departure from the past," though he also notes that this policy had some precedents; Prucha, *American Indian Policy in the Formative Years: The Indian Trade and Intercourse Acts 1790–1834* (Cambridge MA: Harvard UP, 1962): 13–15.

[25] Sosin, *Whitehall and the Wilderness*, 77.

dealing with these matters are longer than in the report and they appear close to the beginning. Emphasis is placed on the dual needs of preventing the excessive extension of the colonies and upholding the promises made to the Indians. Proof of the latter is enlisted through reference to earlier reports, orders and treaties with the Indians. For these reasons, the draft states, the colonies should not be allowed to expand beyond the mountains, and all the land to the west of them

> should be considered as land belonging to the Indians, the dominion of which is to be protected for them by forts and military establishments in proper places.[26]

In the final report, on the other hand, the emphasis is placed elsewhere. Nothing is said about the need to restrain the expansion of the old colonies. Rather, the creation of the Indian country is mentioned along with other areas in contrast to those newly acquired places where some form of government should be established. Occurring almost half-way into the report, it is stated that

> as no such regular civil government is either necessary or can indeed be established, where no perpetual Residence or planting is intended; It will there be sufficient to provide for the free Trade of All Your Majesty's Subjects as is best suited to that End. Such we apprehend to be the case of Newfoundland [...] Such is the case of Senegal [...] And such we apprehend will be the Case of that Territory in North America which in Your Majesty's Justice and Humanity as well as sound Policy is proposed to be left, under Your Majesty's immediate Protection, to the Indian Tribes for their Hunting Grounds; where no Settlement by planting is intended, immediately at least, to be attempted; and consequently where no particular form of Civil Government can be established.[27]

While there is no difference in the actual recommendations concerning the Indian country and trade (which were strongly expressed in Egremont's letter

---

[26] Mr. Pownall's Sketch of a Report, Shelburne Papers 49: 333–64, repr. in Humphreys, "Lord Shelburne and the Royal Proclamation of 1763," 259.

[27] Lords of Trade to Egremont with Report, June 8, 1763, in *Documents Relating to the Constitutional History of Canada* (hereafter *Constitutional Documents of Canada*), 2 vols., ed. Adam Shortt & Arthur G. Doughty (Ottawa: Historical Documents Publication Board, 1918), vol. 1: 139.

and the enclosures[28]), it would seem that the authors of the final report resisted any reference to policy on the expansion of the old colonies, possibly because they disagreed with Pownall's representation or maybe because they found it inappropriate in the report, which was to deal with the *new* acquisitions.[29] It is notable that the wording with regard to the Indian country is completely changed in the report; any reference to "land belonging to the Indians" or "dominion" of the Indians is avoided.

In the Proclamation the wording is again slightly different:

> And whereas it is just and reasonable, and essential to our Interest, and the Security of Our Colonies, that the several Nations or Tribes of Indians with whom We are connected, and who live under our Protection, should not be molested or disturbed in the Possession of such Parts of our Dominions and Territories as, not having been ceded to or purchased by Us, are reserved to them, or any of them, as their hunting grounds.

and a little later:

> And, We do further declare it to be Our Royal Will and Pleasure, for the present as aforesaid, to reserve under our Sovereignty, Protection and Dominion, for the use of the said Indians, all the Lands and Territories not included [in any of the colonies].[30]

It was clearly regarded as important to establish beyond doubt that sovereignty over all the land as far as the Mississippi belonged to the British king. On the other hand, it is arguable that the Proclamation entailed a recognition of the property rights of the Indians to unceded land.

Whether or not there was some disagreement between Pownall and the members of the Board of Trade on the rights of the Indians, the Proclamation essentially embodied the principles in regard to the Indians which Egremont as

---

[28] The document, called "Hints Relative to the Division and Government of the Conquered and Newly Acquired Countries in America," seems to have exerted great influence on Egremont's policy. It is attributed to Henry Ellis, former colonial governor, who was one of Egremont's chief advisors on colonial matters (Sosin, *Whitehall and the Wilderness*, 56–57). The document is printed in *The Mississippi Valley Historical Review* 8 (1921–22): 370–73.

[29] The difference between the draft and the final version does not seem to support the claim made by many scholars of the large influence of the secretary, mentioned in ch. 1.

[30] By the King. A Proclamation, October 7, 1763, in Doughty & Shortt, ed. *Constitutional Documents of Canada*, vol.1, 166–67.

Secretary of State had envisaged as the foundation for improving relations with them.

As early as January 1763, in a letter to Amherst, the Commander-in-chief for the American colonies, Egremont referred to this in his comments on the need to avoid war with the Indians because of settler encroachments:

> His Maty having it much at heart to conciliate the Affection of the Indian nations, by every Act of strict Justice, and by affording them His Royal Protection from any Incroachment on the lands they have reserved to themselves.[31]

The same wish to establish friendly relations by recognizing their rights and preventing abuses against them is emphasized in Egremont's letter to the Board of Trade of May 5. Among other things, the members of the Board were asked to give their opinion on how Indian attacks could be avoided ("the Preservation of the internal Peace and Tranquillity of the Country against any Indian Disturbances"). Egremont allows no room for doubt about the general direction of policy:

> Tho' in order to succeed effectually in this point [maintaining peace], it may become necessary to erect some Forts in the Indian Country, with their [the Indians'] Consent, yet His Majesty's Justice and Moderation inclines him to adopt the more eligible Method of conciliating the Minds of the Indians by the Mildness of His Government, by Protecting their Persons and Property, and securing to them all the Possessions, Rights and Privileges they have hitherto enjoyed, and are entitled to, most cautiously guarding against any Invasion or Occupation of their Hunting Lands, the Possession of which is to be acquired by fair Purchase only.[32]

It may be suggested that underlying the Proclamation was a belief that it was important to improve relations with the Indians and that the best means of achieving this would be to prevent the encroachment of the settlers on Indian land, thereby proving to the Indians the sincerity and goodwill of the British government. As mentioned above, the basic legal and moral right of the Indians to their land was not in question.

This view is further elaborated by an interesting study of treaty relations between Indians and colonizers by Dorothy Jones, who sees the Proclamation as inaugurating a period of conscious policy formulation relating to the Indians

---

[31] Egremont to Amherst, January 27, 1763, CO 5/214: 308.

[32] Egremont to the Board of Trade, May 5, 1763, CO 323/15: 103.

(she calls it a "policy statement on a grand scale"). In Jones's view, the Proclamation marks the beginning of a phase in Indian–British relations where the attempt was made to achieve a mutually satisfactory, lasting solution to the problems disturbing that relationship, focusing particularly on the idea of a boundary as something desirable for both parties.[33]

Alvord, in accordance with his general interpretation, stresses the idea that the provisions of the Proclamation relating to western expansion were regarded by the government as temporary expedients not designed to stand in the way of that expansion.[34] It is true that care was taken to reserve to the government the right to change the provisions concerning the land reserved to the Indians. Thus, both in Pownall's draft and in the final report of the Board, the advice against the extension of settlement as well as in favour of protection of Indian land is modified by the words "for the present at least" or "immediately at least"; the same is repeated twice in Egremont's favourable response to the report. Humphreys also points out that after the Proclamation had finally, and rather hurriedly, been drawn up, the words "for the present" were inserted in two places by Pownall.[35]

Thus it was considered important to allow for future changes of policy; but this need not imply that the provisions of the Proclamation were intended as window-dressing to pacify the Indians. The insertion of these modifications may as well have been intended to 'cover the back' of the government and to allay the fears of the colonists about a permanent prohibition on expansion. A letter from the Board of Trade to William Johnson of August 5 indicates that the policy with respect to the Indians was expected to be long-lasting. The need for a permanent policy towards the Indians is stressed, and the Proclamation is seen as a vehicle for this:

> the necessity there is of speedily falling upon some Method of regulating the Indian commerce and policy, upon some more general and better established system than has hitherto taken place. It is with a view to this object that we have proposed to His Majesty that a proclamation should be issued declarative of His Majesty's final determination to permit no grants of lands nor any

---

[33] Dorothy V. Jones, *License for Empire: Colonialism by Treaty in Early America* (Chicago: U of Chicago P, 1982): 46–47.

[34] Alvord, *The Mississippi Valley in British Politics*, vol. 1, 203; Dickerson (*American Colonial Government*, 349) supports this interpretation.

[35] Humphreys, "Lord Shelburne and the Royal Proclamation of 1763," 254.

> settlements to be made within certain fixed bounds [...] leaving all the territory within these bounds free for the hunting grounds of the Indians.[36]

"His Majesty's final determination" surely suggests that the policy was intended to have some permanency. It would seem that Alvord's emphasis on the temporary character of both the Proclamation and the instructions of 1761 needs to be modified. Alvord supports his interpretation by claiming that most of the politicians and even the king were in favour of more or less rapid expansion to the west.[37] While this is to be borne out by the many private papers consulted by Alvord, it also seems fair to conclude that such ideas did not find any expression in the official policy of the early 1760s.

The urgency referred to in the Board's letter was caused by the news reaching England in July that war with the Indians had broken out. The Indians, under the leadership of Pontiac, had made several successful attacks on the forts in the interior and in fact were sufficiently strong to keep up the offensive until the autumn of the following year.

The causes of the war were widely discussed but no doubt included both resentment at the settlements which the colonists continued to build on Indian land and fear of the consequences of the British victory over the French, possibly increased by rumours started by French settlers. The Indians had been able to exploit the rivalry of the two European powers to their own advantage both economically and politically and were apprehensive of the changes which took place with the end of the war.[38]

It has also been suggested that the decision to refrain from giving the Indians presents, as had been the custom, caused great dissatisfaction. Amherst was

---

[36] Lords of Trade to William Johnson, August 5, 1763, in O'Callaghan & Fernow, ed. *New York Colonial Documents*, vol. 7, 535.

[37] For example, Alvord, *The Mississippi Valley in British Politics*, vol. 1, 178–79, 212–13.

[38] See Francis Parkman, *The Conspiracy of Pontiac and the Indian War after the Conquest of Canada*, 2 vols. (1870; London: Macmillan, 1899), for a vivid account of the struggle and the various circumstances leading to it. Parkman also mentions that attacks were planned by the Indians in both 1761 and 1762 (*The Conspiracy of Pontiac*, vol. 1, 188). Parkman's attribution of overall leadership of the war in 1763 to Pontiac has been contested byHoward Henry Peckham, who suggested that the war was the outcome of attacks by several distinctly organized groups; *Pontiac and the Indian Uprising* (Princeton NJ: Princeton UP, 1947): 107–11 – though Wilbur Ripley Jacobs, in *Dispossessing the American Indian: Indians and Whites on the Colonial Frontier* (New York: Charles Scribner's Sons, 1972: 83–87), offers a number of arguments for why Parkman's original interpretation should be retained.

responsible for this decision; he disliked the Indians and no doubt underestimated their power. Having been ordered to economize, he decided that presents were no longer necessary now that the war was over. It is uncertain whether Egremont knew anything about this fatal decision.[39]

At a rather more sophisticated level of interpretation, the peace treaty itself, in which the French ceded the Northwest to the British, may also be seen as the major cause of the outbreak, since the Indians refused to acknowledge French possession of the area[40] and consequently would not accept British assumption of sovereignty over it.[41] In this way, the Indian war becomes an extension of the war with the French.

The war caused great concern in Britain and made a powerful impression on those involved in it. Official reactions were characterized by outrage (comments referred to "barbarities" and "savage, unprovoked behaviour")[42] and by a desire to bring the hostilities to an end. In a letter from October 1763 to Amherst, Halifax advocated a mixture of sanctions and rewards to achieve peace with the Indians. He first states that he assumes that

> the particular Measure you have taken for chastizing those Indians, whose Treacheries and Barbarities have deserved severe Punishment, will soon have produced the desired Effects.

Later he continues:

> When the Indians shall have been reduced to due Submission, and the Peace of the Country restored, The next great Object of Attention is to secure the Duration of it, by preventing all just Cause of Discontent & Uneasiness among them, in future.[43]

---

[39] Alden claims that Egremont should be held at least partly responsible for the cutback on presents to the northern Indians (and, in turn, for the war) because he was the one who ordered Amherst to economize; *John Stuart and the Southern Colonial Frontier*, 181). On the other hand, in a letter of July 9, 1763 to Amherst, Egremont, having mentioned the rumour that the Indians were dissatisfied, encouraged Amherst, if he thought it a good idea, to support Johnson with further funds to buy presents (Egremont to Amherst, July 9, 1763, CO 5/214: 328).

[40] See Jones, *License for Empire*, 48, 71–73, for examples of the explicit denials by the Indians of French (and British) possession of the west.

[41] Jones, *License for Empire*, 58, 71.

[42] Egremont to Amherst, August 13, 1763, CO 5/214: 336–37.

[43] Halifax to Amherst, October 11, 1763, CO 5/214: 345.

He points out that the Proclamation, which was transmitted with this letter, would be an important means to achieve this.

It is clear from the language in which the acts of the war are described – "chastizing," "Treacheries," "Punishment" – that in some respects, at least, the Indians of the west were regarded as being under the sovereignty of the British king, as is also emphasized in the Proclamation, and therefore required to submit to his military power; the hostilities were also frequently referred to as the "insurrection" or "conspiracy" of the Indians.[44]

It is also clear that the British regarded the war and its causes with great seriousness. The discontent of the Indians had been discussed frequently in the letters before the Indian war, and the decision to publish the policy with regard to the new acquisitions in a proclamation, rather than in the usual and more indirect form of instructions to the governors, was caused by news of the war. It was hoped that it would reassure the Indians of the sincerity of government intentions and put a stop to the clashes between the settlers and the Indians, partly by establishing a firm boundary between them and partly by redirecting the attention of land-seeking settlers to the new colonies in the north and south, where there was supposedly plenty of vacant land.

Although the land policy of the early 1760s was thus firmly based on the wish to curtail the expansion of the settlers, the intentions of the government in London were not generally translated into action. The situation was and remained chaotic, as the works of the many scholars in the field illustrate; on the frontier, colonists persisted in settling on Indian land, with the colonial governments unwilling or unable to stop them, and speculators still purchased huge tracts of land from the Indians, who found it impossible to resist the offers made to them.

Wealthy settlers, often with the backing of monied interests in Britain, formed innumerable land companies with more or less ambitious plans for inland settlement. Petitions for grants were sent unremittingly to the colonial and imperial governments, the governors frequently issued grants contrary to their instructions, and sometimes government officials in Britain even favoured such schemes, though often handicapped by lack of correct geographical in-

---

[44] In other respects, the Indians seemed to be regarded as in large measure retaining their independence; they were, for example, rarely referred to as subjects of the king (in the Proclamation, they were thus the "nations or tribes of Indians with whom we are connected, and who live under our protection"; see above, quotation, 39, and note 30) and when the issue of jurisdiction over the Indian country was discussed it was with regard to the colonists, never the Indians.

formation and knowledge of local conditions.[45] Generally, though, the imperial governments tried to prevent expansion in accordance with the Proclamation and the negotiations for a new boundary in 1768 (see Map 4). The government, however, was essentially powerless to control the settlers, and white settlement continued to move westward, especially after 1768, when there was a veritable explosion of speculative settlement schemes.[46]

The regulation of trade

The other major cause of friction between Indians and colonists, the fraudulent practices of traders frequently mentioned by the superintendents, also received considerable attention in this period.

The Royal Proclamation touched on the problem but left it unsolved, simply permitting trade to all who had a licence issued by the governors, thus following the recommendations of the Board of Trade in their report of June 8 and those of Halifax in his letter of September 1763.[47] In some respects, the provisions of the Proclamation made things worse. John Alden points out that the Proclamation ruled out trading monopolies, one means which the southern colonies had at times employed to impose some kind of regulation on trade.[48] Already at this time, however, a new plan was under consideration;[49] it was finally drafted by the Board under the leadership of Hillsborough, probably in collaboration with Halifax,[50] in July 1764, and sent to the superintendents and governors for comment.

---

[45] The proposal for the colony of Vandalia, which was favourably regarded by many British politicians, was framed within the cession made by the Six Nations in 1768, but beyond the Kanawha River, which was supposed to be the limit of settlement (see quotation in Hillsborough to Johnson, May 13, 1769, in O'Callaghan & Fernow, ed. *New York Colonial Documents*, vol. 8, 166, discussed below).

[46] See, for example, Alden, *John Stuart and the Southern Colonial Frontier*, ch. 13, 15–18; Alvord, *The Mississippi Valley in British Politics*, vol.1, ch. 11 & vol. 2, ch. 4 onwards; Sosin, *Whitehall and the Wilderness*, ch. 5. See also below.

[47] Halifax to Lords of Trade, September 19, 1763, in Doughty & Shortt, *Constitutional Documents of Canada*, vol. 1, 153–55.

[48] Alden, *John Stuart and the Southern Colonial Frontier*, 208.

[49] Halifax to Amherst, October 19, 1763, CO 5/214: 353. The desirability of such a plan was already being pointed out by the Board in November 1757 (Board of Trade to Lyttleton, November 9, 1757, CO 5/403: 202–203) and again in 1762 (Board of Trade to Boone, June 3, 1762, CO 5/404: 172).

[50] Alden, *John Stuart and the Southern Colonial Frontier*, 244; many of the ideas

It foresaw far-reaching changes with complete centralization, putting trade and other Indian matters under the control of imperial officials (the superintendents). All colonial laws concerning Indian affairs would be repealed and even the governors and commanders-in-chief were not to deal with the Indians without informing the superintendents first. The superintendents would be given broad powers to regulate trade (to be conducted at certain posts) and to maintain peace and order. Finally, it reiterated the measures of the Proclamation for preventing the private purchase of Indian land and for establishing a boundary between the Indian country and the colonies.[51]

The reaction of the superintendents was highly favourable – which was natural, since much of the plan was based on their recommendations. However, the stumbling-block was the cost it would entail; it was envisaged, albeit reluctantly, that it could be financed by a tax on the trade, but reactions to the Stamp Act had shown that taxes were not popular and the plan never reached Parliament. Furthermore, fur traders in the north were strongly opposed to conducting trade at specified places, which, they claimed, would be impracticable in an area with such vast distances.

The plan was never officially put into practice, but the superintendents gradually came to implement many of its practical points with the support of the commander-in-chief, General Gage,[52] but without official authority to back their actions. The experiences of the superintendents during the next couple of years were somewhat disappointing; the traders proved almost impossible to control, not least because of their numbers and the size of the country, and the agents employed by the superintendents complained of lack of powers of enforcement. Furthermore, the colonial governments showed little willingness to co-operate in regulating trade.

Another complicating factor was the constantly changing relationship with the Indians, especially in the south, where shifting alliances among the tribes, movements in settlement on the frontier, and the behaviour of the traders

---

contained in the plan had been foreshadowed by Halifax in his report of 1754 as president of the Board of Trade, referred to earlier (for details of the report, see Alden, "The Albany Congress and the Creation of the Indian Superintendencies," 200).

[51] Lords of Trade to Johnson, July 10, 1764, in O'Callaghan & Fernow, ed. *New York Colonial Documents*, vol. 7, 637–41.

[52] Alden, *John Stuart and the Southern Colonial Frontier*, 149, but see also Peter Marshall, "Colonial Protest and Imperial Retrenchment: Indian Policy 1764–68," *American Studies* 5.1 (1971): 1–17, who maintains that Gage's support was somewhat reluctant.

frequently altered the attitude of the Indians towards the English. The superintendents were busily engaged in congresses with the Indians at which they made promises to restrain settlers and traders, which they afterwards found it difficult to keep.[53]

In London, action on regulating trade as well as controlling the advance of settlement slowed right down when there was yet another change of government in 1765. The Rockingham ministry was only in office one year and was succeeded in 1766 by another one headed by Pitt (now Lord Chatham). Finally, in 1767, under the secretaryship of Shelburne, who took time to gather much material on the American situation, a new attempt was made to determine the future of trade and other relations with the Indians. The new plan was marked by a striking departure from past attitudes.

A change of policy?

In October 1767, Shelburne requested the Board of Trade to consider the future management of Indian affairs. The letter was the outcome of a plan Shelburne had been working on since spring and which had been presented to Cabinet in September.[54] The point of departure was the enormous expense of the Indian Department (in large measure caused by the attempt to implement the plan of 1764) and of the management of the forts in the interior. The Board of Trade was asked to consider the position of the superintendents – could they be dispensed with or, conversely, should their powers be increased? Shelburne was in favour of turning over the whole management of Indian affairs to the colonies and clearly placed great weight on a number of petitions he had received

---

[53] See, for example, Alvord, *The Mississippi Valley in British Politics*, vol. 1, ch. 11, and Alden, *John Stuart and the Southern Colonial Frontier*, ch. 14.

[54] Alvord, *The Mississippi Valley in British Politics*, vol. 1, 331–58. Alvord describes the circumstances surrounding the formulation of this policy – pressure exerted by Townshend to reduce costs and the growing hostility towards Shelburne of many of the other cabinet ministers – in great detail. See also Alden, *John Stuart and the Southern Colonial Frontier*, 258–61, and Sosin, *Whitehall and the Wilderness*, ch. 6. Shelburne's dissatisfaction with the plan of 1764 went back at least as far as December 1766, – see Shelburne to Gage, December 11, 1766, in *The Correspondence of General Thomas Gage with the Secretaries of State 1763–1775* (hereafter *Correspondence of Gage*), 2 vols, ed. Clarence Edwin Carter (New Haven CT: Yale UP, 1933): vol. 1, 48–49 and Shelburne to Johnson, December 11, 1766, CO 5/225: 8.

from merchants and land speculators;[55] his formulation of the position is interesting:

> Or how far it may be right to strengthen the Hands of these officers [the superintendents] agreeable to their repeated applications in order to give a more efficient strength to an institution independent both of the civil and military power, but as the general Regulations of Trade attempt[e]d to be carried into execution by the Superintend[en]ts are asserted in these Petitions to be ill suited to the particular circumstances of the several Provinces, and to serve to clog the trade with useless & vexatious restrictions than to remove the evils of which complaint has been made, and as it appears also from the correspondence that the governors of several of the Colonies do not keep up a regular correspondence with these officers, paying little or no regard to the rules laid down by them, if your Lordships should think their further continuance unnecessary you will then state your opinion to his Majesty in what method it may be proper to intrust both the Trade & management of the Indians to the care of the colonies themselves, leaving it to them to judge of their several Interests with those people and to pass laws which shall be adapted to the circumstances of the respective Provinces.[56]

Johnson had continually sent home reports of the difficulties connected with regulating trade and the objections made by the commercial interest,[57] but Shelburne was apparently more inclined to accept the judgement of the merchants and strongly recommend that the regulation of trade be returned to the colonies. Shelburne further suggested that most of the forts might be abolished and the rest turned over to the colonies, who would then be responsible for their upkeep. Finally, he transmitted several letters from the military commanders in America in which it was suggested that three new colonies should be established in the interior; he enumerated the several arguments in favour of this proposition, which he himself regarded in a very positive light.

---

[55] For example, Sosin, *Whitehall and the Wilderness*, 150–68, shows the influence on Shelburne's policy of Benjamin Franklin, Richard Jackson and Jeffrey Amherst in particular (all three biased in favour of the colonies). Sosin, however, also shows that some of the points – those relating to the forts in the interior and the Indian trade – originated in a plan drawn up under the previous ministry by Lord Barrington, Secretary-at-War (who remained in office after the fall of Rockingham) in close cooperation with Gage (see Marshall, "Colonial Protest and Imperial Retrenchment," 9–11.).

[56] Shelburne to Lords of Trade, October 5, 1767, in O'Callaghan & Fernow, ed. *New York Colonial Documents*, vol. 7, 981.

[57] For example, Johnson to Shelburne, December 16, 1766, in O'Callaghan & Fernow, ed. *New York Colonial Documents*, vol. 7, 880–83, in which the objections of Quebec merchants are mentioned.

There is a conspicuous change of tone in the letter with regard to the Indians as compared to earlier ones, even those written by Shelburne himself. In fact, it is rather difficult to determine Shelburne's attitude towards the Indians. In September 1766, he had written to Stuart instructing him to "take every measure that prudence can suggest to appease for the present the too just resentment of the Indian tribes [...] till more regulated measures can be taken."[58] In December of the same year, Johnson was informed that

> when once the Irregularities of these Men [traders] can be restrained for the future [...] it will not be so difficult a Task as is generally imagined to conciliate entirely the Minds of the Indians – As soon as they find that their Boundaries are not encroached upon; that they are not cheated in their Dealings, that Fraudes when committed are punished [...] and that we really mean to cherish and protect them, they will naturally be led to look up to Us as their Guardians and Defenders.[59]

Even in February 1767, Fauquier had been instructed that people encroaching on Indian land must be stopped, since "the Prosperity of the American Colonies, especially their back settlers, depends so much on maintaining Peace and Friendship with the Indians."[60] In this fashion, Shelburne repeats many of the common assumptions about Indian dissatisfaction and the need to preserve their friendship, at a time when he was beginning to work out a new plan which largely disregarded these factors.

Thus, in the letter of October 1767 there is no mention of the need to calm the fears of the Indians in respect of their land (much less any mention of negotiating for the land needed for the new colonies) nor of the prevention of abuses by traders. Indians are mainly considered in the light of raids on the settlers; thus the colonies must themselves pay for what is necessary to achieve "security against Indian Incursions"; the main function of the existing forts is "the forming of a certain Barrier against the Indians for the security of the colonies"; and one of the advantages of the proposed colonies would be that

> being situated behind the other provinces they will be of singular use to keep the Indians in awe and prevent their hostile incursions upon the Frontiers to the eastward, while those savages who are hemmed in by our settlements on

---

58 Shelburne to Stuart, September 13, 1766, CO 5/225: 2.

59 Shelburne to Johnson, December 11, 1766, CO 5/225: 11–12.

60 Shelburne to Fauquier, February 19, 1767, CO 5/1345: 307.

> both sides must either become domiciliated and reconciled to our laws and manners or be obliged to retire to a distance.[61]

This emphasis on the "incursions" of the Indians is in striking contrast to the tenor of Johnson's reports, which almost always stressed the encroachments of the settlers on Indian land and the relative restraint of the Indians.[62] The whole idea of the need to overawe the Indians is diametrically opposed to the earlier attitude of gaining their affections and gradually reconciling them to British rule.

The policy sponsored by Shelburne was thus a departure from earlier measures. The reasons for this are not easy to determine and have been the cause of much debate;[63] Alvord sees Lord Shelburne as one of the major representatives of the expansionist forces in British politics, quite in line with the Pittite radicalism that favoured opening up the west to settlement.[64] While Shelburne's statements and his obvious reliance on American opinion would seem to support this, Sosin modifies this view, claiming that the foremost consideration in the mind of Shelburne was nevertheless the need to reduce expenditure (also consistent with Pittite policies, in this case opposition to enforcing taxation on the Americans).[65] Be this as it may, Sosin is certainly correct in pointing to the inconsistency of policy under Shelburne's stewardship of the colonies.[66]

---

[61] Shelburne to Lords of Trade, October 5, 1767, CO 5/1345: 983.

[62] See also Alden, *John Stuart and the Southern Colonial Frontier*, ch. 13, on the attitude of the southern superintendent.

[63] Besides Alvord and Sosin, see, for example, R.A. Humphreys, "Lord Shelburne and British Colonial Policy, 1766–1768," *English Historical Review* 50 (1935): 257–77.

[64] Alvord, *The Mississippi Valley in British Politics*, vol. 1, ch. 10. Alvord also argues that the repeal of the Stamp Act by the Rockingham ministry in itself necessitated a new western policy, since an important means of funding was thus given up. As this ministry took no steps to carry this out, the whole issue had become quite pressing by the time Shelburne took office – forcing him to adopt a new approach to the problems (Alvord, *The Mississippi Valley in British Politics*, vol. 1, 241–51).

[65] Sosin, *Whitehall and the Wilderness*, 136. Sosin also claims that Shelburne's advocacy of the interior colonies was provoked by the wish to create an extra source of revenue (from the selling of land) (Sosin, *Whitehall and the Wilderness*, 158).

[66] Sosin, *Whitehall and the Wilderness*, 122–27. A further example of this is the fact that after his letter of October to the Board – which essentially favoured abandoning imperial control of the west and Indian affairs – he asked the Board to look into the matter of the boundary-line, which had never been formally established. Establishing a boundary-line (as indeed happened in the course of 1768 on the recommendation of the Board; see Map 4) was ultimately a measure of imperial management, closing the west

In any case, Shelburne's radical measures had less of a lasting effect than they might have had; in January 1768, responsibility for the colonies was removed from his office and placed under the newly created third Secretary of State.[67] It was not until well after Hillsborough had taken up this new office that the Board of Trade finally made its report on Shelburne's letter of October, and Hillsborough would thus have had plenty of time to make his influence felt.

In their report, the Board considered the questions brought up by Shelburne in great detail. On the matter of the office of superintendent, it was pointed out that it had served a good purpose during the war and had also been important afterwards in maintaining good relations with the Indians. Upon careful consideration of the problems connected with encroachments on land and the discontent this had caused, the Board recommended that the superintendents remain in charge of land issues[68] and, furthermore, that steps be finally taken to negotiate the new boundary, as recommended in their report in December.

On the question of trade, however, they went along with Shelburne's idea by recommending that responsibility be returned to the colonies – mainly, it seems, to save money. The Board recognized that the mismanagement of the Indian trade by the colonies before the war was a significant factor in causing the Indian war and declared that they would never make this recommendation if they thought the same would happen again. But, they concluded,

> we trust, that the experience which the old colonies have had of the ill effects of such inattention and neglect, will induce all of them to use more caution and better management for the future.[69]

One wonders what could have induced the Board to draw such conclusions – their hopes were certainly not borne out by the future actions of the colonies.

They also recommended that the forts in the interior be reduced, but left the details to the military department. However, they opposed the establishment of colonies in the interior, declaring that such an idea was "entirely new." They

---

to settlement contrary to the wish of the colonies and thus in continuity with the policy of the early years of the decade (Lords of Trade to Shelburne, December 23, 1767, in O'Callaghan & Fernow, ed. *New York Colonial Documents*, vol. 7, 1004–1005).

[67] See ch. 1, 22 above.

[68] According to Alvord, this was based on a suggestion for compromise made by Shelburne (*The Mississippi Valley in British Politics*, vol. 1, 353).

[69] Representation of Lords of Trade on the State of Indian Affairs, March 7, 1768, in O'Callaghan & Fernow, ed. *New York Colonial Documents*, vol. 8, 25.

claimed that the policy so far had been to confine settlement to the seaboard in order to secure easy access by ship, to the advantage of commerce and the transportation of raw materials. Since they found that this arrangement had been successful, they saw no reason to change it. They furthermore feared that the proposed colonies would attract people from the old colonies engaged in producing goods which Britain needed, which would thus work to the disadvantage of the mother-country. Nor did they accept any of the arguments in favour of the proposition brought forward by Shelburne.

The recommendations of the Board were accepted by the government and executed by Hillsborough. The policy which took effect was a compromise between existing provisions and the radical suggestions of Shelburne. The idea of negotiating a boundary was derived from the proclamation in 1763, hence a mark of continuity with the policy of that year; the abandoning of many of the forts was certainly not opposed to the policy of leaving the western territories to the Indians; nor was the opposition to erecting new colonies in the interior. Both Alvord and Sosin see Hillsborough as chiefly responsible for this latter decision. Lord Clare, the president of the Board of Trade at this time, had declared himself in favour of one interior colony,[70] but had clearly been induced to change his mind before the writing of the report, and it is logical to see in this the influence of Hillsborough.[71] There were several reasons why Hillsborough was against unlimited extenuation of settlement, and the conviction that an Indian war would result was not the least of them.

On the other hand, it is remarkable that in the report of the Board the reactions of the Indians did not figure as an argument against the establishment of the colonies (nor had this been considered in Shelburne's letter). Furthermore, the Board was not completely against expansion, as the boundary-line suggested by them opened up for settlement a considerable area west of the middle colonies – a fact that was emphasized twice in the report.[72]

---

[70] Alvord, *The Mississippi Valley in British Politics*, vol. 1, 352–53. Alvord also states that Clare had been subjected to the persuasive powers of Franklin on this point, while Shelburne had worked on the other members of the Board.

[71] Alvord, *The Mississippi Valley in British Politics*, vol. 2, ch. 1, and Sosin, *Whitehall and the Wilderness*, ch. 7; Hillsborough's resignation in 1772, after being subjected to pressure by the rest of the ministry to accept the establishment of the colony of Vandalia on the Ohio, is perhaps the best evidence of his resistance to large-scale expansion to the west.

[72] Representation of the Lords of Trade on the State of Indian Affairs, March 7, 1768, in O'Callaghan & Fernow, ed. *New York Colonial Documents*, vol. 8, 22, 30.

It is interesting also that the Board, for the first time, now described the provisions of the Proclamation for creating the Indian country as a temporary measure, referring to it as "mere provisional arrangements adapted to the exigencies of the time [i.e. Pontiac's war]."[73] It is also noticeable that although the report shows greater awareness of the significance of Indian discontent than did Shelburne's letter, there is nevertheless a tendency in the report to create the impression that the danger of Indian hostilities caused by settler encroachments had practically disappeared or would do so if only the boundary was negotiated.

Finally, the most significant measure of the report in relation to Indian affairs, the turning-over of the regulation of trade to the colonies, was a dramatic change of policy, the effects of which were to be felt until the Revolution made this point obsolete.

In his comments on the new provisions, William Johnson warned of the consequences, particularly of the improbability that the colonies would take their new responsibility seriously, in view of their previous record in that field and of present settler sentiment towards the Indians. His general description of the latter is illuminating:

> This [the Indians' increasing apprehensions after the Seven Years War] was one of the Natural consequences of our great encrease of our Advancement into their Country and of the enlargement of our connections with them and could only be surmounted by degrees by favours [&] A seemin attention to their Interests, establishments for their Affairs, and some Summary Methods for obtaining Justice – our people are not inclined to do this, They began to think them unworthy attention, they encroached upon them Insulted and Wronged them and altho' they paid dear for this during the Indian War, yet no sooner was it terminated in 1764 than elated thereby, and the Conquest of Canada, and seemingly insensible that this Conquest had encreased the number of our Indian Enemys, and rendered the management of them an affair of much more difficulty than before they pushed on their encroachments and at last began to proceed to Rob and Murder them, the general turn and sentiments of our People will in spight of conviction lead them into these Errors.[74]

Passages like this (merely a repetition of observations made many times before) apparently met with little response in London at this time. In his reply, Hillsborough is much more concerned with expenses, remarking that it is of the

[73] O'Callaghan & Fernow, ed. *New York Colonial Documents*, vol. 8, 21.

[74] Johnson to Hillsborough, July 20, 1768, in O'Callaghan & Fernow, ed. *New York Colonial Documents*, vol. 8, 85.

utmost importance to reduce expenditure. With reference to the colonies, he merely comments that he has no doubt that

> through your assistance, and with your advice, the Colonies will be induced to adopt such regulations for the Commercial parts as will improve the Trade and fix the Affection of the Savages, and in the end produce all those advantages which you seem to think would have been derived from the Execution of the plan suggested by the Board of Trade in 1764.[75]

Since Johnson had pointed to the fact that Hillsborough was one of the authors of the plan of 1764, Hillsborough felt called upon to state that in view of the general circumstances and the attitudes of the colonies "I must confess that I do entirely concur in the measures which have been proposed by the Board of Trade."[76]

All in all, the new policy was a compromise between earlier views and the expedient of reducing the administrative costs of the increasingly troublesome American colonies. Peter Marshall argues that the mere wish to save money is insufficient explanation for the decision to abandon imperial regulation of the Indian trade. He maintains that the whole political situation surrounding the Chatham ministry – "colonial unrest, personal prudence, political instability in England" – must be taken into account.[77] This insight, however, does not alter the fact that the reduction of expenditure, which was closely connected with the factors mentioned by Marshall, was regarded as vital by contemporary politicians and was mentioned without exception as the main reason for the new measures.

The change of tone in reference to the Indians noted in the discussion of Shelburne's letter is perhaps less important, since he did not remain in charge of the Southern Department. The similar, though less marked, tendency in the report of the Board might well be of greater significance, considering its continuing influence on the formulation of Indian policy. However, other letters concerned with Indian affairs leaving London in the spring of 1768 are strongly reminiscent in tone of the earlier correspondence and suggests that the fundamental attitude to Indian matters remained unaltered.

---

[75] Hillsborough to Johnson, October 20, 1768, in O'Callaghan & Fernow, ed. *New York Colonial Documents*, vol. 8, 101.

[76] O'Callaghan & Fernow, ed. *New York Colonial Documents*, vol. 8, 101.

[77] Marshall, "Colonial Protest and Imperial Retrenchment," 17.

For example, in a letter to Johnson written on 12 March (five days after the Board had completed its report, but five days before it was officially sent to the Secretary of State), Hillsborough remarks on the establishment of a boundary:

> The fixing the Boundary Line will, I trust, remove the first great foundation of Jealousy and Discontent from the Minds of the Indians; and be a solid Proof to them of the sincerity of His Majesty's Intentions.

Expecting soon to be able to convey the new plan for managing Indian affairs, designed to prevent, among other things, "the unjustifiable Occupancy of their Lands," Hillsborough expresses the hope that it will "give entire Satisfaction to the Indians in all points."[78]

It may be noted that a certain difference in formulation is discernible in the letters finally transmitting the new orders (in April), depending on whether they were addressed to the superintendents or to the governors. To the former, weight is placed on justifying the new plan with reference to expense and the original purpose of the superintendencies. It is admitted that the previous record of the colonies in relation to trade was dismal, but the pious hopes of improvement voiced by the Board are echoed, and other measures are emphasized, such as the boundary line and the maintenance of the superintendents for dealing with matters regarding land. It is hinted that the reduction in the number of forts will compel the colonies to improve their behaviour for the sake of their own security.[79]

In the letter to the governors, on the other hand, little justification is given for handing over control of trade to the colonies, since such a move would obviously be greeted by them with delight. No reference is made to the past conduct of the colonies, but the greatest part of the letter is taken up with elaboration of the need to reduce the number of forts (leaving the governors to work out the implications for themselves) and with belabouring the fact that the future safety of the colonies would depend on the regulations adopted to prevent abuses towards the Indians.[80]

It is hardly surprising that the letters were formulated according to their addressees; it is an illuminating example of practices in this respect, but it is significant that the letters do not reveal any difference in underlying attitudes towards the Indians. The emphasis is placed differently according to the posi-

---

[78] Hillsborough to Johnson, March 12, 1768, CO 5/69: 112.

[79] Hillsborough to Johnson, April 15, 1768, CO 5/69: 118.

[80] Hillsborough to Governors, circular letter, April 15, 1768, CO 5/69: 115.

tion of the recipient, but the basic view, that somehow amiable relations had to be maintained with the Indians, is the same.[81]

Three years after the new policy on Indian trade was put into effect, it was becoming clear that Johnson's prophesies about its consequences were being borne out. In spite of repeated instructions,[82] the colonies had done nothing to regulate the Indian trade or place any restraints on traders, and relations with the Indians had deteriorated. In December 1771, Hillsborough seemed to be taking back his words on the plan of 1768:

> the plan for Indian affairs [of 1764] which was referred to your consideration when I was formerly in office renders it almost unnecessary for me to say how much I lament that your authority does not extend to redress those grievances which are most material.[83]

He states further:

> I am persuaded that could it have been foreseen that the colonies would have been so negligent in meeting those gracious intentions of the King [...] their [the colonies'] Representations on the subject would have not so far prevailed as to have occasioned such a deviation from the plan at first proposed, as has almost defeated every useful Object it had in view[84]

– which shows that Hillsborough was still – or again – more in favour of the plan of 1764 (which vested control of trade in the Crown) than that of 1768, evidence perhaps that the policy of 1767/68 was really an aberration, caused by Pittite influence, from the general line of thought on both western expansion and Indian policy.

The years between 1768 and 1774 show that the Board of Trade under the leadership of Hillsborough (the secretaryship and the presidency were combined under Hillsborough in June 1768) and Dartmouth basically continued to

---

[81] See also Hillsborough to Gage, April 15, 1768, in Carter, ed. *Correspondence of Gage*, vol. 2, 62, and Hillsborough to Gage, May 14, 1768, in Carter, ed. *Correspondence of Gage*, vol. 2, 67, both of which emphasize the sincere wish to improve relations with the Indians.

[82] For example, Hillsborough to Governors, circular letter, November 15, 1770, in Carter, ed. *Correspondence of Gage*, vol. 2, 254.

[83] Hillsborough to Johnson, December 4, 1771, in O'Callaghan & Fernow, ed. *New York Colonial Documents*, vol. 8, 287. This was repeated in Hillsborough to Johnson, July 1, 1772, in O'Callaghan & Fernow, ed. *New York Colonial Documents*, vol. 8, 302.

[84] O'Callaghan & Fernow, ed. *New York Colonial Documents*, vol. 8, 302.

believe that Indian rights should be protected and western expansion (in most cases) avoided.

This is illustrated by their attitude towards the boundary finally negotiated by Johnson with the Six Nations in November 1768.[85] In the course of negotiations, Johnson accepted the cession of a huge tract of land to the west of Virginia which the Six Nations claimed but which was actually inhabited by the Cherokees (see Map 5).[86] Upon hearing about the matter, Hillsborough wrote to Johnson, ordering him to try and persuade the Indians to take back their cession,[87] and referred the matter to the Board of Trade for consideration. The Board was also thoroughly dissatisfied with this cession, partly because it was feared that this would be a new cause of dissatisfaction among the Indians (especially the Cherokee), but partly also because it had already provoked the Virginians to demand that their boundary be moved further west.[88]

In the letter from Hillsborough to Johnson following the Board of Trade report in which they set forth these objections, it was stated that if the Indians had not been persuaded to change their mind, the cession would be accepted; at the same time, however, Hillsborough pointed out that acceptance of this huge area was not to have any consequences for expansion:

> It is not His Majesty's intention that the settlements of his subjects should be carried beyond the boundary of Virginia as proposed to be fixed near the Kanawha River.[89]

---

[85] The boundary in the south had been negotiated by a series of treaties between 1763 and 1768; see Jones, *License for Empire*, ch. 3, and Alden, *John Stuart and the Southern Colonial Frontier*, ch. 11.

[86] On the circumstances surrounding this cession, see Alvord, *The Mississippi Valley in British Politics*, vol. 2, 70–71, and Jones, *License for Empire*, ch. 4.

[87] Hillsborough to Johnson, January 4, 1769, in O'Callaghan & Fernow, ed. *New York Colonial Documents*, vol. 8, 144. Alvord claims that the rest of the ministry was greatly opposed to these orders; his sources are, however, colonial observers in London, who, since they were all strongly committed to western expansion, may not have been entirely reliable in their reports. Although it is true that in his letter of May 13 Hillsborough changed his orders, this may well have been due to consideration of Iroquois feelings. Alvord, *The Mississippi Valley in British Politics*, vol. 2, 75.

[88] Representation of the Board of Trade to the King upon Sir William Johnson's Treaty with the Indians, April 25, 1769, in O'Callaghan & Fernow, ed. *New York Colonial Documents*, vol. 8, 158–63.

[89] Hillsborough to Johnson, May 13, 1769, in O'Callaghan & Fernow, ed. *New York Colonial Documents*, vol. 8, 166.

This view of British policy on expansion was repeated in 1772 with reference to the same cession:

> instead of being attended with advantage to this kingdom & security to the colonies, [it] is now likely to have no other consequence than that of giving greater scope to distant settlements, which I conceive to be inconsistent with every true principle of policy.[90]

This prediction was borne out by events; in the years following the cession, which was confirmed by a series of treaties with the Cherokee between 1769 and 1774, a large number of petition for land grants were made by small groups of settlers as well as by large interest groups (see Map 6). The largest of these groups, the Ohio Land Company, which was composed of Pennsylvania merchants and British noblemen and other speculators, laid claim to a huge area on both sides of the Kanawha River, in order to found the colony of Vandalia. Hillsborough was opposed to this project, but other ministers and eventually the Privy Council were favourable disposed; the positive treatment which the proposal received obliged Hillsborough to resign. The colony would most probably have come into existence if the War of Independence had not occurred.[91]

The Virginians were opposed to this large invasion of what they considered their rightful area of expansion and tried to forestall it by earlier occupation. In support of this, Lord Dunmore, governor of Virginia, issued large grants of land in opposition to the instructions given him. Although the new Secretary of State, Lord Dartmouth, was less strongly against expansion than Hillsborough, the actions of Dunmore met with severe disapproval from him. Remarking that it had always been the policy to prevent settlement in areas "where they could not fail of exciting the Jealousy and giving Dissatisfaction to the Indians," and that this had been the basis of the Royal Proclamation of 1763, Dartmouth continued:

> and altho' His Majesty was graciously pleased to accept from the Six Nations a Surrender of their Title to the Lands on the South of the Ohio [...] yet such acceptance was accompanied with an order to Sr. William Johnson to assure those Nations of His Majesty's firm Resolution not to suffer any Settlement to be made below the Kanawa River.

---

[90] Hillsborough to Johnson, July 1, 1772, in O'Callaghan & Fernow, ed. *New York Colonial Documents*, vol. 8, 302.

[91] On Vandalia. see, for example, Alvord, *The Mississippi Valley in British Politics*, vol. 2, and Sosin, *Whitehall and the Wilderness*, ch. 8.

Dartmouth further referred to the treaty of Lochaber (one of the treaties agreed with the Cherokee in 1770 as a consequence of the cession by the Six Nations), concluding that, in view of all the pledges which had thus been given to the Indians in the name of the King, any encouragement of settlement beyond the boundary

> can be considered in no other light than that of a gross Indignity and Dishonour to the Crown and of an act of equal Inhumanity and Injustice to the Indians that cannot fail to be attended with fatal consequences.[92]

Although Dartmouth's letter repeats in forceful language many of the views which had been held as early as 1763, it was clear that by this stage the government was fast losing control of the situation. Speculators increasingly purchased land directly from the Indians, and government officials, such as Dunmore, continued to turn a blind eye or even participated actively in the expansionist projects.

Dorothy Jones points out that the Indian outlook was also changing. The Shawnee and other western nations were increasingly opposing the power of the Iroquois confederacy, especially their cession of land in the 1768 treaty, and they attempted to form an alternative power-group to fight against British expansion. To the south, the Cherokee needed a new trading resource as game became depleted, and were therefore willing to sell the land south of the Ohio, to which their rights were not very clear anyway. Thus changing relations between the Indians and the developing needs of individual groups contributed to creating an unstable situation which gave increased scope for speculative forces.[93]

The years following the 1768 plan, which returned part of the control over Indian relations to the colonies, consequently saw a disintegration of policy in respect of land negotiations, an area that was meant to remain under the control of the imperial officials. The Vandalia affair showed that expansionist forces within government circles were influential at this time; on the other hand, the project progressed extremely slowly, being subjected to numerous investigations and reports. By the time it received royal approval, the area had been ceded by the Cherokee as well as by the Iroquois. Thus the official acceptance of Vandalia was not based on disregard for Indian rights, although it did mark a departure from the stated policy of not allowing expansion to the west of the

[92] Dartmouth to Dunmore, September 8, 1771, CO 5/1352: 116–18.

[93] Jones, *License for Empire*, ch. 5.

Kanawha. Official reaction to the Virginia schemes, though, shows a more consistent attempt to uphold that line. The 1768 plan may even have contributed to the failure of this attempt with its renewed encouragement of colonial influence over relationships with the Indians, although, as was shown above, this was not the intended result of that compromise measure.

The last phase

The final attempt by the imperial government to control the management of Indian affairs was made in 1774 when, as part of the Quebec Act, the boundary of said province was extended so that the northern half of the Indian country – as far south as the Ohio – was placed under the jurisdiction of Quebec. The effect of this change and the consequences for the southern half of the territory[94] were never fully felt, because of the intervention of the War of Independence; reference to the new measure in the correspondence is scant.

Lord Dartmouth, in 1773, wrote to Lieutenant-Governor Gramahé in Quebec:

> There is no longer any hope of perfecting that plan of policy in respect to the interior country which was in contemplation when the proclamation of 1763 was issued. Many circumstances with regard to the inhabitance of parts of that country were then unknown, and there are a variety of other considerations that do at least in my judgement induce a doubt both of the justice and propriety of restraining the colony [Quebec] to the narrow limits prescribed in that proclamation.[95]

It is likely, as Sosin points out, that Dartmouth is here referring to increased awareness among government officials of the lack of administrative provisions for the scattered French settlements in the Northwest – a consequence of the exclusion of the interior from the province of Quebec in 1763. By extending the boundaries of Quebec, the government attempted to solve this problem at the same time as they provided a solution to the difficult issue of managing the Indian trade.[96] Like the letter of 1774 quoted above, this letter shows awareness

---

[94] After the death John Stuart and the demise of the Southern Colonial Frontier in 1779, the southern district was divided into two with two superintendents; Alden, *John Stuart and the Southern Colonial Frontier*, 139.

[95] Dartmouth to Gramahé, December 1, 1773, CO 42/32: 93.

[96] Sosin, *Whitehall and the Wilderness*, 237–38. See also the memorandum entitled "Proposed Extension of Provincial Limits" (no author or date), in Doughty & Shortt, ed.

of the fact that the policy current at the time originated in the Proclamation of 1763.

Dartmouth was keenly aware of the dangerous state of Indian affairs, remarking in a letter to Johnson that "there certainly has hardly ever been a time when Indian affairs were in a more critical situation"[97] and in another letter that

> if some method is not soon fallen upon to restrain the numberless frauds and abuses [...] by those who carry on trade and have intercourse with [the Indians], we shall be involved in an Indian war.[98]

He promised to do his utmost to find a solution – the Act of 1774 was probably seen as such, since it would create a proper jurisdictional frame for the northern area. The reduction of the colonies' powers over Indian trade and the inclusion of this huge area within the boundaries of one colony predictably caused an outcry in the colonies, where the Quebec Act was classified as one of the "intolerable acts" (coming at the same time as the punitive measures against Massachusetts), and the Act faced considerable opposition in Parliament.

Before reaching Parliament, the bill was referred to Hillsborough for comment (surely an important indication that he was regarded as knowledgeable in this area); he objected strongly to the changes concerning the Indian country, because he feared that it would upset the Indians and increase the danger of an Indian war. Hillsborough felt that the new measure would encourage settlement in the interior, which he vigorously opposed.[99]

The Cabinet, however, rejected Hillsborough's objections, denying that the intention was to encourage expansion. In a letter to Hillsborough, Dartmouth said that the Cabinet

> are unanimously of opinion that the extension of the Province to the Ohio and Mississippi, is an essential and very useful part of the Bill; it provides for the

---

Constitutional Documents of Canada, vol. 1, 541–43. The editors note that the extension of the boundaries of Quebec was "represented as a direct concession to the Canadian noblesse and clergy in response to their petition" (vol. 1, 541, note 1).

[97] Dartmouth to Johnson, December 1, 1773, in O'Callaghan & Fernow, ed. *New York Colonial Documents*, vol. 8, 404.

[98] Dartmouth to Johnson, September 27, 1772, in O'Callaghan & Fernow, ed. *New York Colonial Documents*, vol. 8, 312.

[99] Lord Hillsborough's Objections to the Quebec Bill in its present Form, April 30, 1774, in Doughty & Shortt, ed. *Constitutional Documents of Canada,* vol. 1, 551–54. See also Sosin, *Whitehall and the Wilderness*, 243–44; Lawson, *The Imperial Challenge*, 131–32.

> establishment of civil government over many numerous settlements of french subjects, but does by no means imply an intention of further settling the Lands included within this extension.[100]

This also came out in the Parliamentary debates, where the boundary provisions were accorded a certain amount of debate and where proponents of the bill claimed that one benefit of this part of the Act would be that it would confine the settlers to the coast. Since the new Act would establish a legal system based on French law in the province of Quebec and also entailed extensive toleration of Catholicism, settlers from the old colonies would find little to encourage them to settle within its limits.[101]

William Knox, under-secretary for the colonies and responsible for drafting the bill, confirmed this interpretation in a pamphlet, saying that the Northwest was made part of Quebec "with the avowed purpose of excluding all further settlement therein, and for the establishment of uniform regulations for the Indian trade."[102]

Policy with regard to the Indians as laid down in this last measure for the west enacted by the British Parliament was very similar to that envisaged in 1763–64; the Indians, in the interest of peaceful relations, were to remain largely undisturbed in their possession of the west, and the fur trade was, to its benefit, to be regulated by imperial officers (a copy of the plan of 1764 was even sent to the governor of Quebec to advise him on this point). Concern for

---

[100] Dartmouth's reply to Hillsborough, May 1, 1774, in Doughty & Shortt, ed. *Constitutional Documents of Canada*, vol. 1, 554.

[101] Speech by the solicitor-general, Alexander Wedderburn, in Henry Cavendish, *Debates of the House of Commons in the year 1774, on the Bill for Making More Effectual Provision for the Government of the Province of Quebec; Drawn up from the notes of Henry Cavendish* (1839; Toronto: Johnson Reprint, 1966): 58. It is notable that considerations of the Indians do not seem to have been mentioned at any time during the debates. See also Alvord, *The Mississippi Valley in British Politics*, vol. 2, 241, and Lawson, *The Imperial Challenge*, 141.

[102] William Knox, *Justice and Policy of the late Act of Parliament for making more effectual Provision for the Government of the Province of Quebec* (London: Adams & Bonwick, 1774), quoted in Alvord, *The Mississippi Valley in British Politics,* vol. 2, 242. Gerald Sandham Graham, *British Policy and Canada 1774–1791: A Study in Eighteenth Century Trade Policy* (London: Longmans, 1930): 25–26, mentions the view of General Haldimand that the boundary was changed so as to prevent the colonists from gaining control over the interior. Graham himself believes that the clause was included in the Act to secure British power over the area against the ever-present threat of a renewed struggle with France.

the Indians played a less significant role in the correspondence at this point than in the early 1760s, which is perhaps understandable in view of the unruliness of the colonies at this time. As the months went by, the colonists came to pose a much greater threat to British hegemony in North America than the Indians did.

In fact, by May 1775, when the Act was to come into operation, the first shots had already been fired in the War of Independence and all efforts were directed towards that struggle; interest in the Indians hereafter focused on securing them as allies. The British were more successful in this than they had been in the previous war. The Indians had little to gain from supporting the colonists, knowing very well that if they won, their own battle would thereby be lost. Consequently, Indian support for the British was widespread, although some chose to support the rebels.[103]

Nevertheless, the extent of their loss came as a shock to the Indians when they realized that the British, by the terms of the peace treaty signed at Versailles in 1783, had recognized American sovereignty over the entire region east of the Mississippi as far north as the Great Lakes – over most of the area designated "Indian country" in the Royal Proclamation. Not only did the Indians feel betrayed by their allies, they also felt strongly that the British had no right to accede to those terms, since the Indians had never recognized British sovereignty over the area (just as they had not recognized French sovereignty over it twenty years earlier).

The British were aware of Indian feelings, reported by various officials in Canada, and acknowledged that they had been unfairly treated. Lord North in April 1783 referred to the "Justice and necessity" of continuing to give "presents" to them,[104] and in a letter from Whitehall to General Haldimand in August 1783 the obligations towards the Indians were further specified:

> These People [the Mohawk] are justly entitled to our peculiar attention, and it would be far from either generous or just in us, after our Cession of their Territory and Hunting Grounds, to forsake them. I am, therefore, authorized

---

[103] See Sosin, "The Use of the Indians in the War of the American Revolution: A Re-Assessment of Responsibility," *Canadian Historical Review* 46.2 (June 1965): 101–121, and S.F. Wise, who makes the point that the Indians participated in the war not so much to support the British as to remove the settlers from their land; Wise, "The American Revolution and Indian History," in *Character and Circumstance: Essays in Honour of Donald Grant Creighton*, ed. John S. Moir (Toronto: Macmillan of Canada, 1970): 198–200.

[104] North to Haldimand, April 10, 1783, CO 42/44: 56.

> to acquaint you, that the King allows you to make those offers to them, or any other nations of the Friendly Indians who may be desirous of withdrawing themselves from the United States, and occupying any Lands which you may allot to them within the Province of Quebec.[105]

Like the Loyalists, they were usually settled on land along the border with the United States so as to serve as a barrier against any incursions from the south (as is openly stated in the letter). That the reception of the Indians was not motivated solely by notions of justice and generosity is indicated in the continuation of the letter:

> It is to be hoped that from thence [the Indians' new settlements] they will be able to carry on their Hunting from their former Grounds and return with their Furs and Peltry, where the British traders can meet them, with their Wives and Children in security, and being under our Protection, their attachment to His Majesty may continue and this Country may enjoy the advantages of their Trade.[106]

In this way, groups of Indians were resettled on land in Canada purchased from local Indians.

Contrary to the treaty provisions, the British, under various pretexts, also continued to hold the northwestern posts, from which they issued provisions to the Indians and counselled them on their conduct with the Americans, who, predictably, were moving westward at an ever-increasing rate.

While the continuation of the fur trade was important to the British, Robert Allen has argued that the main reason why the British continued this involvement with the Indians on what they recognized to be American territory was the desire to maintain the friendship of the Indians and thereby avoid retaliatory measures from them in the undefended parts of western Canada.[107]

This is confirmed by a despatch from Lord Sydney to Lieutenant-Governor Hope of Quebec in April 1786 in which he discussed the position of the British in the eventuality of war between the Indians and the Americans:

---

[105] Whitehall (unsigned) to Haldimand, August 8, 1783, CO 42/44: 160–62.

[106] Whitehall (unsigned) to Haldimand, August 8, 1783, CO 42/44: 162.

[107] Robert S. Allen, *A History of the British Indian Department in North America (1755–1830)* Manuscript Report no 109 (Ottawa: Department of Indian Affairs and Northern Development, 1971): 54–55, 126; James Rodger Miller, *Skyscrapers Hide the Heavens: A History of Indian–White Relations in Canada* (Toronto: U of Toronto P, 1989): 78.

> To afford them [the Indians] open and avowed Assistance, should Hostilities commence, must at all events in the present State of the Country be avoided; but His Majesty's Ministers at the same time do not think it either consistent with Justice or good Policy entirely to abandon them [...] as from motives of resentment it is not unlikely that they might hereafter be led to interrupt the Peace and Prosperity of the Province of Quebec.[108]

The struggle between the Indians and the Americans which evolved in the course of the next ten years saw some British activity 'behind the lines', but when it came to actual fighting the British refused any assistance, much to the dismay of the Indians.[109] British disengagement was further emphasized when the western posts were finally turned over to the Americans as a consequence of Jay's Treaty, signed in 1794.

The War of 1812 between the British and the Americans saw the last instance of British alliance with the Lakes Indians, whose hopes of reviving the struggle for their land led them once again to support the British. Although significant conquests were made during the brief war, all were relinquished in the peace treaty of Ghent in 1814, once more disappointing Indian expectations.

The end of this war marked a watershed in British–Indian relations, in several respects. The military significance of the Indians as allies of rival European colonizers was nullified; the cessation of hostilities between the British and Americans meant that the Indians lost their best chance of playing one side off against the other to improve their situation; and one good reason for the British to seek the friendship of the Indians had disappeared.

Furthermore, British connections with tribes south of the border were clearly at an end; from this time onwards, British policy towards the indigenes was confined to dealing with the Canadian Indians, but on the basis of the rather different cultural and political background pertaining to that area.

Finally, and as a consequence of the first two points, British policy towards the Indians underwent a dramatic change. In the course of the next decades the ever-present demands made on the Indian Department[110] to save money con-

---

[108] Sydney to Hope, April 6, 1786, in Doughty & Shortt, ed. *Constitutional Documents of Canada*, vol. 2, 807.

[109] Allen, *A History of the British Indian Department*, ch. 3–4.

[110] Headed by Sir John Johnson, William Johnson's son, as superintendent general from 1782 to 1828. See Bruce Wilson, "The Struggle for Wealth and Power at Fort Niagara 1775–1783" in *Interpreting Canada's Past*, ed. J.M. Bumsted (Toronto: Oxford UP, 1986), vol. 1, for details on the Indian Department in British North America.

tributed to the gradual development of a new system for managing Indian affairs. It was envisaged that the Indians would be gathered onto reserves where they could be christianized and 'civilized', hence assimilated to European ways. Removed from their land in this fashion, the Indians would no longer stand in the way of the expansion of white settlement.[111]

The Indian a human being?

So far, the present chapter has shown that policy towards the Indians during the period 1763–1783 was in the main determined by the issues of land and trade, since it was these that affected the Indians and influenced their attitude and behaviour towards the colonists. Thus policy was to a large extent dependent on the practical experience of British officials in America and the reaction to this on the part of the metropolitan governmentn. In the correspondence of this period there are, however, also a few cases which are not directly related to one of these main issues but which are interesting for the way they shed light on the attitudes of British government officials towards the Indians.

One such occasion was the visit of three Cherokee chiefs to London in 1762. Their interpreter had died on the voyage and nobody had been able to understand them, but as Egremont wrote to Governor Boone in South Carolina that "every possible attention has been paid to them." Boon was asked to

> direct proper Compliments to be made to them, in the King's Name, & express to them his Majesty's Concern at the Loss of their Interpreter, which must have subjected them to many inconveniences, during their stay in England, & you will assure them, that it was the King's particular Order that the utmost attention should be paid to them; and in case you shall perceive, that they have been offended or disgusted with anything that may have happened, you will endeavour to remove any ill Impressions they may have conceived by availing yourself of the Circumstance of the Death of their Interpreter, & our not being able to understand what they might wish to have,

---

[111] Miller, *Skyscrapers Hide the Heavens*, ch. 5; see also John L. Tobias, "Protection, Civilization, Assimilation: An Outline of the History of Canada's Indian Policy," in *As Long as the Sun Shines and Water Flows: A Reader in Canadian native Studies*, ed. Ian A.L. Getty & Antoine Lussier (Vancouver: U of British Columbia P, 1983): 39–55. Cf Maitland to Bathurst, November 29, 1821, and Cole to Hay, May 3, 1829, both in *British Colonial Developments 1774–1834; Select Documents*, ed. Vincent Todd Harlow & Frederick Madden (Oxford: Clarendon, 1953): 588–92.

> which, you will assure them, would have been, in every respect, complied with, as far as possible.[112]

It is difficult to know what actually happened during the stay of the chiefs or why they wished to visit England. However, even if the object of their visit received no attention, the tone of the letter suggests a sincere wish to be courteous towards the visitors and a desire to communicate this even after their departure. While it is difficult to say whether behaviour towards the Indians was truly polite or whether it was condescending or even worse, the letter at least indicates that the Cherokee chiefs were perceived to be sufficiently important to warrant the respect and proper diplomatic treatment accorded other foreign visitors of significance.

Two other cases, both from 1765, support the idea that the Indians in general were regarded as fellow human beings by members of the administration (as opposed to the view of some of the colonists). In March of that year, the Board of Trade was directed by the House of Lords to prevent the public exhibition of two Indians in London; in letters to the lieutenant-governor of New York and to William Johnson, the affair was referred to as "so scandalous a proceeding" and it is mentioned that orders had been given for "proper care to be taken of these Indians, and that their passage back to New York should be defrayed at the public expense."[113]

The other case concerned a number of settlers in Virginia who had forcibly rescued some prisoners sentenced for murdering "several Indians in alliance and friendship with Us."[114] In the instructions sent to the Governor of Virginia in October 1765, the killings are described as having happened in "a most Savage and Atrocious manner"; furthermore, it is stated that the settlers involved "have openly and publicly declared, that the killing a Savage is an action for which no Man ought to suffer." The Instructions then declared that

> it is highly necessary and expedient, that such dangerous and illegal Acts and proceedings, founded in Principles so irreligious and Inhuman, should be discouraged and suppressed.[115]

---

[112] Egremont to Boone, August 7, 1762, CO 5/214: 288–89.

[113] Lords of Trade to Lieutenant-Governor Colden, March 16, 1765, in O'Callaghan & Fernow, ed. *New York Colonial Documents*, vol. 7, 708.

[114] The murderers were never subsequently apprehended; Alden, *John Stuart and the Southern Colonial Frontier*, 218.

[115] Additional Instruction, October 10, 1765, CO 5/1368: 286.

In order to do so, the governor was directed to use military force to prevent similar occurrences in the future. In both cases, objection was made at an official level to treatment of the Indians by the settlers as sub-human or as beasts, and the ministry used its power as far as possible to put a stop to such practices.

Principles of humanity were again invoked in 1770, with the prospect of a new Indian alliance and war. As a consequence of the regroupings taking place among the Indians, referred to earlier, the Cherokee had suggested that the Six Nations join them in fighting the southern and western tribes, but the Six Nations had made their answer depend on the advice of William Johnson, to be obtained at a general Indian congress. As Johnson put the matter to Lord Hillsborough, the alternative, to "permit these people to cut each others throats," would be to "risque their discharging their fury on our Traders and defenceless frontiers" because of the general discontent of the Indians.[116]

To this Hillsborough answered that to encourage a war between the Indians would be "irreconcilable with the principles of humanity" – on the other hand, an attack on the frontier would have to be avoided at all costs; consequently,

> the King however unwillingly, cannot but approve of your adopting the alternative, and making the security of his subjects and the peace of the frontiers, the principal object of your attention at the congress, but it would be most pleasing to His Majesty, if it could be obtained without encouraging the Savages in their barbarous attacks on each other.[117]

From John Alden's description of policies in the south, it appears that the strategy of depending on internal strife among the Indians, or even fanning the flames, was frequently employed by the superintendent to prevent attacks on frontier settlers until he was censured by Lord Shelburne in December 1766.[118] Alden claims that previous Secretaries of State had not been opposed to such a policy, and nor was Hillsborough after Shelburne, although he does not, unfortunately, offer any evidence to support this claim.[119] If the letter quoted

---

[116] Johnson to Hillsborough, February 10, 1770, in O'Callaghan & Fernow, ed. *New York Colonial Documents*, vol. 8, 204.

[117] Hillsborough to Johnson, April 14, 1770, in O'Callaghan & Fernow, ed. *New York Colonial Documents*, vol. 8, 211.

[118] Shelburne to Gage, December 11, 1766, in Carter, ed. *Correspondence of Gage*, vol. 2, 51.

[119] Alden, *John Stuart and the Southern Colonial Frontier*, 229. Alden rejects Carter's point that Gage, who was in favour of setting the Indians against each other, knew

above represents a consistent attitude, it can hardly be said that Hillsborough thought positively of such measures.

Expedience vs. justice

A few tendencies may be suggested on the basis of the material discussed in this chapter. The policy with respect to the Indians in North America pursued by the British government in the period between 1756 and 1783 was marked by a handful of successes and many more failures; the appointment of the superintendents was a success, in the sense that it helped Britain acquire a number of very important allies in her war with France. After the war, it also had the beneficial effect of maintaining communication with the Indians, even at critical times, and of avoiding conflicting messages, which had been an obvious problem while the colonies were in charge of Indian affairs. The establishment of a boundary-line between the Indians and the colonies, first decided on formally in 1763 and maintained throughout the period, was also a success, in the sense that it was a measure which had the approval of the Indians and therefore secured their goodwill, at least temporarily.[120]

The failure of the boundary-line is, however, far more conspicuous. The British government proved to be utterly unable to control the colonies and enforce this regulation, and never managed to set a limit to western expansion. While the focus here has been on the desire to prevent encroachment on Indian land and on the ensuing struggles, there were other reasons for the anti-expansionist policy of this period; these included the fear that if the settlers moved away from the seacoast they would be beyond the reach of British goods and

---

that this ran counter to London's wishes (Carter cites only Shelburne as evidence of this attitude; Carter, ed. *Correspondence of Gage*, vol. 2, 193).

[120] Note should be made at this point of Jones's objection to the common presentation of policy and action as if the Indians were "little more than stage props in a drama that was written, directed, and acted by the British" (Jones, *License for Empire*, 214). She makes a major contribution towards showing the Indians as active participants in shaping policy, in terms both of their actions and of their aims. In particular, she sees the policy of the period 1763–68 as the outcome of the desires of two centres of authority – the British government and the Iroquois confederacy. Neither of them had power enough to enforce the system that was established. See also John S. Milloy, "The Early Indian Acts: Developmental Strategy and Constitutional Change", in Getty & Lussier, ed. *As Long as the Sun Shines*, 56–64. Milloy refers to the "coincidence of imperial and Indian interests" (56) and generally considers the conduct of British policy to have been a success.

would start their own manufacturing, to the detriment of British commerce; the belief that the establishment of new colonies in the interior would be too costly because they would necessitate administrative and military arrangements; and the fact that expansion would damage the fur trade, which was vigorously protected by influential merchants. However, at various times – most markedly while Shelburne was Secretary of State and while the colony of Vandalia was under consideration – opposing arguments favouring the extension of settlement gained in strength. This struggle between opposing views on expansion in London probably contributed to a situation in which unscrupulous men far away from the centre of government could ignore the law and follow their own inclinations to settle and grab large profits.

In terms of the Indian trade, government policy was only marginally more successful, in that, in the period between 1764 and 1768, the superintendents, with the support of government officials, managed to impose some semblance of order on the trade. As mentioned earlier, this was by no means generally achieved, however, and with the decision of 1768 to turn over regulation to the colonies, this aspect of Indian policy collapsed. The measures regarding the west which were enacted in the Quebec Act of 1774 indicate that the British wished to improve on this situation, but one is tempted to suggest that even if the War of Independence had not taken place, the colonists had by this time acquired such strength and independence of mind that it would most likely not have made a great deal of difference.

Irrespective of successes and failures (which are always measured with the benefit of hindsight), the documents discussed in this chapter show that the Indian policy of the British was to a large extent marked by continuity of means and aims (perhaps excepting the influence exerted by Lord Shelburne in 1767–68), though not always by great intensity. It is suggested that this continuity was based on a fundamental attitude towards the Indians which remained fairly constant throughout the whole period.

There is little doubt that expediency was a powerful factor in determining British action towards the Indians.[121] The British were in North America to establish and maintain colonies for various reasons – reasons perceived by them to be sufficiently good to make it worth the cost and trouble. The Indians

---

[121] Expediency is clearly considered the main motive behind British policy throughout Sosin's work (Sosin, *Whitehall and the Wilderness*, e.g., 46, 231). Jones's evaluation of that policy is based on her basic view that it was shaped as much by Indian actions as by British ones.

possessed considerable military strength, which could be both useful and dangerous and which it was therefore important to control; consequently, when it became obvious that the colonies were not handling relations with these people very well, it became necessary for the imperial government to take over and attempt to maintain friendly relations with the Indians by preventing the abuses of which the latter complained.

On the other hand, in the years following the war with the French, which had been very expensive, it became increasingly important to reduce expenditure; and as the colonies were opposed to contributing to expenses, it had to be done by cutting down on existing arrangements. Thus a number of the forts in the interior were abandoned and imperial control of the Indian trade was relinquished. These measures were directly opposed to the goal of maintaining the friendship of the Indians. Yet an attempt was made to counter this by concentrating on carrying out the provision of establishing a boundary-line in the west. In a manner typical of governments, policy became based on piecemeal solutions to general problems.

Yet expediency cannot wholly account for the orders and comments relating to the Indians. On the one hand, evidence of insincerity is occasionally found in the official orders, as when Egremont in 1763 gave orders for the congress of Augusta with the southern Indians and, among other things, suggested that Stuart could hold out an offer to consider the abandonment of the interior forts in order to appease the Indians – only to state in a later letter that this did not mean actually promising to abandon them, which proposal was apparently not approved by the commander-in-chief.[122]

On the other hand, the correspondence shows that this was not the overall perception of how Indian affairs should be conducted. Instigating inter-tribal warfare was not, as a rule, approved of, the justness of Indian complaints was generally admitted, acts of violence and cruelty towards the Indians by the settlers were deplored. Justice and the concomitant values of honour and decency were frequently invoked when problems and solutions were discussed.

On this basis, it is suggested that the concept of justice played a role in the formulation of policy, alongside considerations of a more practical nature. Obviously, the British colonization of North America, based as it was on de-

---

[122] Egremont to Governors (circular), March 16, 1763, CO 323/16: 103 and Egremont to Amherst, July 9, 1763, CO 5/214: 328. Egremont may, of course, also simply have found that he had committed the government further than he was warranted to do. See also discussion of congress of Augusta in Alden, *John Stuart and the Southern Colonial Frontier*, ch. 11, and in Jones, *License for Empire*, ch. 3.

priving the original inhabitants of their land, was a gross violation of the rights of the Indians. To the eighteenth-century mind, this could be rationalized and legitimized in terms of general theories of exploitation of the land; this, however, did not solve the problem of finding a manner of dealing with the people actually confronted, who exhibited no doubt about their prior claim on the country. As seen at the beginning of this chapter, the British accepted their claim and recognized the legal right of the Indians to the land as the original owners.

Working on this fundamental assumption, government officials dealing with the colonies developed the perception that the Indians had a moral and legal claim to being justly treated. Although it would have been possible both to deal with and to discuss the indigenous population in more ruthless terms, the official exchange of letters reveals an awareness of a theoretical obligation to deal with the Indians in a morally justifiable way, and it was this attitude, together with the need to control the military potential of the Indians, that determined policy in this area.

3 New South Wales c. 1784–98

Britain's convict problem

ONE OF THE CONSEQUENCES of the war with the American colonies was the internal problem of disposing of the convicted criminals crowding the prisons; it had been the custom to transport a number of these across the Atlantic, but the war made this impossible, and finding a solution to this difficulty soon became a pressing concern for the authorities. Thus, at the same time as battles were being fought in America, the House of Commons in 1776 and again in 1779 appointed committees to consider the condition of the prisons and the hulks in the Thames which were used as a temporary hold for those sentenced to transportation. In response to the report of the second committee, Parliament in 1779 enacted a bill which both provided for transportation "beyond the seas" and for the building of new prisons. However, very little action was taken and in 1784 a new Act was passed, which among other things ordered the resumption of transportation, to any place decided on by the government.[1]

The problem of finding a suitable place to send the convicts was attacked in different ways. A number of piecemeal and temporary attempts were made to find outlets for the growing number of convicts. As early as 1781, a group was sent to the British slaving post, Cape Coast Castle, on the Guinea Coast in an area which was notorious for its high death-rate among Europeans. The experiment was not a success, as most of the convicts had either died or escaped within a year. In 1783 another plan to re-establish transportation to America

[1] Alan Frost, *Convicts and Empire: A Naval Question 1776–1811* (Melbourne: Oxford UP, 1980): 8–18.

proved unsuccessful, and attempts in 1784 and in 1785 to land some convicts in Honduras also miscarried.[2]

In the period 1783–86, a number of proposals were made to the government for the solving of the convict problem, some of them tacking their solution on to a project otherwise concerned with the possibility of a profitable trade. Most of the plans proposed sending the convicts abroad (to such different places as Africa, South America or Australia), though some suggested various employment at home.[3]

The government was attracted to the idea of sending the convicts to Africa, in the first instance to Lemain, an island in the river Gambia. However, the Committee on the Return of Felons, under the chairmanship of Lord Beauchamp, examined the scheme in 1785 and did not recommend it. The evidence heard by the committee ruled out the scheme by showing that the convicts would most probably die from local diseases shortly after arrival.[4] Having heard evidence on other places, the committee, in its final report, issued in July 1785, recommended a penal colony at Das Voltas Bay on the southwest coast of Africa.[5]

An expedition was dispatched soon after the committee report was published, returning almost a year later to report that the place was wholly unsuitable for settlement. Soon after this report, in August 1786, the government decided to send the convicts to Botany Bay in New South Wales instead. After long preparations, the so-called First Fleet sailed for New South Wales in May 1787, under the leadership of Captain Arthur Phillip, the first governor of the settlement.

Such, in brief, are the steps leading to the establishment of the colony of New South Wales. There has been vigorous debate among Australian historians as to whether any underlying motives existed for the founding of the colony. Some historians have argued repeatedly for explanations of the decision taken in 1786 that offer more plausible alternatives to the traditional 'dumping of convicts' theme prevalent among earlier scholars. Some have attempted to show that the possibility of strengthening trade in the east in the

---

[2] Frost, *Convicts and Empire*, ch. 1, and Hugh W. Oldham, ed. *Britain's Convicts to the Colonies by Wilfried Oldham* (Sydney: Library of Australian History, 1990): ch. 5.

[3] David Mackay, *A Place of Exile: The European Settlement of New South Wales* (Oxford & Melbourne: Oxford UP, 1985): 55.

[4] First Report from the Committee, May 9, 1785, HO 42/6: 373–83.

[5] Report, June 21, 1785, HO 42/7: 3–22.

context of the East India Company's desire to increase the China trade weighed heavily with the government.

Other scholars have taken as their point of departure the tense atmosphere existing between the British and the French following the American War of Independence, and have claimed that the British considered the establishment of strategic outposts as well as the availability of naval stores as essential to their possessions in Asia, and that the founding of New South Wales should be seen in this context.[6]

The basic point remains, however, that in the early 1780s the British government was keen to find a place to which convicts could be easily and inexpensively transported, preferably without the possibility of returning when their sentence had expired. Whether or not the British government had ulterior motives for making the decision they did, and regardless of whether this can be traced in the available documents, the establishment of New South Wales meant that the British were confronted with a hitherto scarcely known people and had to formulate a policy towards them. For the purposes of the present study, the debate about underlying motives for government action is therefore not so essential, although some of the details which have been brought up in this prolonged debate as well as some of the implications of the general conclusions do have an important bearing on the discussion.

An attempt will be made in the present chapter to characterize the official attitudes towards the original inhabitants of that distant country during the first decade or so. Such an attempt must rest primarily on the documents relating to the establishment of the colony; however, government policy towards Aborigines is nowhere discussed at the length or with the frequency of the North American documents. After a discussion of the documents which do refer to the Aborigines, some additional material will therefore be considered. The reports about New South Wales available to the government provide an opportunity to discuss the assumptions underlying the decision to establish the colony. Likewise, documents relating to other places which were considered for occupation may indicate the general attitude towards indigenous peoples at this particular time. Finally, the policy pursued by Phillip may give an idea of what the government found acceptable. Although any conclusions drawn on

---

[6] See Ged Martin, ed. *The Founding of Australia: the Argument about Australia's Origins* (Sydney: Hale & Iremonger, 1978), for an easily accessible collection of essays central to this debate, and Alan Atkinson, "The First Plans for Governing New South Wales 1786–1787," *Australian Historical Studies* 24 (1990–1991): 22–24, on some recent contributions to it.

this basis must necessarily be tentative, it is the only way in which anything can be said about the development of attitudes towards the indigenous population of New South Wales in the early years of European settlement.

The documents relating to the establishment of Botany Bay

Many scholars have argued that the decision to settle New South Wales was made by a rather desperate government in a hasty and not very thorough manner, just as the preparation of the First Fleet was insufficient.[7] Others, most notably Alan Frost, have claimed that the decision was based on careful consideration over a long period; likewise, the provisioning of the ships has been claimed to have been more than plentiful.[8]

The official documents relating to the decision, however, are sparse and do not reveal much about the deliberations made by the Pitt ministry on this occasion. A memorandum, probably from December 1784, shows that New South Wales was considered alongside Lemain at that time,[9] but since no action was taken the suggestion must have been shelved. In January 1786, while the expedition to Das Voltas Bay was still under way, Evan Nepean, the permanent under-secretary, made enquiries about the cost of transporting convicts to New South Wales[10] – which may be an indication that at some level Botany Bay was still considered a possibility.

After the west coast of African had been effectively ruled out, Nepean again took up the work of making reliable estimates on the cost of the New South Wales scheme with the help of the Treasury and other officials,[11] and, at some point in August 1786,[12] the Cabinet decided on New South Wales as the future place of transportation.

---

[7] For example, Mackay, *A Place of Exile*, ch.5; see also A.G.L. Shaw, *Convicts and the Colonies: A Study of Penal Transportation from Great Britain and Ireland to Australia and other Parts of the British Empire* (London: Faber & Faber, 1966): 54.

[8] Frost, *Convicts and Empire*, 121–41, and *Botany Bay Mirages: Illusions of Australia's Convict Beginnings* (Carleton, Victoria: Melbourne UP, 1995): ch. 5 & 6.

[9] Memorandum of matters to be brought before Cabinet, undated but dated by Frost to December 10, 1784 Dixson Add. Ms Q 522, reproduced in Frost, *Botany Bay Mirages*, 104–105.

[10] Frost, *Botany Bay Mirages*, 108.

[11] HO 42/7: 23 and HO 42/10: 425. See also Frost, *Convicts and Empire*, 127.

[12] Frost believes this to have happened on 19 August (*Convicts and Empire*, 129), while Mackay suggests the 15th (*A Place of Exile*, 56).

Letters signed by Sydney, Secretary of State in the government of William Pitt the Younger, communicated the decision to the Lords of the Treasury on 18 August and to the Lords of the Admiralty on 31 August. Although very detailed, the letter to the Treasury makes no mention of the indigenous population of the place,[13] but the letter to the Admiralty does refer briefly to them; in a passage pertaining to the directing of the supply of ships and marines, it is further stated that

> it has been thought adviseable that some Military Establishment shall be made at the New intended Settlement, not only to enforce due Subordination and Obedience, but for the defence of the Settlement against Incursion of the Natives.[14]

Both letters were accompanied by a document entitled "Heads of a Plan for effectually disposing of Convicts, and rendering their Transportation reciprocally beneficial both to themselves and to the State, by the Establishment of a Colony in New South Wales." One parenthetical reference to the indigenous people is made in the plan; it was suggested that two companies of marines should be included

> to form a military establishment on Shore (not only for the protection of the Settlement, if requisite, against the Natives, but for the preservation of good order).[15]

The authorship and date of origin of this document are unknown and have been an issue of debate among historians. Frost has suggested that someone within the Home Department, possibly the permanent under-secretary, Evan Nepean, was the author and that it was written as an outline of the project in preparation for the cabinet meeting when the final decision was made.

David Mackay, on the other hand, argues that the document shows evidence of having been written by someone outside the administrative circle aiming at persuading the government and confirming the decision (references are made to "the views of the government," "government should immediately provide" etc).[16] Be that as it may, the inclusion of the plan in the letters to the Treasury

---

[13] Sydney to Treasury, August 18, 1786, HO 35/1.

[14] Sydney to the Lords of the Admiralty, August 31, 1786, Adm 1/4152.

[15] Heads of a Plan, undated, HO 35/1.

[16] Mackay, *A Place of Exile*, 59.

and the Admiralty and the reference to it as "a Sketch of the Plan for forming this New Settlement"[17] show that it had the stamp of official approval.

No great significance need be granted the reversal of the order of the two objectives in the Admiralty letter and the Plan. They both show that the ability to defend the settlement was considered a natural prerequisite of the venture just as was the ability to keep the convicts under control. Perhaps more significantly, the qualification in the plan shows that a certain amount of uncertainty prevailed in regard to the disposition of the indigenous inhabitants.

A similar kind of uncertainty is suggested in the first commission issued to Phillip (in October 1786). Phillip was appointed governor of "all towns, garrisons, castles, forts, and all other fortifications or other military works, which now are or may be hereafter erected upon this said territory."[18] In the second and final commission (April 1787), the idea that any buildings might exist was eliminated by omitting the words "now are" from the otherwise identical passage.[19] Thus the first commission illustrates the lack of knowledge about the place under which the officials laboured.[20] The second commission was much longer than the first, but although it did not include this obvious mistake it still made no provision for establishing a relationship with the inhabitants of the area.

In Phillip's instructions, by contrast, the indigenous population was referred to on three occasions; Phillip's first action after landing was to take

> measures for securing yourself and the people who accompany you as much as possible from any attacks or interruptions of the natives of that country.[21]

Secondly, the possibility that Phillip might trade with the inhabitants was allowed for:

---

[17] Sydney to Treasury, August 18, 1789, HO 35/1.

[18] Governor Phillip's First Commission, October 1786, in Frederick Watson, ed. *Historical Records of Australia* (Sydney: Government Printer, 1914–1925), vol. 1: 1.

[19] Governor Phillip's Second Commission, April 1787, in Watson, ed. *Historical Records of Australia*, vol. 1, 2.

[20] It may, of course, also have been a result of simply copying from instructions issued to someone else in a different situation, in which case it would, rather, illustrate bureaucratic inefficiency.

[21] Instructions to Arthur Phillip, April 25, 1787, in Watson, ed. *Historical Records of Australia*, vol. 1, 11.

> a quantity of arms and other articles of merchandise to be provided and sent out in the ships under your convoy, in order to barter with the natives either on the territory of New South Wales or the islands adjacent.

Thirdly, Phillip was to obtain the friendship of these people

> You are to endeavour by every possible means to open an intercourse with the natives, and to conciliate their affections, enjoining all our subjects to live in amity and kindness with them. And if any of our subjects shall wantonly destroy them, or give them any unnecessary interruption in the exercise of their several occupations, it is our will and pleasure that you do cause such offenders to be brought to punishment according to the degree of the offence. You will endeavour to procure an account of the numbers inhabiting the neighbourhood of the intended settlement, and report your opinion to one of our Secretaries of State in what manner our intercourse with these people may be turned to the advantage of this colony.[22]

Interpretations of Phillip's instructions have varied. Jan Kociumbas has seen the main point of the orders to lie in a wish to exploit the possibilities which might arise from better knowledge of the people,[23] while Robert King has emphasized the qualifications surrounding the injunction to offer protection to the inhabitants ("The rights and well-being of the Aborigines were to be protected only insofar as they were consonant with the overall safety and prosperity of the colony").[24]

Although both these points may certainly be inferred from the passage quoted above, they do not do justice to the general tenor of the orders, which is focused on establishing an amicable relationship with the inhabitants; as far as possible, they were to be left in peace, and anyone who disturbed them was to be punished. Rather than suggesting a profound disregard for the inhabitants, it indicates a belief that it would be possible for the two groups to coexist – that there would be "room enough for everyone" even if the British settled there.

While the fact that Phillip was provided with "arms" as a trade good may be seen as indicating the expectation that friendship was to be the rule between the settlers and the original inhabitants, it is somewhat contrary to the instruction that the Fleet be prepared to defend the settlement.

---

[22] Watson, ed. *Historical Records of Australia*, vol. 1, 13.

[23] Jan Kociumbas, *The Oxford History of Australia*, vol. 2: *1700–1860 Possessions* (Oxford & Melbourne: Oxford UP, 1992): 51.

[24] Robert King, "Terra Australis: Terra Nullius aut Terra Aboriginum," *Journal of the Royal Australian Historical Society* 72 (1986): 80.

It is more striking, though, that there is no provision in the instructions for negotiating with the inhabitants for land on which to place the settlement. This has been seen as the main reason why there have never been any treaties or land purchases in Australia, and it has commonly been interpreted as a conscious decision by the British from the very beginning not to negotiate with the Aborigines.[25]

However, this may not be the correct understanding of the instructions or of British attitudes at this time. As suggested by Henry Reynolds, the omission could simply have been a mistake; alternatively, it could be taken as an indication that the traditional approach was simply assumed to apply.[26] King believes that Phillip was expected to discover whether negotiation for the land was required.[27] Although there is no direct proof of this, it may well be suggested that the function of the last sentence was to hold the government's position in reserve until more was known about the inhabitants of the country.

While the number of documents revealing anything about the government's attitude towards the indigenous population in New South Wales is very small, the conclusion that this was due to indifference towards them is contradicted by Phillip's instructions. There is a clear indication of a desire to establish a positive relationship with the inhabitants, and the way is left open for further measures to be taken to achieve this. However, in order to be able to determine more accurately how this reflected government attitudes towards indigenous peoples at that time, it is necessary to get some idea of what prior knowledge the government had of the Aborigines, since this would obviously form the basis for the decisions made and the policy formulated.

Material influencing government

It is generally very difficult to determine the significance of various kinds of information in forming opinions and attitudes towards a particular topic. One could go through the accounts of Australia written until 1786 and synthesize the image of the Aborigines created in them, but there would be no way of knowing if this was indeed the picture which the relevant government officials

---

[25] See, for example, Frost, *Botany Bay Mirages*, ch. 9.

[26] Henry Reynolds, *The Law of the Land* (Ringwood, Vic: Penguin Australia, 1987): 42, and *Frontier* (Sydney & Boston MA: Allen & Unwin, 1987): 183–84.

[27] King, "Terra Australis," 82.

entertained. Fortunately, there is some indication of what formed the source of information of the Home Department at this time.

In the above-mentioned letter to the Treasury of 18 August, Sydney states that

> His Majesty has thought it adviseable to fix upon Botany Bay [...] which according to the Accounts given by the late Captain Cook, as well as the representation of Persons who accompanied him during his last Voyage, and who have been consulted upon the Subject, is looked upon as a place likely to answer the above purposes [of disposing of the convicts].[28]

As pointed out by Mackay, there is some confusion about Cook's voyages here, since it was his first and not his last one which took him to New South Wales and it was some of the people who participated in that first voyage who supplied additional information about New South Wales.[29] Nevertheless, the passage shows that the writings of Cook and a number of others were indeed taken into account in forming government opinion on this new country. The identity of these other informants is revealed by the existence of their letters and proposals in the official records, though some caution is still called for in determining the weight which these should be accorded. The material will be dealt with here in chronological order of appearance.

Captain Cook's journal of his voyage 1768–71, submitted to the Admiralty on his return to England, was the first account of New South Wales to be received by the government. Besides a wealth of nautical and astronomical observations, the journal contained a detailed account of all the countries visited, of their geographical nature, their climate, wildlife and inhabitants. Cook thus also made a number of observations on the inhabitants of what he decided to call "New South Wales."

As well as numerous references to smoke from fires and occasionally to the people themselves observed as the *Endeavour* sailed along the east coast of Australia, Cook provides more detailed descriptions of the Aborigines, in particular of their disposition towards the intruders in connection with the two major landings, at Botany Bay and at Endeavour River. At Botany Bay two of the inhabitants tried to prevent Cook's party from getting ashore by throwing spears at them, withdrawing only after several shots had been fired by Cook's

---

[28] Sydney to Treasury, August 18, 1786, HO 35/1.

[29] Mackay, *A Place of Exile*, 57. Mackay concludes that Cook's account was not used and that the government primarily relied on "Banks's testimony in 1779 and on Matra's plan and testimony"; however, he offers no evidence for these conclusions.

men.[30] On three other occasions during their stay at Botany Bay, the Aborigines made a stand against a party from the ship (though with fewer threats of violence),[31] but otherwise they avoided contact completely despite the attempts made by Cook and others to meet them, and they barely ever touched the things which were offered to them.[32]

In his concluding remarks about the bay, Cook summarizes his view on the inhabitants:

> The Natives do not appear to be numberous neither do they seem to live in large bodies but dispers'd in small parties along by the water side.

He goes on to remark on their appearance, their "lack" of clothing, their subsistence on fish and their means of catching these. but he concludes that

> we could know very little of their customs as we never were able to form any connections with them, they had not so much as touch'd the things we had left in their hutts on purpose for them to take away.[33]

At the Endeavour River, which the expedition entered in order to repair the ship after it had run aground on the Barrier Reef, several weeks passed before any contact was made with the inhabitants. Eventually four Aboriginal men ventured close to the ship and accepted a few things from the crew.[34] After this the relationship evolved until some of the Aborigines came on board the ship; on seeing a number of recently caught turtle on the deck they tried to take some of them and when they were prevented from doing so they became angry and set the nearby grass on fire. Cook fired a shot at them, wounding one, but afterwards peace was restored.[35]

---

[30] J.C. Beaglehole, ed. *The Journals of Captain James Cook on his Voyages of Discovery;* Part 1: *The Voyage of the Endeavour 1768–1771* (Cambridge: Cambridge UP, 1955): 305. Beaglehole used the so-called Canberra Manuscript as the basis for his text but in his annotations made note of significant variations in the other manuscripts, including the one that the Admiralty received (which is now in the Public Record Office); see his "Textual Introduction," cxciii–ccxiv.

[31] Beaglehole, ed. *The Voyage of the Endeavour*, 306, 308 and 310.

[32] *The Voyage of the Endeavour*, 305–12. On one occasion, a member of the crew came upon an old man and woman with a child, but they did not want to have anything to do with him (their reaction was interpreted as fear; *The Voyage of the Endeavour*, 309).

[33] Beaglehole, ed. *The Voyage of the Endeavour*, 312.

[34] *The Voyage of the Endeavour*, 357.

[35] *The Voyage of the Endeavour*, 361.

The final meeting with the Aboriginal people was recorded on the day when the last landing was made:

> we saw a number of People upon this Island arm'd in the same manner as all the others we have seen [....] From the appearance of these People we expected that they would have opposed our landing but as we approached the Shore they all made off and left us in peaceable possession of as much of the Island as served our purpose.[36]

In his general remarks about the country, Cook sums up his findings about these people, saying among other things:

> I do not look upon them to be a warlike People, on the Contrary I think them a timorous and inoffensive race, no ways inclinable to cruelty [...] Neither are they very numerous, they live in small parties along by the Sea Coast, the banks of Lakes, Rivers creeks &ca. They seem to have no fix'd habitation but move about from place to place like wild Beasts in search of food, and I believe depend wholy upon the success of the present day for their subsistance [....] In short these people live wholy by fishing and hunting, but mostly by the former, for we never saw one Inch of Cultivated land in the whole Country.[37]

The description of the Aborigines and the meetings with them were observed by Cook and represented in his journal in a way which creates an image of the inhabitants of this country as a retiring people who – apart from a few cases of heroic opposition – were easily frightened off. They withdrew from contact with the newcomers, showing little curiosity about their presence or the things they offered. There were apparently not very many of them and they did not seem to be attached to any particular place. It should be noted, though, that Cook himself was aware that most of his conclusions were based on conjecture, because he had not managed to establish proper contacts with the people.[38]

Cook's speculations about the possibilities for agriculture –

> In this extensive Country it can never be doubted but what most sorts of Grain, Fruits, Roots &ca. of every kind would flourish here were they once brought hither, planted and cultivated by the hand of Industry, and here are Provender

---

[36] *The Voyage of the Endeavour*, 387.

[37] *The Voyage of the Endeavour*, 396.

[38] Reynolds has discussed in detail the various patterns of reaction towards the new people among Aborigines, though focusing mostly on the time after the initial settlement, in *The Other Side of the Frontier* (1981; Ringwood, Victoria & Harmondsworth: Penguin, 1982).

> for more Cattle at all seasons of the year than ever can be brought into this Country[39]

– unencumbered by considerations about the people already living on the land, may also have conveyed the impression that there would indeed be no problem in establishing an agricultural settlement, since the inhabitants did not "use" the land for their subsistence.

While Cook's journal was received and (presumably) read at the Admiralty, the preparation of the journal for publication was handed over to John Hawkesworth, a well-known essayist of the day. Hawkesworth was also allowed to use Sir Joseph Banks's journal, and his two volumes on the voyage turned out to be a mixture of the two texts with additional observations and speculations of his own. It was claimed that the original authors had read and accepted the work before it was published, a claim Cook vigorously disputed when he became acquainted with the account upon his return from his second voyage to the Pacific. The work had a mixed reception and was commented upon in a rather critical manner by many. However, it exercised great fascination among educated circles and was widely read, as shown by the fact that it went into a second edition shortly after its first appearance.[40]

It is therefore open to question whether the "accounts given by the late captain Cook," mentioned in Sydney's letter and quoted above, referred to Cook's own journal or to Hawkesworth's edition of it; it is, consequently, necessary to examine briefly what was said about the Aborigines in the latter work as well.

Hawkesworth's account of the encounter with the inhabitants of New South Wales is rather more elaborate than Cook's, using more words than he does and incorporating bits and pieces from Banks's journal. In a few places there are significant changes, but generally Hawkesworth follows the account given by Cook.[41] After describing the stay in Botany Bay, Hawkesworth reproduces some of the remarks made by Cook:

---

[39] Beaglehole, ed. *The Voyage of the Endeavour*, 397.

[40] *The Voyage of the Endeavour*, ccxlii–ccliii.

[41] John Hawkesworth, *An Account of the Voyages undertaken by the Order of His Present Majesty for making Discoveries in the Southern Hemisphere and successively performed by Commodore Byron, Captain Wallis, Captain Carteret, and Captain Cook drawn up from the Journals which were kept by the several Commanders and from the Papers of Joseph Banks, Esq.*, 3 vols. (London: W. Strahan & T. Cadell, 1773). Hawkesworth, for example, hypothesizes on the effect of firearms on the minds of the Aborigines (vol. 3, 500); he also transfers part of Cook and Banks's concluding remarks about the Aborigines to the description of the inhabitants of Tierra del Fuego (vol. 2, 59).

> All the inhabitants that we saw were stark naked: they did not appear to be numerous, nor to live in societies, but like other animals were scattered about along the coast.[42]

Hawkesworth also makes note of the fact that the ship's company could form very little opinion of their way of life, as they were unable to communicate with them; however, the comparison with "other animals" here seems to be his own.

Hawkesworth again commented on the number of the inhabitants in his final description of New South Wales, noting that

> [it] appears to be very small in proportion to its extent. We never saw so many as thirty of them together but once, and that was at Botany Bay,[43]

continuing that even when they tried to oppose the intruders they "never could muster above fourteen or fifteen fighting men." Echoing Banks, Hawkesworth did not consider that the interior would be inhabited –

> there is great reason to believe that this immense tract is either wholly desolate, or at least still more thinly inhabited than the parts we visited[44]

– basing his view on the belief that the people could only survive when they could get food from the sea. He also makes the comment that "They appear to have no fixed habitations, for we saw nothing like a town or village in the whole country," and in general creates the impression that the Aborigines lived rather cumbersome lives assisted by few tools or other instruments. Hawkesworth wavers on the question of their courage, noting on the one hand that their opposition to the landing at Botany Bay was a sign of considerable bravery, while "their precipitate flight from every other place that we approached, without even a menace [...] was an indication of uncommon tameness and

---

On the latter point, cf Glyndwr Williams, "'Far more Happier than We Europeans': Reactions to the Australian Aborigines on Cook's voyage," in *Through White Eyes*, ed. Susan Janson & Stuart Macintyre (Sydney: Allen & Unwin, 1990): 62; and Bernard Smith, *European Vision and the South Pacific 1768–1850* (Oxford: Clarendon, 1960): 22.

[42] Hawkesworth, *Account of the Voyages*, vol. 3, 506.

[43] *Account of the Voyages*, vol. 3, 631.

[44] *Account of the Voyages*, vol. 3, 631.

timidity."[45] The account of the Aborigines concluded with the comment that "I have faithfully related facts, the reader must judge of the people for himself."[46]

Besides Cook's work, a number of other "representations" were reported by Sydney to have been taken into account by the government. The first of these was probably the testimony given by Banks to the House of Commons Committee on Transportation in April 1779. Banks, who had accompanied Cook on his first voyage as a botanist, was by now President of the Royal Society and in other ways an active and influential person whose opinion would have been of interest to the committee.[47]

He was asked by the committee to suggest which place would be most suitable for him if

> it should be thought expedient to establish a Colony of convicted Felons in any distant Part of the Globe, from whence their Escape might be difficult, and where, from the Fertility of the Soil, they might be enabled to maintain themselves, after the First Year, with little or no Aid from the Mother Country.

Banks answered that Botany Bay seemed to him to answer to that purpose, observing further:

> that he apprehended there would be little Probability of any Opposition from the Natives, as, during his Stay there, in the Year 1770, he saw very few, and did not think there were above Fifty in all the Neighbourhood, and had reason to believe the Country was very thinly peopled; those he saw were naked, treacherous, and armed with Lances, but extremely cowardly, and constantly retired from our People when they made the least Appearance of Resistance.[48]

This summary corresponds fairly well to the picture of the Aboriginal peoples that emerges from Banks's journal;[49] along with detailed description of their appearance, housing, food, weapons, etc., Banks drew various general conclu-

---

[45] Hawkesworth, *Account of the Voyages*, vol. 3, 644–45.

[46] *Account of the Voyages*, vol. 3, 645.

[47] See Glyndwr Williams, "'The common centre of we discoverers,' Sir Joseph Banks, Exploration and Empire in the Late Eighteenth Century," in *Sir Joseph Banks: A Global Perspective*, ed. R.E.R. Banks et al. (Kew: Royal Botanical Gardens, 1994): 177–191, for details about Banks's career after the *Endeavour* voyage.

[48] *Journals of the House of Commons* 37 (1778–1780): 311.

[49] John Manning Ward claims that Banks "modified his conclusions" when giving testimony, though Ward seems mostly to be thinking of Banks's statements about the appearance of the land; Ward, *British Policy in the South Pacific* (Sydney: Australasian Publishing Company, 1948): 3; cf Frost, *Botany Bay Mirages*, 87–91.

sions, such as the belief that there was not much difference in customs between geographically distinct groups, that their main source of food was the sea, that partly for this reason the interior would most likely be uninhabited, and that in any case the sea-coast was very sparsely populated ("thinly inhabited even to admiration").[50]

A paper among the Colonial Office documents entitled "Africa, Convicts, Memorandum" contains a summary of part of the evidence heard by the committee; it includes extensive notes on Banks's evidence, twice referring to the number of inhabitants. It followed Banks's observations quite closely: "few Natives in 1770. believes there are few Inhabitants, naked and timorous." Banks's word "treacherous" from the official report is here replaced by "timorous"; it is, of course, impossible to determine whether this was merely due to a mistake by a clerk or something else, but it recalls Cook's characterization quoted above. Towards the end of the lengthy summary, the inhabitants are mentioned again (although Banks did not do so): "not fifty natives residing in that part of the Country."[51]

Obviously the number of inhabitants was considered sufficiently important to make sure that all the information about it was included.

Banks's recommendation of New South Wales carried little weight with the Committee; in their report they did not mention it as a possible place of transportation. Then again, nor did they mention any of the other places on which they heard evidence, though they did, no doubt as a reflection of this, suggest a division of convicts, sending the hardened ones to "unhealthy places" and the young ones to "some distant Part of the Globe, and in New-discovered Countries."[52]

---

[50] J.C. Beaglehole, ed. *The Endeavour Journal of Joseph Banks 1768–1771* (Sydney: Trustees of the Public Library of New South Wales in association with Angus & Robertson, 1963): 122, 123–37. Banks's journal was not published in the eighteenth century (or, indeed, the nineteenth) except for the parts included in Hawkesworth's edition; for this reason, only brief reference is made to it here to indicate the background against which Banks formulated his response to the two Commons committees he appeared before. For a discussion of differences and similarities between the journals of Cook and Banks, see Williams, "'Far more Happier than We Europeans'."

[51] Africa, Convicts, Memorandum, undated, HO 42/5: 412–13. Cf Frost, *Botany Bay Mirages*, 101. Mackay calls it a "report" of ministerial deliberation and dates it to December 1784 (see Mackay, *A Place of Exile*, 32, 105 note 26).

[52] *Journals of the House of Commons* 37, 314.

The east coast of New Holland was brought to the attention of the government again in August 1783 when James Maria Matra submitted to the Home Department an unsolicited proposal for colonization there. Matra participated as midshipman in the *Endeavour* voyage, where he incurred Cook's disapproval as "one of those gentlemen, frequently found on board Kings Ships, that can very well be spared."[53] Banks seems to have thought more kindly of him, since he apparently helped him to various appointments later on.[54]

Matra was an American loyalist who, like other countrymen of his, found himself in a difficult position after the Revolution. His proposal to establish a colony in New South Wales (which he claimed had Joseph Banks's approval) was an attempt to create new opportunities for the loyalists. Matra refers once to the indigenous inhabitants, on the first of nine pages – mentioning the coast of New South Wales, he says:

> In this immense tract of more than 2000 miles there was every variety of Soil, & great parts of it were extremely fertile, peopled only by a few black Inhabitants, who in the rudest state of Society, knew no other Arts than such as were necessary, to their mere animal Existence, & which was almost entirely sustained by catching Fish.[55]

In March or April 1784, Matra was granted an interview with Lord Sydney, surely a sign that his proposal was accorded some interest. There are no records of the interview, but an extended version of Matra's proposal, submitted in April, suggests that Sydney had asked about the prospects for transporting convicts to New South Wales, an idea Matra immediately took up and added to his own plan.[56]

---

[53] Beaglehole, ed. *Voyage of Endeavour*, 323.

[54] Frost, *Convicts and Empire*, 11–13.

[55] James Matra to Lord North, August 23, 1783, CO 201/1: 57. Matra is sometimes suggested as the author of the first, anonymous, book on New South Wales, which was published in 1771, two years before the official account of the voyage (see Beaglehole, ed. *Voyage of Endeavour*, cclvi–cclix). The description of the inhabitants might well have been Matra's; they were described as "entirely naked and black" and at the Endeavour River the general comment was made that "They were ignorant, poor and destitute, not only of the conveniences, but of many of the necessaries of life"; Anon., *Journal of a Voyage round the World in His Majesty's Ship Endeavour in the Years 1768, 1769, 1770 and 1771, undertaken in pursuit of natural Knowledge at the Desire of the Royal Society* (London: T. Becket & P.A. De Hondt, 1771): 111, 122.

[56] Matra to Nepean, April 6, 1784, quoted in Martin, ed. *The Founding of Australia*, 14–16. Mollie Gillen points out that in fact the suggestion might well have been made by

Towards the end of the year, the "memorandum of matters to be brought before Cabinet" refers (as "Matra's Plan") to the idea of making a settlement in New South Wales both for loyalists and convicts,[57] and on 25 December Lord Howe, head of the Admiralty, was consulted by Sydney on the feasibility of Matra's ideas,[58] both signs that Matra was taken seriously by government even though the plan was not acted upon.

Two other people made representations to the government on the topic of New South Wales; one was John Call, who, after some twenty years in India, came back to England, became a member of Parliament and submitted numerous proposals to government on various subjects, some of which received serious consideration.

Call's scheme was broader than Matra's, in that he considered New Zealand, New Caledonia, Norfolk Island and New South Wales in the light of commercial interests as well as in terms of their being suitable places for loyalists and convicts. His reference to the inhabitants was also more extensive; on New South Wales he says:

> In his concluding observations, Captain Cook does not indeed give the most favourable Account of the Soil, Timber, vegetable or animal Productions, or even of the Inhabitants that he saw, nor does he suppose the latter are very Numerous.[59]

Call goes on to say that since Cook did not visit the interior and, furthermore, was unable to communicate with the people he met, it would be a fair assumption that in other places it was possible to grow food enough for "Millions of People," but he does not go further and conclude that perhaps there were also many more inhabitants in other parts of the country.

About Norfolk Island, Call has this to say:

> This Island has an advantage not common to the Others by not being inhabited, so that no Injury can be done by possessing it, to the rest of Mankind.

Matra himself; see "The Botany Bay Decision, 1786: Convicts, not Empire," *English Historical Review* 97 (1982): 744.

[57] Memorandum, December 1784, see Martin, ed. *The Founding of Australia*, 17–18.

[58] Howe to Sydney, December 26, 1784, HO 28/4: 386.

[59] Paper left with Lord Sydney by Colonel Call, undated, HO 42/7: 52. The year 1786 is suggested with a question mark, but seems too late, since Call and George Young applied for permission to settle Norfolk Island in June 1785; the general proposal must have been earlier than this. Frost suggests August 1784 (*Convicts and Empire*, 203 note 13), to which Mackay objects (*A Place of Exile*, 31–32).

He devotes some space to the further consideration of this question, both from a moral and from a practical (though not from a legal) point of view, in connection with other places. Thus he maintains that even though the Society Islands or the New Hebrides may be more attractive, they are so densely populated that occupation of them could not take place without bloodshed, something that he considers "repugnant to human Nature"; and further:

> In Reply to this it may be urged that the same difficulty will occur at New Holland, New Zealand or New Caledonia, because these are all inhabited – The Objection seems natural; but as these Countries are much larger, and not so fully inhabited, there is apparently room for much greater degrees of Population, and the most extensive Improvement of Cultivation.

The impression that a country could be less than "fully populated" carries the natural conclusion that others could settle there without necessarily infringing on the way of life of the original inhabitants. This belief was also noted in connection with Phillip's instructions above. Call, however, wanted to add yet more weight to his claim that it was permissible to settle in a country occupied by others, and he did so by pointing out all the material and (particularly) moral advantages the indigenous inhabitants would gain by it – arguments that were to gain much ground in subsequent decades:

> And to reduce the Objection still more, it must be allowed that the Natives want many of the Necessaries of Life, which it would be Charity to furnish them with – That they are in a very uncivilized State – That to instruct, and inform them better, would be doing them no Injury – That by communicating the Principles of the Christian Religion, They would receive an invaluable Blessing

Most significantly, he then observes:

> – and lastly, it is probable a Purchase might be made of a Part of the Country from the native Inhabitants for Articles more agreable and useful to them.[60]

This is one of the very few occasions before 1788 on which suggestions for land purchase were made in the context of New South Wales. Another was the hearing of evidence by the Commons Committee of 1785, of which, significantly, Call was a member. There is unfortunately no actual evidence that Call's proposal had any influence with government, though one may speculate

---

[60] Colonel Call, undated, HO 42/7: 54.

that, being a member of the 1785 committee and with his India experience, he may well have been looked upon as knowledgeable on these issues.

Finally, Sir George Young, a naval officer and Call's brother-in-law by second marriage, also submitted a proposal to the Secretary of State on New South Wales. Like Call, he emphasized both the commercial benefits to be derived from that place and the possibility of placing both loyalists and convicts there. Young made no reference whatsoever to the original population.[61]

As with Call, there is no direct evidence that Young's plan (which is found among the official documents in several versions[62]) was considered by government, but there are indications that it may have been. The plan of January 1785 was transmitted by Pepper Arden, the Attorney-General, with encouraging comments and a reference to Lord Mansfield's interest in the subject; both men, one can assume, would have assured the plan at least a reading. Furthermore, Young and Matra joined forces to some extent,[63] just as Call and Young did a little later; the three of them seem in some way interconnected.

On the other hand, a later letter written by Young shows that he himself did not feel that he had been taken into account on this business,[64] and neither he nor Call comes under the description of "persons who accompanied him [Cook]" – referred to in Sydney's letter as those who had been consulted on New South Wales. Mackay claims that the main purpose of the proposals of all three men was to secure government employment or commercial benefits for the authors and that their ideas have "had a much greater impact on historians

---

[61] Sir George Young's Plan, transmitted to Lord Sydney through the Attorney-General on 13 January 1785, quoted in Martin, ed. *The Founding of Australia*, 19–22.

[62] Sir George Young's Plan, January 1785 CO 201/1: 52–53, 55–56 (a printed version, probably also early 1785); another printed version, dated April 21, 1785 CO 201/8: 152–53; and Young to Pitt, undated, PRO 30/8/342: 283–84, pt. 2. I am grateful to Glyn Williams for pointing out to me that the proposals made by George Young have been published in *Dreams of a Pacific Empire: Sir George Young's proposal for a colonization of New South Wales (1784–1785)*, ed. Alan Frost (Sydney: Resolution Press, 1980).

[63] See Matra to Nepean, October 1, 1784, CO 201/1: 66; Young to Davidson, February 3, 1793, CO 201/8: 148; and Frost, *Convicts and Empire*, 27. But cf also Alan Atkinson, "Whigs and Tories and Botany Bay," in Martin, ed. *The Founding of Australia*, 193. Atkinson also discusses the political affiliations of the three men but does not provide conclusive evidence that these had any impact on the reception of their proposals ("Whigs and Tories," 191–200).

[64] Young to Davidson, February 3, 1793, CO 201/8: 148.

than they had on the ministry of William Pitt"; he does, however, believe that their plans were nevertheless accorded some consideration by government.[65]

It may be added that by early 1785 the government had decided in favour of Lemain in Africa, rendering redundant the schemes and other evidence on New South Wales.

Banks and Matras, however, were heard on New South Wales again in May 1785 at the hearings of the Commons Committee on Transportation that put a stop to the Lemain scheme.[66]

Matra appeared on three occasions. The minutes of the first interview have been lost; on his second and third appearance no reference was made to the inhabitants of New South Wales, but he did testify that Cook had "taken possession" of the coast and that it was believed that no "European powers" had ever visited it.[67]

Banks, on the other hand, was asked several questions about the people during his interview. As has been pointed out by Reynolds, both the questions and the answers are interesting; I quote them in full here:

> "Is the Coast in general or the particular part you have mentioned much inhabited?"
>
> "There are very few inhabitants"
>
> "Are they of a Peaceable or hostile Disposition?"
>
> "Though they seemed inclined to Hostilities they did not appear at all to be feared. We never saw more than 30 or 40 together"
>
> "Do you apprehend in Case it was resolved to send Convicts there any District of the Country might be obtained by Cession or Purchase?"
>
> "There was no probability while we were there of obtaining any thing either by Cession or Purchase as there was nothing we could offer that they would take except Provisions and those we wanted ourselves"
>
> "Have you any Idea of the Nature of the Government under which they lived?"
>
> "None whatever, nor of their Languages"[68]
>
> [....]
>
> "Do you think that 500 Men being put on Shore there would meet with that obstruction from the Natives which might prevent their settling there?"

---

[65] Mackay, *A Place of Exile*, 34–37. Mackay is particularly concerned to deny the significance of these proposals in indicating government motives, such as trade or strategy, in founding New South Wales.

[66] Call and Young were also interviewed – but on Africa, rather than on New South Wales.

[67] Matra's evidence, May 23, 1785, HO 7/1: 85.

[68] Banks's evidence, May 10, 1785, HO 7/1: 72–73.

"Certainly not – from the experience I have had of the Natives of another part of the same Coast I am inclined to believe they would speedily abandon the Country to the New Comers"

"Were the Natives armed and in what Manner?"

"They were armed with spears headed with Fish Bones but none of them we saw in Botany Bay appeared at all formidable"

"Do you know of any place you think preferable to this for the purpose of sending Convicts to it?"

"From the Fertility of the Soil, the timid Disposition of the Inhabitants, and the Climate being so analogous to that of Europe I give this place the preference to all that I have seen."[69]

Banks's testimony here was very similar to that given to the Committee in 1779, claiming essentially that the country was very thinly inhabited and that the people who lived there were so fearful that they would not put up any resistance to the invasion of their country. It should be noted that Banks does not say that the Aborigines had no form of government or that it would be unnecessary to come to an arrangement with them about the land, although some scholars have interpreted his statements to that effect.[70] Banks confines himself to reporting his observations, which were basically that it had not been possible to trade with the Aborigines nor to get any information about their political organization (or to learn their language), though later he does conclude that they would give up their land.

The questions show very clearly what was considered important:[71] the number of inhabitants, perhaps in order to assess whether the country was "fully inhabited"; the disposition of the people and, importantly, whether they would be willing to sell any part of the land; this question is evidence both of the presupposition that the inhabitants owned the land and of the assumption that establishing a settlement would require obtaining some of this land from the inhabitants.[72]

---

[69] Bank's evidence, May 10, 1785, HO 7/1: 75–76. Banks's testimony is also quoted in Reynolds, *The Law of the Land*, 53–54, and King, "Terra Australis," 77.

[70] See, for example, A.G.L. Shaw, "British Policy towards the Australian Aborigines 1830–1850," *Australian Historical Studies* 25 (1992–1993): 266; and Jonathan King, ed. *In the Beginning... The Story of the Creation of Australia from the Original Writings* (Melbourne: Macmillan, 1985): 51.

[71] Cf Mackay, who points out that the questions deemed most important by the committee in connection with all the places they considered were those relating to the climate and the disposition of the inhabitants (*A Place of Exile*, 52).

[72] This conclusion is also reached by Reynolds, *The Law of the Land*, 53–54.

The answer to this question must have been puzzling; reluctance to part with their land would have been well-known from North America but refusal to trade at all, whether in land or in anything else, would probably not have been encountered before and would have been very hard for the British to understand. Perhaps the question about their form of government was an attempt to arrive at an explanation of this strange situation.

Considering the amount of evidence on New South Wales which the Committee heard, it is surprising that they did not mention the place at all in their report but discussed only the southwest coast of Africa, on which they had heard evidence by Edward Thompson.[73] Frost suggests that the government had Call give the Committee a plan on Das Voltas Bay, though there is little conclusive evidence to support this.[74] Even if the government did prefer to work actively towards the African solution, there is no reason to believe that their decision was based on considerations about the inhabitants in either place.

In any case, the government found itself with few options except New South Wales when Das Voltas Bay proved unsuitable. It is difficult to establish whether the evidence on Australia heard by the Committee had any influence with the government; Alan Atkinson points out that Lord Beauchamp, the chairman, belonged (like the chairman of the 1779 committee) to the opposition and as such cannot be assumed to reflect government policy.[75] While this observation is obviously relevant in the present context, it does not rule out the possibility that there may have been points of agreement between the two parties. In any case, it is more likely than not that the government followed the proceedings with interest.

All in all, then, there exists quite a considerable amount of material which may have played a role in forming the opinion of the government about the indigenous population of the place where they were about to establish a penal settlement. The authors of the various accounts stress different aspects, no doubt according to their personal outlook and the aim of their work. Some compare the Aboriginal way of life to that of wild animals subsisting from day to day, and make note of their colour or their nakedness; in some of the ac-

---

[73] Frost, *Botany Bay Mirages*, 107.

[74] Frost, *Convicts and Empire*, 41; Mackay is rather more inclined to believe that the government simply followed the recommendations of the Committee (*A Place of Exile*, 48).

[75] Atkinson, "Whigs and Tories," 187–88. Atkinson's point occurs as a contribution to the debate about motives for the foundation of New South Wales; he does not refer to attitudes towards indigenous peoples.

counts, the limited knowledge acquired about this group of people is mentioned; and some mention the inhabitants' attempts to defend their country, but hasten to add that this was soon replaced by a tendency to retire before the intruders.

While there is no evidence that the first of these observations had any impact on the attitude towards the inhabitants of New South Wales, the last one may be reflected in the provisions for defence made in Sydney's letter to the Admiralty, in the "Heads of a Plan," and in Phillip's instructions. The qualifying "if required" of the plan may reflect the limited knowledge possessed about the intentions of the inhabitants.

Variations apart, however, the accounts have one point in common: they all state as a fact that the number of inhabitants was very small, and it is safe to conclude that whatever else the Home Office drew from the accounts of New South Wales, the impression would have been gained that this area was very thinly populated.[76]

Evan Nepean summarized the assumptions about New South Wales upon which the government worked, in a letter to the Irish government in October 1786. He mentions that the convict settlement was intended to be at Botany Bay, a place which

> according to the Accounts of the late Captain Cook, as well as others who accompanied him upon his Voyages, appears to be a Country peculiarly adapted for a Settlement

on account of the supplies of fuel and water, the soil and the supply of fish. Three pages later he refers to "the advantage of Ground Fruit, which the very few Natives inhabiting the Neighbourhood have raised in great Quantities."[77] Although the reference to the inhabitants thus appears well after the initial characterization of the country and in a parenthetical clause, it shows beyond doubt that the government had accepted the general view on their numbers. They would probably have concluded that for this reason problems with the inhabitants were unlikely to occur – that, indeed, it was quite possible that the original inhabitants would leave the place when the settlers arrived.

---

[76] Cf Reynolds, *The Law of the Land*, 32 and 55, who concludes that it was a widespread assumption that New South Wales was practically uninhabited. See also King, ed. *In the Beginning*, 76.

[77] Nepean to Sackville-Hamilton, October 21, 1786, HO 100/18: 369–73.

The idea that there would be room enough for everybody, as intimated in Phillip's instructions, may well be traced to such impressions; and the order to ascertain the numbers of the inhabitants could be seen as a wish to make sure that this was true.

The information about New South Wales possessed by the government thus throws considerable light on the orders contained in the official documents. In particular, the lack of provision for negotiating with the inhabitants for cession of land is more understandable in this context. It is highly probable that the belief that the country was practically uninhabited led the government to conclude that there was no need to insert such a provision.

Comparison with official statements in connection with other areas in a similar situation shows that New South Wales was an exceptional case, and in turn gives additional support to the idea that a particular view of that country probably gave rise to the departure from the established pattern.

Government action in other areas[78]

The acquisition of new territory was considered by the British government on a number of occasions in this period; as a starting-point, part of Cook's instructions for his first voyage to the South Seas in 1768 may be quoted. He was ordered

> With the consent of the natives to take possession of convenient situations in the country in the name of the King of Great Britain or if you find the country uninhabited take possession for His Majesty by setting up proper marks and inscriptions as first discoverers and possessors.[79]

A distinction is made here between inhabited and uninhabited land and it is stated that in the former case permission had to be obtained from the inhabitants to make a claim to the territory (against other colonizing powers). It is difficult not to see this as evidence that at this time the official policy of expansion in Britain recognized the right of indigenous peoples to their land and the need to negotiate with them for permission to settle. Other cases, closer in time to the settlement of New South Wales, confirm this impression.

---

[78] Alan Frost has also surveyed the material mentioned here, in *Botany Bay Mirages*, but although his immediate conclusions are much the same as those drawn here, his general thesis on this and related issues is different, as will appear later. But cf Reynolds, *The Law of the Land*, 51–53.

[79] Beaglehole, ed. *The Voyage of the Endeavour*, cclxxxii.

Lemain is an obvious candidate for comparison, being in many ways parallel to Botany Bay: it was considered mainly from the point of view of getting rid of the convicts; the deliberations about it were carried out in haste (though Edward Thompson – who later suggested Das Voltas Bay – was sent to survey the area); it was based on suggestions made by people outside the government (in this case, John Barnes of the Company of Merchants); the letter sent by Lord Sydney to the Treasury announcing the decision to establish a settlement there was similar to the one on Botany Bay and it was likewise accompanied by a "plan" setting out the details.[80]

In his letter to the Treasury of February 1785, Sydney explains that a man called Richard Bradley had been sent to the Gambia

> with Instructions for entering into Engagements with the native Chiefs for obtaining, upon the payment of such Annual Custom as may be agreed upon, the Island of Lemain.[81]

Provision is also made for goods to be sent out with which trade could be carried on with the neighbouring inhabitants. The enclosed plan, entitled "A Description of the Island Lemain collected from the Information of Gentlemen who have been Members of the African Committee," painted a rather rosy picture of the place. Among other things, it stated that "the Natives are hospitable and inoffensive," that any amount of land could be "possessed upon Payment of a small annual Custom to the Chief of the Country," and that trade in general could be conducted with the Africans.[82]

Limited as the official documents relating to Lemain are, they nevertheless show a clear awareness of the presence of the original inhabitants of the area under consideration, take their disposition into account, and regard it as the most natural thing in the world to take measures for obtaining their permission to establish the settlement.

The northwest coast of Africa was relatively well-known from the long experience gained by the Africa Company and the Company of Merchants in

---

[80] For information about the Lemain scheme, see John Milner Gray, *A History of the Gambia* (Cambridge: Cambridge UP, 1940): 277–280; Frost, *Convicts and Empire*, 28–37; and Oldham, *Britain's Convicts to the Colonies*, ch. 6.

[81] Sydney to Treasury, February 9, 1785, HO 35/1.

[82] "A Description of the Island of Lemain," February 9, 1785, HO 35/1. See also Bradley to Sydney, November 9, 1785, T 1/641: 44–45, a report from Bradley on his expedition to the Gambia, where he did indeed purchase or lease Lemain (although some of the chiefs put up resistance to the proceedings).

the process of trading for slaves and valuable goods, both in the Senegambia region and on the Guinea Coast. The British were familiar with the Africans and knew that the area was well-populated, and that some arrangement would be necessary with the local chief. In other words, relying on the available information and expertise, the British government based the establishment of the settlement on the foundation of such relations with the inhabitants as were necessary for the success of the venture, just as in the case of the establishment of successful trading relations.[83]

That this was the normal process in this area is indicated by a paper entitled "Thoughts upon the Establishments to be made in the River Gambia," probably written a few years earlier.[84] Discussing the power-relations between Britain and France in the area, it argues for the acquisition of Bunnion Point at the mouth of the river, and then states that

> The first Point to be attained is the purchase or Lease [....] to send the Governor out with proper persons under him to make the purchase in Question.

Furthermore, the author speculates that the French might prevail upon the Africans to

> Refuse Us a Settlement on the Main which by the bye they always have done, & we were allowed to wood, water & bury our dead at Gillipee only upon payment of a Yearly acknowledgment & without having a *Settlement*.

Assuming that "they" refers to the Africans rather than the French, both passages confirm the impression that local ownership of the land was accepted without question and that this issue had to be given serious consideration in the planning of future ventures.

---

[83] See also Kent McNeil, *Common Law Aboriginal Title* (Oxford: Clarendon, 1989): 124–30, who shows that in the case of both Sierra Leone and the Gold Coast the British negotiated with the inhabitants for cession of land.

[84] "Thoughts upon the Establishments to be made in the River Gambia," undated, CO 267/20: 381–82. The document is contained in a box labelled "Africa, 1781–84, Miscellaneous Papers." Frost suggests that it was written by the Law Officers in early 1784 but offers no evidence to support this. From the style of the paper it is likely, at least, that it was written by some government official, rather than by an outside party submitting a proposal. On the basis of the reference to the "guaranty of Gambia River by France," it may be concluded that the document was written after the Treaty of Versaille was signed in September 1783 (cf Gray, *History of the Gambia*, 273).

The orders given on the survey of Das Voltas Bay also show concern about the local inhabitants; in Sydney's August 1785 letter to the Admiralty ordering the survey, the following directive is issued:

> Your Lordships will [...] take especial care that the Commander of the Ship to be sent upon this Service be particularly instructed to avoid giving any sort of Offence, or cause of Complaint, in the mode of conducting it, to the peaceable Natives.[85]

An incomplete memorandum, undated and unsigned but referring to this particular topic, recommends Das Voltas Bay as a place for convicts, pointing out that

> although the interior part is very little known or indeed even the Coast, it has been ascertained by Ships that have touched at places upon that Coast that the Natives are not inclined to Act with Hostility, and that they are amply.[86]

For the purposes of this chapter it is particularly frustrating that the memo stops in the middle of a sentence describing the inhabitants – all the more so as it is noteworthy that although Sydney gives instructions not to disturb the inhabitants (and both the letter and the memo state that they are peaceable), there is no provision for buying land from them as there is in the Lemain case; this of course makes it somewhat comparable to Botany Bay, and it would have been very interesting to know if the continuation of the memorandum contained any further indications of how this was perceived (if, for example, the land was considered to be very sparsely inhabited – as indeed it was).

The report of the 1785 Committee, which recommended Das Voltas Bay for transportation, refers quite extensively to hearsay reports about the place, and the hospitality and friendly nature of the inhabitants are mentioned several times. This leads the Committee to conclude

> That it appears to them highly probable that the Natives would without resistance acquiesce in ceding as much Land as may be necessary for a stipulated Rent.[87]

---

[85] Sydney to Admiralty, August 22, 1785, HO 28/5: 119–20, based on a government memorandum with nearly the same wording, 16 August 1785, HO 28/5: 116–17.

[86] Memorandum, undated, HO 42/1: 402. The date 1782 is suggested on the following sheet, but this surely cannot be right. From the contents it can be dated with a great degree of certainty to spring or early summer 1785.

[87] Report, June 21, 1785, HO 42/7: 17.

As in the Committee's questioning of Banks, this statement is evidence of an assumption that the territorial rights of the inhabitants would have to be recognized and extinguished before a settlement could be properly established. It is of course impossible to say whether the Committee's expectations would have been borne out if the scheme had been further developed.

Examples from other parts of the world where the British were much involved indicates that this assumption was shared by government.

One of the major concerns of the British in the eighteenth century (as indeed at other times) was to safeguard their route to the east and their trade there, particularly in the case of war. This concern always gained urgency when there were rumours of increasing French hostility, as happened regularly towards the end of the century. The Board of Control, who supervised the East India Company, was therefore engaged constantly in a discussion of how and where to acquire additional naval stations to support them in defending the Indian possessions.

Most of the places considered were on the Malaysian peninsula or the Indonesian islands.[88] The British always conducted negotiations with the rulers of these countries and in some cases gained cessions of land sufficient to establish a trading post and harbour (often in return for military aid), but the political structure and social organization of these peoples as well as their experience in foreign policy and trade were very different from those of hunter–gatherer or pastoral societies; consequently, these places do not, perhaps, provide the best cases for comparison.

However, the Board also considered the Andamans and the Nicobars, islands in the Bay of Bengal, both of which groups were inhabited by "tribal" peoples. The islands were considered in a number of memoranda, in which no reference was made to any inhabitants – the territories were considered solely

---

[88] See, for example, Instructions to Captain Forrest, May 31, 1784 (on acquiring the island of Rhio), and Orders to Lord Cornwallis, 1786 (on Penang) in *British Colonial Developments, 1774–1834, Select Documents*, ed. Vincent Todd Harlow and Frederick Madden (Oxford: Clarendon, 1953): 11–13, 52–54. See also Vincent Todd Harlow, *The Founding of the Second British Empire 1763–1793*, 2 vols. (London: Longmans & New York: Green, 1952–1964), for an overview of the complex issues involved in British actions in the east. Madagascar was also suggested as a possible way-station (e.g. Blankett to Nepean, November 1786, HO 42/10: 418–22; and Young to Davidson, February 3, 1793, CO 201/8: 148–51) and occasionally the coast of southern Africa (Dalrymple to Devayne, September 1785, PRO 30/8/128).

from the point of view of their utility to the British;[89] but in a letter to the British government in India from 1785, which ordered an expedition to the Nicobars to establish the situation there with respect to European posts, directions were given

> to take immediate Possession of them [the Islands], & to use every Means to conciliate the Affections of the Natives & obtain their Consent.[90]

It may well be argued that the order "to take possession" was concerned primarily with establishing the British right to the islands as against other European powers, whereas the direction to "obtain their Consent" would be the way actually to gain sovereignty over the area they were interested in. In the event, nothing came of the scheme.[91]

The best-documented case from this period is probably that of the northwest coast of North America, where a controversy raged for a couple of years with the Spanish monarch over possession of Nootka Sound.

The first British party to visit the area was Cook's third and final expedition in 1778 (it is considered unlikely that Drake ever got that far north); the Russians may have been there before and the Spanish had sent the first of a number of expeditions along the northwest coast in 1774.[92] Several trading expeditions were sent to Nootka Sound by enterprising merchants to buy furs for the China trade, but in 1789 a conflict developed when a Spanish commander seized some English ships and held the crews prisoners, claiming that the whole of the American coast belonged to Spain as a consequence of papal commission, various treaties, and de-facto possession.[93]

A diplomatic crisis ensued in which both nations prepared for armed struggle, but the controversy was eventually solved by a mutual agreement which in essence granted both the British and the Spanish the right to trade and establish settlements on the northwest coast. While it is not necessary to dis-

---

[89] For example, Board of Control Memorandum, May 25, 1788, PRO 30/8/360: 108–14; Board of Control Minute, October 1788, CO 77/26: 35.

[90] India Board to Governor-General and Council at Bengal, April 9, 1785, FO 41/1.

[91] Harlow, *The Founding of the Second British Empire*, 361–63. Cf discussion in ch. 5, below, "Acquiring title to colonies against other colonizers."

[92] W.L. Cook, *Floodtide of Empire* (New Haven CT: Yale UP, 1973): ch. 3.

[93] John M. Norris, "The Policy of the British Cabinet in the Nootka Crisis," *English Historical Review* 70 (1955): 562. For information on the crisis see also William Ray Manning, "The Nootka Sound Controversy," *Annual Report of the American Historical Association, 1904* (Washington DC: Government Printing Office, 1905): 283–479.

cuss the details of the controversy here, a number of interesting points about the Indians was made in the documents produced in this connection.

It appeared from a memorial written by a Captain Meares who was involved in the expedition to Nootka Sound in 1789 that a piece of land had been bought from the Indians the previous year for the purpose of building a trading post; furthermore, several Indian chiefs had been paid for the right to carry on trade with them (to the exclusion of anyone else). However, it does not seem that any attempt had been made to claim sovereignty over the area.[94]

After news had reached Britain of the seizure of British property (but before Meares's memorial had been received), the government decided to send an official expedition from India to the northwest coast

> for the protection of the Trade of His Majesty's subjects, and for forming an Establishment upon the said Coast[95]

It would thus appear that the British intended to occupy the area and form a colony there. A few pages later this important order was given:

> In the whole of this service, but particularly in the establishment of the intended Settlement, you are to do your utmost to maintain a friendly intercourse with the Natives; and, if you find any person or number of persons among them who appear to have any right or Sovereignty over the Territory which you shall fix upon for the Settlement, you are to endeavour to purchase their consent to the formation of the Settlement, and a Grant of Land for that purpose, by the presents with which you are furnished.[96]

Although the expedition was called off and the order thus not put into practice, this passage contains an important indication of British government perceptions of the policy to be pursued on the founding of a new settlement at this time. It is regarded as essential to maintain friendly relations with the Indian inhabitants, and provision is made for buying land from them; however, it would seem to be the first time that any doubt is expressed about the existence of territorial rights among the inhabitants. It is nevertheless clear that an intention existed to observe whatever rights the British believed the inhabitants had.

---

[94] Meares to Grenville (Memorial), April 30, 1790, HO 28/61: 291–304, though Norris seems to think that Meares said that territorial claims had been made ("The Policy of the British Cabinet in the Nootka Crisis," 570).

[95] Instructions to the Captain of the Frigate to be dispatched from the East Indies, March 1790, HO 28/61: 273.

[96] Instructions to the Captain of the Frigate, HO 28/61: 276.

This is also indicated in the first representation made by the British *charge d'affaires* in Madrid; it was claimed that British subjects had a right to

> the Possession of such Establishments, as they may form, with the Consent of the Natives, in Places unoccupied by other European Nations.[97]

When the conflict had been resolved, instructions were issued for a new expedition which was to survey the coast and receive from the Spanish the property which they had confiscated in 1789; however, the commander, Vancouver, was not directed to gain possession of any land or establish a settlement. Grenville wrote to the Admiralty that

> In the execution of every part of this Service, it is very material that the Commanding Officer should be instructed to use every possible Care to avoid disputes with the Natives of any of the Parts where he may touch, and that he should be particularly attentive to endeavour, by Presents and by all other means, to conciliate their friendship and confidence.[98]

These are familiar tones by now; it may quite safely be stated that, common to all the ventures undertaken by the British in the period between 1760 and 1790 which involved an encounter with indigenous people, orders were unfailingly given to try and establish friendly relations with them – a sensible policy, considering the trouble these people could create if hostilities developed. It also appears that in all cases where a settlement was planned (except New South Wales and Das Voltas Bay) orders were given to purchase land from the inhabitants.

None of these places was exactly like New South Wales, and perhaps it is somewhat incautious to atempt to subject them to strict comparison: Lemain was in an area over which the British claimed sovereignty and where they had previously bought land from the local chiefs for their posts; in neither the Nicobars nor Nootka Sound was such a claim made, but in both cases a (potential) conflict existed with other European powers in which reference to purchase from the inhabitants could strengthen a British claim; however, the point remains that orders were given in these cases for such purchases, implying as it did a recognition of the ownership of the land by the original inhabitants.

---

[97] Mr Merry's Representation to the Spanish Court, May 4, 1790, FO 72/17: 19.

[98] Grenville to Admiralty, February 11, 1791, ADM 1/4156.

Das Voltas Bay and New South Wales apparently deviated from this pattern. While it is difficult to say anything about the former on the basis of the scant material existing, an attempt can be made to explain the case of New South Wales. Henry Reynolds points to the lack of competition from other European nations for the area as a factor that helps to explain why no provision was made for cession of the land.[99] This may indeed have relieved some of the pressure felt by the British, though later developments suggest that they were not entirely sure of French intentions in the Pacific. However, on the basis of the general tenor of British dealings with indigenous peoples as illustrated in this and the previous chapter, this does not provide a complete and satisfactory explanation. Some other factor must have influenced the men writing Phillip's instructions to leave out any mention of land settlement – my suggestion would be that it was the belief that New South Wales was largely uninhabited: as indicated above, an important element in most of the assumptions about the place.

Also inferring from the other instances examined in this study, it is most likely that had a treaty with the Aborigines been recommended by the governor, the government in London would have agreed to it. However, the most puzzling thing about official policy towards the inhabitants of New South Wales is the fact that in the decades following settlement, there seems to have been no consideration of such a thing, even though knowledge about the inhabitants was greatly increased and their hostility towards settlement on their land was being clearly displayed.

Developments after 1788

For a long time after the first landing, official policy towards the indigenous population was not only conducted through Phillip but also laid down by him. (The first dispatch was not drafted in London until the late summer of 1789 and did not arrive in New South Wales until the spring of 1790.) Thus Phillip's actions and intentions, which were communicated to the Secretary of State for his approval, are important in suggesting the direction of views on the Aboriginal population of the area.

Before his departure, Phillip had informed the Home Office of his expectations and intentions, among other things with regard to the Aborigines. In a memorandum written in 1786, Phillip described the need for some measure of

[99] Reynolds, *The Law of the Land*, 53.

defence against "the Natives, who tho' only seen in small Numbers by Capt Cook, may be very numerous on other parts of the Coast." This apprehension about the numbers of the inhabitants is further specified later on, when he says: "I am not of the general opinion that there are very few Inhabitants in this Country, at least so Few as have been represented" (incidentally confirming the view that this was the prevailing opinion).

He showed concern about the way in which to cultivate their friendship and avoid conflict; first, he intended to prevent any contact between them and the convicts or the sailors. Secondly, he would like to make a few of them live in the settlement so that he could give them "every thing that can tend to Civilize them, & to give them a high Opinion of their New Guests." Thirdly, he would punish anyone who did not treat the indigenous women well, if they were allowed to intermarry with the settlers.[100]

Phillip obviously gave the relationship with the original inhabitants serious thought and sincerely wished to succeed in this respect. However, given his scepticism with regard to the number of inhabitants, it is odd that he did not reflect on the need for negotiation with them for a cession of land. This apparently did not occur to him, and may be explained by the fact that Phillip was primarily a naval officer, not highly educated, and although he had formed an opinion against slavery, he would most likely not have been very well informed about government policy towards indigenous peoples.[101] Thus Phillip's background would not have furnished him with the means necessary to comprehend the more profound consequences of the encounter between the Aborigines and the British.

The development of relations after the convict ships had anchored in Sydney Cove has been frequently described.[102] After initial shows of hostility by the

---

[100] Botany Bay Memorandum, 1786, CO 201/2: 91–93.

[101] See Alan Frost, *Arthur Phillip 1783–1814: His Voyaging* (Melbourne: Oxford UP 1987): 1–133, for Phillip's life before the voyage to New South Wales.

[102] For example, Marjorie Barnard Eldershaw, *Phillip of Australia: An Account of the Settlement at Sydney Cove 1788–1792* (London: George G. Harrap, 1938); C.M.H. Clark, *A History of Australia* (Carlton, Victoria: Melbourne UP, 1962): vol. 1; Richard Broome, *Aboriginal Australians: Black Response to White Dominance 1788–1980* (Sydney: Allen & Unwin, 1982); Geoffrey Blainey, "Sydney 1788," in *Australians: An Historical Library;* Part 1: *Australians to 1788*, ed. Derek John Mulvaney & Peter J. White (Broadway, NSW: Fairfax, Symes & Weldon, 1987): 412–32; as well as many of the works used in the present section; the account given in W.E.H. Stanner, "The History of Indifference thus Begins," *Aboriginal History* 1.1 (1977): 2–26, is probably

Aborigines, more friendly scenes followed when Phillip walked among them, unarmed and offering presents, hoping in this way to secure their friendship. In spite of this, it took more than two years before any Aborigines came voluntarily into Port Jackson (three had been captured and forced to live there, but they had all either died or escaped), and even then clashes with the convicts, which began shortly after their arrival, despite Phillip's intentions to keep them separate, continued on the outskirts of the settlement.

The logic of Phillip's actions has been questioned by some; in the 1968 Boyer lectures, W.E.H. Stanner described developments in a way which highlighted the inconsistency of Phillip's intentions; he even questioned the motives underlying his wish to create greater intimacy with the Aborigines, emphasizing Captain Tench's claim that it was in order to learn about the resources of the country. Stanner characterizes Phillip by 1790 as "brave, magnanimous and good-hearted as ever, but, we must now conclude, rash and rather wrong-headed."[103]

Others, such as Marjorie Barnard Eldershaw and Alan Frost, have praised Phillip for his intentions as well as for his actions and have found no inconsistency in his policy.[104] The variation depends to a large extent on the point of view adopted; seen with the benefit of present-day knowledge about Aboriginal society, Phillip committed many blunders, and the goal of friendly coexistence was in any case destined to fail from the start. From a contemporary perspective, however, Phillip's reactions and interpretations would have seemed quite consistent and logical; furthermore, although it took longer than he expected, eventually he succeeded in establishing the kind of relationship he had desired, as the Aborigines of the Port Jackson area, from 1791 onwards, often gathered in large numbers in the settlement and became acquainted with the settlers – as described by David Collins, Judge-Advocate, in an appendix (written in September 1796) to his journal:

> after many untoward occurrences, and a considerable lapse of time, that friendly intercourse with the natives which had been so earnestly desired was

---

the most detailed one made. See Map 5 for distribution of Aboriginal groups on the southeast coast.

[103] W.E.H. Stanner, *After the Dreaming* (Sydney: Australian Broadcasting Commission, 1968): 7–11 (and "The History of Indifference thus Begins," 24). Cf also King, ed. *In the Beginning*, 83, who finds that "it is difficult not to accuse Phillip of simple-mindedness in presuming that he could avoid disputes with the natives."

[104] Eldershaw, *Phillip of Australia*; and Frost, *Arthur Phillip*.

> at length established; and having never been materially interrupted, these remote islanders have been shown living in considerable numbers among us without fear or restraint; acquiring our language; readily falling in with our manners and customs; enjoying the comforts of our clothing, and relishing the variety of our food [....] By slow degrees we began mutually to be pleased with, and to understand each other.[105]

To Phillip and his fellow officers, this would doubtless have been taken as evidence that the original inhabitants had become reconciled to their presence.[106]

In accordance with his instructions, Phillip in an early despatch commented on the number of inhabitants in the area. He noted that were far more people than he had been led to expect (thus confirming his own expectations):

> The natives are far more numerous than they were supposed to be. I think they cannot be less than fifteen hundred in Botany Bay, Port Jackson, and Broken Bay, including the intermediate coast. I have traced thirty miles inland and having lately seen smoke on Landsdown Hills, which are fifty miles inland, I think leaves no doubt but that there are inhabitants in the interior parts of the country.[107]

Although this was substantially more than had been expected, it was still not a very large number if seen with the eyes of the Europeans, whose own settlement at the outset numbered some one thousand inhabitants. Furthermore, as a result of the smallpox epidemic raging among the Aborigines in 1789, their

---

[105] David Collins, *An Account of the English Colony in New South Wales with Remarks on the Dispositions, Customs, Manners, etc. of the Native Inhabitants of that Country* (1798–1802; Sydney: A.H. & A.W. Reed for the Royal Australian Historical Society, 1978): vol. 1, 451.

[106] Stanner, "The History of Indifference thus Begins," and King, ed. *In the Beginning*, 84–86, discuss how it must have seemed to the Aborigines.

[107] Phillip to Nepean, July 9, 1788, in Watson, ed. *Historical Records of Australia*, vol.1, 56. Part or all of the same information is mentioned several times in the first series of despatches from Phillip, sent from New South Wales in July 1788 and received in London in June 1789. See Phillip to Sydney, May 15, 1788, in Watson, ed. *Historical Records of Australia*, vol. 1, 29–30; Phillip to Sydney, July 9, 1788, in Watson, ed. *Historical Records of Australia*, vol. 1, 49–50; Phillip to Stephens, July 10, 1788, in Watson, ed. *Historical Records of Australia*, vol. 1, 62; Phillip to Sydney, July 10, 1788, in Watson, ed. *Historical Records of Australia*, vol. 1, 65. Cf Reynolds, *The Law of the Land*, ch. 3, who quotes several First Fleet journals and accounts on the surprisingly large number of inhabitants.

numbers were decimated, so that the whites must by then have outnumbered the original inhabitants of the area.

When most of the ships had left Sydney Cove, making it clear to the Aborigines that the white people intended to stay, Phillip was in no doubt about their displeasure. Commenting on a meeting, Phillip observed:

> they were friendly, but as I have ever found them, since they find we intend to remain, they appeared best pleased when we were leaving them, though I gave them many useful articles; and it is not possible to say whether it was from fear or contempt that they do not come amongst us.

Again, a little later in the same letter, worrying that the Aborigines might try to burn down the crops:

> they certainly are not pleased with our remaining amongst them, as they see we deprive them of fish which is almost their only support.[108]

The Aborigines were naturally reacting against the invasion of their territory and the depletion of their food resources, though Phillip is mostly to have been thinking about the latter. The struggle over limited amounts of food caused incidents like the one described in the following passage:

> Yesterday twenty of the natives came down to the beach, each armed with a number of spears, and seized on a good part of the fish caught in the seine. The coxswain had been ordered, however small the quantity he caught, always to give them a part whenever any of them came where he was fishing, and this was the first time they ever attempted to take any by force. While the greatest number were seizing the fish, several stood at a small distance with their spears poised ready to throw them if any resistance was made, but the coxswain very prudently permitted them to take what they chose, and parted good friends. They, at present, find it very difficult to support themselves.[109]

Phillip's order to share the catch with the Aborigines indicates both humanity and an awareness of the predicament in which the Aborigines had been placed by the European presence. The next sentence, however, has an ominous sound: "In consequence of what happened yesterday, no boat will in future go down the harbour without an officer."

---

[108] Phillip to Sydney, September 28, 1788, in Watson, ed. *Historical Records of Australia*, vol. 1, 76–77.

[109] Phillip to Nepean, July 10, 1788, in Watson, ed. *Historical Records of Australia*, vol. 1, 66–67.

Recording his despair over the lack of contact in October 1788, Phillip reflected a little further on the cause of Aboriginal distance:

> The natives still refuse to come amongst us [....] I now doubt whether it will be possible to get any of those people to remain with us, in order to get their language, without using force; they see no advantage that can arise from us that may make amends for the loss of that part of the harbour in which we occasionally employ the boat in fishing.[110]

A more precise expression of Aboriginal territorial possession is given in the journal written by Collins, who, besides being Judge-Advocate, was also Secretary of the colony and may be presumed to have had opportunities to discuss these matters with Phillip. In February 1791, Collins expressed his regret

> that we have not yet been able to reconcile the natives to the deprivation of those parts of this harbour which we occupied. While they entertain the idea of our having dispossessed them of their residences, they must always consider us as enemies; and upon this principle they made a point of attacking the white people whenever opportunity and safety concurred.[111]

Henry Reynolds concludes that within the first couple of years it was realized among the British (at least, those who wrote journals) that the original inhabitants were organized in groups with particular territorial connections (although the details of their social and territorial organization were very imperfectly understood).[112] Phillip himself recorded that there were territorial groupings around Port Jackson, but he apparently did not draw the rather natural conclusion that the settlement would upset the existing pattern of land ownership.[113]

It is unclear whether the clashes between convicts and Aborigines, which began soon after the arrival of the British, were attempts to protect the land in

---

[110] Phillip to Sydney, October 30, 1788, in Watson, ed. *Historical Records of Australia*, vol. 1, 96.

[111] Collins, *An Account of the English Colony in New South Wales*, vol. 1, 122. In the appendix to his journal, Collins describes the customs and way of life of the Aborigines in a very thorough manner. On property, he says: "Strange as it may appear, they have also their real estates. Bennillong, both before he went to England and since his return, often assured me, that the island Me-mel (called by us Goat Island) close by Sydney Cove was his own property" (*An Account of the English Colony in New South Wales*, 497).

[112] Reynolds, *The Law of the Land*, ch. 3.

[113] Phillip to Sydney, February 13, 1790, in Watson, ed. *Historical Records of Australia*, vol. 1, 160.

general or retaliation for specific wrongs suffered by the Aborigines; Phillip certainly perceived them as the latter. In the early years, few incidents with the Aborigines were attributed by the British to the attempt to defend their land from intrusion (apart from the frequent show of hostility on first encounter). Even though it is quite likely that the inhabitants of the Sydney area tried to defend their land, just as later Aboriginal groups did all over Australia, Phillip and his men did not generally see this.

In any case, in spite of the ongoing battle and the reluctance of the Aborigines to become friends with the Europeans, Phillip never suggested that some arrangement should be made in order to gain their assent to settlement. Nor did he consider the indigenous inhabitants a menace to the small settlement; in February 1790, he wrote to Sydney:

> It will appear to your Lordships, after what has been said of the natives, that a less force will be wanted for the security of the settlement than what I considered as necessary soon after my arrival in this country, although that was not considerable.[114]

This was expanded on in a later dispatch:

> settlers have little to fear from the Natives, against whom I have never thought any Defence necessary more than what our Houses and Barracks afford us [....] I believe there is little Reason to think that the Natives will ever attack any Building and still less to suppose they will attack a number of armed Men; not that I think they want innate Bravery; they certainly do not – but they are sensible of the great Superiority of our Arms. Setting fire to the Corn I most feared, but which they never have attempted; and as they avoid those Places we frequent, it is seldom that any of them are now seen near the Settlement.[115]

One would imagine that such statements would have carried considerable weight with the government in London and would no doubt have given them the impression that there was no need to make any further arrangements, indeed, initially the prediction made by Banks and others that the inhabitants would abandon their land seems to have been borne out.

After 1790, the business of running the settlement became more complex and took up most of Phillip's despatches until his departure in December 1792;

---

[114] Phillip to Sydney, February 13, 1790, in Watson, ed. *Historical Records of Australia*, vol. 1, 161.

[115] Phillip to Grenville, February 17, 1790, CO 201/5: 139.

the Aborigines fades from view.[116] In the despatches written from London to Phillip, there was only one reference to the original inhabitants.

This was in the first despatch, written in June 1789, in which Grenville, who had just become Secretary of State, commented briefly on the situation:

> The Soil at Port Jackson [....] does not appear to be as fertile as could have been wished and, exclusively of that consideration, the number of Natives inhabiting its vicinity must render its Cultivation both difficult and dangerous, particularly whilst they continue to avoid any friendly intercourse with the Settlement. From these Circumstances, Norfolk Island, where the Settlers possess the advantage of a luxurious Soil, and carry on their operations unmolested by any other Inhabitants, is, I conceive, the most favourable position, and were it not from the great labor and expence incurred already at Port Jackson, I should have been inclined to have recommended that Island's being made the principal Settlement.[117]

Grenville goes on to instruct Phillip to send more convicts to Norfolk Island and, if he finds "a similar Situation equally advantageous," also to establish a settlement there. While it is difficult to conclude anything on the basis of a single document, a few suggestions can be made. For one thing, the Home Office officials had read Phillip's despatches closely enough to gather that the number of indigenous inhabitants was relatively large, and they had concluded that this could make it dangerous to cultivate the land. However, this did not prompt the Secretary of State to suggest negotiating with them for permission to live there.

On the other hand, it is plain from the recommendation of uninhabited areas that such a place was considered preferable because incidents with the inhabitants would thereby be avoided. One might wonder why it was not decided to make Norfolk Island the main settlement from the start; but, again, the explanation may lie in the belief that the number of inhabitants on the mainland was inconsiderable.

In the draft of another early despatch containing instructions to Phillip on the granting of land, the Aborigines are mentioned once, though not because they are considered the owners of the land; it is recommended that settlers are grouped in townships – among other things, for the sake of preserving

---

[116] Cf Stanner, *After the Dreaming*, 11. See CO 201/6. See Map 6 for extent of colony in 1792.

[117] Whitehall to Phillip, June 20, 1789, CO 201/3: 151–52.

> the Security, they have already acquired against the Insults and Insurrections of Neighbouring Indians.[118]

This passage, however, was crossed out and replaced by "their Security"; whether this was because it was found unnecessarily detailed or unsupported by the reports from Phillip (the instructions were written before Phillip made his remarks on defence quoted above) is difficult to say; "Insults and Insurrections" are certainly not easy to trace in Phillip's letters, he always blamed the convicts for any conflicts that arose. The use of the word "Neighbouring" may perhaps again suggest that the two groups were perceived in England to be living in separate communities.

Most other letters from the Secretary of State to Phillip were concerned with the business of sending convicts and provisions.[119]

Phillip thus laid down policy according to his instructions and his own intentions and preconceptions. These involved basic goodwill towards the original inhabitants and a desire to protect them and promote good relations with them. However, in a reappraisal of traditional interpretations, Reynolds has shown that this is only one aspect of Phillip's policy towards the Aborigines. Reynolds has drawn attention to his use, or threat, of force against them and points out that on several occasions Phillip ordered what might be seen as early punitive expeditions (though they were all unsuccessful). Some of Phillip's fellow officers commented on the need to keep the Aborigines at a distance. Reynolds also sees Phillip's discussion of the number of marines needed to defend the settlement as evidence of this aspect of Phillip's policy.[120] This is no doubt an important corrective to the understanding of early policy and it is not at odds with Phillip's instructions, which, as shown above, included provision for defence and both for peaceful relations.

As pointed out above, Phillip showed little awareness of the fundamental question of territorial ownership and rights, and made no attempt to address this problem or suggest it to his superiors in London. Furthermore, at a fairly early point he drew the important conclusion that in spite of frequent clashes and other signs of discord, there was no real apprehension about the safety of the settlement.

---

[118] Whitehall to Phillip, August 24, 1789, CO 201/4: 34. Reference to the Aborigines as "Indians" was quite common; see, for example, Banks's journal.

[119] See dispatches in CO 201/4–7.

[120] Reynolds, *Frontier*, 32–37.

Judging from the letters Phillip received from the Home Office, his conclusions were not questioned by the government in London and they therefore came to represent official policy. This acceptance of policy as laid down by the governor continues in the years following Phillip's departure.

There is only one other reference to the Aboriginal inhabitants in the London despatches from the first ten years of the colony's existence.[121] This was in a letter from Portland to Hunter, Phillip's successor, from June 1796. Captain Paterson of the New South Wales Corps, who was in charge of the colony for ten months before Hunter's arrival, had ordered what must have been one of the first successful punitive expeditions against the Aborigines, who had resisted the settlement of ex-convicts on the Hawkesbury River. A number of Aborigines were killed and others were taken prisoner.[122] Portland comments thus:

> The Steps taken by Captain Paterson for the protection of that part of the Settlement which is on the Hawkesbury River, and for instilling into the Minds of the Natives a proper Degree of Respect and regard for the Colony appear to have been highly proper.[123]

This sets a rather new tone in government attitudes towards the treatment of indigenous peoples; "instilling [...] a proper degree of respect" is a world apart from "conciliating their affections." There is little to suggest that it was any particular view of the Secretary of State which was responsible for this change of attitude. Descriptions of Portland vary from one extreme to the other, but none of them suggests that he took a special interest in New South Wales or in the treatment of indigenous peoples.[124] Rather, there is little doubt that this new attitude was a reflection of the increasingly hostile relationship between Aborigines and settlers that had arisen during the first years of settlement and which

---

[121] This conclusion is based on a survey of CO 201/1–14.

[122] Kociumbas, *1700–1860 Possessions*, 56. Paterson apparently developed something of a reputation for punitive expeditions later on at Port Dalrymple (*1700–1860 Possessions*, 97). See also Collins's report of the matter, *An Account of the English Colony in New South Wales*, vol. 1, 348–49 (where he refers to the situation at the Hawkesbury during the preceding period as one of "open war").

[123] Portland to Hunter, June 1796, CO 201/12: 70.

[124] David Mackay, "Direction and Purpose in British Imperial Policy 1783–1801," *Historical Journal* 17.3 (1974): 495; and Helen Taft Manning, *British Colonial Government after the American Revolution 1782–1820* (New Haven CT: Yale UP, 1933): 90.

continued to escalate after Phillip's departure.[125] It would seem that the Secretary of State had accepted the view of the situation presented by the colonial government and based his comments on the assumption that the Aborigines, as aggressors, had to be taught a lesson.

Later developments

In the next decades, hostilities developed into a full-scale guerrilla war, spreading to the rest of the continent in the course of the century.[126] Incidents from this struggle and the steps taken to control the 'natives' were regularly mentioned by successive governors in their despatches. The punitive measures undertaken by the settlers, which the governors tried to regulate but did not prevent, weighed most heavily in the reports.[127] Conversely, governors also sometimes reported attempts to protect the Aborigines and to persuade them into peaceful coexistence with the settlers. Missionary efforts to convert them and make them adopt European ways of life, which were also seen as means to this end, began with the establishment of "native institutions" during the governorship of Macquarie.[128]

---

[125] It appears from Collins's journal for the period 1788–1796 that the relationship which developed after 1791 was sharply divided in the minds of the settlers between friendly association with the groups of Aborigines who came into Sydney, and hostile relations with other groups who did not come into town and who continued and even increased their attacks on settlers on the outskirts (see Collins, *An Account of the English Colony in New South Wales*, vol. 1).

[126] See, for example, C.D. Rowley, *The Destruction of Aboriginal Society* (Ringwood, Victoria: Penguin, 1972), as well as Reynolds's work.

[127] See, for example, Hunter to Portland, November 12, 1796, in Watson, ed. *Historical Records of Australia*, vol. 1, 688; King to Hobart, October 30, 1802, in Watson, ed. *Historical Records of Australia*, vol. 3, 581–93; King to Camden, July 20, 1805, in Watson, ed. *Historical Records of Australia*, vol. 3, 497; Macquarie to Bathurst, May (?) 1816, in Watson, ed. *Historical Records of Australia*, vol. 9, 141–45; Darling to Bathurst, May 6, 1826, in Watson, ed. *Historical Records of Australia*, vol. 12, 269.

[128] See, for example, Hunter to Portland, January 2, 1800, in Watson, ed. *Historical Records of Australia*, vol. 2, 401–22; King to Hobart, December 20, 1804, in Watson, ed. *Historical Records of Australia*, vol. 5, 165–66; Macquarie to Bathurst, February 24, 1820, in Watson, ed. *Historical Records of Australia*, vol. 10, 262–72 and quotations in Anthony Hewison, ed. *The Macquarie Decade: Documents illustrating the History of New South Wales 1810–1821* (Melbourne: Cassell Australia, 1972): 26–30. Cf Reynolds, *The Law of the Land*, 60.

Occasionally, the Secretaries of State referred to these issues in their letters to the governors. The dual nature of the policy pursued towards the Aborigines is nowhere better illustrated than in two orders from London to Governor Darling, written within a few days of each other in July 1825. In Darling's instructions, the following reference was made to relations with the Aboriginal people:

> it is Our further will and pleasure, that you do to the utmost of your power promote religion and education among the Native Inhabitants of Our said Colony, or of the Lands and Islands thereto adjoining; and that you do especially take care to protect them in their persons and in the enjoyment of their possessions; and that you do by all lawful means prevent and restrain all violence and injustice which may in any manner be practised or attempted against them; and that you take such measures as may appear to you [...] to be necessary for their conversion to the Christian faith, and for their advancement in civilization.[129]

The desire to protect and assimilate the Aborigines is unmistakable; while their "possessions" are mentioned and a need to avoid "injustices" is acknowledged, it is clear that this is not intended to cover rights to the land or to their original mode of existence. The original inhabitants were to be assisted in becoming part of colonial society.

However, in the letter conveying Darling's instructions, the Secretary of State, Lord Bathurst, made a comment of quite another nature on relations with the Aboriginal people:

> In reference to the discussions, which have recently taken place in the Colony respecting the manner, in which the Native Inhabitants are to be treated when making hostile incursions for the purpose of Plunder, you will understand it to be your duty when such disturbances cannot be prevented or allayed by less vigorous measures, to oppose force by force, and to repel such Aggressions in the same manner, as if they proceeded from subjects of any accredited State.[130]

---

[129] Instructions to Governor Darling, July 17, 1825, *Parliamentary Papers, House of Commons* 19.261 (1831): 9.

[130] Bathurst to Darling, July 14, 1825, in Watson, ed. *Historical Records of Australia*, vol. 22, 21. Why the instructions should have been dated after the letter enclosing them is something of a mystery; it has not been possible to investigate this further, and is perhaps less important than the fact that the two orders were written more or less simultaneously.

The line taken towards the Aborigines in Portland's despatch from 1795 is here further developed; the governor was actually being ordered to use force against the Aborigines although other means were supposed to have been tried first. The emphasis is so clearly on the use of power, despite the reference to "less vigorous measures," that the Aborigines in this passage become an enemy to be conquered. Any perception of friendly relations or indigenous rights has been completely lost sight of. The passage indicates that the government in London had accepted the view of the settlers that the Aborigines had to be subdued or even killed so that the settlement could flourish, though there are other signs that as the 1820s turned into the 1830s more emphasis was placed on protective and "civilizing" measures.[131]

The scarcity of comment on policy towards the Aboriginal population in the letters from the Secretary of State during the early decades of the colony's existence is inherently difficult to assess. It may indicate real agreement with what was represented in the despatches received and, when there were no such representations, a willingness to assume that all was well. It may also indicate indifference towards the issue.[132] Then again, it may be a reflection of the fact that at least after 1793 the government was preoccupied with other matters (such as the war with France). In any case, the upshot is that both the interpretation of the situation offered by Phillip and his successors and the measures they adopted stand as official policy towards the indigenous population.

Thus, a reformulation of the initial instructions to include some kind of land settlement, which might have been expected on the basis of attitudes and policy towards other indigenous peoples, was never made. In its stead is found general acceptance of the local assessment of the situation. The result of this was a

---

[131] See, for example, "Copies of all Correspondence between Lieutenant–Governor Arthur and his Majesty's Secretary of State for the Colonies, on the Subject of Military Operations lately carried on against the Aboriginal Inhabitants of Van Diemen's Land," *Parliamentary Papers, House of Commons* 19.259 (1831): 177–232 and "Copies of Instructions given by his Majesty's Secretary of State for the Colonies, for promoting the Moral and Religious Instruction of the Aboriginal Inhabitants of New Holland and Van Diemen's Land," *Parliamentary Papers, House of Commons* 19.261 (1831): 153–169. See also Shaw, "British Policy towards the Australian Aborigines," and Reynolds, *The Law of the Land*, ch. 4.

[132] A survey of general government policy towards New South Wales in the early years shows, if not indifference, then at least a very narrow conception of the colony, which prevented any development in visions about it; David Mackay, "Far-Flung Empire: A Neglected Imperial Outpost at Botany Bay 1788–1801," *Journal of Imperial and Commonwealth History* 9.1 (October 1980): 125–45.

dramatic change in official attitude towards the inhabitants, from the early desire not to cause any disruption to their way of life to a view which accepted force as the appropriate means of coming to terms with them, combined with a long-term view which envisaged assimilation for the survivors. This development may have been foreshadowed in the dual provisions for defence and peace of Phillip's instructions and in his conduct of affairs in the early years, but it was no doubt mainly the result of reports of clashes on the frontier, which figured more prominently in the despatches than accounts of peaceful relations.

From ignorance to informed injustice

The official attitude towards the Aborigines thus falls into two stages, the transition from one to the other occurring in the course of the first decades after the establishment of the settlement.

The documents relating to New South Wales before 1788, though few in number and only occasionally referring to the inhabitants there, do reveal something about the policy to be pursued towards these people. Provision was made for defence against attacks as well as for the establishment of friendly relations, a policy quite consistent with that pursued in North America and elsewhere in connection with indigenous peoples, although a deviation from this is suggested by the absence of instructions to acquire permission from the inhabitants to settle on their land.

This apparent aberration calls for an explanation, the most likely one being suggested by the sources on which the government relied for information about this country. They all agreed that the population of the places visited in New South Wales was very small, and the importance of this can hardly be exaggerated; if there were only "very few Natives inhabiting the Neighbourhood" (in the words of Nepean), there would be plenty of space for a penal settlement, which, although further shipments of convicts were planned, was not at that time expected to grow to any considerable size. There would be no problem comparable to that encountered with the Indians – and the settlers – in North America. The conclusion drawn by Banks – that the few people living in the area would most likely remove themselves at the appearance of the settlers – would merely have further encouraged this line of thinking.

The consequence of this reasoning would be that there was probably no need to negotiate over land. As King suggests, this belief may have been strengthened by the report that the inhabitants had no conception of property or trade, though the provision in the instructions for barter goods indicates that this had not been taken too seriously.[133] The way was left open, however, for future revision of policy as more information about the Aborigines was gathered. The obvious limitations to the knowledge acquired by Cook and his companions would have made this seem a prudent provision.

Thus it may be suggested that the policy outlined by the government at the outset of the colonization of New South Wales was not out of line with that pursued elsewhere but, rather, was adapted to what was perceived to be the situation in this place. While Frost would probably agree with this statement, he objects very strongly to the view that the British believed the country to be "effectively uninhabited." Frost maintains instead that the British "adjusted their views of indigenous peoples according to the levels of culture that they saw these people as having attained."[134] In other words, the British made no provision for purchasing the land or gaining permission to settle, because they believed that the Aborigines did not have the governmental or social institutions necessary for such transactions.

As evidence for this view, Frost relies on the comments made by Cook and Banks about the Aborigines and interprets them as he believes they would have been understood by their contemporaries. While the descriptions furnished by Cook and Banks and their place in the intellectual world of the eighteenth century will be discussed in a later chapter, the point to be made here is that there is no indication in the government documents leading up to the settlement of New South Wales that the Aborigines were considered to be different from other 'natives', more 'primitive' or anything else. Nor is there any evidence in the official documents from this period that indigenous peoples in general were perceived as having relative positions on any kind of cultural or racial scale or that official policy was influenced by considerations of this sort. On the other hand, there is evidence (as pointed out above) that the government had reflected on the size of the population in New South Wales, so that it is more reasonable to base any attempt to explain government policy on this aspect.

The policy which took shape after 1788, however, gradually diverged further and further from the established pattern. Rather than coming to see the need for negotiation with the Aborigines and perhaps finding some way of

---

[133] King, ed. *In the Beginning*, 81.

[134] Frost, *Botany Bay Mirages*, 189. Frost's views will be taken up again in Chapter 5. See also Shaw, "British Policy towards the Australian Aborigines ," 266, who adopts the same point of view as Frost.

separating the area inhabited by them from that occupied by the settlers (as happened in North America), the authorities in New South Wales and, apparently in consequence of this, in London ended up pursuing the radically different end of eradicating Aboriginal resistance to settler encroachment, followed either by the destruction of the original inhabitants or their enforced adaptation to colonial society. From the late 1820s onwards, humanitarian influence favoured the latter.

A number of explanatory factors may be tentatively suggested for this striking development. The Aborigines resisted the invasion of their country fiercely and came to represent a real danger to outlying settlements, but their organization for war and the tactics they employed meant that they were never regarded as a military threat. Furthermore, the situation in Australia was such that the Aborigines were never requested to act as allies of the British, either against a foreign nation or against the settlers. Consequently, the need to cultivate their friendship was not as urgent as if these elements had been present.

As was pointed out in Chapter 1, the administrative apparatus for governing the colonies was at a low ebb during the closing decades of the century, and this affected the efficiency and understanding with which colonial affairs were conducted. Furthermore, around the turn of the century the British were engaged in a strenuous war with the French, which necessarily meant that less attention could be paid to the internal affairs of the colonies. While even at the best of times New South Wales as a penal settlement commanded less interest than the profitable and more self-confident colonial possessions in the Caribbean or in India, such factors would have made it highly expedient to leave the running of the colony as much as possible to the people on the spot, whose attitude to the Aborigines was coloured by their desire for expansion. Thus in the early, formative years of the colony's existence various circumstances helped subject the shaping of policy towards the indigenous inhabitants to local influences.

However, when bureaucratic changes were beginning to be noticeable in relation to the colonies and the French wars were over, the despatches sent from London continued to indicate agreement with the policy pursued in New South Wales. Mention of indigenous rights to their land or their just complaints about the settlers, so frequent in connection with North America, is conspicuous by its absence from the letters relating to New South Wales in the early decades of the nineteenth century. By this time, indifference can no longer be attributed to mistaken notions about the number of the original inhabitants; much information had been gathered about the Aboriginal peoples and their way of life, including the size of the population.

The lack of imperial concern with the rights of the Aborigines during the first forty-odd years is obviously connected with the fact that no strategic considerations forced the British government to correct materially the policy laid down by local authorities; but the conspicuous change of tone in the official despatches from London calls for further explanation. It may be speculated that the very different way of life and culture of the Aborigines may at this time have started to filter through to the Colonial Office, exerting an influence on official attitudes towards this group of people. It may even be possible that the experience gained from New South Wales was an important factor in shaping imperial attitudes towards indigenous peoples encountered later on. The passage relating to the Indians at Nootka Sound from 1790, which for the first time entertains the possibility that the people might or might not have 'rights over' the land, may be a reflection of a new outlook wholly or partly caused by the government's understanding of the situation in New South Wales. It is thus possible that Frost's interpretation of government policy as differentiating between different peoples may be applicable after 1788, though not before it.

4 The Cape of Good Hope c. 1795–1814

The acquisition of the Cape

THE OUTBREAK OF THE WAR WITH FRANCE in 1793 had numerous implications for the British and their empire, not the least of which was the decision to occupy the Dutch settlement at the Cape of Good Hope. As soon as the war began, the question of the Cape came up for consideration in Britain because of its importance as a way-station on the route to India as well as its military usefulness; the nation holding the Cape had an extremely powerful position in times of war.[1] For these strategic reasons, Britain in 1795 sent a fleet to the Cape which took possession of the settlement in September that year.[2] Following the Peace of Amiens, Britain handed over the

[1] Numerous documents show the significance attributed to the Cape (though some of them also state the undesirability of acquiring more colonies); see, for example, Dundas to Grenville, April 23, 1793, in *British Colonial Developments 1774–1834, Select Documents*, ed. Vincent Todd Harlow & Frederick Madden (Oxford: Clarendon, 1953): 17; Baring to Dundas, January 4, 1793, in Harlow & Madden, ed. *British Colonial Developments*, 17–19; Blankett to Nepean, January 25, 1795, in Harlow & Madden, ed. *British Colonial Developments*, 19–21. The Cape had also been considered on earlier occasions – see, for example, the Chairman and Deputy Chairman of the East India Company to Hillsborough, October 25, 1781, in Harlow & Madden, ed. *British Colonial Developments*, 4–7; and Dundas to Grenville, September 2, 1787, in Harlow & Madden, ed. *British Colonial Developments*, 15; cf L.C.F. Turner, "The Cape of Good Hope and the Anglo-French Conflict, 1797–1806," *Historical Studies, Australia and New Zealand* 9 (1959–61): 368.

[2] *Britain at the Cape 1795–1803*, ed. Maurice Boucher & Nigel Penn (Houghton: Brenthurst, 1992): ch. 1.

Cape to representatives of the Batavian Republic in February 1803, only to retake the colony in January 1806. In August 1814, following the first peace with France in May, the British possession of the colony was conclusively confirmed by the Dutch.[3] It is fairly certain that the first British occupation was only intended to be temporary, but there are several indications that when the Cape was taken for the second time, attitudes on this issue had changed. Military considerations during the first phase of the Napoleonic Wars had shown the significance of the place to be beyond doubt, and other reservations about the Cape subsided after the turn of the century, to the point that British retention of the colony after the war would have seemed very likely.[4]

The colony which the British occupied in 1795 was a small settlement with a complex population pattern. The Dutch burghers and the employees of the Dutch East India Company constituted the majority of the European inhabitants. Most of the settlers lived in the western Cape, though increasing numbers were moving further east in search of grazing for their cattle.[5] A large number of slaves were held in the western wheat- and wine-growing areas;[6] fewer slaves were found in the east, where the farmers relied mainly on the labour of the Khoisan under conditions varying from near-slavery to semi-independence.[7]

---

[3] Boucher & Penn, ed. *Britain at the Cape*, ch. 6; and George McCall Theal, ed. *History of South Africa from 1795 to 1872* (1888–93; London: Allen & Unwin, 1915–20), vol 1: 276–79.

[4] Turner, "The Cape of Good Hope," 377. Vincent Harlow's suggestion that the Cape was retaken primarily from considerations of trade have been refuted, see Ronald Hyam, "British Imperial Expansion in the Late Eighteenth Century," *Historical Journal* 10.1 (1967): 123.

[5] See, for example, Gerrit Schutte, "Company and Colonists at the Cape, 1652–1795," in *The Shaping of South African Society, 1652–1840*, ed. Richard Elphick & Hermann Giliomee (Pinelands: Maskew Miller Longmans, 1989): 283–323; and M.F. Katzen, "White Settlers and the Origin of a New Society, 1652–1778," in *A History of South Africa to 1870*, ed. Monica Wilson & Leonard Thompson (London: Croom Helm, 1982): 187–232.

[6] James C. Armstrong & Nigel A. Worden, "The Slaves, 1652–1834," in Elphick & Giliomee, ed. *The Shaping of South African Society*, 109–83. Some of the slaves were occasionally manumitted and continued to live in the area as so-called "free blacks," cf Anna Jacoba Böeseken, *Slaves and Free Blacks at the Cape, 1658–1700* (Cape Town: Tafelberg, 1977).

[7] Cf Hermann Giliomee, "The Eastern Frontier 1770–1812", in Elphick & Giliomee, ed. *The Shaping of South African Society*, 430–31.

The Khoisan were the original inhabitants of the Cape area; some of them were nomadic pastoralists, others hunters and gatherers.[8] When the Dutch arrived in 1652, they found groups of both living on the coast at the Cape, but because of their desire to secure the supply of meat for the visiting ships, they primarily came into contact with the Khoikhoi, bartering with them for cattle and sheep.[9] As white settlement became firmly established and then began to expand, the Khoisan were gradually deprived of their livelihood, the Khoikhoi in terms of both livestock and grazing land, the hunters through loss of their hunting grounds.[10] Some responded by moving further east, others by working for the settlers, often as herdsmen. Eventually the hunters were driven into the mountainous and desert areas to the northeast (which were unattractive to the cattle farmers), from where they carried out attacks and raids against the settlers and sometimes against the Khoikhoi. When the latter could no longer find land on which to graze their stock, they became absorbed in the white community as labourers (and marksmen in the punitive expeditions – the

---

[8] In the past, they were commonly referred to as "Hottentots" and "Bushmen" respectively; more recently these terms have frequently been replaced by "Khoikhoi" and "San," though some scholars such as Elphick avoid "San" altogether, both because it was used as a derogatory term by the Khoikhoi and because of its uncertain application; it is, however, used here in accordance with what seems common usage. See, for example, Monica Wilson, "The Hunters and Herders," Wilson & Thompson, ed. *A History of South Africa to 1870*, 35–37, 41; and Richard Elphick, *Khoikhoi and the founding of White South Africa* (Johannesburg: Ravan, 1985): xv, xxi–xxii, for comments on terminology. It is beyond the scope of this chapter to discuss the theories about the origins and distribution of these peoples, but see Wilson, "The Hunters and Herders," 41–74; Elphick, *Khoikhoi and the Founding of White South Africa*, pt 1; and Richard Elphick & V.C. Malherbe, "The Khoisan to 1828," in Elphick & Giliomee, ed. *The Shaping of South African Society*, 3–7. See Map 9 for distribution of the Khoikhoi and the San at the time of first settlement.

[9] See the accounts in Van Riebeeck's journal, reproduced in *The Record, or a Series of Official Papers relative to the Condition and Treatment of the Native Tribes of South Africa*, ed. Donald Moodie (1838; Amsterdam & Cape Town: A.A. Balkema, 1960), part 1: 1–30.

[10] There were several wars between the Khoikhoi and the settlers during the first half century of Dutch occupation, cf Moodie, *The Record*, pt 1, 31–446; and Elphick, *Khoikhoi and the Founding of White South Africa*, ch. 5–6. Like the Australian Aborigines and other indigenous peoples, the Khoisan were also seriously reduced in numbers by smallpox and other introduced diseases (Elphick, *Khoikhoi and the Founding of White South Africa*, xvii).

commandos – against the San).[11] Sexual relations between colonists and Khoikhoi women were frequent, and some of their offspring, the so-called Bastaards, in time came to form the semi-independent Griqua communities.

To the east, the expansion of, first, the Khoikhoi and then the Dutch was halted by the settlement of Bantu-speaking Nguni peoples, mainly the Xhosa (other large groups such as the Ndebele and the Zulu lived further east). They cultivated the land and had large herds of cattle; they were more numerous and stationary than the Khoisan and therefore presented a more obdurate obstacle to settler expansion than the former. The situation was further aggravated by the slow movement west of Xhosa groups who also wanted more land and game for their increasing population (see Map 10). Contact between colonists and Nguni increased throughout the eighteenth century, initially as a result of trade and also cattle raiding and then, as the century wore on, in the struggle for the land. By the 1770s, the two groups were both occupying land between the Sunday and Great Fish Rivers. In 1779, mounting tension erupted into the first "Kaffir" or frontier war and some of the Xhosa were temporarily forced to move east of the Fish River, which in 1780 was officially declared to be the boundary of the colony. The period which followed saw escalating fighting between the two parties, eventually leading to the second frontier war in 1793.[12]

The acquisition of the Cape thus brought the British into contact with new groups of indigenous peoples whose relations with the colony had already been established under the rule of another European power. The relationship between indigenous peoples and colonists had entered a new phase by the late eighteenth century, which created an explosive situation, especially in the

---

[11] On fighting with the San, see Andrew Bank, "Liberals and their Enemies: Racial Ideology at the Cape of Good Hope 1820–1850" (unpublished doctoral dissertation, Cambridge University, 1995): 52–54. The account given here is of necessity the merest sketch of the developments taking place after the Dutch invaded the Cape; for more detail, see, for example, Elphick, *Khoikhoi and the Founding of White South Africa*, pt 2–4; Elphick & Malherbe, "The Khoisan to 1828"; and Wilson, "The Hunters and Herders." Earlier authorities include William Miller Macmillan, *The Cape Colour Question: A Historical Survey* (London: Faber & Gwyer, 1927), and Johannes Stephanus Marais, *The Cape Coloured People 1652–1937* (1939; Johannesburg: Witwatersrand UP, 1957).

[12] For details on the Nguni and the frontier situation, see Wilson & Thompson, *South Africa to 1870*, ch. 3, 6, and Giliomee, "The Eastern Frontier", 421–39. See also William Miller Macmillan, *Bantu, Boer and Briton: The Making of the South African Native Problem* (London: Faber & Gwyer, 1928).

eastern part of the colony. Throughout the two occupations of the Cape, the British had to deal with the conflicts that arose out of this situation. Developments in this period provide the basis for further illustration of official attitudes towards indigenous groups around the turn of the century; however, although the events that occurred were quite momentous and caused considerable activity on the part of the colonial government, comments in the official despatches from London remained relatively few, albeit increasing as the nineteenth century wore on. As in the case of New South Wales, it is therefore necessary to trace the policy pursued in the colony in order to evaluate the scarcity of official response from that perspective. From the mid-1820s onwards this situation changed considerably; the final section of the chapter touches on some of the developments taking place at this point, in order to illustrate the direction in which policy moved after the early years.

The first British occupation

The earliest indication of official British attitudes to the indigenous peoples in the Cape area appears in the instructions to the first governor, Lord Macartney, who arrived in the colony in May 1797. In the 24th paragraph of his instructions, Macartney was directed to

> enquire and report to Us thro' One of Our Principal Secretaries of State whether it may be necessary to erect any new Forts or Posts in any interior parts of the said Settlement either for the protection and security of Our Subjects against the Caffres and Hottentots or other Savage Tribes, or for establishing or carrying on a Commerce with them, and you are to use your best endeavours to conciliate their affections and to induce them to trade with Our Subjects, and in order to prevent any improper conduct towards the said Natives. It is Our further Will and Pleasure that you do report to Us, thro' one of Our Principal Secretaries of State, the best accounts you can obtain of the Trade, that is or may be carried on with them, and how the same may, in your opinion, be extended and improved.[13]

The instructions are similar in many respects to earlier ones issued in connection with other colonies. The relationship with the indigenous peoples is still thought of in the dual terms of security and friendly relations. The main stress, however, is on trade, which the governor is induced to promote.[14] No doubt the

[13] Instructions to the Earl of Macartney, December 13, 1796, CO 49/9.

[14] Steps in this direction had already been taken, as is shown by a letter from acting Governor General Craig to Henry Dundas, April 12, 1796, in which it is mentioned that

rumour of profitable trade goods contributed to this interest. Soon after his arrival, Macartney took steps to produce the desired information about the extension of this trade; he sent his private secretary, John Barrow, on a tour of the colony, among other things to find out

> What Commerce or Intercourse might be carried on with the Hottentots, Caffres or other savage nations on our Boundary with safety, propriety and advantage. Whether the Caffer Country abounds, as it is said, with Ivory, Gold dust and other valuable articles of trade, and, if so, how the Natives dispose of them, and with what Nations do they now traffic.[15]

The emphasis on trade is reminiscent of the great significance attributed to trade with the Indians in North America; clearly, the thought of a trade as lucrative as the fur trade would have seemed attractive to the British. All in all, then, the instructions to Macartney are in line with policy obtaining both in North America and in New South Wales at the beginning of settlement. The lack of provision for any protection of indigenous rights to the land in this case may be attributed to the fact that the British had gained the colony by conquest from the Dutch and therefore would, very conveniently, have proceeded on the assumption that indigenous title had been extinguished by the former colonizers. The case is roughly parallel to the British conquest of Quebec during the Seven Years War, through which the British were considered to gain all the rights that the French had acquired.[16]

The provision in Macartney's instructions for protection of the indigenous inhabitants against the treatment of the settlers may be seen as a general precaution based on experience, such as also occurred in Philip's instructions in New South Wales; however, it may also be evidence of an awareness of the particular tensions between the colonists and the original inhabitants at the Cape.

---

three "Caffres" had visited Cape Town in order to "see the new nation." Craig states that he had been at pains to secure their friendship because trade with them would be of advantage to the colony; George McCall Theal, ed. *Records of the Cape Colony* (Cape Town: Government of the Cape Colony, 1897–1905), vol. 1: 354.

[15] Macartney to Barrow, June 30, 1797, in Theal, ed. *Records of the Cape Colony*, vol. 2, 111.

[16] The case of the land west of the Alleghenies which was addressed in the Royal Proclamation was different from that of Quebec because it had not been settled by colonists; it was therefore still debatable what rights the French had acquired there.

The existence of a vague knowledge of problems of this sort is indicated in other early documents; for example, Henry Dundas, the Secretary of State for War under whose responsibility the Cape fell as a conquest in the war, discussed in a memorandum the limitations of the economic system imposed by the Dutch, seeing this as responsible for "the discontent in the districts, hence the poverty of the colonists, hence the humiliating situation of the natives."[17] In a report for government use, written in 1796 on the basis of old Dutch accounts of the Cape, it is stated that the colonists seemed to "have practised deceit and cruelty" against the indigenous peoples.[18] It is likely, though, that the British had little prior notion of the extent of the prevailing animosity.

The Khoikhoi rebellion 1799–1803

However, soon after the British had taken over, the situation at the eastern Cape exploded into open fighting and rebellion. In the easternmost district of Graaff Reinet, established in 1786, the Dutch colonists had for some time been in a state of militant dissatisfaction with what they perceived as government lack of support. In 1796 the British brought the unrest to an end by cutting off the supply of ammunition and other essentials to the district. When unrest broke out again in 1799, the colonial government sent a force consisting of British and Khoikhoi troops to restore peace.[19]

However, the appearance of the soldiers and the defeat of the colonists (who were disarmed by the British troops) triggered off a major uprising by the Khoikhoi working on the Boer farms. They deserted the farms in great numbers, often taking the Boers' cattle, guns and other belongings with them and in some cases killing the farmers and burning down their homesteads. Many of them then sought protection among the British troops, while others joined the neighbouring Xhosa settlements, from which both they and the Xhosa raided ever larger tracts of the country. The British failed to give the refugee Khoikhoi the reassurances they wanted (basically, protection against the colonists and

---

[17] Official Memorandum by Henry Dundas, July 29, 1796, in Boucher & Penn, ed. *Britain at the Cape*, 77. Cf also Memorandum by Charles Grant, Director of the East India Company, to H. Dundas, ca. 1796, in Boucher & Penn, ed. *Britain at the Cape*, 85.

[18] Sketches of the Political and Commercial History of the Cape of Good Hope, no author given, but presumably written at the Cape, 1796, BO 222: 29.

[19] Giliomee, "The Eastern Frontier", 440–42; and Susan Newton–King & V.C. Malherbe, *The Khoikhoi Rebellion in the Eastern Cape (1799–1803)* (Communications no 5; Cape Town: Centre for African Studies, 1981): 12–14.

grants of land on which they could live) and when most of the troops left for Cape Town they, too, joined the Xhosa.

By mid-year the joint Khoikhoi–Xhosa forces had succeeded in driving the colonists out of the southeastern part of the district. However, in August the acting governor, Major-General Francis Dundas, arrived in Graaff Reinet with reinforcements. Initially intending to subdue the rebellion by force, Dundas gradually changed his mind under the impression of the great numbers of Khoikhoi and Xhosa, and in October peace negotiations were successfully carried out. The Xhosa settled to the west of the Great Fish River were allowed to remain; the Khoikhoi were enjoined to return to the colonists and were promised some protection against abuse, including a "register of servants" kept by the *landdrost*.

After less than two years of uneasy coexistence and occasional raids by Khoikhoi who had not returned to the service of the settlers, the struggle broke out again. Despite greater resistance by the colonists this time, by late 1802 a large area had again been laid waste by raids. At this time, the British were beginning to withdraw from the Cape, and it was left to the Dutch to make a peace settlement with the Khoikhoi and those Xhosa who had again joined the battle.[20]

In the course of this prolonged struggle, the colonial government officials referred to matters connected with it in a large number of letters to persons within the colony, and several despatches to London also set out the course of events. Comments from London, however, were exceedingly sparse. With regard to the first signs of settler unrest, it was remarked that

> From the habits and temper of the Inhabitants of the district of Graaff Reinet, and from the great distance of this Dependency of the Cape from the seat of Government, it is probable that they will continue more or less troublesome and difficult to manage and control during the War.[21]

The despatch continues by noting the influence of hopes for independence, encouraged by contact with the "enemy," and approval is given to the way in which the situation had been handled.

---

[20] For accounts of the Khoikhoi Rebellion, see Newton-King & Malherbe, *The Khoikhoi Rebellion in the Eastern Cape*, 15–57; Boucher & Penn, ed. *Britain at the Cape*, 220–223; Giliomee, "The Eastern Frontier", 442–43.

[21] War Office to Macartney, January 26, 1798, in Theal, ed. *Records of the Cape Colony*, vol. 2, 224.

Only one letter from Henry Dundas refers at all to the role of the indigenous peoples in the hostilities; in a letter from July 1800, Dundas says

> With respect to the disturbances which broke out at Graff Reynit, there can be no doubt that their origin is in a great degree to be attributed to the cruel and oppressive treatment of the Hottentots, Cafres and Natives by the white Inhabitants.[22]

Dundas had obviously formed an opinion on this issue, and despite its brevity the statement leaves no doubt about where his sympathies lie. This attitude reflects the opinion prevailing among the officials of the colonial government, although Governor Yonge's expression of it is somewhat more muddled than that of either Andrew Barnard, colonial secretary, or Francis Dundas. Especially the latter, who had been present in Graaff Reinet during part of the rebellion and who had been responsible for concluding the first peace in 1799, had formed a detailed impression of the causes underlying the hostilities. He placed particular emphasis on Boer maltreatment of the Khoikhoi (stating that the Khoikhoi had "long lived in a state of Slavery and under oppression") as well as on the necessity for maintaining good relations with the Xhosa, whom he considered powerful enough to cause great damage to the colony. Nor did he leave any doubt as to his attitude towards the Dutch settlers, whom he characterized as "the strongest compound of cowardice and cruelty, of treachery and cunning, and of most of the bad qualities with few very few of the good ones, of the human mind."[23]

In spite of Francis Dundas's very detailed report, Yonge seems to have been somewhat confused about the causes and developments of the rebellion; in his letter of March 1800, to which the above-quoted despatch by Henry Dundas was an answer, Yonge appeared to suggest that not only the colonists but also the Khoikhoi were inspired by "Jacobin" sentiments, and he spoke of a tradition of "mutual Violence and Oppression" between the two groups, suggestions which find little support elsewhere;[24] as appears from the quotation above, however, Dundas was in no doubt about the causes of indigenous discontent.

---

[22] Henry Dundas to Yonge, July 28, 1800, CO 49/9: 142.

[23] Francis Dundas to Yonge, February 20, 1800, and Answers to questions proposed by Sir George Yonge, February 24, 1800, in Theal, ed. *Records of the Cape Colony*, vol. 3, 51, 58. See also Barnard to Henry Dundas, September 13, 1799, in Theal, ed. *Records of the Cape Colony*, vol. 3, 79–84.

[24] Yonge to Henry Dundas, undated "but probably March 29, 1800" (Theal's comment), in Theal, ed. *Records of the Cape Colony*, vol. 3, 88–90. Yet, in a later dispatch,

Yonge was. in general, more concerned with Boer sentiments, and suggested as a means of preventing future disruptions that measures should be taken to extend law and order to the furthest parts of the colony by appointing more magistrates and directing judges from Cape Town to make annual circuits round the country. It is in response to these ideas that Henry Dundas continues his despatch of July 1800 by saying

> Considering the extent of Country over which the latter are dispersed, the rude and uncultivated state in which they have hitherto lived, and the wild notions of Independence which prevail among them, I am afraid that any attempts to introduce Civilization and a strict administration of Justice, will be slow in their progress, and likely, if not proceeded upon with caution and management, rather to create a spirit of resistance, or a disposition to migrate still further from the seat of Government, than to answer the beneficent view in which they might be undertaken.[25]

Dundas recommended that they were left in control of "their domestic concerns [relations with the Khoikhoi?] and interior Economy" and that it was better to view them as "distant Tribes dependant upon His Majesty's Government" than as "subjects necessarily amenable to all the Laws and Regulations." He further recommended that "Barter and Commercial Intercourse" should be the main link with these people and that "a strict adherence to good Faith and Justice" should be observed towards them.[26]

Yonge understood this part of Dundas's despatch to refer to the indigenous peoples; he stated

> On the Subject of the rude uncultivated State of the Caffres, Hottentots, Boshiesmen, and other Wild Tribes, on the Confines of the Colony, what you are pleased to observe Is perfectly applicable to them in the State they were in before the late troubles, and as long as they Continue to remain in that State the Policy of regarding them as Independent Tribes, Is very Just [...] however, many of them are no longer in such a situation so that, so far from rejecting or being averse to any proposals for their Civilization, or the Protection of Gov-

---

Yonge also emphasizes Dutch "Cruelty to the Hottentots and Boshiesmen"; Yonge to Henry Dundas, January 5, 1801, in Theal, ed. *Records of the Cape Colony*, vol. 3, 369.

[25] Henry Dundas to Yonge, July 28, 1800, in Theal, ed. *Records of the Cape Colony*, vol. 3, 142–43.

[26] Theal, ed. *Records of the Cape Colony*, vol. 3, 143.

> ernment [...] they now look up to Government for their Protection, and to the Administration of Justice, as their best Security.[27]

Although the phrases employed by Dundas are strikingly similar to formulations generally used when discussing relations with indigenous peoples, there can be little doubt that "the latter" in the opening sentence of the second quotation from his despatch refers to "the white Inhabitants" in the sentence immediately preceding it (quoted above) and not to the indigenous peoples. It would thus seem that Yonge misunderstood Dundas.

The issue is of considerable importance apart from what it reveals about the occasional obstructions in communication between imperial officials; if Dundas meant his words to refer to the indigenous peoples it would indicate a strong opinion on how relations with these peoples should be conducted and significant evidence of tolerance towards their different way of life. If, as it seems, he meant to refer to the Boers (and it would correspond well to the sentiments expressed earlier on the question of Dutch discontent), then the comment about hostilities originating in Dutch maltreatment remains the only indication of the government attitude towards – or, indeed, awareness of – the situation of the Khoikhoi in the eastern Cape.

There are no means of investigating the question further. The despatch from London which answered Yonge's letter of January 1801 did not refer to this matter (although it mentioned the Boer prisoners convicted for the rebellion in early 1799, as well as the institution of the system of circuit courts); furthermore, both sender and recipient had by this time changed – Lord Hobart had replaced Henry Dundas as Secretary of State, and Francis Dundas was again acting governor after Yonge's dismissal.

The only other reference to the rebellion is framed in general terms. In a despatch from Henry Dundas to General Dundas of August 1800, the former expressed "His Majesty's approbation"

> particularly of the Zeal and Activity which marked Your proceedings in putting an end to the troublesome and dangerous insurrection in the District of Graaf Reynett.[28]

It is likely that by using the terms "dangerous insurrection" Henry Dundas meant to refer to the Khoikhoi rebellion and not just to settler unrest; if this is

[27] Yonge to Henry Dundas, January 5, 1801, in Theal, ed. *Records of the Cape Colony*, vol. 3, 368.

[28] Henry Dundas to Francis Dundas, August 6, 1800, CO 49/9.

the case, then obviously Dundas's remark shows that the government approved of the peace negotiated with the Khoikhoi and the Xhosa. There is no evidence to the contrary; in any case, it might be assumed that had the government disapproved of the actions of the colonial government it would have been stated in this connection. There seem to be no despatches from London touching on the renewed fighting in 1802, probably because of the imminent return of the colony to the Dutch. On the basis of the rather meagre evidence, it may be concluded that the official attitude in London to the Khoikhoi rebellion was based on recognition of the unenviable situation of the Khoikhoi and on general acceptance of the policy pursued by officials in the colony.

A central characteristic of colonial government policy was the consistent distinction between different groups of indigenous peoples. Thus, in the peace negotiations in 1799 very different terms were offered to the Xhosa and to the Khoikhoi.[29] The Xhosa were guaranteed their right to live on the western side of the Great Fish River as long as they did not attack the settlers, and presents were sent to Ngqika, one of the chiefs of the area east of the river, to secure his cooperation in securing the return of fugitive Boers. An attack on the Xhosa by the colonial troops early in the struggle was seen as a regrettable mistake caused by Boer misrepresentations. In the words of Susan Newton–King and V.C. Malherbe, the Xhosa were seen as "a powerful neighbouring nation."[30]

The Khoikhoi, on the other hand, were seen as "rebellious subjects of the colonial government" who were merely promised better protection against the colonists, to whose service they should return;[31] except in a few cases, no promises of land were made to them and very few obtained any, although throughout the struggle Khoikhoi leaders had made it clear that they wanted land and to be able to return to their former way of life.[32] The Khoikhoi were seen as having "no property in the Country, having been deprived of the Cattle and lands by the European Settlers in Africa" – obviously a matter of the past and beyond the power or concern of the British; all that remained to be done for

---

[29] Some, such as Andrew Barnard, were against the negotiation of a peace at all, believing that it would have been better to have defeated the rebels militarily; see Barnard to Wellesley, April 20, 1802, A 1415 (74): 145.

[30] See Francis Dundas to Yonge, February 20, 1800, in Theal, ed. *Records of the Cape Colony*, vol. 3, 54, 56; and Newton–King & Malherbe, *The Khoikhoi Rebellion in the Eastern Cape*, 29–30.

[31] *The Khoikhoi Rebellion in the Eastern Cape*, 29–30.

[32] *The Khoikhoi Rebellion in the Eastern Cape*, 16–17; Elphick & Malherbe, "The Khoisan to 1828," 33.

them was to secure tolerable conditions for them as labourers.[33] Some sympathy for their situation was expressed, but there is little indication of a sense of fundamental injustice on their behalf.

The third group of indigenous people, the San, living in the mountains to the north and northeast, had not figured prominently in the rebellion, although some of them had probably taken part in it; they had, however, been the object of some concern during Lord Macartney's brief governorship. In May 1797 Macartney had issued a proclamation authorizing commandos against the San in the northern part of the district of Stellenbosch; in the proclamation, Macartney emphasized the point that it was the duty of the settlers to join commandos against such "depredators of private property and disturbers of the public peace."[34] A year later, however, Macartney issued another proclamation in which he pursued a line entirely different from this adherence to the traditional one of hunting down the San.

As mentioned above, in 1797 and the first part of 1798 Macartney had dispatched his private secretary, John Barrow, on several tours of the country. In his reports, Barrow described the San very carefully and, though elaborating on what he considered their physical ugliness, he had many positive comments on their mental character: "In his disposition he is lively and cheerful; in his person active. His talents are far above mediocrity; and averse to idleness, they are seldom without employment."[35] He remarked on the cruelty of the commando system and the settler habit of taking women and children as prisoners, whom they treated worse than slaves, and he stated that "the first step" towards improving relations "would be to abolish [that] inhuman practice."[36] Barrow also mentioned the more positive fact that some groups of San had been given cattle and sheep by the colonists in the hope of making them settle and become productive pastoralists. He also noted the plans of missionaries to work among them and expressed the hope that they would be able to gain the confidence of the San and "shew them that the colony is now in the hands of a government

---

[33] Francis Dundas to Yonge, February 20, 1800, in Theal, ed. *Records of the Cape Colony*, vol. 3, 53.

[34] Proclamation of May 20, 1797 by the Earl of Macartney, *Parliamentary Papers* 39.50 (1835): 52–53.

[35] John Barrow, *An Account of Travels into the Interior of Southern Africa, in the years 1797 and 1798* (London: T. Cadell Junior & W. Davies, 1801): 283. This book and a second volume published in 1804 were based on the reports made by Barrow.

[36] Barrow, *An Account of Travels into the Interior*, 290.

that will no longer sanction the cruelties under which they have so long and lately groaned."[37]

As suggested by Nigel Penn, it is likely that the report by John Barrow influenced Macartney to change government policy towards the San.[38] In the proclamation of July 1798, Macartney issued directions for a policy of "civilizing and conciliating the Bosjesmen" by giving them livestock and encouraging them to elect their own leaders, who were to be given symbols of government recognition of their position. Furthermore, these people were to be given land in the far northeastern corner of the colony. In this way it was hoped that the hunters would acquire "a sense of the benefits arising from permanent property" and from being under the protection of the government. It was emphasized that the San were no longer to be "molested, nor their children taken from them, or made slaves or servants of"; in conclusion, it was stated that "the reclaiming these Bosjesmen from their present savage and deplorable state is not only of the greatest importance to the colony, but highly interesting to humanity."[39]

Thus the policy pursued by the first British colonial government at the Cape was marked by recognition of the power of the indigenous groups of people to disrupt the functioning of the colony – sufficient to encourage attempts to ameliorate their condition. In the case of the San, the policy laid down by Macartney promised the goal of enabling them to pursue an independent life, whereas the provisions made by his successors in relation to the Khoikhoi merely attempted to improve their present subservient situation. In the case of the more powerful Xhosa bordering the colony, more overt endeavours were made to placate their feelings and avoid hostilities.

From the existing evidence, it appears that the government in London acquiesced in this policy, though the very few comments made on this point (despite the occurrence of several important events and decisions) suggest that relations with the indigenous peoples were not considered particularly important by the London officials. It is more than likely that the expectation that the Cape would at some stage be handed back to the Dutch militated against any great degree of involvement in the internal affairs of the colony.

---

[37] Barrow, *An Account of Travels into the Interior*, 399.

[38] Nigel Penn, "The Northern Cape Frontier Zone, 1700–c.1815" (unpublished doctoral dissertation, Cape Town University, 1995): 388–92. Penn also mentions the influence of a Dutch official, Floris Visser (399–404).

[39] Proclamation of July 24, 1798 by the Earl of Macartney, *Parliamentary Papers* 39.50 (1835): 53–54.

The second British occupation

In respect of the Khoikhoi, colonial policy pursued after 1806 was similar to that of the earlier period. The most significant manifestation of that policy is found in the proclamation issued by the governor, Lord Caledon, in 1809. This so-called "Caledon Code" had two aspects; on the one hand, it stipulated that Khoikhoi had to have "a fixed place of abode" which had to be registered, and that they were not allowed to move about without a certificate, which they had to produce on demand. On the other hand, the proclamation contained a number of rules applying to the hiring of Khoikhoi, such as the writing of a formal contract, the paying of wages, the lodging of complaints against masters, etc., all of which was subject to the supervision of the *landdrost* or the fiscal.

The purpose of the latter provisions were quite clearly to protect the Khoikhoi against the well-documented abuses which they suffered from the colonists, and as such were quite in line with what was offered to the Khoikhoi in the peace negotiations of 1799. The purpose of demanding that the Khoikhoi have permanent places of residence was, equally clearly, to compel them to seek employment with the settlers – practically the only means the Khoikhoi had of finding employment. The reason for this was stated in the preamble: it was necessary for the prosperity of the colony that everyone, including the Khoikhoi, should be "subject to proper regularity in regard to their places of abode and occupations"; furthermore, it was better that the Khoikhoi should be induced to work for the settlers than that they should lead "an indolent life" ("by which they are rendered useless both for themselves and the community at large").[40]

There has been much discussion about the intentions and impact of the Caledon Code. Some scholars have placed much emphasis on the protection which it meant to give the Khoikhoi and have seen it as a beneficent measure.[41] Others have focused on the inadequacy of that protection, regarding the proclamation as a further means of subjecting the Khoikhoi.[42] There is some truth

[40] Proclamation by the Earl of Caledon, November 1, 1809, *Parliamentary Papers* 39.50 (1835): 164–66.

[41] For example, Marais, *The Cape Coloured People*, 121–23; H.A. Reyburn "Studies in Cape Frontier History," *The Critic* 3.1 (October 1934): 51–52 (Reyburn calls the proclamation "a compromise)." Cf also T.R.H. Davenport, "The Consolidation of a new Society: the Cape Colony," in Wilson & Thompson, ed. *A History of South Africa to 1870*, 303.

in both points of view; the code was both inconsistent and oppressive. However, this was doubtless not the way it was perceived at the time it was issued.

To the contemporary British mind, it was generally considered to be the lot and the duty of the poor anywhere to work for their subsistence under whatever conditions were offered to them.[43] The Code, with its provisions for making the Khoikhoi take up their allotted place in society, was thus in line with the general outlook at the time, while the attempt to improve their situation merely placed them on a level comparable to that of many British labourers.[44] The Code may even be indicating that the Khoikhoi were by this time regarded as a more or less integrated part of the population of the colony rather than as an "alien" element like the San or Xhosa on the borders.[45]

It may be suggested that to the British ruling classes the Code was a rather unexceptional piece of legislation designed to create order in the labour supply

---

[42] For example, Macmillan, *The Cape Colour Question*, 164. Newton–King sets the Code in the context of the general labour shortage at the Cape, which was aggravated by the abolition of the slave trade in 1807: Newton–King, "The labour market of the Cape Colony, 1807–1828," in *Economy and Society in Pre-Industrial South Africa*, ed. Shula Marks & Anthony Atmore (London: Longman, 1980): 176–178.

[43] There were, of course, many differences between the conditions of the Khoikhoi and those obtaining among the labourers in Britain, but also some interesting similarities; thus, for example, for much of the eighteenth century a certificate from the parish officer was necessary to move from one parish to another; see John Lawrence & Barbara Hammond, *The Village Labourer 1760–1832: A Study in the Government of England before the Reform Bill* (1927; London: Longman, 1978): 70–71. It is also striking, as pointed out by Davenport, "The Consolidation of a new Society," 303, that when missionaries later objected to the code it was chiefly because it did not apply equally to everyone, rather than because it forced the Khoikhoi to work as labourers. Cf Timothy Keegan, *Colonial South Africa and the Origins of the Racial Order* (Cape Town: David Philip, 1996): 54–56.

[44] This does not necessarily alter the point that the immediate cause of the proclamation was a desire to reconcile settler demands for labour with missionary complaints about the treatment of the Khoikhoi; it perhaps modifies the idea that Caledon's policy was a departure from the policy pursued during the initial occupation (Penn, *The Northern Cape Frontier Zone*, 463).

[45] Further support for the suggestion that the Khoikhoi were coming to be seen in much the same light as other workers is found in the fact that in 1818 a proclamation was issued prohibiting white indentured servants from leaving their masters without written permission; first offences were punished with prison and a fine, second ones with corporal punishment; the difference between these provisions and those of the Caledon Code is one of degree rather than of kind; see Newton–King, "The Labour Market of the Cape Colony," 185.

of the colony. Perhaps this explains the fact that the proclamation elicited no comment from the Secretary of State; neither the letter from Caledon to Castlereagh transmitting the proclamation nor the reply from Liverpool in which the receipt of that letter was acknowledged made any mention of it.[46] The same may apply to another regulation proclaimed in 1812 by which it was made legal to take Khoikhoi children who had been brought up on farms until their eighth year and "apprentice" them to the farmers for ten years. J.S. Marais points out that this proclamation was made "at the very time when the last remnants of the Elizabethan apprenticeship system were swept away in England." While Marais sees this as evidence for the extremely conservative character of this measure, at the same time it serves as a reminder that the apprenticeship system was no colonial invention.[47]

Like Macartney, Caledon obtained information about the distant parts of the colony by sending a trusted official, in this case Colonel Collins, on a tour of the country. Collins submitted a number of reports to Caledon on the state of affairs, concluding with recommendations on various points. Judging from the high degree of similarity, there is little doubt that Collins's suggestions on the question of the Khoikhoi formed the basis for the Caledon Code.[48] However, Collins was in fact not sent on his journey to investigate the situation of the Khoikhoi but, rather, that of the "Bosjesmen" in the northern part of the colony and the "Caffre People" in the east (perhaps again underlining the perceived difference between the Khoikhoi and the latter peoples).[49]

Collins's report on the San in the northern region expressed some surprise at the fairly peaceful relations between hunters and settlers; although he did not approve of the steps taken by Macartney, it is likely that the provision of the San with cattle and sheep by the farmers was responsible for the decrease in hostilities.[50] Collins strongly recommended establishing mission stations among the San, in order "to rescue this unfortunate race from the deplorable state of barbarism to which they have been so long condemned." At the mis-

---

[46] Caledon to Castlereagh, November 2, 1809, in Theal, ed. *Records of the Cape Colony*, vol. 7, 217; Liverpool to Caledon, March 3, 1810, in Theal, ed. *Records of the Cape Colony*, vol. 7, 266.

[47] Marais, *The Cape Coloured People*, 127.

[48] Cf Penn, *The Northern Cape Frontier Zone*, 465.

[49] The journals and reports of Colonel Collins are reproduced in Moodie, *The Record* part 5, 1–60.

[50] Moodie, *The Record* part 5, 33–38. Cf Penn, *The Northern Cape Frontier Zone*, 466–67.

sions, the San would learn useful trades and could eventually be transferred to the settlers as labourers. As Penn points out, Collins thus envisaged that the missions would fulfil the same function as the Caledon Code was expected to do in relation to the Khoikhoi.[51] In this case, however, the reaction of the government in London is on record; Collins's report was sent to the Secretary of State, Lord Castlereagh, who, although not particularly optimistic about the results, responded favourably to the "interesting" report by saying that "I can have no hesitation in authorizing Your Lordship to make an experiment with the Kraal best situated for such an undertaking," adding that it was further recommended by the fact that it would not be very expensive.[52]

Missions were already well established in the Cape colony and beyond. The Moravian Brethren had built a mission in the east as early as 1737 and, after this first attempt had failed, had started afresh in 1792. Missionaries from the London Missionary Society had arrived in 1799, among other things establishing a mission to the San at the Sak River in the north and to the Khoikhoi, first at Botha's Farm and later at Bethelsdorp in the eastern Cape. Although the Sak River Mission closed down in 1806, the mission to the Khoikhoi proved long-lived. Van der Kemp and later James Read became deeply involved in the plight of the Khoikhoi, attempting to intervene in the fighting in the last years of the rebellion, and afterwards continued to draw attention to the deplorable conditions of these rural labourers, no doubt in part contributing to the drawing-up of the protective measures contained in the Caledon Code.

The missionaries often occupied a precarious position in the colony, labouring under the distrust and sometimes overt hostility of the colonists and a somewhat ambiguous attitude on the part of the colonial government.[53] Governors clearly perceived them as useful intermediaries – for example, making use of Van der Kemp to negotiate with one of the Khoikhoi leaders during the

---

[51] Penn, *The Northern Cape Frontier Zone*, 469.

[52] Castlereagh to Caledon, May 12, 1809, GH 1/5. Collins' proposal, however, does not seem to have been carried into immediate effect; cf Penn, *The Northern Cape Frontier Zone*, ch. 14.

[53] Governor Yonge gave an early account of missionary activity which was very negative, reporting missionaries to be interested solely in economic gain, and perhaps even subversive; Yonge to Henry Dundas, October 22, 1800, in Theal, ed. *Records of the Cape Colony*, vol. 3, 338–40. This was probably an extreme instance, but cf Somerset's despatch of January 28, 1825 (see below, note 88).

rebellion[54] – but were equally aware of their potentially disruptive role in depriving the colonists of their labour supply. The missionaries, on their part, made use of all the means at their disposal to achieve the improvement of the situation of their protégés and, in time, their conversion. Thus, beside making representations to the local authorities and to the governor, they made extensive use of their mother organizations in Europe to attempt to influence the British government.

Secretaries of State often gave such representations a hearing, transmitted them to the governor, and left it up to him to take further action; for example, in 1807 Windham, in a despatch to Caledon, mentioned the situation of the Moravians, proceeding to "recommend the Establishment and the Individuals composing it, who are represented to have always conducted themselves extremely well, to your Lordship's Protection."[55] Again, in 1813, Bathurst, also with reference to the Moravians, instructed Cradock to confirm certain grants of land, noting the "uniform good conduct" of the missionaries and the "influence which they have already produced upon the manners and morals of those Hottentots under their care."[56]

On occasion, missionary endeavours elicited more engaged response from London, as in the case of James Read, part of whose journal and letters on a number of murders of Khoikhoi had been transferred to Liverpool by the London Missionary Society; in this case, it made enough of an impression on the minister for him to write to Lieutenant-General Cradock

> It is needless for me to recommend the subject of it [the enclosed extracts] to Your most serious attention, or to point out to You (should these statements prove correct) that the Interests of Humanity and Justice and the Honor of the British Name demand the immediate adoption of the most effectual measures to secure the exemplary punishment of such atrocious crimes and to shield the injured Natives from the Barbarity of their oppressors in future.[57]

---

[54] See Newton–King & Malherbe, *The Khoikhoi Rebellion in the Eastern Cape*, 45–48.

[55] Windham to Caledon, January 31, 1807, GH 1/1.

[56] Bathurst to Cradock, December 3, 1813, GH 1/11: 155. The Moravians were again mentioned in a despatch from Bathurst to Somerset, October 19, 1815, GH 1/17: 3, recommending further favours.

[57] Liverpool to Cradock, August 9, 1811, GH 1/6. Cradock was already engaged in an investigation of the charges (cf Bird to Cuyler, February 28, 1811, in Theal, ed. *Records of the Cape Colony*, vol. 7, 496–99). The accusations made, especially by James Read,

For the first time in a despatch from London concerned with the indigenous peoples of the Cape, the word "justice" occurs; it is striking that the context was the accusation of tangible crimes against their person rather than the more abstract ones of depriving them of their land, which was the context for the use of the same word in the case of North America some fifty years earlier. The letter indicates an attitude of concern to prevent oppression and cruelty towards indigenous peoples.

While missionary influence on Secretaries of State was to increase considerably, these early examples of their impact already show a degree of willingness to respond favourably to missionary requests; this suggests that the suspicion towards the early missionary movement among colonists and colonial officials identified by some scholars, and referred to above, did not generally influence the government in Britain.[58] There was little hesitation to approve, at least on paper, these early missionary endeavours to improve the lot of indigenous peoples.[59]

The missions to the San on the northern boundary, suggested by Colonel Collins, were not established, though the London Missionary Society on their own initiative did build two missions in the far north in 1814 and 1816 respectively; both of them were closed again after a short period of time.[60] Nevertheless, in 1812 Cradock felt able to say that

> The Bosjesman Nation are now in perfect Amity with the Inhabitants, and many of them are in the Service of the Farmers – Indeed I have every reason to hope that of late Years, oppression and misconduct have much ceased, and that the pains that have been taken, to create new Principles and benevolent Proceedings have not been thrown away.[61]

This was certainly an exaggeration of the situation in the north, where San and colonists continued to struggle until the former had been completely overcome; yet Bathurst was eager to believe Cradock, replying:

---

eventually led to special investigation by the second circuit court in 1812, the so-called "black circuit."

[58] For example, Penn, *The Northern Cape Frontier Zone*, ch. 14.

[59] See, for example, Andrew Ross, *John Philip (1775–1851): Missions, Race and Politics in South Africa* (Aberdeen: Aberdeen UP, 1986): 35. See also discussion of missionary influence in ch. 6 below.

[60] Penn, *The Northern Cape Frontier Zone*, 470. Other missions were established to serve the Khoikhoi and the Griqua in the north.

[61] Cradock to Liverpool, June 10, 1812, GH 23/4: 59.

> The improvement which you represent to have taken place in the conduct of the Inhabitants of the Settlement towards the Hottentots & Bosjesmen is extremely gratifying and I cannot but contemplate with satisfaction the impossibility which now exists of perpetrating with impunity any cruelties similar to those which formerly disgraced the Colony.[62]

The willingness to believe that future atrocities would be impossible or would at least be discovered and punished is hard to accept, considering the many stories that reached Britain about relations between colonists and indigenous peoples; maybe it is wishful thinking. It is interesting that Bathurst refers to "Hottentots" as well as "Bosjesmen," although Cradock had in fact made no mention of the former – an indication, perhaps, of a certain confusion about the indigenous groups in the Colonial Office.

The fourth frontier war

Of the various groups of indigenous peoples, the neighbouring Xhosa excited the greatest attention from the home government during the second occupation. Ever since the first arrival of the British at the Cape (and before then the Dutch), an ambiguous policy had been pursued with respect to these people. Macartney had issued a proclamation in 1797 which prohibited Xhosa from entering the colony unless they had received "badges of authority" and had also stipulated that all Xhosa in the service of the colonists should be discharged so that they could return to the eastern side of the Great Fish River.[63] This policy of creating a barrier between the Xhosa and the colonists was occasionally reinforced by armed attempts to force the Xhosa living on the western side of the river across to the other side; the most recent attempts had taken place in 1799 and 1802, when British troops and settler commandos were defeated by the Xhosa, the attacks no doubt reinforcing the inclination on the part of the Xhosa to support the rebellion of the Khoikhoi. This policy was, however, offset by periodic recognition of Xhosa settlements to the west of the Great Fish River, as in the peace agreement of 1799, which was confirmed by the Dutch in 1803. Cattle raiding and mutual hostility, already endemic to the area, worsened when the fragile balance between the two groups was upset by official action.

---

[62] Bathurst to Cradock, November 30, 1812, GH 1/7: 42.

[63] Proclamation by Macartney, June 27, 1797, in Theal, ed. *Records of the Cape Colony*, vol. 2, 107.

This was illustrated by events in 1809–10; the proclamation prohibiting the employment of the Xhosa had been renewed and troops were sent to the districts of Graaff Reinet and Uitenhage to enforce the proclamation. However, the result was that the many displaced labourers, in order to survive, joined other Xhosa under some of the less powerful chiefs to engage in cattle raiding within the colony. The situation in the eastern Cape – the result of internal power-relations among the Xhosa and of the increasing pressure exerted by the colonists and the colonial power – was once more highly unstable.[64]

In his report, Colonel Collins had stated that the only solution to the problem was a decisive armed effort to remove all Xhosa far to the east of the Great Fish River; he believed it was necessary to secure the boundary of the colony partly by extending it where convenient (from the colonial point of view – though it was proposed to be achieved by purchase from the Xhosa) and partly by settling the area adjoining it more closely than had hitherto been the custom. Collins was one of the first to have suggested that an area of neutrality should be imposed between the Xhosa and the settlers (in his proposal, the land between the Keiskamma and Great Fish Rivers).[65] The *landdrost* of Uitenhage, Cuyler, also repeatedly recommended military action against the Xhosa. Almost immediately after his arrival, Governor Cradock, in October 1811, ordered troops to move to the east in order to remove all the Xhosa to the other side of the colony's boundary.[66]

Soon after this, Cradock informed the Secretary of State of his decision to "enter upon some measures of more effectual operation against the ill disposed of the Caffre Tribes" than those of his predecessors.[67] In this and subsequent letters, Cradock was at pains to justify the decision to take up arms against the Xhosa. If the "repeated aggressions" – wholly unprovoked – of the Xhosa were not stopped, the colonists would leave their farms and a valuable part of the colony would be lost; indeed, if not stopped, the Xhosa would advance even further into the colony and seriously diminish it; any hope of peace would lie in a complete separation of the settlers from the Xhosa, for which action a military presence would be necessary; "Forbearance and conciliation" had been tried and had failed but would hopefully be more successful once there was force to back up the rhetoric; somehow the decision to use force against the

---

[64] Giliomee, "The Eastern Frontier," 447.

[65] Moodie, *The Record*, 17–19.

[66] Giliomee, "The Eastern Frontier," 448.

[67] Cradock to Liverpool, October 18, 1811, GH 1/7: 6.

Xhosa seemed in Cradock's view "peculiarly to accord" with the annual circuit courts, which were intended to scrutinize "the State of the Interior and [to] promote the Course of Justice and Good Order." Cradock sums up by stating that "I anxiously hope that they [these measures] will meet with the approbation of His Majesty's Government."[68]

The official response from London to Cradock's decision is of more than passing interest. In December 1811, Liverpool expressed "much regret" at the news; while accepting the need to prevent "the repeated aggressions of the wandering Kraals of the Caffres" and to maintain a "distinct and acknowledged boundary," Liverpool states that

> It were much to be wished that an arrangement for this purpose could have been amicably concluded and I trust that every attempt to affect it by conciliation will have failed before compulsion is resorted to.[69]

There are two reasons for this opposition to open hostilities, though, as Liverpool is careful to point out, he did not mean to find fault with Cradock. For one thing, Liverpool instructs Cradock to make absolutely sure that the Xhosa really are the aggressors and that their actions "are *not* measures of Retaliation" against settler injustices. Curiously, Liverpool proceeds to refer to "The Proclamation issued by Lord Macartney at a former period," which

> sets forth that the wretched Natives are compelled to have recourse to robbing and various other irregularities in order to support life in consequence of the injury which their peaceful Possessions sustained from the [settlers] who reduce them to misery and wants.[70]

Expecting that such "disgraceful Proceedings" have been stopped, Liverpool shows no awareness that the people whom Macartney's proclamation referred to were the hunters ("Bosjesmen") on the northern boundary rather than the Xhosa on the eastern one – which, as Cradock later pointed out in a reply, was "all together a Separate question."[71] Although this illustrates British metropolitan confusion and ill-informedness about the indigenous peoples of

---

[68] Cradock to Liverpool, October 18, 1811, GH 1/7: 6–8; and Cradock to Liverpool, June 10, 1812, GH 23/4: 58.

[69] Liverpool to Cradock, December 20, 1811, CO 49/10: 86.

[70] Liverpool to Cradock, December 20, 1811, CO 49/10: 86–87 (emphasis in original).

[71] Cradock to Liverpool, June 10, 1812, GH 23/4: 59.

the Cape colony, it does not alter the fact that Liverpool was inclined to question the truth of the claim that the Xhosa were the first aggressors.

It is, however, clear that there was another reason for Liverpool's lack of enthusiasm about the prospect of hostilities with the Xhosa. This rested on what Liverpool termed "the impolicy of a systematic War with the Caffre Nation," which he believed could carry "little benefit," even if successful. In Liverpool's view, it would be better for the colony if the attacks of the Xhosa were defeated when they made them rather than through mounting a full-scale war. It is not quite clear why Liverpool would have had this opinion, since one might expect – as the colonial authorities did – that if the war were successful it would have the advantage of consolidating the boundary between colonists and Xhosa. It is likely, though, that Liverpool was more concerned with the prospect of prolonged warfare, knowing very well that there was a tendency for one war to lead to another. Perhaps the sentiments of his successor, Lord Bathurst, may be used to throw light on Liverpool's views. In his letter of July 1812, Bathurst professed to be in complete agreement with the opinion about the impolicy of systematic warfare:

> I fear that there will be little cause to rejoice at the Success of your attempts to expel them [the "Caffres"] from the Tracts which they occupied if the permanent employment of a regular Force is required to secure the recovered land from future inception [?].[72]

In other words, this kind of war was inexpedient, because it drew too heavily on the military forces of the colony. Bathurst further elaborated on this aspect by referring to the war with France, which placed a heavy drain on all available troops. With this in view, Bathurst stated:

> His Majesty's Government would have been most anxious that the whole of the Troops under your Command should have been left entirely disposable for the defence of the Colony from external Attacks

– and had they been able to foresee that so many soldiers would have been detained for so long in the east, they would probably have discouraged the war.[73] Bathurst here comes close to outright disapproval of the war and he stresses the desirability of bringing it to an end as soon as possible, even if it means leaving some of the Xhosa on the western bank of the Great Fish:

---

[72] Bathurst to Cradock, July 29, 1812, CO 49/10: 94–95.

[73] Bathurst to Cradock, July 29, 1812, CO 49/10: 95.

> If so desirable an object cannot be secured without restoring to the Caffres some part of the Land from which they have been expelled it would not perhaps be inconsistent with sound Policy to make the sacrifice if it will not interfere with the Rights of other Individuals.[74]

Considering the aim of the war, Cradock would most certainly have disagreed with this proposal, which would have rendered the whole war futile. Thus, in this letter, Bathurst was less perceptive than Liverpool was about the colonial views that had prompted the war, or perhaps less sympathetic.

Both Liverpool and Bathurst recognized the territorial rights of the Xhosa to the land on the eastern side of the Great Fish River, Liverpool referring to the territories "belonging to the Caffre Tribes" and Bathurst to "their own Country." This sentiment was generally shared by colonial officials. But Bathurst also expressed the hope that before allowing this war, Cradock would have obtained "the most satisfactory proof that the Caffres had no Claim of Right to the Territory which they have occupied" to the east of the river, a possibility discounted in the colony, although the Xhosa chiefs affected frequently claimed to have purchased the land on which their cattle were grazing.[75]

Finally, both Secretaries of State emphasized the need to treat the Xhosa humanely and to maintain control over the settlers and soldiers involved in the struggle. Liverpool advocated the "utmost humanity [...] consistent with the Security of Property and the tranquillity of the Settlement" and noted with "apprehension" one letter written to the governor which asked for such "confidence" to be placed in the writers as would enable them to act efficiently, promising that "no more Caffres shall be shot than will be found absolutely requisite to the attainment of the desired End of exterminating them from the Zuurveld." Liverpool drily commented: "I trust that no such confidence as is required in this letter has been reposed."[76]

Bathurst, who in the meantime had received the despatch from Cradock containing his famous statement that "there has not been shed more Kaffir blood than would seem to be necessary to impress on the minds of these

---

[74] Bathurst to Cradock, July 29, 1812, CO 49/10: 96.

[75] J.B. Peires, *The House of Phalo: A History of the Xhosa People in the Days of their Independence* (Johannesburg: Ravan, 1981): 57–58.

[76] Liverpool to Cradock, December 20, 1811, CO 49/10: 87.

savages a proper degree of terror and respect,"[77] echoed Liverpool's sentiments, noting that "unnecessary Acts of Severity" would

> inevitably tend to produce an irritation and desire of Revenge in the Sufferers which must oppose [sic] the greatest obstacles to complete reconciliation.[78]

It is thus reasonable to conclude that the government in London did not extend wholehearted support for the war against the Xhosa that Cradock had started. Although he was not officially reprimanded, there were sufficient indications in the letters from London to show that the government had doubts about the reasonableness and expedience of it. For this reason, it might seem somewhat incongruous that when commenting on the conclusion of that war Bathurst not only communicated to Cradock the conventional observation that "His Royal Highness has learnt with peculiar satisfaction the termination of the Warfare with the Kaffre Tribes" but also "His entire approbation of the conduct of Colonel Graham" and all his men. Bathurst, of course, would not have been informed of the bloody details of the struggle, even Cradock may not have been fully aware of them; in his letter to Bathurst, he merely stated that the actions of Graham's forces "does the greatest Credit to their discretion and humanity."[79] Bathurst's comment therefore does not necessarily condone the indiscriminate shooting that apparently took place at times, but it does indicate approval of the war and the ends achieved through it.

Moreover, Bathurst, upon referring to the measures taken by Cradock for preserving the newly won peace in the east (including the decision to maintain a considerable number of troops there), observed that these measures "appear well calculated to secure the Colony against future Invasion."[80] Bathurst apparently had withdrawn his reservations once the war against the Xhosa had been brought to a – from the colonial point of view – successful conclusion. This impression is further strengthened by a passage in an 1814 letter from Bathurst to Cradock's successor, Lord Somerset, in which he writes:

---

[77] Cradock to Liverpool, March 7, 1812, quoted in Ben Maclennan, *A Proper Degree of Terror* (Johannesburg: Ravan, 1986): 128.

[78] Bathurst to Cradock, July 29, 1812, CO 49/10: 96.

[79] Cradock to Liverpool, June 10, 1812, GH 23/4: 58. Maclennan, *A Proper Degree of Terror*, seems to provide the only detailed description of the war; but see also Giliomee, *The Eastern Frontier*, 448, and Peires, *The House of Phalo*, 60.

[80] Bathurst to Cradock, November 30, 1812, GH 1/7: 42.

> The Colony is also much indebted to Sir John Cradock for the Rescue of its frontier Provinces from the predatory incursions of the Kaffre Tribes. Your Lordship will at once see the necessity of adhering to the line of Policy which he has uniformly followed.[81]

There would thus appear to have been a shift in official attitude towards the war against the Xhosa during the years 1812–14. Liverpool was the most uneasy about Cradock's decision, displaying a considerable degree of concern about the reasonableness of a war against "the Misguided Natives," though not to the extent of stopping it (which would of course have been impossible, the greater part of the fighting being over by the time Liverpool's letter reached Cape Town).

While Bathurst repeats many of Liverpool's points, his letter is marked to a greater degree by concern for expedience: the war should be ended because it was making use of troops wanted elsewhere; the Xhosa should be allowed to stay if this would make it easier to achieve peace; excessive violence should be avoided because it would lead to retaliation. This probably explains why Bathurst extended his full approval once the war was over, since at that point it would have seemed a complete success. Furthermore, by the time Bathurst made his unreserved praise of Cradock's policy, the war against France appeared to be at an end and Bathurst's worries about the availability of troops thus no longer relevant.

The official despatches sent from London during the second British occupation of the Cape indicate a certain degree of variation in attitude towards the different indigenous groups. The working conditions of the Khoikhoi received little attention; it is tempting to see this as an instance of official indifference, but against this view can be set the concern expressed at settler maltreatment of Khoikhoi and San and the favourable comments on missionary endeavours to bring them the benefits of Christianity. The greatest attention, however, was focused on the emergence of open hostility between the colony and the Xhosa, to a large extent marked by considerations of a practical nature, tempered by some concern for rights and proper treatment. Altogether, though, the most pervasive impression left on reading the despatches from London is one of inaction on the part of the Secretaries of State; rarely did they exert themselves to achieve anything in relation to these peoples or to modify the measures taken in the colony with respect to them, with the result that colonial policy, guided

[81] Bathurst to Somerset, July 30, 1814, GH 1/14: 6.

by the desire to aid the settlers and to protect the boundaries of the colony even at the expense of the rights of the indigenous peoples, was left to stand.

Changing attitudes?

Policy towards the indigenous population continued in much the same vein in the years immediately following the permanent acquisition of the Cape by the British.

Relations with the Xhosa remained troubled. The attempt to end the conflict once and for all through military operations in the war of 1811–12 had for the first time involved the colonial government in a major altercation over the boundary problems of the east. This in itself was significant, because it turned the hitherto existing balance of power between the Dutch settlers and the Xhosa decisively in favour of the settlers. Nevertheless, the success achieved in driving the Xhosa over the Great Fish River proved illusory. Before long, the starving Xhosa (who had lost vast amounts of cattle and corn during the war) were back in the colony raiding the farmers as never before. In 1818, the increasingly unstable internal power-relations among the Xhosa chiefs led to war between the government ally, Ngqika, and his chief enemy, Ndlambe; when the colonial government entered the war to restore Ngqika, hostilities escalated and by 1819 all the Xhosa were forced to retreat further east across the Keiskamma, with Governor Somerset demanding the cession of the land between the Great Fish and Keiskamma Rivers from Ngqika (see Map 11). In the period after this fifth frontier war, groups of Xhosa who refused to abandon the "ceded territory" were alternately expelled and permitted to stay, and conflicts with the settlers moving east inevitably continued. Thus the relationship between the colony and the Xhosa was marked by raids followed by armed retaliation combined with expansion of colonial territory – a pattern that continued until the Xhosa were finally destroyed.[82]

The Khoikhoi continued to work for the settlers under the oppressive rules of the proclamations of 1809 and 1812. In 1819, the provisions for apprenticing Khoikhoi children to farmers was extended by a further proclamation to include Khoikhoi orphans. By this time, practically none of the Khoikhoi re-

[82] Giliomee, "The Eastern Frontier," 480–84; Monica Wilson, "Co-operation and Conflict: The Eastern Cape Frontier," in Wilson & Thompson, ed. *A History of South Africa to 1870*, 250–56; Peires, *The House of Phalo*, 61–81; Maclennan, *A Proper Degree of Terror*, 150–225.

mained as independent groups, the only options to settler service left for them being life on one of the missions or enrolment in the Cape Corps.[83]

Relations between the San and the colonists were less closely regulated than those between the Khoikhoi and the colonists, and the San consequently could still attempt to survive in independent groups at or beyond the northern boundary of the colony, though once they became employed by the settlers they were subject to the same regulations as the Khoikhoi.[84] Hostile engagement with the colonists continued when the latter formed commandos to recover stolen cattle, in the process often killing a large number of the San, especially the men, whereas the women and children continued to be taken back to the farms as servants. In order to check this latter practice, a proclamation was issued in 1817 ostensibly prohibiting it – but at the same time rules were established for how San children (if there was "some well-grounded apprehension" for their lives – something extremely difficult to check in the more remote parts of settlement) could be "apprenticed" to the settlers for up to ten years.[85]

It was not until the 1820s that events took place which suggest some change of attitude towards the situation of these peoples. In 1829 it was decided to make a settlement for the Khoikhoi on the Kat River as a protective and civilizing measure. However, the benevolent impression created by this step is somewhat diminished by the fact that it was caused to a large extent by a desire to expel Ngqika's son Maqoma from the same area.[86]

A more unequivocally beneficent measure for the Khoikhoi was the 50th Ordinance, drawn up the year before by Bourke, the acting governor. According to this ordinance, Khoikhoi or "other free persons of colour" were no longer to be forced to work for settlers or anyone else and the requirement that all Khoikhoi carry passes when travelling was abolished. Khoikhoi could not enter into contracts of work for more than a year at a time, though these could be renewed, and children living with their parents at a farm were no longer

[83] Elphick & Malherbe, "The Khoisan to 1828," 42–46.

[84] Penn, *The Northern Cape Frontier Zone*, 486–88.

[85] Proclamation by Somerset, August 8, 1817, *Parliamentary Papers* 39.50 (1835): 166–67, and correspondence between Colonial Secretary Bird and Landdrost Stockenstrom, May–June 1822, *Parliamentary Papers* 39.50 (1835): 67–69. Cf Elphick & Malherbe, "The Khoisan to 1828," 44.

[86] Peires, *The House of Phalo*, 89–90, and, by the same author, "The British and the Cape, 1814–1834," in Elphick & Giliomee, ed. *The Shaping of South African Society*, 484.

liable to being apprenticed by the farmer, though this could still be done in the case of orphans. Detailed provision was made for complaints to be lodged by the contracting parties with the magistrates or justices of the peace of the relevant district. Furthermore, the ordinance refuted the widespread notion that Khoikhoi were legally prohibited from owning land; it confirmed all "grants, purchases and transfers of land" hitherto made and declared it to be lawful for any Khoikhoi who was "born or having obtained deeds of burghership in this colony" to acquire land.[87]

By thus repealing the proclamations of 1809 and 1812, the ordinance removed the legal sanction of the oppressive labour and living conditions of the indigenous groups of people within the colony who had hitherto been made to work for the settlers. As might be expected, though, the ordinance did not have any dramatic consequences for the position of these people except in such cases as the Kat River settlement, where the Khoikhoi received an actual grant of land which gave them an economic basis for an independent existence. There was no provision in the ordinance for further grants of land, nor any mention of other means of compensation for the loss of land suffered by the original inhabitants of the Cape. Nevertheless, the ordinance was clearly a liberal measure, intended to bring reform to the appalling conditions of part of the population of the Cape colony, who were indisputably regarded as "His Majesty's Subjects," though the application of the ordinance to "Hottentots and other free persons of colour" showed the basic inequality underlying it.

In view of the far from liberal line of policy pursued by the colonial government up to that point, it is important to make clear the motives behind the ordinance in order to highlight the direction policy was taking at this stage. There were in fact two parallel processes leading to this important development. Missionary activity again played an important role, this time primarily in the case of John Philip. He had arrived in Cape Town in 1819 as superintendent of the mission stations of the London Missionary Society. His main task was to improve relations between the colonial government and the missionaries, which had deteriorated in the years immediately before his arrival. Initially, therefore, Philip devoted his time to this endeavour,[88] but after a few years in

---

[87] Ordinance of his Honour the Lieutenant-governor in Council, for improving the Condition of the Hottentots and other Free Persons of Colour at the *Cape of Good Hope* and for consolidating and amending the Laws affecting those Persons, *Parliamentary Papers* 25.339 (1829): 2–8.

[88] His endeavours to conciliate the colonial government were hampered by the fact that he made a personal enemy of the governor, Lord Somerset, who had come to regard

the colony, he became aware of the situation of the indigenous peoples, in part due to the influence of James Read, and started his long struggle for the improvement of their situation.[89]

In 1826, Philip returned to Britain in order to further his cause. He first secured the support of the London Missionary Society, which in January 1827 submitted a memorial to the Secretary of State.[90] He also contacted influential people from the anti-slavery movement such as William Wilberforce and Thomas Fowell Buxton and even gained a meeting with the Secretary of State.[91] To support this lobbying, he wrote a tract, *Researches in South Africa: Illustrating the Civil, Moral and Religious Condition of the Native Tribes*, designed to illuminate the ill-treatment of the indigenous peoples of South Africa. In this work, Philip described in great detail the condition of the Khoikhoi and the San and the effects of the legislation concerning them, and demanded that all such legislation be abolished and equality before the law for all inhabitants be established.

Philip's powerful work, which earned him a libel case at the Cape and whose truthfulness has been debated ever since by historians,[92] achieved its purpose when the issue was taken up by Buxton. On 15 July, 1828, he moved a resolution in the House of Commons, which in part said

> that this House has observed with great satisfaction that the original Natives of South Africa have always been recognised by the British Government, as a free People, having a lawful abode in the Colony; and that the British Government has promised to protect their persons, property and possessions, the same as those of other free People; That this House humbly solicits His Majesty to cause such Instructions to be sent to the Colony of the Cape of Good Hope, as shall most effectually secure to all the Natives of South Africa,

---

him as subversive, referring to "the insidiousness of this dangerous Man's character"; Somerset to Bathurst, January 27, 1825, in Theal, ed. *Records of the Cape Colony*, vol. 19, 481.

89 Ross, *John Philip*, ch. 4.

90 Hankey to Bathurst, January 22, 1827, in Theal, ed. *Records of the Cape Colony*, vol. 30, 119–28.

91 Ross, *John Philip*, 104–11. Cf Keegan, *Colonial South Africa*, 102–103.

92 See, for example, Ross, *John Philip*, 77, 105–11; John S. Galbraith, *Reluctant Empire: British Policy on the South African Frontier 1834–1854* (Berkeley: U of California P, 1963): 82–84.

> the same freedom and protection as are enjoyed by other free people of that Colony, whether English or Dutch.[93]

It was further requested that various documents relating to the indigenous peoples of the Cape be laid before the House. The motion was passed, apparently with the approval of the government,[94] and was duly sent to the governor at the Cape. In the letter transmitting the resolution, the Secretary of State, George Murray, remarked

> As I have not, as yet, received any report from His Majesty's commissioners of Enquiry relative to the condition of the Hottentot and Bushmen, I must defer furnishing you with any specific instructions

"In the meantime," as he said,

> I only fulfil His Majesty's especial Commands in recommending the original Natives of the Cape, who are residing within the limits of Your Government, to your special attention, in order that you may, upon all proper occasions, exert the authority which is entrusted to you for the purpose of securing to the Hottentots and Bushmen, their freedom and the protection of the Laws.[95]

This somewhat bland or at best neutral statement was further elaborated upon in a letter written the following day. In this letter, Murray transmitted the writings of John Philip – further testimony to his influence – and reminded the governor that "you will of course feel yourself empowered to take measures for remedying any well substantiated causes of complaint" which were brought forward by Philip. Murray himself drew particular attention to the provision (which he believed stemmed from the proclamation of 1809 but which in fact was part of the one of 1812) for apprenticing farm-raised children into the control of the farmers, stating that "I think this enactment of the Proclamation should be repealed." He also mentioned "the Laws respecting Vagrancy, which at present is very loosely defined" but again deferred giving any particular instructions until he had received the report of the Commissioners of Enquiry.[96]

---

[93] Murray to Lowry Cole, August 2, 1828, GH 1/70: 12–14.

[94] Ross, *John Philip*, 109; and Galbraith, *Reluctant Empire*, 83. Philip, in the preface to his *Researches*, went into great detail about the negative attitude of Lord Bathurst to the whole issue; Philip, *Researches in South Africa: Illustrating the Civil, Moral and Religious Condition of the Native Tribes* 2 vols.(1828; New York: Negro UP, 1969), vol. 1: xxii–xxv.

[95] Murray to Lowry Cole, August 2, 1828, GH 1/70: 9–11.

[96] Murray to Lowry Cole, August 3, 1828, GH 1/70: 16–22.

The 50th Ordinance, which sounds tailor-made to the demands of the resolution and Murray's instructions, was, however, dated July 17, 1828, two days before the resolution was moved and a couple of weeks before Murray's letters. The circumstances of its creation therefore require additional explanation. In part, this may be found in the Commission of Enquiry alluded to by Murray. It was appointed in 1822 at a time of unrest among the large group of British settlers who had arrived in the colony in 1820; the Commission was instructed to investigate the conditions of the settlers but also to examine other aspects of the administration of the colony. Inasmuch as they recommended reforms in the legal system, the civil service and the economic foundations of the colony, it is perhaps not surprising that the commissioners also suggested reforms in the legislation concerning Khoikhoi.[97] The commissioners noted the heavy restrictions placed on the freedom of movement of the Khoikhoi and their poor working conditions, including low wages, and they recommended that the demand for passes be abolished and that small grants of land be made as an inducement to industry.[98] Although some of their recommendations were made at a later date, there can be little doubt that the views of the commissioners were well known in the colony in 1828. Their reformist attitudes may thus well have influenced the acting governor, himself described as a Whig committed to "liberal ideals."[99] It is also claimed that the advice of influential men in the colony had an impact on the formulation of the ordinance.[100]

Bourke's letter to the Secretary of State conveying the ordinance reveals little of his motivation; he merely states that "The necessity for an enactment of this nature has been apparent to me from a very early period after my arrival in the Colony."[101] It may be suggested that since missionary attitudes and influence in Britain would have been well known in Cape Town, Bourke would in

---

[97] Peires, *The House of Phalo*, 494–99.

[98] Report of the Commissioners of Enquiry to the Right Honourable William Huskisson upon the Police at the Cape of Good Hope, May 10, 1828, in Theal, ed. *Records of the Cape Colony*, vol. 35, 147–51; for some disagreement among the commissioners as to the abolition of the regulations on vagrancy, see Bigge to Huskisson, May 12, 1828 and Colebrooke to Huskisson, May 14, 1828, in Theal, ed. *Records of the Cape Colony*, vol. 35, 200–207. The final report on the Khoikhoi and San was submitted later: Report upon the Hottentot Population of the *Cape of Good Hope*, and of the Missionary Institutions, January 28, 1830, *Parliamentary Papers* 21.584 (1830) : 140–162.

[99] Peires, "The British and the Cape," 495. Cf Bank, *Liberals and their Enemies*, 123.

[100] Galbraith, *Reluctant Empire*, 83; and Marais, *The Cape Coloured People*, 156.

[101] Bourke to Huskisson, July 22, 1828, GH 23/8.

any case have been able to sense in what direction things were moving and anticipate orders from home, which were certain to arrive.

Newton–King considers the ordinance in a different light when she argues that it was basically part of the same attempt as the Caledon Code to improve the labour situation of the colony. Thus she believes that an important motivation behind the ordinance was the belief that forced labour had increased Khoikhoi resistance, thereby making them less productive as workers; "emancipation" would create a more willing supply of labourers. Ideally, it would also remove much of the attraction of the missionary stations.[102] Although these expectations were not fulfilled, the belief that the ordinance would improve the labour situation may very well have contributed to the willingness of the colonial government to make the ordinance.[103]

Upon reception in Britain, the ordinance was submitted to the legal counsel of the Colonial Office, James Stephen. In view of Stephen's later position in colonial affairs, his comments may be taken to indicate official reaction to the proposed legislation.[104] His general comments are indeed unreservedly favourable despite the neutral language:

> A careful consideration of the whole subject induces me humbly to submit to you my opinion that this is an Act of great value introducing many most important amendments of the former law, and highly deserving not merely of the sanction but of the approbation of His Majesty.[105]

In his view, the ordinance appeared to deal with all the complaints that had been made about the treatment of the Khoikhoi. In his further discussion of the ordinance, Stephen takes his point of departure in a number of comments submitted by Philip a month earlier. Some of these points are technical details or of minor importance. However, Stephen agrees that, considering the traditional

---

[102] Newton–King, "Labour Market of the Cape Colony," 197–200. Ordinance 49, passed at the same time, was more overtly directed towards this goal by allowing groups of refugee Xhosa to enter the colony as labourers. Keegan, *Colonial South Africa*, 104, does not believe that considerations of labour were of great significance in formulating the ordinance.

[103] Clifton C. Crais, *White Supremacy and Black Resistance in Pre-Industrial South Africa* (Cambridge: Cambridge UP, 1992): 73–76. Bank, on the other hand, argues that missionary influence at the Cape, supported by "urban professional-merchant liberalism" there, was the primary force behind the ordinance, *Liberals and their Enemies*, 123–25.

[104] Cf Chapter 1: 36 above.

[105] Stephen to Murray, January 9, 1829, CO 323/46: 263.

attitude of the colonists against the Khoikhoi, it would have been preferable if it had been stated directly that all "free persons" were to be considered equal before the law. While he rejects Philip's point that there should be no separate legislation for any groups of free subjects, he does allow for the possibility that the colonial government might later wish to alter this piece of legislation; consequently, he suggests that an addition may be made stating that the ordinance can only be altered with royal approval.[106] Finally, Stephen acknowledges the danger of Khoikhoi being detained by colonists on grounds of alleged debts.[107]

In the order in council giving assent to the ordinance, a paragraph was accordingly added to deal with these problems. It was stated, "for the prevention of any doubt," that

> all Hottentots and other free persons of colour, lawfully residing within the said Colony, are and shall be, in the most full and ample manner, entitled to all and every the rights, privileges and benefits of the law, to which any other His Majesty's subjects.[108]

It was further stated that no Khoikhoi could be held back in order to work to pay off a debt; finally, the ordinance could not be changed without the assent of the King. The addition of these measures, obviously designed further to protect the Khoikhoi and others affected by the measure, as well as Stephen's long and detailed discussion of it, indicate that the ordinance was supported by the government, who showed a desire to ensure the beneficent intention perceived to underlie it. The general attitude of the government to the ordinance is stated in the letter acknowledging its receipt, in which Murray says: "I have much pleasure in acquainting you that His Majesty's Government highly approve the Regulations contained in that Ordinance."[109]

There is no reason to doubt that this was indeed the official attitude. It is also clear that the government would have given instruction for a similar measure had none been forthcoming from the colony. It is obvious, though, that the

---

[106] In 1834, the colonial government submitted a vagrancy bill which would have seriously undermined the provisions of the ordinance. It was, however, disallowed by the Colonial Office. Stephen to Murray, January 9, 1829, CO 323/46:263–268.

[107] Stephen to Murray, January 9, 1829, CO 323/46: 269.

[108] "Ordinance of his Honour the Lieutenant Governor in Council for improving the Condition of the Hottentots and other Free Persons of Colour at the *Cape of Good Hope*, and for consolidating and amending the Laws affecting those Persons, *Parliamentary Papers* 25.339 (1829): 147.

[109] Murray to Lowry Cole, January 10, 1829, GH 1/72.

impetus for this came to a large extent from the missionary circles outside the government and there is no way of knowing whether the same steps would have been taken without this pressure – even with the forthcoming report of the commissioners;[110] yet the response of the government to events and their reception of the ordinance indicate that they were indeed willing to take up this cause in an active manner. At the very least, it shows that a change of attitude towards the problems of the indigenous peoples and the means of handling these problems was under way.

The correspondence on the problems connected with the Xhosa further illustrates this gradual change of attitude. The problems on the eastern frontier continued unabated, with cattle raiding and retaliation both in the colony and in the "ceded country." Both in January 1823 and in March 1824, Somerset received Bathurst's sanction for measures against the "depredations and Outrages committed by the Kaffir people."[111] A further example of Bathurst's attitude to the problems of the eastern Cape is provided by a despatch from July 1826. In this document, Bathurst comments on the decision by Bourke to abolish commando-incursions into the territory of the Xhosa to recapture stolen cattle. Bathurst has reservations about this decision; on the one hand, he says

> I am fully aware of the many inconveniences which must occasionally arise from permitting the Borderers to take the Laws into their own hands.[112]

On the other, as Bathurst had not received details about the system to replace it (both in order to "indemnify the Borderers" and to "punish the Caffres who may steal them [the cattle]"), he could only "express [his] hope that [Bourke has] made this change after due enquiry."[113] Bathurst's concern about expedi-

---

[110] Galbraith, *Reluctant Empire*, ch. 5, claims that the "power [of missionary influence] has been overstated." Insofar as this refers to its impact in the colony itself, this may be true; however, in line with what was said earlier on the attitude of the government in London towards the missionaries, their influence at this time among officers of the British government seems to have been very much in the ascendance. Cf George M. Frederickson, *White Supremacy: A Comparative Study in American and South African History* (New York: Oxford UP, 1981): 319 (note 54), who notes this controversy but concludes that although missionaries may not have been the only source of influence, they, particularly Philip, played a certain role.

[111] Bathurst to Somerset, January 1, 1823, in Theal, ed. *Records of the Cape Colony*, vol. 15, 200–201; Bathurst to Somerset, March 13, 1824, in Theal, ed. *Records of the Cape Colony*, vol. 17, 142–43.

[112] Bathurst to Bourke, July 2, 1826, CO 49/9: 57–58.

[113] Bathurst to Bourke, July 2, 1826, CO 49/9: 57–58.

ency here clearly took precedence over any notions of benevolence towards the Xhosa. Bathurst continued to be in favour of the policy towards these people that had been established by 1814, which was essentially one of repelling them by force.

In May 1829, when the colonial government again decided to expel Maqoma from the "ceded territory," the new Secretary of State, Murray, continued Bathurst's line of policy when he responded by saying "I am happy in having to express to you my entire approbation of the measures which you have taken for ensuring the tranquillity of the eastern frontier of the colony."[114] However, when the question of populating the "ceded territory" came up in 1830, Murray adopted a rather more ambiguous tone; he noted with regret that the area continued to be inhabited by numerous Xhosa (many of whom had returned after the expulsion, as on former occasions) and continued:

> This is undoubtedly a great evil; for while, on the one hand, it is not to be expected that these people will ever voluntarily evacuate the colonial territory, I am not, on the other hand, prepared to authorize you to expel them by force of arms from the land of their birth. At the same time it is clear that, without entirely abandoning the policy which sought to set up a bar of separation between the Caffres and the colonists, the former cannot be allowed to remain as owners of the soil in permanent occupation of the colonial territory.[115]

The dilemma with which the Secretary of State (and the governor) was thus confronted introduced an aspect which had hitherto been almost wholly backgrounded in framing policy with regard to the Xhosa: by referring to "the land of their birth" from which the Xhosa could not be expelled without good reason, Murray was obviously influenced by moral considerations about the rights of the Xhosa. However, this was countered by considerations about the consistency of a policy of which Murray highly approved; the creation of an empty tract of land between the two groups was in Murray's view "a wise measure," as much implemented for the sake of "remov[ing] them [the Caffres] from the temptations which must attach to their close proximity to the borders of the colony" as for the security of the settlers. This led Murray to conclude that it would be "sacrificing the ultimate hope of their civilization" if the Xhosa were allowed to remain in the "ceded territory" without "some effectual guarantee" against disturbances. His solution to the problem was that this guarantee

---

[114] Murray to Lowry Cole, October 15, 1829, *Parliamentary Papers* 39.252 (1835): 44.

[115] Murray to Lowry Cole, May 6, 1830, *Parliamentary Papers* 39.252 (1835): 54.

> should be their peaceable conduct; and it must be fully understood, that every attempt which they shall make to plunder the farms or property of the colonists, will, as in the case of Makomo, be visited by the immediate expulsion of the tribe to which the plunderers shall belong.[116]

Murray believed that this would be the only way of "leading those people to adopt the habits of civilized life." It is striking that this "civilization" could be achieved only with the assistance of the threat of expulsion. However, the fact remains that Murray had decided in 1830 that the remaining Xhosa should be allowed to stay in the "ceded territory." This position, together with Murray's long discussion of the way in which to deal with the Xhosa, his consideration on the one hand of their rights and on the other of the need to "civilize" them in order to obtain security at the frontier, does indeed confirm the suggestion made above that changes in official attitudes were taking place.

The culmination of this change is found in the well-known despatch by Secretary of State Lord Glenelg, from December 1835, at the end of the sixth frontier war. This war, begun by the Xhosa in October 1834, was instigated by the wounding of one of their chiefs by a patrol, although the deeper causes for this as for the previous wars was to be found in the continuous struggle for land and cattle between the settlers and the Xhosa.[117] After their attack was repelled, the colonial troops proceeded against Hintsa, one of the major chiefs of the Xhosa, whom they killed while holding him hostage for the surrender of the original attackers. Peace was made in September 1835, no real conclusion having been reached in the fighting. However, governor D'Urban announced the annexation of the territory between the Keiskamma and Kei rivers, which he called the Queen Adelaide Province, thus adding several thousand Xhosa to the population of the Cape colony (see Map 11).[118]

In his very long despatch, Glenelg condemned in no uncertain terms the entire policy conducted towards the Xhosa since 1811; noting the inconsistency of that policy and the injustice of depriving the Xhosa of their land between the Great Fish and Keiskamma rivers as well as the persistent retaliatory raids made by the colonists, Glenelg was convinced that such measures had forced the Xhosa to attack the colony in 1834. Glenelg was not against defensive measures against the Xhosa; thus it was D'Urban's "clear and indispensable

---

[116] Murray to Lowry Cole, May 6, 1830, *Parliamentary Papers* 39.252 (1835): 54.

[117] Galbraith, *Reluctant Empire*, 108–11.

[118] Peires, *The House of Phalo*, 109–15; Galbraith, *Reluctant Empire*, ch. 6. Cf Keegan, *Colonial South Africa*, 139–45.

duty to arrest the progress of the invaders, and to compel them to retire within their own territory," which amounts to much the same thing as repelling their "depredations and Outrages." However, it is obvious that Glenelg was much more careful than his predecessors in inquiring whether "the Caffres [were] provoked by such wrongs as afforded them a legitimate cause of war" and his conclusion that they "had a perfect right to hazard the experiment, however hopeless, of extorting by force that redress which they could not expect otherwise to obtain" is unprecedented in the official despatches from London to the Cape.[119]

Furthermore, Glenelg strongly rejected the idea of expanding the territory of the colony:

> The general principles by which the British policy towards the Aborigines of Southern Africa should be governed, are obvious, and beyond the reach of doubt. The extension of His Majesty's dominions in that quarter of the globe, by conquest or cession, is diligently and anxiously to be avoided. Hostilities with the tribes in our vicinity may occasionally be inevitable for the protection of the King's subjects; but on every other ground they cannot too earnestly be deprecated.[120]

In consequence of this, Glenelg directed that unless D'Urban could present material of such a fundamental character that it would change Glenelg's view of the situation, the Queen Adelaide Province was to be given up. D'Urban had urged that it was necessary for the security of the colony, but Glenelg brushed this aside with the statement that "His Majesty would never consent to consult expediency at the expense of justice."[121] Moreover, new conquests would inevitably bring on new wars and contact with new "uncivilized" and "barbarous" tribes. Treaties were to be entered into with the individual chiefs, a government agent was to be appointed to live on the eastern side of the boundary, and a lieutenant-governor was to be in command of the eastern Cape.

In the course of his despatch, Glenelg remarked that he had detected in the official documents written by D'Urban signs of an attitude towards the Xhosa

---

[119] Glenelg to D'Urban, December 26, 1835, *Parliamentary Papers* 39.279 (1836): 63.

[120] Glenelg to D'Urban, December 26, 1835, *Parliamentary Papers* 39.279 (1836): 68.

[121] Glenelg to D'Urban, December 26, 1835, *Parliamentary Papers* 39.279 (1836): 69. In Galbraith's view, the decision to renounce his annexation did not come as something wholly unexpected for D'Urban, who knew that he had moved beyond his instructions for retrenchment as outlined by Stanley; Galbraith, *Reluctant Empire*, 114.

which he could not accept. Strongly objecting to D'Urban's comparison of the Xhosa with wolves and his characterization of them as "irreclaimable savages," Glenelg took pains to point out that the opposite was in fact true, with reference to the missionary endeavours among the Xhosa which had gathered momentum since 1817:

> In the midst of all the calamities incident to their situation in our immediate neighbourhood, the Caffres, under the guidance of their Christian ministers, have built places of public worship; have formed various congregations of proselytes, of learners; have erected school-houses, and sent their children thither for instruction. In the meanwhile no inconsiderable advance has been made in agriculture and in commerce.[122]

In other words, the Xhosa were well on their way to becoming "civilized," due to the influence of missionaries and education, agriculture and commerce. In summing up the policy to be pursued, Glenelg said

> It cannot be too often or too importunately pressed on our conviction as a plain practical truth, that the safety of the colony, which after all is the first object, is to be derived from observing in our dealings with the frontier tribes the most rigid justice, respect for their feelings and prejudices, regard for their real interests, conciliatory kindness when it can be properly shown, and above all, an unwearied anxiety to diffuse among them the blessings of education and of Christian knowledge.[123]

Glenelg's exceptionally long and carefully worded despatch provides an unusually explicit statement of government policy towards part of the indigenous population of the Cape colony. It may be suggested that while there were few overt changes of policy in this statement (the government had never, for example, sanctioned a vast extension of the territory of the Cape colony), there was a striking change of attitude towards the way in which that policy was to be carried out. The suggestion of a concern for moral justification which was noted in Murray's despatch from 1830 becomes a certainty in Glenelg's letter; the actions of colonists and colonial government are scrutinized and rejected, and those of the Xhosa found to be more justified (even according to the laws of war). Furthermore, also in line with Murray's letter, great emphasis is placed

---

[122] Glenelg to D'Urban, December 26, 1835, *Parliamentary Papers* 39.279 (1836): 64.

[123] Glenelg to D'Urban, December 26, 1835, *Parliamentary Papers* 39.279 (1836): 70.

on the belief that relations with the Xhosa were to be improved through efforts to "civilize" them.

Glenelg's despatch has customarily been seen as the product of the influence of missionaries who attempted to protect the Xhosa against the colonists and who tried to convert them to Christianity. John Galbraith, however, has argued that this influence in the despatch has been exaggerated; he places greater emphasis on the view that the despatch expressed the ideas of the entire cabinet, which "certainly was not dominated by 'humanitarian' influence."[124] Rather, Galbraith suggests, the decision not to accept the annexation of the new territory was determined by economic considerations.[125] The point that economy was an important motive for resisting expansion certainly finds support in the despatch; thus Glenelg comments:

> Whence the necessary revenues for defraying the additional establishments, civil and military, are to be extracted, is a question to which your consideration does not appear to have yet been given, and to which I have directed my own in vain.[126]

Similarly, the king's resistance to Glenelg's despatch and the cabinet's determination to withstand this resistance shows that a fairly united cabinet was indeed behind the measures.[127]

However, the evidence for outside influence presented by Galbraith himself is quite clear. Glenelg stated that he had relied on material presented to him by interested peersons, and some of this was obviously from missionaries and their societies. Although, as Galbraith points out, some of the missionaries may have been in favour of extending British rule, whereas Glenelg was not, there is little doubt that in respect of the beneficial effects of christianization they would have been in full agreement.[128]

---

[124] Galbraith, *Reluctant Empire*, 124.

[125] Galbraith, *Reluctant Empire*, 127–29. Keegan makes the same point, seeing humanitarian influence as providing the "public rhetoric," while it was the "commitment to economy [...] that dictated policy," *Colonial South Africa*, 148.

[126] Glenelg to D'Urban, December 26, 1835, *Parliamentary Papers* 39.279 (1836): 69

[127] Galbraith, *Reluctant Empire*, 129–31.

[128] Galbraith, *Reluctant Empire*, 126–27. It is generally recognized that the second half of the 1830s saw the climax of humanitarian influence in British government circles; see Bank, *Liberals and their Enemies*, 138.

A final example of the change in attitude may be given with reference to the northern boundary of the colony. In June 1833, Governor Cole issued a proclamation and then an ordinance which renewed Macartney's proclamation on commandos against "the wild Bosjesmen" from 1797. The ordinance was transmitted to James Stephen for legal comment, and on this occasion his language was anything but tepid. He declared:

> It would seem sufficiently established that the Commandos have been marked by the most atrocious and wanton disregard of human life, and by Cruelties alike disgraceful to those who sanctioned & destructive to those who endured them ... this system has been a fearful Scourge to the native Population & an indelible Stain upon the national Character of Holland and of Great Britain.

Rather than accepting that the ordinance was merely a continuation of the early policy laid down by Macartney, Stephen proceeds to reject the latter – politely but firmly; were it not for the governor's introduction to the ordinance, he states, he "should have not hesitated to say that Lord Macartney's Proclamation could have been quoted only to be condemned, in the most unequivocal Manner":

> I could refer to no other example of the Establishment of an Enactment of this nature, not as a temporary Measure to meet some extreme Exigency, but as a permanent rule for the habitual conduct of the Magistracy and of the People at large.

Stephen then examines the ordinance in detail, concluding that "I can only say that so far as I can understand the Subject, it appears to me that this Ordinance is indefensible and ought to be disallowed."[129] In language which closely echoed Stephen, the Secretary of State, Stanley, shortly afterwards signified to Cole's successor, D'Urban, that the ordinance was rejected. Stanley directed D'Urban to establish another way of protecting the northern boundary. Well aware of the difficulty of this job, Stanley nevertheless pointed out that this should be achieved by "ordinary means of precaution":

> I would especially call your attention to the propriety of cultivating an intercourse with the chiefs of the Caffre tribes [....] many of those chiefs might be gradually induced in return for small annual presents of stores, to become responsible for the peaceable conduct of their followers; and by degrees they might learn to appreciate the solid advantages of an authorized barter.[130]

---

[129] Stephen to Stanley, November 4, 1833, CO 323/49: 234–34.

[130] Stanley to D'Urban, November 27, 1833, *Parliamentary Papers* 39.252 (1835): 65–66.

Although Stanley confuses the San and the other peoples living in the north with the "Caffre tribes" and although his suggestion for an alternative policy might seem somewhat naive in the face of the development of relations since the first arrival of the British at the Cape, his intentions are clear enough. Commandos were not to be tolerated, because of their cruelty and their irresponsible delegation of power to people unqualified to hold it. Instead, measures were to be pursued which would teach the indigenous people the "civilized" ways of honest interaction.

These examples show amply that by the late 1820s and early 1830s official attitudes in Britain towards the indigenous peoples of the Cape colony and the policy to be pursued with respect to them had undergone a quite dramatic shift. Concern with the treatment accorded these peoples was becoming evident, some consideration was expressed for their rights, and there were even instances of a certain degree of emotional involvement.

Furthermore, Secretaries of State and their staff were becoming actively involved in the measures which were put into force, and were beginning to express a consistent line of thinking in relation to the treatment due to these people. Leslie Duly has detected a similar tendency in the Colonial Office approach to land policy at the Cape. The first three decades of the century he terms "the Age of Neglect and Administrative Infancy in the Colonial Office"; in the late 1820s, he finds, this "general apathy" was replaced by greater eagerness to intervene in colonial policy. Duly believes that this change was to a large extent inspired by the reports of the Commission of Enquiry and the influence of proponents of Wakefieldian systematic colonization.[131] Comparable developments have been identified by Isobel Edwards, who studied the impact of the complaints of the "1820 settlers" on the policy of the Colonial Office; in this case, too, outside influence contributed to forcing officials into action.[132] There is a close parallel between the processes at work in these areas of policy which suggests that the changes which took place during the 1820s and 1830s were caused at least in part by general developments that were not necessarily related specifically to the question of indigenous peoples.

---

[131] Leslie Clement Duly, *British Land Policy at the Cape, 1795–1844: A Study of Administrative Procedures in the Empire* (Durham NC: Duke UP, 1968): 141–42. Cf Macmillan, *The Cape Colour Question*, 42–48.

[132] Isobel Eirlys Edwards, *The 1820 Settlers in South Africa: A Study in British Colonial Policy* (London: Longmans, Green, 1934): ch. 6–7.

From inactivity to protection

The official attitude in London towards the indigenous peoples of the Cape during the first fifteen to twenty years of British rule is by no means easy to assess. Early comments indicate a certain sympathy with the oppressed situation of the Khoisan, in some measure induced by missionary agitation on their behalf, to which the Colonial Office was favourably disposed. The slightness of official engagement with the situation of these peoples, however, suggests that there was little active interest in their fate, and in any case has the effect, as in the case of New South Wales, of endorsing the policy pursued in the colony. Although some attempts were made in the colony to improve the situation of the San and the Khoikhoi, particularly the latter were clearly perceived as a source of labour, and policy towards them was firmly based on the premise that such labour should be made available to the colonist.

Policy towards the Xhosa received more attention from the government in London. This was undoubtedly so because the British became involved in a war with these people, a factor which usually aroused the interest of government. Various elements could be discerned in the attitude towards the Xhosa war of 1812–13 but the overall impression by the end of it is one of expediency. Bathurst almost invariably advocated measures calculated to reduce trouble or expenses, a line of policy which continued throughout the long period during which he was Secretary of State. As pointed out earlier, the general impression gained of the official attitude towards issues connected with indigenous peoples at the Cape is one of inactivity on the part of the British government.

The peculiar circumstances surrounding the British presence at the Cape may afford some explanation for this. Especially during the first occupation, there was every expectation that the colony would at some stage be handed back to the Dutch. Consequently, while the men on the spot had to deal with the conflicts that arose, the British government would have felt little inclination to get involved in problems which they would have seen as essentially none of their concern. Dundas' phlegmatic response to the rebellion of the Dutch colonists at Graff Reinet confirms this view.

During the second occupation, however, the belief was probably widespread that the Cape would remain British. The policy of the colonial government reflects this, since several measures of considerable importance were carried out during this period. The slight increase in comments from London may also be seen as a reflection of this. The fact that Britain was still at war during this period could, on the other hand, explain why the increase was so inconsiderable. This explanation is supported by the steady increase in documents after

1815, at which time the war was over and the colony confirmed as in British possession.

The change which took place from the late 1820s onwards was characterized by several closely connected factors: a dramatic increase in official material relating to the indigenous peoples; an increase in the level of active policy-making, frequently involving alterations or additions to the measures suggested by the colonial government; and, most importantly, an attitudinal change in relation to these peoples, which emphasized moral concern and perhaps even responsibility towards "uncivilized" peoples who obviously needed help to obtain the religious and material benefits which should be extended to them.

The 50th Ordinance, although not the work of the Colonial Office, was highly approved of by the government. In some respects there is a close similarity between this measure and the abolition of slavery; both were designed to release unfortunate groups of people who through no fault of their own had been subjected to the cruel treatment of others; both sought to establish these groups on an equal footing with "free" people; and both measures envisaged that the "liberated" people would take up a position among the "labouring classes" of their respective societies. Both these movements were sponsored by the same people in London. It is probably no coincidence that they were so close in time to each other.

Taking this parallel a little further, it may be suggested that perhaps the British perceived the Khoikhoi, whom they had never encountered as an independent people, to be rather more like slaves or even ordinary labourers than like an indigenous people. Although their past was of course well-known, their situation in the early nineteenth century was very different from, for example, that of the Xhosa, who were at this time still resisting their subjection. The majority of the Xhosa were fighting against the expanding colony from beyond its limits, whereas the Khoikhoi (except briefly during the rebellion) had been wholly submerged within the colonial boundaries. Perhaps this may explain, at least in part, why the government in London never exhibited as much interest in this group of people as in others, so that almost all policy towards them has to be traced through the actions of the colonial government until some of the same forces as worked for the abolition of slavery took up the cause of the Khoikhoi.

The change that occurred between the early years of the century and the third decade is perhaps most clearly illustrated in relation to the Xhosa. Glenelg's reversal of colonial policy, his criticism of previous policy and his admission of the Xhosas' view of the situation are evidence of a concern for indigenous peoples, the strength of which is quite unprecedented. Equally important is the consistent emphasis placed on the desire to "civilize" the Xhosa, based on a conviction of the immeasurable advantage flowing from conversion to Christianity and, closely connected with this, the British way of life. Moral indignation at the behaviour of the colonists and even at times at the policy suggested by the colonial government is clearly discernible in connection not just with the Xhosa but also with the San.

It has already been mentioned several times that a very important source for this development was the influence exerted by missionaries involved in the conversion of indigenous peoples. Many of the missionaries became deeply engaged in the problems of the people they got to know, and through their efforts official attention was drawn to these problems. The impact of missionary efforts had been felt for decades, but it reached its highest point in the 1830s, as is so amply illustrated by the case of the Cape colony.

Maps

MAP 1
Select Indian groups in North America east of the Mississippi at the time of first contact with the Europeans.

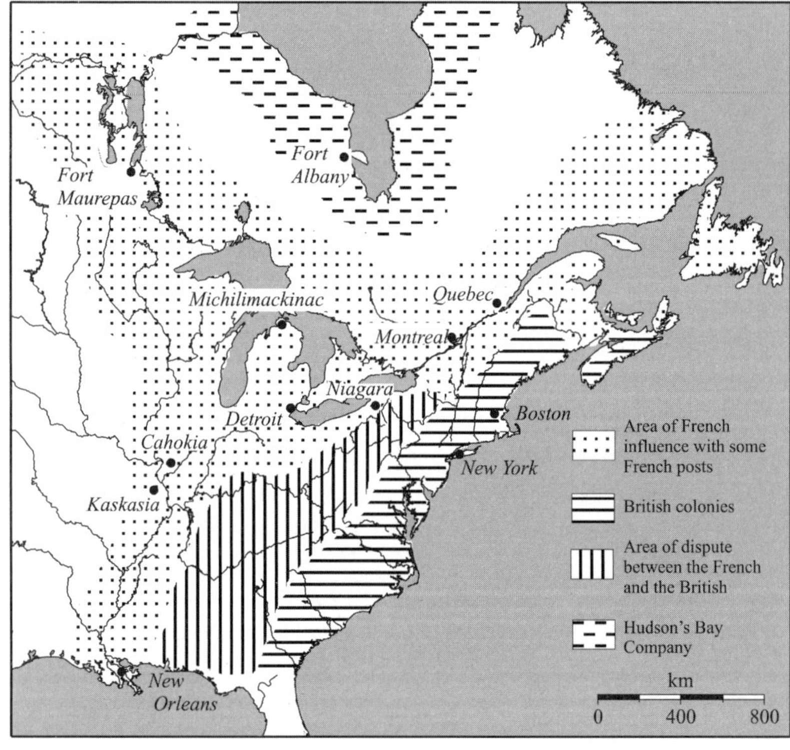

MAP 2:
Approximate extent of French trade and settlement in North America by the first half of the eighteenth century.

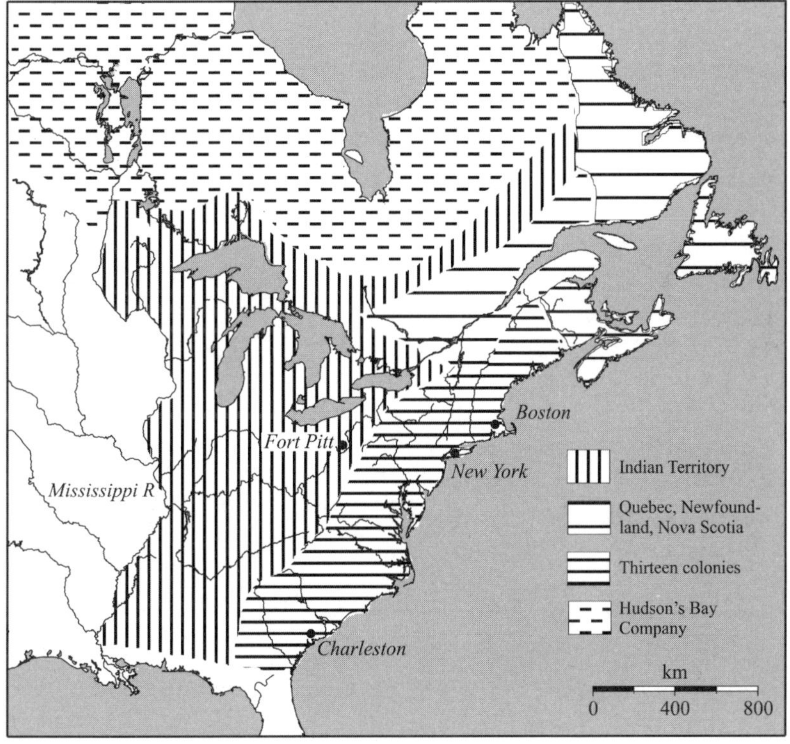

MAP 3:
The division of North America according to the Royal Proclamation, 1763.

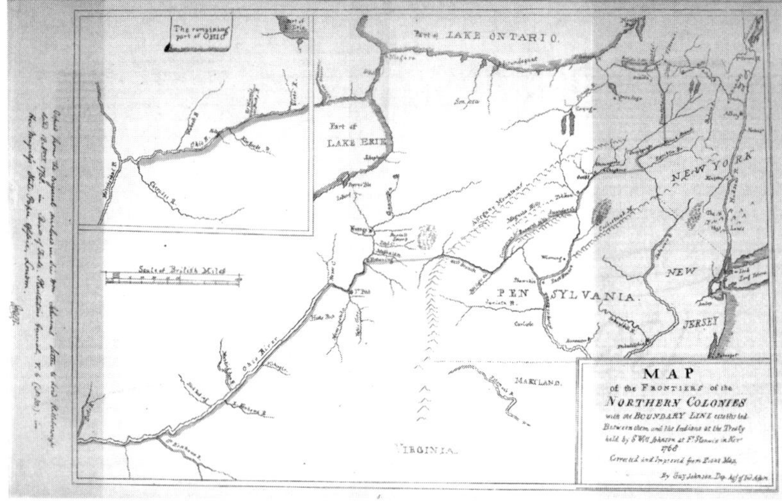

MAP 4:
The northern boundary between the colonies and the Indians ordered by the Board of Trade, January 1768.

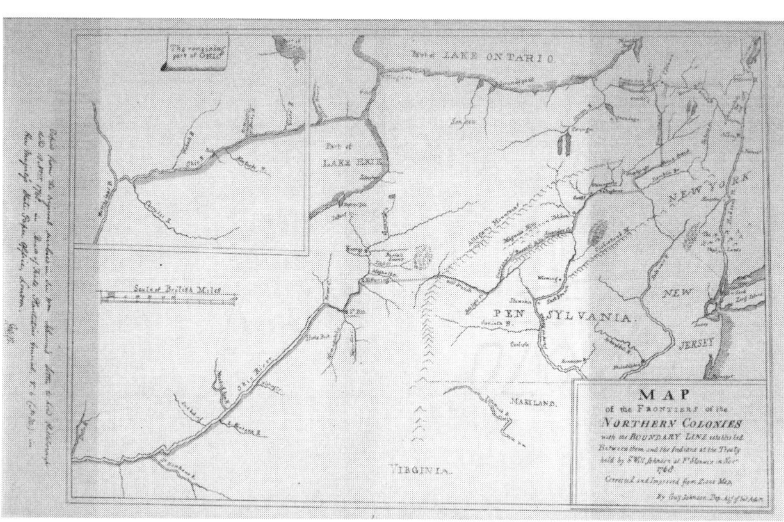

MAP 5:
The northern boundary negotiated at Fort Stanwix, October 1768.

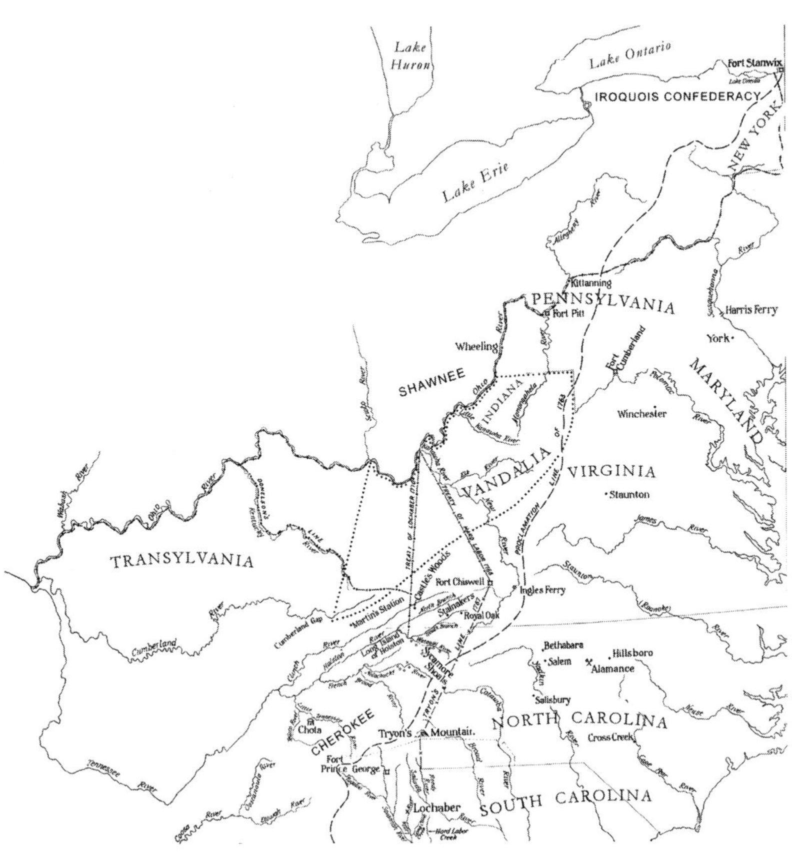

MAP 6:

The cessions and treaties negotiated with the northern Indians between 1763 and 1775.

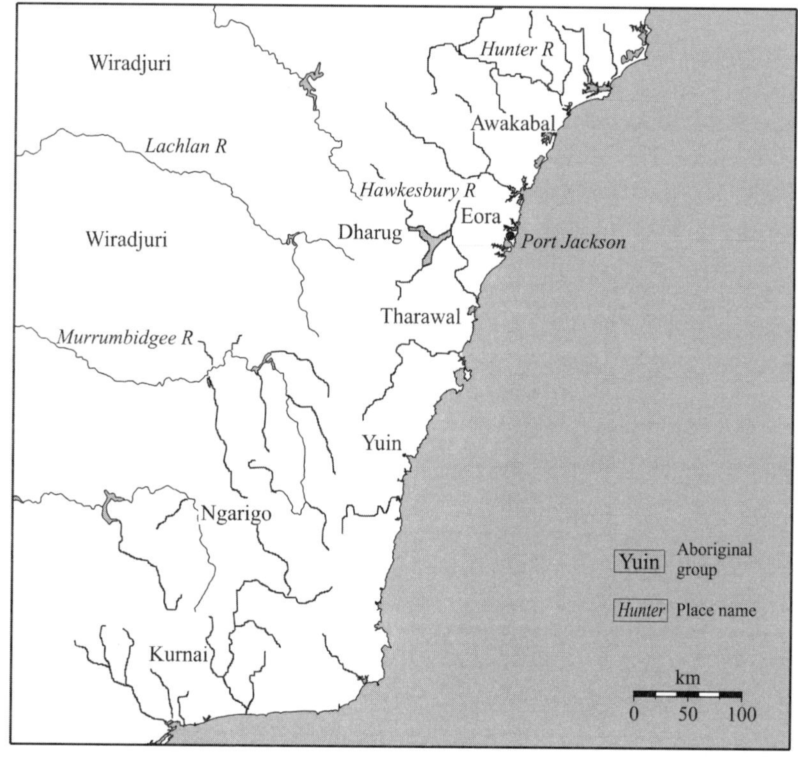

MAP 7:
Select Aboriginal groups on the southeast coast of Australia at the time of first contact with the British.

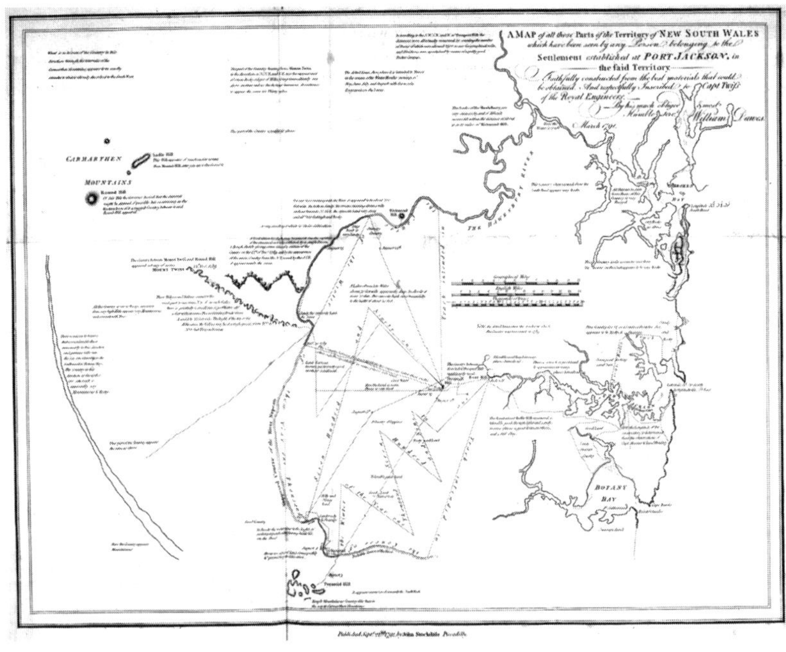

MAP 8:

Map of Sydney area and southeast Australia from 1792.

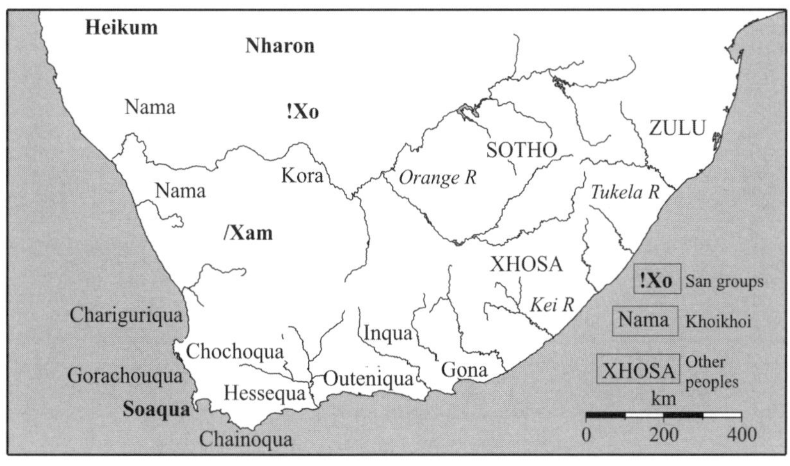

MAP 9:
Select San and Khoikhoi groups in western South Africa at the time of first contact with the Dutch.

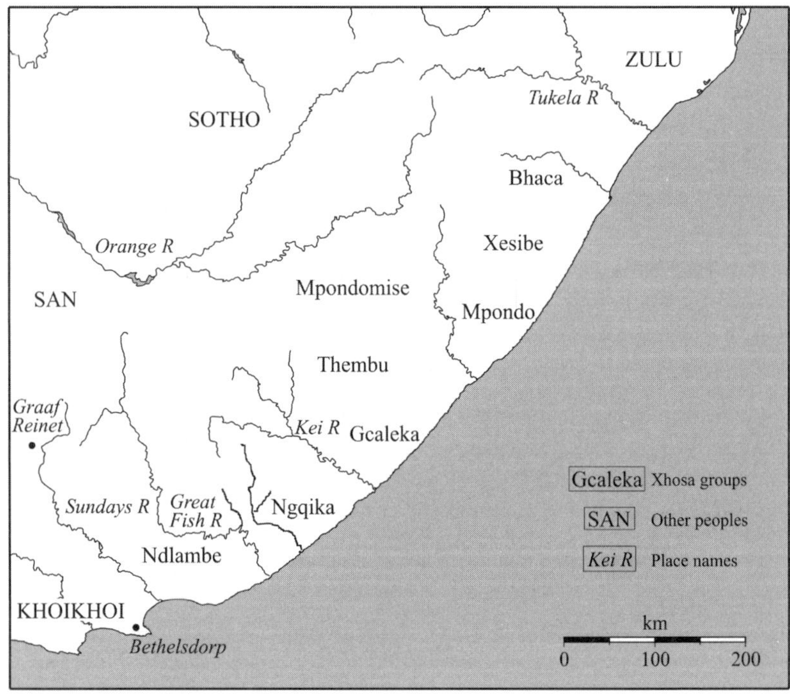

MAP 10:
Select Xhosa groups in the eastern Cape colony around 1800.

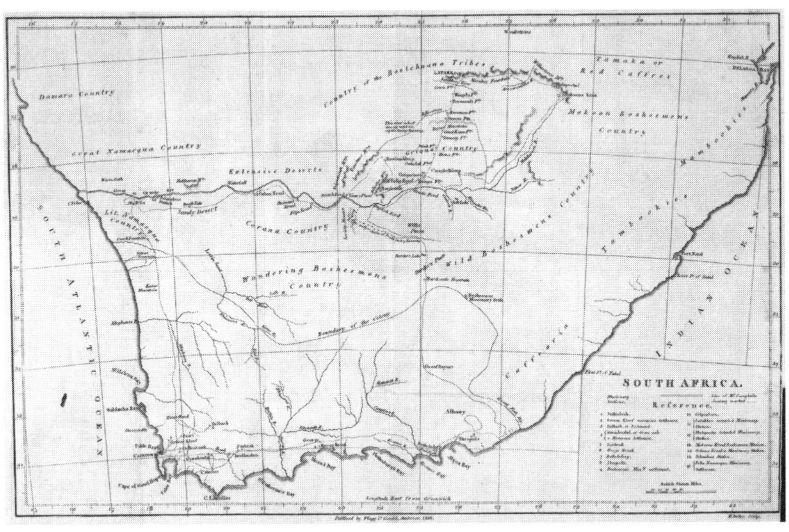

MAP 11:
Extent of the Cape colony around 1800.

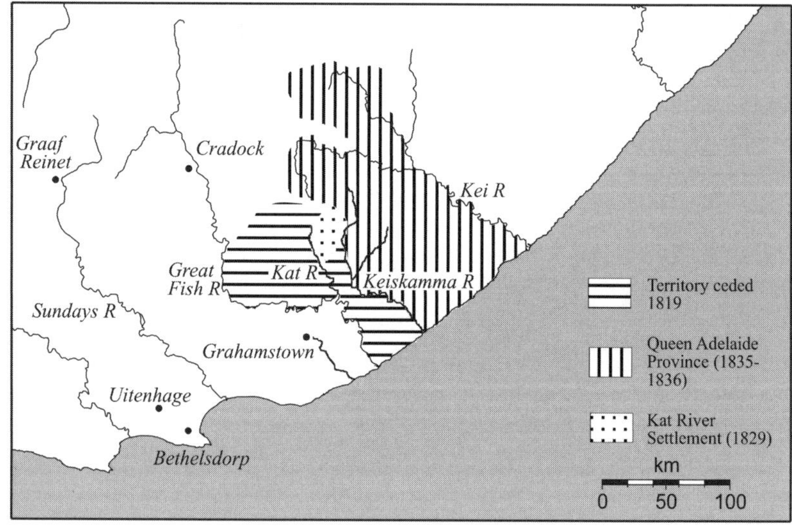

MAP 12:
The area of struggle between colonizers and Xhosa in the Eastern Cape, showing the "ceded territory" and the Queen Adelaide Province annexed in 1835.

5 The Legal View

THROUGHOUT THE ERA of European colonization, the legal questions connected with the acquisition of land belonging to other peoples attracted considerable attention. From the beginning of Spanish expansion in America, learned people discussed the right of the Crown to dispossess the Indians, and the debate was continued in the following centuries by leading European scholars engaged in developing a system of international law, as well as by jurists concerned with the implications for the domestic law of their own nation. Others perhaps less well versed in legal doctrines, such as authors writing about the new possessions and the companies often involved in running them, also expressed their views on the issues involved in this debate. Gradually, bodies of law were developed which were perceived to regulate – and justify – the acquisition of colonies and to define the rights of their original as well as their later inhabitants.

In recent years there has been a vast amount of discussion of these legal consequences of colonization; the position vis-à-vis indigenous peoples has been not the least of the subjects examined. Much of this work has been carried on with the aim of creating a body of law regarding the rights of these peoples in the postcolonial era.[1] Legal and official opinion through the centuries has

[1] Influential scholars in the field of aboriginal title at common law include Kent McNeil, *Common Law Aboriginal Title* (Oxford: Clarendon, 1989); Paul McHugh, *The Maori Magna Carta: New Zealand Law and the Treaty of Waitangi* (Auckland: Oxford UP, 1991); Geoffrey S. Lester – for example, *Inuit Territorial Rights in the Canadian Northwest Territories: A Survey of the Legal Problems* (Nunavut: Tungavik Federation, 1984); Brian Slattery – for example, *Ancestral Lands, Alien Laws: Judicial Perspectives on Aboriginal Title* (Saskatchewan: University of Saskatchewan Native Law Centre,

been used as the source material from which to develop a coherent doctrine of "aboriginal title" to be applied by the courts in litigating land rights and other cases. Although historical material is thus used and interpreted, it is most often with a view to illustrating and supporting a contemporary theory of how the law should be understood. Similarly, when the courts apply previous decisions to the case before them, their procedure is based on careful selection aimed at pronouncing the law as it is perceived to be and should not be taken as an exercise in history-writing (although the combined efforts of the courts over the centuries have resulted in the creation of legal history, accepted or disputed by later jurists).

In the present chapter, no attempt is made to present the theories of modern scholars on how indigenous rights should be applied today. The aim here is to show the historical development which the view of the law in this area underwent in the period under consideration in this study, from a discussion of influential sources such as the writings of legal authorities, legal decisions and occasionally other work. The intention is to examine the legal opinions which were current and to compare them with the official views and attitudes discussed in the previous chapter.

It should be pointed out that the documentation is so voluminous, especially since material from the sixteenth and seventeenth centuries has to be included, that exhaustive treatment cannot be attempted. Although the main focus is on understanding how the legal issues involved in the colonization of land inhabited by indigenous peoples were regarded in the eighteenth century, this is so closely connected with the developments of the previous centuries as to necessitate a discussion of this as well. Furthermore, at the end of the eighteenth century important changes took place, and in order to assess the impact of these it is also necessary to outline some nineteenth-century developments.

Several distinct issues are involved in a discussion of the legal consequences of territorial acquisition. One group of questions centres on the rights perceived to exist at the point of contact: were the inhabitants recognized by the Europeans as having rights to their land, and, if so, were they property rights in the land itself or territorial rights of sovereignty (or both); and by what right was the European nation perceived to acquire title to the land, and did it acquire sovereignty only or also rights of a proprietary nature? Distinct from this is the question of how rights to the newly discovered areas were regulated among the

---

1983); Richard H. Bartlett, *Native Title in Australia* (Chatswood, NSW: Butterworths, 2000).

competing European nations. Another group of questions is concerned with the rights the indigenous inhabitants were regarded as having after colonization of their land; were they seen as being governed by their own laws and retaining a measure of independence, or were they subjects of the new monarch, obliged to obey the laws of that nation?

These issues, however, were not dealt with in any systematic fashion by contemporary writers; often, little distinction is made between property rights and sovereignty, and frequently the rights of the inhabitants have to be inferred from general statements. This is to a certain extent reflected in the pages which follow in which authors are dealt with largely in chronological order; at the end of sections an attempt is made to summarize the main points somewhat more systematically.

To start with, an outline is provided of the dominant views on the way in which European nations vied with each other to lay claim to new territory; as this is relevant only as background to the position against indigenous inhabitants, it requires only very brief treatment.

Acquiring title to colonies against other colonizers

In the earliest phase of European expansion during the fifteenth and early sixteenth century, the Church, by virtue of the Pope's global jurisdiction, was perceived to be the body controlling international relations. Thus the Portuguese gained rights to the Canary Islands by papal bull in the early part of the fifteenth century, as Spain did to the islands found by Columbus towards the end of the century. In a later bull (the Treaty of Tordesillas), the Pope divided the newly discovered part of the world between Spain and Portugal.[2]

It is commonly agreed among scholars, however, that from the late sixteenth century onwards, as the Pope's powers began to be questioned by some nations, the acts of 'discovering' and 'taking possession of' a formerly unknown country came to be regarded by European powers as that which gave the nation performing these acts a right to that area over competitors. It appears, though, that there was considerable disagreement about what was required to take possession of a country and even to discover it. John Juricek has demonstrated

[2] Robert A. Williams, Jr., *The American Indian in Western Legal Thought* (Oxford & New York: Oxford UP, 1990): ch. 2.

that a basic distinction existed between the approach of the Iberian powers and the nations of the rest of Europe.[3]

To the Spanish and the Portuguese, the sighting of one island could give them rights to all the adjoining land, and symbolic acts of taking possession in the form of reading a proclamation, firing a volley of shots from a ship's cannons, or pinning a brass plate on a tree would be sufficient to show all the world that those making landfall now had rights to this area. As pointed out by Juricek, this way of laying claim to large areas was eminently suited to the purposes of the first explorers of the 'new' world who wanted rights to as large a share of their discoveries as possible.[4]

It is therefore also logical enough that the European nations which in the succeeding centuries joined in the quest for colonies should have found means of disputing the extensive claims of the Portuguese and especially the Spanish. They claimed that possessing an area was an integral part of discovering it, so that until this had occurred others could 'discover' it anew. Furthermore, taking possession of a territory involved not only symbolic acts but also actual occupation. In other words, the Spanish could only claim title to areas which they had actually settled.

It is interesting that as the seventeenth century progressed the English began to adopt the Spanish position: that symbolic acts of possession were enough to secure English rights to an area. In explaining this, Juricek points to the fact that as they became increasingly involved in expansion in North America, the English increasingly referred to the early voyages of John Cabot as giving them a superior title to the area as compared to the Dutch and the French, their main rivals; the Stuart monarchs' highly developed belief in the extent of their royal powers also contributed to the development.[5] Once established, however, this practice continued, as was apparent in the Pacific voyages of exploration, in which sea captains continually "took possession" of territory on behalf of their

---

[3] John Juricek, "English Territorial Claims in North America under Elizabeth and the Early Stuarts," *Terra Incognitae* 7 (1976): 7–22. See also Lester, *Inuit Territorial Rights*; Brian Slattery, "Did France Claim Canada Upon Discovery?" in *Interpreting Canada's Past*, 2 vols., ed. J.M. Bumsted (Toronto: Oxford UP, 1986), vol. 1: 2–26; F.A. Freiherr von der Heydte, "Discovery, Symbolic Annexation and Virtual Effectiveness in International Law," *American Journal of International Law* 29 (1935): 448–71.

[4] Juricek, "English Territorial Claims in North America", 10.

[5] Juricek, "English Territorial Claims," 22. See also McHugh, *The Maori Magna Carta*, 26, who sees the English charters in North America as laying claim to the territory against other Europeans but not against the Indians.

sovereign. As mentioned in preceding chapters, the British government was fully aware of the significance of this.

This issue of regulating what was perceived as the right to establish colonies against competitors should, then, be distinguished from the question of how legal title was considered to be acquired from the original possessors of the country. This issue is considered below, partly on the basis of works on international law and partly on that of British legal work. This distinction has been made because international and British law constitute separate systems, their foundations are not the same, and their development varies somewhat. Furthermore, since this study is concerned with British attitudes it was important to distinguish between British and other European developments.[6] However, the impact of international law on British law, although difficult to assess, may have been quite significant, as will become clear below.

Acquiring title against the indigenous inhabitants – before the eighteenth century

European attempts to justify the acquisition of land inhabited by other peoples were long influenced by the frame of reference established by the Christian church. Medieval notions of Christian rights against infidels still exerted considerable influence. In the Middle Ages, the Pope, by ordering their conquest and compulsory conversion, could punish any "non-believers" who violated the law of nature. The acts which entitled the Pope to call a crusade included the worship of "idols," resistance to peaceful missionary activity, and "immoral" or "barbarous" customs.[7]

When Columbus returned from his voyage to describe what he had found, the Pope's sanction was immediately sought to legitimize Spanish actions towards the Indians. In the bull issued by the Pope in 1493, the Indians were described as a people "well disposed to embrace the Christian faith" and the Spanish monarch, as the Pope's vicar, was given the right to rule and convert them. Although the Indians were thus not considered to have violated natural law, the christianizing mission remained the factor justifying the Conquest. In effect, the position held in Spain in the early sixteenth century was that the mere discovery of non-Christian territory by a Christian nation was sufficient

---

[6] For this reason, Alberico Gentili is discussed together with other scholars writing in Britain, rather than in the section on international law.

[7] Williams, *The American Indian in Western Legal Thought*, ch. 1.

grounds for the Pope to issue authorization for wholesale conquest of that territory and its people.

Although the Spanish conquest of America soon became the subject of heated controversy when the Dominicans (not least the renowned friar Bartolomé de Las Casas) attacked the way in which the indigenous inhabitants were treated, the Spanish monarchs continued to maintain that they acted according to Divine Will. The famous *Requerimiento*, a proclamation composed in 1513 by the court jurist, Juan López de Palacios Rubios, exemplified the current legal opinion. Based on the doctrine that the Pope was in charge of the entire world, it served notice on the Indians that they were 'required' to submit to his rule through his intermediary, the kings of Castile, and to listen to the preaching of the gospel. If they refused, they would be compelled to submit on pain of war, enslavement, and confiscation of wives and goods.[8] The document had to be read aloud to the Indians by a notary and through an interpreter before the beginning of battle and was perceived to safeguard the Spanish against any accusations of wrongful action.

However, in the following decades the underlying assumptions of this point of view began to be questioned. One of the best-known of the Spanish scholars to consider these issues was Francisco de Vitoria, a Dominican professor of theology at the University of Salamanca. In 1532 he gave a lecture on the rights of Spain to the "Indies," published for the first time in 1557 from students' notes. Vitoria began by considering the rights of the Indians; disposing of possible objections to their capacity as owners of property (that they were "sinners or were unbelievers or were witless or irrational),"[9] Vitoria concluded that

> the aborigines undoubtedly had true dominion in both public and private matter, just like Christians, and that neither their princes nor private persons could be despoiled of their property on the ground of their not being true owners.[10]

In rejecting the view that the Indians were of "unsound mind," Vitoria stated that they "have, according to their kind, the use of reason." Evidence for this was found in the fact that they had a system of government, trade and social

---

[8] Williams, *The American Indian in Western Legal Thought*, 88–93.

[9] Francisco de Victoria, *De Indis et de Iure Belli Relectiones, being part of Relectiones Theologiae*, tr. John Pauley Bate, ed. Herbert Francis Wright, intro. Ernest Nys (1696; Washington DC: Carnegie Institute, 1917): 120.

[10] Victoria, *De Indis et de Iure Belli*, 128.

organization and "a kind of religion."[11] Vitoria, however, did not idealize the Indians, as appears from his concluding remark: "I for the most part attribute their seeming so unintelligent and stupid to a bad and barbarous upbringing," a trait which, according to Vitoria, they had in common with ordinary Spanish peasants.[12]

Having established the proprietary rights of the Indians, Vitoria proceeded to discuss the possible titles under which the Spanish could claim to hold the land of the Indians. He distinguished between "legitimate" and "illegitimate" claims to title; among the latter Vitoria counted the propositions that Christians as a group, under the authority of the Roman Emperor, or that of the Pope automatically had divinely ordained rights to wage war on and subdue the Indians. Vitoria did not believe that the Pope had temporal or spiritual power over them.[13] Nor did he believe that mere discovery gave any rights to their land:

> Not much need be said about this third title of ours, because, as proved above, the barbarians were true owners, both from the public and from the private standpoint. Now the rule of the law of nations is that what belongs to nobody is granted to the first occupant [...] as the object in question was not without an owner, it does not fall under the title which we are discussing [...] by itself it gives no support to a seizure of the aborigines any more than if it had been they who had discovered us.[14]

In what was clearly a radical re-interpretation of the powers and rights of Christians, Vitoria thus discarded some of the most common justifications for the conquest of the American Indians. As a consequence, he also rejected the underlying notions of the right to impose Christianity on non-Christians; the true faith could not be forced on others. Even if the Indians rejected it after it had been sincerely demonstrated to them by argument and example (which Vitoria did not believe had happened in America), it would still not be right to make war against them.[15] Finally, Vitoria denied the right of Christians to punish the Indians for transgressing the laws of nature by cannibalism or

---

[11] Victoria, *De Indis et de Jure Belli*, 127.

[12] *De Indis et de Jure Belli*, 127.

[13] "Christians have no just cause of war against them either on the ground that the Pope has made a gift of their lands on the footing of absolute lord or that they do not recognize the lordship of the Pope"; *De Indis et de Jure Belli*, 138.

[14] *De Indis et de Jure Belli*, 139.

[15] *De Indis et de Jure Belli*, 139–45.

incestuous behaviour, basically because the Pope had no jurisdiction over the Indians.[16]

While Vitoria refused to recognize the divinely inspired causes of conquest, he accepted that there might be other reasons for such an action. He considered that the relationship between peoples was governed by rules laid down by natural law; if a people suffered a wrong according to these rules, it would constitute a legitimate cause for war. Vitoria believed that by the law of "natural society and fellowship" the Spanish had a right (provided they behaved peacefully and did no harm) to travel among the Indians, to trade with them or to share things with them which did not belong to anybody; if they were prevented from doing so and no peaceful means could change the situation, war would be lawful. The same would be the case if the Indians prohibited the preaching of the gospel or if they persecuted converts.[17]

Beyond this, Vitoria found that if the rulers or the laws of the country were such that "they work wrong to innocent folk there" (as in the case of rules of human sacrifice) it would be the duty of the Spaniards to intervene and rescue the people (even if they did not want to be rescued).[18] Vitoria also mentioned the possibility (though, as he said, "I dare not affirm it at all, nor do I entirely condemn it") that if the Indians could be shown to be incapable of taking care of their own affairs it would be right for the Spanish to take over for the good of the Indians.[19]

Vitoria's discussion of the rights of Spain to land in America was remarkable for its time; his rejection of much of the theological basis for the Spanish title pointed towards the future separation of theological and secular law, as did his emphasis on the law of nations as regulating relations between different peoples. Although some were opposed to his views and his discussion incurred the wrath of the Spanish king, he acquired a considerable following among Spanish theologians and jurists who came to form the so-called Salamanca School.[20]

Robert Williams repeatedly emphasizes the point that the legitimate reasons for war suggested by Vitoria were based on notions of a law of nations that

---

[16] Victoria, *De Indis et de Jure Belli*, 145–48.

[17] *De Indis et de Jure Belli*, 151–58.

[18] *De Indis et de Jure Belli*, 159.

[19] *De Indis et de Jure Belli*, 161.

[20] Cf Anthony Robin Pagden, *The Fall of Natural Man: The American Indian and the Origins of Comparative Ethnology* (Cambridge: Cambridge UP,1986): 60, 106.

were entirely eurocentric. The rights and duties flowing from it were all discovered in European, Christian culture and given universal application; since this was naturally inappropriate, the effect was that it provided an alternative justification for Spanish colonization. Similarly, by considering the possibility that the Indians' inability to rule themselves might necessitate Spanish intervention, Vitoria inaugurated the European doctrine of guardianship over indigenous peoples.[21]

While all this is clearly true (and remains so for much later work on international law), Vitoria's innovative and moderating role in the debate about Spanish rights to conquest of other peoples should not be completely overshadowed by this insight. In his conclusion, Vitoria gave a significant indication of the implications of his theories; if on examination it were found that there was indeed no just cause for subduing the Indians (which, as it appears throughout the work, he did not think there was), this would not mean giving up all relations with – and profit from – America; trade, import duties and the well-being of converts would ensure continued connections with the area.[22] Obviously, Vitoria was opposed to the practices of his countrymen abroad and wished through his university lectures to try to influence developments in a direction more conducive to Indian rights and peaceful coexistence.[23]

Vitoria's lectures on the Indies were issued in several editions from various places in Europe during the sixteenth century and his thoughts had an immense influence on later writers dealing with related subjects.[24]

Thus Hugo Grotius, the Dutchman whose work *De Jure Belli ac Pacis* (1625) has been described as the first systematic account of the law of nations, referred to Vitoria several times when discussing similar issues. Grotius removed his theories even further than Vitoria from a papal basis towards a conception of natural law which, although laid down by God, was discoverable by human reason (though still drawing mainly on the Bible for evidence of this).[25]

---

[21] Williams, *The American Indian in Western Legal Thought*, 96–108.

[22] Victoria, *De Indis et de Jure Belli*, 161–62.

[23] See Pagden, *The Fall of Natural Man*, 6, who points out that the *relectio*, of which Vitoria's on the Indies was an example, was a special occasion at the end of the year, well attended by both students and professors.

[24] See Williams, *The American Indian in Western Legal Thought*, 169, and Ernest Nys in the introduction to Victoria, *De Indis et de Jure Belli*, 96–100.

[25] Joseph Gabriel Starke, *An Introduction to International Law* (1947; London: Butterworths, 1963): 20.

Although Grotius's work is not as narrowly focused, as were Vitoria's theories, on the rights of indigenous peoples or on the possibility of acquiring title to their land, it is nevertheless possible to find statements in his work which have a bearing on these issue.

Under the heading of unjust causes of war, Grotius disposed of a number of justifications commonly put forward for acquiring land in America. Thus he considered the claim of the Christian church to have jurisdiction over the whole world as false, and wars based on this claim as unjust,[26] though he did believe that if a people violated the law of nature by, for example, eating human beings or through piracy they could be punished by war.[27] Other commandments of God which were less self-evident would not justify such action; thus those who "erred" against the laws of God by worshipping natural or animalistic objects or the like were not to be persecuted. Nor could such people be forced to accept Christianity. On the other hand, if they persecuted converts they could be justly attacked.[28]

Grotius also rejected the notion that people could be conquered on the ground that it would be for their benefit ("Not less iniquitous is it to desire by arms to subdue other men, as if they deserved to be enslaved, and were such as the philosophers at times call slaves by nature").[29] Most significantly in the present context, Grotius refused to consider discovery of land inhabited by indigenous peoples as a justifiable reason for subjection:

> Equally shameless is it to claim for oneself by right of discovery what is held by another, even though the occupant may be wicked, may hold wrong views about God, or may be dull of wit. For discovery applies to those things which belong to no one.[30]

His reference to Vitoria as authority for this statement would seem to prove that Grotius regarded this as applying to the situation of the American Indians. His recognition of the territorial rights of indigenous peoples is further streng-

---

[26] Hugo Grotius, *De Jure Belli ac Pacis Libri Tres, in quibus Jus Naturae & Gentium, item Juris Publici praecipua explicantur : Editio Nova cum Annotatis Auctoris, ex postrema ejus ante Obitum cura multo nunc Auctior* 2 vols., tr. Francis W. Kelsey, ed. & intro. James Scott Brown, (1646; Washington DC: Carnegie Institute & Oxford: Clarendon & London: Humphrey Milford, 1913–1925), vol. 2, book 2: 553.

[27] Grotius, *De Jure Belli ac Pacis*, vol. 2, book 2, 505–506.

[28] *De Jure Belli ac Pacis*, vol. 2, book 2, 515–17.

[29] *De Jure Belli ac Pacis*, vol. 2, book 2, 551.

[30] *De Jure Belli ac Pacis*, vol. 2, book 2, 550.

thened by his comment that "for the exercise of ownership neither moral nor religious virtue, nor intellectual excellence, is a requirement."[31]

In another passage, however, Grotius seems to take a different view:

> Again, if within the territory of a people there is any deserted and unproductive soil, this also ought to be granted to foreigners if they ask for it. Or it is right for foreigners even to take possession of such ground, for the reason that uncultivated land ought not to be considered as occupied except in respect to sovereignty, which remains unimpaired in favour of the original people.[32]

It should be pointed out, though, that the passage occurs in a section dealing with the rights of foreigners in need, rather than in the context of just causes for war; thus the paragraph before it is concerned with the right to take up residence in another country if one has been driven out of one's home. The statement that sovereignty remained with the original inhabitants also shows that Grotius was not referring to the acquisition of colonies.

The German jurist Samuel Pufendorf made further revisions in the perception of the rights of European nations to make war against the American Indians. In his massive work *De Jure Naturae et Gentium* (1672), he maintained that it could not be held to be a general right, granted by the law of nations, that strangers had a right to visit another country regardless of the numbers in which they arrived or of the intention of such a visit; thus he rejected Vitoria's first cause for just war against the Indians (with specific reference to the Spanish scholar).[33] He likewise rejected Vitoria's claim that it was lawful for the Spanish to make war against the Indians if they refused to trade with them ("if I am satisfied with my own products, on what grounds can any one force upon me, against my will, those of another people").[34]

Pufendorf also stated that even if the Indians violated the law of nature, they could only be attacked if by doing so they actually hurt innocent foreigners; considering very carefully all aspects of the issue, he stated that he did not agree that

---

[31] Grotius, *De Jure Belli ac Pacis*, vol. 2, book 2, 550.

[32] *De Jure Belli ac Pacis*, vol. 2, book 2, 202.

[33] *De Jure Belli ac Pacis*, vol. 2, book 2, 364–65.

[34] Samuel von Pufendorf, *De Jure Naturae et Gentium Libri Octo*, 2 vols., tr. Charles Henry & William Abbott Oldfather, ed. James Scott Brown, intro. Walter Simons (1688; tr. 1710 & 1717 [Basil Kennett]; Oxford: Clarendon & London: Humphrey Milford, 1934), vol. 2: 370.

> sufficient cause for waging war upon the Americans can be found in the fact that they can be held condemned by the very law of nature, because it is their custom to sacrifice men and eat human flesh. On this matter we should carefully consider whether a Christian prince can attack the Indians, as men condemned by nature, merely because they eat human flesh like any other food, or because they eat the flesh of men of their own religion, or because they eat that of strangers. And in connexion with their treatment of strangers we must again inquire, whether those foreigners come to their shores as enemies and robbers, or come as innocent guests, or driven by storms. For only in the last case does a right of war lie with those whose citizens are treated with such cruelty, not in the others.[35]

In this painstaking fashion, Pufendorf further consolidated the idea that a nation had a just cause for war only if it had received an injury; punishment for disobeying the law of nature did not constitute a sufficient reason for conquest.

Thus it will be seen that some of the most prominent writers on international law in the sixteenth and seventeenth centuries gradually left the theologically based justifications for conquest of indigenous peoples behind and increasingly turned to a concept of natural law as governing relations between nations. Similarly, notions were rejected that the mere discovery of a country inhabited by hunters and gatherers or other peoples would be sufficient justification for the subjection of the inhabitants. Insofar as there were a just reason for colonizing such land, it would always be based on conquest, justified by a transgression of the law of nations whereby citizens of the "visiting" nation had been seriously wronged. Perceptions of what constituted such "wrongs" have narrowed considerably in the course of the two centuries.

English opinion before the eighteenth century

There is no doubt that the common European heritage of theological assumptions at the beginning of European expansion also exerted its influence in England in spite of the separation from the Church of Rome. The idea that land inhabited by non-Christians could be conquered by any Christian nation is clearly illustrated in the early charters. Thus, in 1584 Walter Raleigh was authorized to go to "remote heathen and barbarous landes Contries and territories not actually possessed by any Christian Prynce and inhabited by Christian people" and to "have holde occupy and enjoye [whatever by] discovery

---

[35] Pufendorf, *De Jure Naturae et Gentium*, vol. 2, 1297.

subduing and possessing shall be there gotten or obteyned."[36] Wilcomb Washburn calls this kind of charter "speculative" because any actual rights to the land depended on whether the grantee would be able to "subdue" the inhabitants; the charter itself did not grant anything except the right to make the attempt.[37]

The justification for these attempts to make settlements in non-Christian countries was the conversion of the inhabitants to Christianity; as the Pope's authority to grant rights to the whole world was denied by the English, it was only logical that the monarch would assume the power to commission the conversion of the "heathen." In the first charter to the Virginia Company, issued by James I in 1606, the king acknowledged the Company's desire for

> the propagating of Christian Religion to such People, as yet live in Darkness and miserable Ignorance of the true Knowledge and Worship of God, and [which] may in time bring the Infidels and Savages, living in those Parts, to human Civility, and to a settled and quiet Government.[38]

The idea that the inhabitants might even welcome conversion and foreign rule, which was also suggested in the papal bull granting the Caribbean to the Spanish, is elaborated in a charter from 1613 to Robert Harcourt, permitted by James I to attempt the conquest of Guiana. On a previous visit, Harcourt was said to have found

> the naturall people and inhabitants thereof very tractable and desirous of some civil governors, magistrates and government that might direct and instruct them

The king further speculated that

> finding upon deliberate consideration of the premises that we are tied and bound by our duty to Almighty God and our Regal Office to procure and endeavour the in Largement of the territories of the Christian Church in all partes of the World, and well knowing that the said countreys lyeing waste and being savage so that by the law of nature and nations we may by our Regall authority possess ourselves and make grants thereof without doing

[36] Quoted in Juricek, "English Territorial Claims in North America," 12.

[37] Wilcomb Edward Washburn, *Red Man's Land/ White Man's Law* (Norman: Oklahoma UP, 1995): 30.

[38] Quoted in Williams, *The American Indian in Western Legal Thought*, 201.

> wrong to any other prince or state considering it is not actually possessed by any Christian prince[39]

and he therefore proceeded to grant rights to the territory. Geoffrey Lester has seen the description of territory as "lyeing waste and being savage" as an indication that indigenous peoples were regarded as being "beyond the pale of civil law" and that their land was there for the taking.[40] Lester sees this grant as an early example of the later dominant equation of indigenous land with uninhabited land. Although the idea of land lying waste even if inhabited does point forward to later views, this statement and the omission of any reference to conquest of the inhabitants may not mean very much in this case. Since it was claimed that the inhabitants desired British government, it would not only have been difficult to claim the country by conquest, it would also have been unnecessary, while the passage in general clearly shows the same assumptions about the rights of Christians to acquire non-Christian land as the other early charters.

The famous judgement in Calvin's Case by the Lord Chief Justice, Edward Coke, in 1608 provides strong evidence of the currency of the doctrine of conquest. In this case, which had nothing to do with overseas possessions or indigenous peoples, the court was nevertheless led to consider the position of "aliens" under English law. A distinction was made between aliens who were friends, and those who were enemies, the latter being divided in turn into temporary and perpetual enemies. Of the latter Coke then said:

> But a perpetual enemy (though there be no wars by fire and sword between them) cannot maintain any action, or get any thing within this realm. All infidels are in law [...] perpetual enemies (for the law presumes not that they will be converted, that being [...] a remote possibility) for between them, as with the devils, whose subjects they be, and the Christian, there is perpetual hostility, and can be no peace.

and a little later:

> if a Christian King should conquer a kingdom of an infidel and bring them under his subjection, there *ipso facto* the laws of the infidel are abrogated, for

---

[39] Quoted in Geoffrey S. Lester, "Primitivism versus Civilization: A Basic Question in the Law of Aboriginal Rights to Land," in *Our Footprints are Everywhere*, ed. Carol Brice–Bennett (Nain: Labrador Inuit Association, 1977): 358.

[40] Lester, "Primitivism versus Civilization," 358.

> that they be not only against Christianity, but against the law of God and of nature.[41]

According to this exposition of the law, the English were always at war with all non-Christians, and as such the judgement shows that at this time the prevailing view must have been that title against indigenous inhabitants was acquired by conquest.

This conclusion is also supported by the fact, pointed out by some legal scholars, that in English law during this period all titles to land were derivative and that consequently there were only two ways of acquiring territory: through conquest (or cession), or through inheritance.[42] The notion that Christians had a right to conquer these peoples was a denigration of their standing as independent nations, based on eurocentric assumptions about the significance of Christianity. This is also exemplified with abundant clarity by Coke's statement that as a matter of course the laws of conquered infidels ceased to exist when the English took over. Nevertheless, the idea of conquest rests on an implicit recognition of the territorial rights of the indigenous people (otherwise there would be no need for conquest) and is therefore evidence that the indigenous people were regarded as possessing their land.

Coke's extreme views were not universally followed in Britain during this early period of expansion.[43] Another treatment of the rules governing war with other peoples, in *De Iure Belli* (1589) by the Oxford professor Alberico Gentili, shows a somewhat more moderate attitude, influenced by the same concepts of natural law as were noted in connection with the Continental theorists.

Gentili maintained that lack of faith in Christianity did not provide a just cause of war; no-one should be persuaded by force to accept any religion. He cited Vitoria (and other Spaniards) as authority for the view that "religion was not a just reason for the war of his Spanish countrymen against the Indians."[44]

---

[41] Calvin's Case, 1608. Coke's Reports, part 7, 1A in *English Law Reports* 77 (1907): 377–411.

[42] Lester, *Inuit Territorial Rights*, 16; Geoffrey S. Lester & Graham Parker, "Land Rights, the Australian Aborigines have lost a Legal Battle, but …," *Alberta Law Review* 11 (1973): 197; McNeil, *Common Law Aboriginal Title*, 112–13. Grotius' acceptance of the possibility of original title to uninhabited land is based on the Roman civil law prevalent in continental Europe.

[43] Cf McHugh, *The Maori Magna Carta*, 88.

[44] Alberico Gentili, *De Iure Belli Libri Tres* 2 vols., tr. John C. Rolfe, ed. James Scott Brown, intro. Coleman Philipson (1612; Oxford: Clarendon & London: Humphrey Milford, 1933), vol. 2: 39.

He did not accept that the Spanish were justified in waging war because the Indians refused to listen to their preaching, for, as Gentili put it, "this is only a pretext of religion."[45] The Indians could only be converted through peaceful means and by their own will. Gentili did admit that if a people were to be found who had no religion whatsoever, it would be lawful to make war against them, because they would be violating the law of nature. However, he immediately deflated this point by stating that he did not believe such a people existed anywhere.[46] Gentili, finally, also considered the view that non-Christians could be regarded as not having "realms of their own because of their heresy and infidelity, since a heretic and an infidel has no true jurisdiction" but rejected this with great firmness: "this argument is utterly inane; for it is God who confers jurisdiction upon them."[47]

In other sections, Gentili accepted several alternative reasons for just war. Among them were violation of such "natural rights" as that of passing through someone's country and of trading with other people. Thus he commented:

> And that is one reason why the warfare of the Spaniards in that part of the world seems to be justified, because the inhabitants prohibited other men from commerce with them

but he immediately continued (with a – for the times – suitable bias against the Spanish):

> it would be an adequate defence, if the statement were true [...] But the Spaniards were aiming there, not at commerce, but at dominion. And they regarded it as beyond dispute that it was lawful to take possession of those lands which were not previously known to us; just as if to be known to none of us were the same thing as to be possessed by no one.[48]

However, Gentili recognized that the Indians might have broken other "laws of nature" and thereby justified their own conquest by the Spanish:

> I approve the more decidedly of the opinion of those who say that the cause of the Spaniards is just when they make war upon the Indians, who practised

---

[45] Gentili, *De Iure Belli*, 123.

[46] *De Iure Belli*, 41.

[47] *De Iure Belli*, 39.

[48] *De Iure Belli*, 89.

> abominable lewdness even with beasts, and who ate human flesh, slaying men for that purpose. For such sins are contrary to human nature.[49]

If "idolatry is joined with the slaughter of innocent victims" this would also be a violation of natural law and would call for punishment in the form of war.[50]

Gentili thus rejected the notion that non-Christians may be subdued as of right by Christians, simply because of religious difference, thereby representing a different view of the law from that of Coke, one which was eventually to become dominant as the law grew increasingly divorced from its theological roots.

In line with other writers on international law at the time, he accepted that interaction between nations was determined by certain laws of nature, which were regarded as universal and which the Indians were therefore expected to obey. There is, however, no doubt that even if this created new openings for acquiring Indian land, this remained a matter of conquest of peoples who were regarded as possessing their land. Gentili's statements reveal that he did not regard America as ownerless.

In another context, Gentili referred to "unoccupied land" and noted that "those who take it have a right to it, since it is the property of no one." This extended even to land under the sovereignty of some ruler, because it was against the law of nature that land should lie waste. However, he emphasized that "lands which are not vacant ought not to be taken";[51] there is no indication that he regarded the lands of the Indians as vacant.

Gentili's work contributed to the development of the law of nations (Grotius's debt to him is evident) and to the introduction of this line of legal thinking in England. Although Gentili's point of departure was thus different from that of Coke, who developed his theory within the framework of English common law, the work of both may still be taken as indications of the historical development of legal thought in Britain on the issues dealt with here.[52] Their work shows that legal opinion in Britain was influenced by both the old theologically inspired doctrine of Christian rights to dominate the world and by the developing law of nations (based on natural law), the latter gradually becoming the dominant element in the debate.

---

[49] Gentili, *De Iure Belli*, 122.

[50] *De Iure Belli*, 123.

[51] *De Iure Belli*, 80–81.

[52] McHugh, *The Maori Magna Carta*, 71, briefly discusses the distinction between the two systems of law.

In the course of the century, the question of the rights of the English (and the Indians) to the land in North America was brought up in many connections. The colonial companies were at times forced to consider matters related to the issue, essays were written and sermons preached which touched on it, and the colonial governments were constantly faced with problems arising from the matter.

The Virginia Company, which may be taken from this wealth of material as a good example, vigorously upheld the belief that full sovereignty over the area rested with the Company, no doubt as a consequence of the charter which they had received from the King. It is possible that the Company perceived the charter itself to be an "act of conquest."[53] In any case, they strongly opposed any suggestion that the Indians retained rights of this kind. This is illustrated by Barkham's Case (1622), in which Barkham had been granted land by the governor in Virginia on condition that the grant was accepted by Opechancanough, the Indian chief succeeding Powhatan. The Company objected to this:

> this Graunt of Barkhams was held to be verie dishonourable and prejudicall to the Companie in reguard it was lymitted with a Proviso to compound with Opachankano, whereby a Soveraignty in that heathen Infidell was acknowledged, and the Companies Title thereby much infringed.[54]

Yet there are suggestions that at least in the early years of the colony the Company was somewhat less outspoken about their absolute rights to the area. Before the first settlers left for Virginia, it had been suggested that a justification for the venture should be circulated to oppose false accusations from opponents; recognizing that this would involve not only countering the claim of the Spanish but also the rights of the Indians (a "disputation of [...] much intricacy, perplexity, and replication"), a majority of the council decided to avoid this "vnnessisary way of prouication" and "reserue ourselues to ye defensiue part, when they shall offer anything agaynst vs,"[55] words which do not indicate a great deal of self-assurance. Robert Williams suggests that the judgment in Calvin's Case, which was made only a few years later, was "intended

---

[53] Lester, *Inuit Territorial Rights*, 19, 27, maintains that in the course of the seventeenth century the charters came to be seen this way.

[54] W. Stitt Robinson, ed. *Early American Documents, Treaties and Laws, 1607–1789*, vol. 4: *Virginia Treaties 1607–1722*, general editor Alden T. Vaughan (Washington DC: UP of America, 1983): 28.

[55] Susan Myra Kingsbury, ed. *The Records of the Virginia Company of London* (Washington DC: Government Printing Office, 1906–1933), vol. 3: 2–3.

as the written legal justification" for the Company's activities in America that the Company had thus declined to give themselves.[56]

Similarly, the peculiar ceremony conducted in Virginia, commonly referred to as the "crowning of Powhatan," was ordered by the Company and used in London as legitimizing propaganda. Powhatan had been induced to allow a crown to be placed on his head, ostensibly as a token of submission to the English King, though the meaning of the ceremony must have been at least ambiguous to those participating in it. It was then claimed that Powhatan had received "voluntarily a crown and a sceptre, with full acknowledgement of duty and submission" and had "licensed us to negociate among them, and to possess their country with them."[57] This does seem to indicate a recognition of Indian title to the land and of the need to make mutually satisfactory arrangement with the Indians for transfer of land in order for the English to gain a title to Virginia.

In any case, existing doubts about the legality of the settlement were put to rest after 1622 when the large-scale attack by the Indians was returned by the setters in what was seen as a just war. In their orders for taking revenge, the Company advised that "as they [the Indians] have merited let them have a perpetuall warre without peace or truce."[58] In the Company's account of the event it was noted that the settlers "may now by right of Warre, and law of Nations, invade the Country" and any Indian survivors could be regarded as truly conquered.[59]

This "discourse of conquest," as Williams terms it,[60] was supplemented by other means of providing the English with a just title to America. A great variety of alternatives were offered in the course of the century; Samuel Purchas provides a good example of this in his essay "Virginias Verger," in which he listed all the justifications for the English settlement in Virginia that he could think of. He echoes the writer from the Virginia Company, quoted above, in his reflections on the question of just war; by attacking the English, the Indians had violated the law of nations and "disloyall treason hath now confiscated whatsoever remainders of right the unnaturall Naturalls had, and made both them

---

[56] Quoted in Williams, *The American Indian in Western Legal Thought*, 204.

[57] Williams, *The American Indian in Western Legal Thought*, 208.

[58] Stitt Robinson, *Virginia Treaties 1607–1722*, 43.

[59] *Virginia Treaties 1607–1722*, 37.

[60] Williams, *The American Indian in Western Legal Thought*, e.g., 6–7.

and their Country wholly English."[61] To Purchas, conquest finally sealed English title to the land, otherwise gained by "first discovery, actuall possession, chargeable continuation, long prescription, voluntary subjection, delivery of seisin, naturall inheritance of English there borne, reall sale, legall cession, regall vassallage."

However, the entitlement to America was based first and last on God's commands. Having started his essay with a long account of man's relation to God which led him to conclude "that Christians have and hold the world and the tings thereof in another tenure, whereof Hypocrites and Heathens are not capable," he then stated:

> we have a naturall right to replenish the whole earth: so that if any Countrey be not possessed by other men, (which is the case of Summer Ilands, and hath been of all Countries in their first habitations) every man by Law of Nature and Humanities hath right of Plantation and may not by other after-commers be dispossessed, without wrong to human nature. And if a country be inhabited in some parts thereof, other parts remaining unpeopled, the same reason giveth liberty to other men which want convenient habitation to seat themselves, where (without wrong to others) they may provide for themselves.[62]

God's command to people the earth justified the acquisition of those parts which were uninhabited or less densely inhabited than Europe. It is interesting, however, that the two categories were seen as separate; Purchas did not consider Virginia to be uninhabited, and the Indians had a title to the land they used by the law of nature and through God's generosity,[63] though later he described them as "more brutish then the beasts they hunt, more wild and unmanly then that unmanned wild Country, which they range rather then inhabite."[64]

The divine origin of Purchas's last justification is even clearer: "Loe here the scope of Christians Plantations to plant Christianity, to produce and multiply Christians, by our words and works to further the knowledge of God in his Word and Workes."[65] The command to convert the heathen was the final and

[61] Samuel Purchas, *Hakluytus Posthumus or Purchas His Pilgrimes, Contayning a History of the World in Sea Voyages and Lande Travells by Englishmen and others* (1625; New York: AMS, 1965), vol. 19: 224, 229.

[62] Purchas, *Hakluytus Posthumus*, vol. 19, 222.

[63] *Hakluytus Posthumus*, vol. 19, 219.

[64] *Hakluytus Posthumus*, vol. 19, 231.

[65] *Hakluytus Posthumus*, vol. 19, 230.

strongest claim the English could invoke to demonstrate their right to settle among the Indians.

Purchas's essay illustrates the diversity of arguments that were employed to explain the lawfulness of the English colonizing venture. The crusading spirit of perpetual war against the infidel was not so strong here, but the basic justifications were still perceived to stem from God. This was also apparent in the works of many other writers throughout the century.[66]

One of the most extended and systematic examples of this is perhaps found in *Two Treatises on Government*, written by John Locke around 1680.[67] Locke was involved to a considerable extent with the colonies during his lifetime, investing in the slave trade and in the company developing the Bahamas, advising the proprietors of Carolina, and as secretary to the Council of Trade and Plantations in 1673–74 and then as Commissioner of the Board of Trade in 1696–1700.[68] It may be presumed, therefore, that his use of the American Indian in his discussion of the origins of property was based on thoughts formed over some time. Taking his point of departure in the words of God, he said:

> God, who hath given the World to Men in common, hath also given them reason to make use of it to the best advantage of Life, and convenience.[69]

What the "best advantage" amounts to is clarified a little later:

> God, when he gave the World in common to all mankind, commanded Man also to labour [...] God and his Reason Commanded him to subdue the Earth, *i.e.* improve it for the benefit of Life [...] He that in Obedience to this Command of God, subdued, tilled and sowed any part of it thereby annexed to it something that was his *Property*.[70]

---

[66] See Harry Culverwell Porter, *The Inconstant Savage: England and the North American Indian 1500–1660* (London: Duckworth, 1979): esp. ch. 17 and 18; Williams, *The American Indian in Western Legal Thought*, ch. 4 and 5; Lester, "Primitivism versus Civilization," 356–57; Robert F. Berkhofer, Jr., *The White Man's Indian: Images of the American Indian from Columbus to the Present* (New York: Alfred A. Knopf, 1978): 115–26.

[67] John Locke, *Two Treatises on Government*, ed. Peter Laslett (1690; Cambridge: Cambridge UP, 1970): intro., ch. 3.

[68] Wayne Glausser, "Three Approaches to Locke and the Slave Trade" in *Race, Gender and Rank: Early Modern Ideas of Humanity*, ed. Maryanne Cline Horowitz (Rochester NY: U of Rochester P, 1992): 32–36.

[69] Locke, *Two Treatises on Government*, 304.

[70] *Two Treatises on Government*, 309.

Divine decree had thus laid down that agriculture was the ultimate way of using the earth;[71] as Locke believed that property arose as a consequence of applying ones labour to something, it followed that the land one cultivated became one's private property (and one did not need the consent of one's fellow beings to acquire it). This principle also applied to the American Indian:

> The Fruit, or Venison, which nourishes the wild Indian, who knows no Inclosure, and is still a Tenant in common, must be his.[72]

The property of the Indian in the results of his labour, defined as hunting and gathering, were recognized, but because no individual by applying his labour to the land had "inclosed it from the common" it had not yet become the property of anyone. Conveniently ignoring Indian cultivation of the land, Indian ownership of the land was denied because it was held in common, not being subject to private property, the only form of property which was recognized by Locke.

Although it was not the primary purpose of his work, Locke thus provided a – divinely inspired – rationale for settling in America which was not (necessarily) based on conquest but, rather, on the notion that the original inhabitants did not own the land. Based as it was on insufficient knowledge (and misrepresentation) of the way of life of the Indians, it could also easily be combined with the common belief that the Indians had more land than they could make use of (as noted in the passage from Purchas quoted above), making colonization entirely justifiable. Locke was himself implying as much when he said "he that leaves as much as another can make use of, does as good as take nothing at all," and later, even more clearly:

> let him plant in some in-land, vacant places of *America*, we shall find that the *Possessions* he could make himself upon the *measures* we have given, would not be very large, nor, even to this day, prejudice the rest of Mankind, or give them reason to complain.[73]

---

[71] This was further stressed later on when Locke, enlarging on the value of labour, said: "There cannot be a be a clearer demonstration of any thing, than several Nations of the Americans are of this, who are rich in Land and poor in all the Comforts of Life [...] for want of improving it [the land] by labour, have not one hundredth part of the Conveniences we enjoy" (*Two Treatises on Government*, 314–15).

[72] Locke, *Two Treatises on Government*, 305.

[73] *Two Treatises on Government*, 311.

In the interpretation of Locke's theory of property by Herman Lebovics, Locke's use of America is further extended to become one of his fundamental premisses. Lebovics suggests that Locke saw the large areas of "waste" land in America as the means whereby the great non-propertied classes in England could acquire property and thereby participation in the political life of the nation.[74] This interpretation adds further significance to Locke's statements on the Indians and their perceived lack of property and points to the impact which the 'new world' was to have in attempts to understand the workings of the 'old' one.

Common to the theories that attempted to explain and justify the settlement of the English on Indian land was, however, the fact that they often did not accord very well with the realities which the settlers experienced. Any illusion that the land became English through some imagined conquest, as a result of Christian destiny or divine command, was shattered by Indian insistence that the land belonged to them and by their willingness to part with it only in return for favours or desired goods – or if forced by use of superior military power.

Colonial practice almost immediately adapted to this situation and the purchase of land became widespread, as did actual warfare with the Indians.[75] Gradually, the theoretical position came to reflect the reality of the colonial experience. Thus, as pointed out by L.J. Priestley, after the peace treaty between settlers and Indians in Virginia in 1646, Indians were perceived to belong to two groups: "dependent" and "foreign"; whereas the former were seen as part of the colony whose rights were defined by the treaty, the latter were perceived as "independent groups of aliens, with whom war was waged and treaties made and who were regarded as having territorial rights."[76]

The need to purchase land from the Indian tribes with whom the colonists came into contact was buttressed by orders from the companies and proprietors based in England[77] – which surely indicates a recognition of Indian possession of the land. Similarly, in a memorial from 1697 the Board of Trade referred to

---

[74] Herman Lebovics, "The Uses of America in Locke's *Second Treatise of Government*," in Horowitz, *Race, Gender and Rank*, 59.

[75] Cf Washburn, *Red Man's Land/White Man's Law*, 41–42.

[76] L.J. Priestley, "Communal Native Title and the Common Law: Further Thoughts on the Gove Land Rights Case," *Federal Law Review* 6 (1974): 156.

[77] Peter A. Cumming & Neil H. Mickenberg, ed. *Native Rights in Canada* (Toronto: Indian–Eskimo Association of Canada / General, 1972): 15–16, 67–68.

"the five Nations of Indians [...] possessing the Lands to the Westward, and North West of that Plantation [New York]."[78]

Two legal opinions written within thirty years of each other exemplify the great range of the legal view on the rights of the Indians and the entitlement of the English to their land. In an opinion from 1675 on the standing of the title of a number of settlers to land in New York, it was stated that

> Tho it hath been & still is the Usuall Practice of all Proprietors to give their Indians Some Recompence for their Land & and So Seems to Purchase it of them yet that is not done for want of Sufficient title from the King or Prince who hath the Right of Discovery but out of Prudence & Christian Charity.[79]

On the other hand, in the initial phase of the case of the Mohegan Indians v. Connecticut, Lord Northey, the attorney-general, in 1703 found that the charter of Connecticut was not "intended to dispossess the Indians who before and after the Grant were Owners and possessors of [their lands]."[80]

Thus, as Brian Slattery points out, the legal views which developed during the seventeenth century concerning title to North America and the rights of the Indians were somewhat contradictory.[81] Any attempt to reconcile the different opinions of the legal position of the Indians is probably futile; the best conclusion would be that during this and the previous century legal theorists and others concerned with these issues struggled to make sense of the novel situation created by the 'discovery' of America and its peoples.

---

[78] Memorial of the Right of the British Crown over the New-York Indians, 1697, in Edmund Baily O'Callaghan & Berthold Fernow, ed. *Documents Relative to the Colonial History of the State of New York procured in Holland, England and France by Romeyn Brodhead* (hereafter *New York Colonial Documents*) (Albany NY: Weed & Parsons, 1856–1883), vol. 5: 75.

[79] Councells Opinion concerning Coll. Nicholls pattent and Indian Purchases, 1675 in O'Callaghan & Fernow, ed. *New York Colonial Documents*, vol. 13, 487. But cf Lester's comment that this was a "partisan document," *Inuit Territorial Rights*, 18. It should be noted also that this case was concerned with a claim by certain settlers that they could buy land directly from the Indians without permission from the Crown, a position which British courts have always denied (see McNeil, *Common Law Aboriginal Title*, 221–35).

[80] Quoted in Lester, *Inuit Territorial Rights*, 28. See also Joseph Henry Smith, *Appeals to the Privy Council from the American Plantations* (New York: Columbia UP, 1950): 422–42, and James Youngblood Henderson, "Unraveling the Riddle of Aboriginal Title," *American Indian Law Review* 5 (1975): 97–99.

[81] Slattery, *Ancestral Lands, Alien Laws*, 4.

Sovereignty over the east coast was variously claimed by reference to conquest (either notional or actual) or to divine command of one sort or another; the acquisition of sovereignty was in some cases perceived to extinguish the property rights of the Indians in the land, but in most instances this did not automatically follow, perhaps supporting the suggestion made by some scholars that the rights of the Indians were recognized to an increasing extent as the century proceeded.[82] The distinction between sovereignty and ownership of the land was somewhat blurred in British perception during the seventeenth century, owing to the continuing influence in legal theory of feudal notions of lordship based on royal possession of all land. According to Lester, however, this began to change towards the end of the century. Perhaps these circumstances may to some extent explain the inconsistencies and lack of clarity.[83]

In any case, however, it is safe to conclude that in general the Indians were implicitly or explicitly recognized to have – or at least to have had – some kind of right to the land on which they lived. In other words, while the acquisition of colonies in North America by the English was in most cases justified by pointing to the superior rights of Christians as compared to other peoples, it was not based on wholesale denial of the rights of those peoples; the land was not regarded as if it was uninhabited.

It would thus seem that English law retained the crusading tradition of the Middle Ages or, at least, notions derived from it for longer than was the case in writings on the law of nations. This is perhaps not surprising; the common-law basis of English law, with its strong reliance on precedent, ensured a great deal of continuity in legal views. On the other hand, the law of nations, an emerging body, drew on new ideas among a relatively small number of legal thinkers. Still, while the idea of Christian conquest of infidels remained significant throughout the seventeenth century in England, the fact that other justifications for taking possession of Indian land were offered may indicate that changes were taking place here as well. Although these justifications still had theological foundations, ideas such as the duty to subdue the earth and cultivate the land were quite closely related to the notion that there existed certain natural laws which all had to obey. The natural law upon which international law was being based was, of course, also perceived originally to have been laid down by God.

---

[82] Lester, *Inuit Territorial Rights*, 27; McHugh, *The Maori Magna Carta*, 35.

[83] Lester, *Inuit Territorial Rights*, 27.

The eighteenth century

The law of nations continued to develop very rapidly during the eighteenth century; most noticeable is the fact that the context changed in which land inhabited by indigenous peoples was considered. Where the implicit question had formerly been whether or not a European nation could wage just war on such peoples, it now tended to become a question of use and ownership of land.

One of the continental writers on international law most frequently cited by the British (at least during the nineteenth century)[84] was the Swiss jurist Emerich de Vattel. In his *Law of Nations*, published in 1758, he discussed among other things the possession and acquisition of territory. In the section called "Occupation of a Territory by a Nation," Vattel maintained that "the earth belongs to all mankind"; however, in order to be able to feed everybody it was necessary to adopt agriculture as the mode of subsistence, and this was the origin of ownership of the land. As a group of people came together in a "civil society," they acquired sovereignty over the land they owned and inhabited. Vattel considered that it was still possible to come across uninhabited land which could then be taken possession of:

> When [...] a Nation finds a country uninhabited and without an owner, it may lawfully take possession of it, and after it has given sufficient sights of its intention in this respect, it may not be deprived of it by another Nation[85]

– though Vattel was quite firm that a nation could not attempt to lay claim to more than it could actually occupy and make use of. He continued:

> There is another celebrated question which has arisen principally in connection with the discovery of the New World. It is asked whether a Nation may lawfully occupy any part of a vast territory in which are to be found only wandering tribes whose small numbers can not populate the whole country.[86]

---

[84] See the introduction by Albert de Lapradelle to Emerich de Vattel, *The Law of Nations or the Principles of Natural Law, applied to the Conduct and to the Affairs of Nations and of Sovereigns*, 3 vols., tr. Charles G. Fenwick, ed. James Scott Brown, intro. Albert de Lapradelle (*Le Droit de Gens, ou Principes de la Loi Naturelle, appliqués a la Conduite et aux Affaires des nations et de Souverain*, 1758; tr. 1759; Washington DC: Carnegie Institute, 1916), vol. 3, though Lapradelle also notices the frequent criticism of Vattel by other jurists, including British ones. Cf Alex C. Castles, *An Introduction to Australian Legal History* (Sydney: Law Book Company, 1971): 14.

[85] Vattel, *The Law of Nations*, vol. 3, 84.

[86] *The Law of Nations*, vol. 3, 85.

As Vattel himself pointed out, he had already answered this question in an earlier section, in which he had maintained the extreme importance of agriculture to the state; in fact, it was "an obligation imposed upon man by nature" because

> The whole earth is destined to furnish sustenance for its inhabitants; but it can not do this unless it be cultivated. Every Nation is therefore bound by the natural law to cultivate the land which has fallen to its share.[87]

Not surprisingly, given this view, Vattel looked sternly upon those who did not obey this "law"; those who preferred to "live by plunder" rather than work on the land "deserve to be exterminated like wild beasts of prey." There are also those

> who, in order to avoid labor, seek to live upon their flocks and the fruits of the chase. This might well enough be done in the first age of the world when the earth produced more than enough, without cultivation, for the small number of its inhabitants. But now that the human race has multiplied so greatly, it could not subsist if every people wished to live after that fashion. Those who still pursue his idle mode of life occupy more land than they would have need of under a system of honest labor, and they may not complain if other more industrious Nations, too confined at home, should come and occupy part of their lands [....] The peoples of those vast tracts of land rather roamed over them than inhabited them.[88]

This, then, was Vattel's general view, which was made more explicit in his answer to the question posed about the New World:

> Their [the Indians'] uncertain occupancy of these vast regions can not be held as a real and lawful taking of possession; and when the Nations of Europe, which are too confined at home, come upon lands which the savages have no special need of and are making no present and continuous use of, they may lawfully take possession of them and establish colonies in them [...] we are not departing from the intentions of nature when we restrict the savages within narrower bounds[89]

In Vattel's view, hunters (and pastoralists) had more land than they needed, or would need if they cultivated it, and others might therefore settle on part of it. The command to "subdue the earth," which was used by Locke to establish the

---

[87] Vattel, *The Law of Nations*, vol. 3, 37.
[88] *The Law of Nations*, vol. 3, 38.
[89] *The Law of Nations*, vol. 3, 85.

existence of property in the land, is here explicitly developed to determine the territorial rights of a people. In Vattel's work it is turned into a legal principle that a nation can only claim as much land as it needs to subsist by agriculture and the rest may be occupied by others.

Vattel here seems to offer a complete vindication of the colonization of North America by the European nations, and he has been quoted to that effect many times. Indeed, he himself said:

> while the conquest of the civilized Empires of Peru and Mexico was a notorious usurpation, the establishment of various colonies upon the continent of North America might, if done within just limits, have been entirely lawful.[90]

However, this interpretation of Vattel needs to be modified. First and foremost, only part of the land over which the Indians "roamed" could be taken: only that which they made "no present and continuous use of" or "had no special need of" might be occupied; the Indians might be "restricted within narrower bounds" but there were "just limits" to how little land could be left for them. Thus Vattel did not regard indigenous peoples to be without rights to the land; although they could not, in his view, be regarded as possessing all of America, they clearly were entitled to part of it. In a later passage, less frequently quoted, Vattel in fact says even more than this:

> When a country is occupied by wandering families, like those of pastoral tribes, which move from place to place according to their needs, it is possessed by them in common. They hold it to the exclusion of other peoples, and they can not be justly deprived of lands of which they are making use.

Vattel realized that he was in danger of contradicting himself here, so he attempted to incorporate his earlier view:

> But let us repeat again [...] that the savage tribes of North America had no right to keep to themselves the whole of that vast continent; and provided sufficient land were left to the Indians, others might, without injustice to them, settle in certain parts of a region, the whole of which the Indians were unable to occupy.[91]

Although he did not quite escape the contradiction, these passages prove beyond doubt that Vattel did not deny Indian possession over the land which they "actually used." This is also shown by the fact that, like Purchas, he did

[90] Vattel, *The Law of Nations*, vol. 3, 38.
[91] *The Law of Nations*, vol. 3, 143.

not regard land inhabited by hunters or pastoralists as falling within the category of "uninhabited land," which, as shown above, he discussed separately. Obviously, then, Vattel envisaged a situation (far removed from reality as it was) where it would be possible for the colonists to settle on such lands as the original inhabitants (in the eyes of the Europeans) made no immediate use of. The latter would be confined to smaller areas but would not otherwise be prevented from continuing their previous way of life, and they could not be subjected by force to the rule of the colonists.[92]

In important ways, Vattel thus built on the thought of the previous century about the right of Europeans to "replenish and subdue" other parts of the world, but in a way that, however contradictory it may seem now, upheld the rights that the existing inhabitants had to their land according to the law of nature.

A contemporary of Vattel's, the German jurist Christian Wolff, however, stated the rights of the latter much more clearly and unequivocally. In his work *Jus Gentium* (1749), Wolff dealt extensively with ownership and acquisition of territory. He placed less emphasis than Vattel had on the duty to cultivate the land, and much more on the inviolability of territorial possession. He rejected the idea, accepted by Grotius, that foreigners may occupy unused land belonging to another nation (Vattel also rejects this idea).[93] In fact, the only land that could be acquired was that which was uninhabited:

> Islands arisen or discovered in the ocean, and other lands not subject to ownership and sovereignty or uninhabited by any nation can be occupied and colonies established in them.[94]

Wolff specifically dealt with land occupied by non-Europeans in the section headed "Whether territories inhabited by a nation may be occupied, because they are unknown." He first of all stated that such an occupation was not lawful; he then went on to qualify this by saying that "groups of men dwelling together

[92] "No one may lay claim to sovereignty over that country [inhabited by independent families], for this would subject those families against their will, and no man has the right to rule over persons born free unless they submit voluntarily to him"; Vattel, *The Law of Nations*, vol. 3, 143.

[93] Christian Wolf, *Jus Gentium, Methodo Scientifica Pertractatum*, 2 vols., tr. Joseph H. Drake, ed. James Scott Brown, intro. Otfried Nippold (1764; Oxford & London: Clarendon, 1934), vol. 2: 141. Vattel, *The Law of Nations*, 140. Wolff is also quoted extensively in Henry Reynolds, *Aboriginal Sovereignty: Reflections on Race, State and Nation* (St. Leonards, NSW: Allen & Unwin, 1996): 49–52.

[94] Wolff, *Jus Gentium*, vol. 2, 147–48.

in certain limits but without civil sovereignty are not nations," but offered no examples of such groups.

However, he defined the rights of "separate families dwelling together in a certain territory," distinguishing between "families" who had ownership of individual blocks of land and "families" who had not settled on any particular piece of land but "wander through uncultivated lands." In the former case, land which was the property of no-one might be acquired by the first comer; but in the second case, the whole area through which the inhabitants "wander" was owned communally by them and there were no vacant places

> if the families have no settled abode but wander through the uncultivated wilds, in that case, nevertheless, they are understood to have tacitly agreed that the lands in that territory in which they change their abodes as they please, are held in common, subject to the use of individuals, and it is not to be doubted but that it is their intention that they should not be deprived of that use by outsiders.[95]

Wolff is here breaking new ground by distinguishing between what was perceived to be the original state in which all land was in common (what he called "primitive community-holding") and the actual joint ownership of hunters and gatherers ("mixed community-holding"), which he recognizes as a form of proprietary right wholly comparable to individual ownership (private property). He goes on to discuss the possibilities of occupying such lands:

> Since lands subject to private use or to the use of individuals in that territory in which separate families wander hither and thither are subject to the mixed community-holding of those families, and consequently, since those who are not in the number of those families are excluded from the ownership which they have in those lands, those lands can be occupied by no-one coming into the territory inhabited by these families, even if at the time those who inhabit the territory are not using those lands. Ownership is not lost by non-use. And if separate families wander through uncultivated places, they intend a use of the places only in alternation, a thing which is readily evident, if only you turn your attention to the reason which impels them to wander through uncultivated places.[96]

Having thus laid down what appears to be the complete inviolability of tribal communal ownership, Wolff then finally rejected the last means of acquiring the lands possessed by indigenous peoples:

---

[95] Wolff, *Jus Gentium*, vol. 2, 158.

[96] *Jus Gentium*, vol. 2, 159.

> By nature all men are free and by the introduction of ownership the status of freedom is not destroyed. Therefore, since a right born with him can be taken from no man, but since it certainly is taken away in part, if any are subjected to civil sovereignty against their will; in either hypotheses no one has the right to subject to the civil sovereignty separate families dwelling in a certain territory or staying there.[97]

Wolff specifically rejected the argument that it would be for the benefit of the people themselves to be subjected to the 'civilizing' forces of Europe as sufficient justification for occupation. He also rejected the idea that because these peoples did not use the land "properly" (i.e., though agriculture) it would be justifiable to take it from them.[98]

Wolff was very thorough in his treatment of the law of nations, and his work is rather heavy reading. Vattel, who was the pupil of Wolff and who in the introduction to his own work acknowledged his great debt to his teacher, claimed that his chief aim was to make Wolff's work accessible to the general public.[99] However, it is clear from the passages quoted above that on the issue of the rights of nomadic peoples to their lands there is a difference between the two. The contradiction noted in Vattel's discussion of the property rights of these peoples can be traced, on the one hand, to his attempt to follow Wolff in his upholding of these rights, and, on the other, to his over-ruling belief in the duty to cultivate the land.

Of the two, Wolff obviously had the greater understanding of actual conditions and formulated a comprehensive theory of different kinds of property rights, based on this, which left very little scope for territorial expansion to the colonizing nations of Europe. Against this background, it is understandable that Vattel should have gained a wider audience than Wolff, at least in Britain.

Although Vattel, as pointed out, in certain respects links up with some of the thinking about indigenous title to land from the seventeenth century, whereas Wolff manifestly does not, they do have several things in common. They both reflect a belief in natural rights; furthermore, it is clear, as suggested earlier, that their works show no continuity in the notion of conquest as a just means of acquiring land.

---

[97] Wolff, *Jus Gentium*, vol. 2, 159.

[98] "for no right is created to that which belongs to another, because he does not use and enjoy his own property as much as he could, however much it would have helped you, if he used it and enjoyed it in another way"; Wolff, *Jus Gentium*, vol. 2, 160.

[99] Vattel, *The Law of Nations*, vol. 3, 7a–8a.

Wolff rejected the idea that crimes against the law of nature or idolatry might present a just cause of war; he specifically said that the only justifiable reason for war was if an "irreparable wrong" had been committed against a nation.[100] Although Wolff recognized the duty of "learned and cultivated" nations to influence "barbarous and uncultivated" ones, as well as the duty to attempt to disseminate the Christian faith, resistance by the recipient was entirely lawful and did not constitute a cause for war.[101] In general, no nation could be forced to obey the law of nature, and refusal to follow its dictates did not constitute an injury to another nation; this only happened if a nation was "rendered unfit to attain the purpose of its state."[102]

Similarly, Vattel regarded only self-defence as constituting a lawful reason for war against another nation – he certainly did not regard the desire to acquire land as a just cause of war:

> I do not offer conquest or the desire to usurp the property of another as one of the purposes of offensive war; such a purpose, lacking even a semblance of right, is not the object of formal war, but of brigandage.[103]

It was also seen in the discussion of Vattel's views that he did not hold the Spanish conquest of the "civilized Empires of Peru and Mexico" to be lawful.

Thus the development noticed in the earlier period picked up steam during the eighteenth century; influential writers on international law all but excluded the possibility of conquest as a means of acquiring territory inhabited by indigenous peoples. Insofar as colonies were to be established in such areas, it would have to be on land not used by these peoples; Vattel thought that such a possibility existed, whereas Wolff did not leave much scope for this.[104]

British opinion in the eighteenth century

It is pointed out by Lester that from the turn of the seventeenth into the eighteenth century a distinction began to come into existence in Britain between territories acquired by conquest and those acquired by "plantation." It appears

[100] Wolff, *Jus Gentium*, vol. 2, 314–27.

[101] *Jus Gentium*, vol. 2, 89, 133–34.

[102] *Jus Gentium*, vol. 2, 84–94.

[103] *The Law of Nations*, vol. 3, 243, 36.

[104] Cf. the extensive discussion of Wolff and Vattel in Reynolds, *Aboriginal Sovereignty*, 49–54. Reynolds also finds that neither of the two provides support for colonization based on disregard for the rights of existing inhabitants.

that the distinction turned primarily on deciding what law existed in the respective colonies, the king ruling by prerogative in countries gained by conquest, the common law running in "plantations."[105] The distinction was applied in a memorandum by the Privy Council in 1722 (the so-called "Case 15 – Anonymous"), in which it was stated

> That if there be a new and uninhabited country found out by *English* subjects, as the law is the birthright of every subject, so, wherever, they go, they carry their laws with them, and therefore such new found country is to be governed by the laws of *England.*

In the next sentence, reference was made to Barbados, where a particular statute was held not to apply. However, since Barbados was apparently uninhabited when the British settled it in 1625,[106] it does not indicate a change of opinion regarding land inhabited by indigenous peoples.

In the second paragraph of the short opinion, it was said:

> Where the King of *England* conquers a country, it is a different consideration: for there the conqueror, by saving the lives of the people conquered, gains a right and property in such people; in consequence of which he may impose upon them what laws he pleases.[107]

Until the king made any changes, the existing laws continued to be in force "unless where these are contrary to our religion, or enact any thing that is *malum in se*, or are silent; for in all such cases the laws of the conquering country shall prevail." Thus, this opinion upheld the decision in Calvin's case, which distinguished between the conquest of infidels and others. It also upheld the view that inhabited country was conquered. Thus the rule that automatically transferred English law only applied to the settlement of truly uninhabited land.

---

[105] Lester, *Inuit Territorial Rights*, 16–17; cf McHugh, *The Maori Magna Carta*, 42–44; McNeil, *Common Law Aboriginal Title*, 113–15.

[106] McNeil, *Common Law Aboriginal Title*, 136; Peter Hulme & Neil L.Whitehead, ed. *Wild Majesty: Encounters with Caribs from Colombus to the Present Day; An Anthology* (Oxford: Oxford UP, 1992): 63; J.H. Parry, Philip M. Sherlock & Anthony P. Maingot, *A Short History of the West Indies* (Basingstoke: Macmillan Caribbean, 1987): 51.

[107] Case 15 – Anonymous, 1722, *Reports of Cases collected by Peere Williams 1695–1734* 2 (1826): 75–76.

William Blackstone, who is one of the acknowledged authorities on common law, also reflected on this question in his *Commentaries of the Laws of England*, the first volume of which was published in 1765. Under the heading "Of the Countries Subject to the Laws of England," Blackstone referred among other things to "our more distant plantations in America and elsewhere" where English law might apply. In order to determine this, he began:

> Plantations or colonies, in distant countries, are either such where the lands are claimed by right of occupancy only, by finding them desert and uncultivated, and peopling them from the mother-country; or where, when already cultivated, they have been either gained by conquest, or ceded to us by treaties. And both these rights are founded upon the law of nature, or at least upon that of nations.[108]

Blackstone is here following the decision in Case 15, which he in fact paraphrases (and refers to) a little further down when he says about the first category of colonies (those "claimed by occupancy only"):

> For it hath been held, that if an uninhabited country be discovered and planted by English subjects, all the English laws then in being, which are the birthright of every subject, are immediately there in force.

To Blackstone, then, "desert and uncultivated" meant "uninhabited," and a territory of this description could be occupied by the English (according to the law of nations) and English law would apply there.[109] This opinion is in line with that of others discussed above. As to the second category of colonies, Blackstone states:

> But in conquered or ceded countries, that have already laws of their own, the king may indeed alter and change those laws; but till he does actually change them, the ancient laws of the country remain, unless such as are against the law of God, as in the case of an infidel country. Our American plantations are principally of this latter sort, being obtained in the last century either by right of conquest and driving out the natives (with what natural justice I shall not at present inquire,) or by treaties.[110]

Again Blackstone is in line with the opinion seen so far. Inhabited country was held by conquest and was subject to royal prerogative. Following Calvin,

---

[108] William Blackstone, *Commentaries on the Laws of England in four Books* 4 vols., ed. William Draper Lewis (1765–1769; Philidelphia PA: Rees Welsh, 1902), vol. 1: 93.

[109] Cf Slattery, *Ancestral Lands, Alien Laws*, 5.

[110] Blackstone, *Commentaries on the Laws of England, vol.* 1, 94.

Blackstone maintained that if the inhabitants were infidels their laws immediately ceased to exist. Blackstone made it quite clear that the colonies in America were held by conquest or cession, and the reference to infidels makes it likely that Blackstone was following Coke in this respect as well.

The case of Campbell v. Hall from 1774 also has a bearing on these issues. This case was concerned with the question of the king's prerogative in a country gained by conquest – in this case Grenada, acquired from the French in the Seven Years War. In his judgement, Lord Mansfield upheld Coke's dictum that in a country conquered by the British, the king could alter the laws of the inhabitants, but that until this happened they continued in force. However, he made this important statement:

> The absurd exception as to pagans mentioned in *Calvin's Case* shows the universality and antiquity of the maxim. For that distinction could not exist before the Christian era, and in all probability arose from the mad enthusiasm of the Crusades.[111]

Mansfield rejected the idea that the laws of "infidels" cease to exist immediately on conquest; by implication, he also rejected the notion of a constant condition of war between Christians and non-Christians and thus finally rid English law of the last traces of the old crusading tradition. Mansfield upheld a distinction between types of colonies based on whether they were conquests or not; he quoted the opinion of two lawyers on Jamaica which operated according to two possibilities: whether the island was "still to be considered as a conquered island" or whether it was "to be considered in the same light as the other colonies." Mansfield continued by referring to "the island being in one state or in the other" and said, again with reference to the two lawyers: "Whether it remained a conquest or was made a colony they did not examine." The point here is not that Mansfield was considering other possibilities of acquiring territory (a little earlier he had mentioned with approval Coke's view that there were two means: conquest and inheritance) but, rather, tendering the view that the status of a territory depended on the way in which it was ruled. If the area continued to be ruled through the king's prerogative it "remained a conquest"; if an assembly was commissioned by the king it "was made a colony," subject to the legislative power of that assembly and Parliament.

[111] Campbell v. Hall, 1774, *All England Law Reports Reprint, 1558–1774, revised and annotated* (1968): 254.

The first British case of a judicial character to deal specifically with the rights of the Indians in North America was that of the Mohegan Indians v. Connecticut, which, as mentioned above, began in the early eighteenth century. The Indians, who with their "guardian," John Mason, initiated the case, claimed that they had been illegally deprived of their land; for the other side, the colonial government pointed to several deeds and treaties from the late seventeenth century (some of which the Mohegans regarded as fraudulent) which they believed had transferred property rights to the colony.

It is not easy to work out the proceedings of the case, nor, indeed, the outcome of it. In the course of the ensuing seventy years, a number of Royal Commissions were appointed by the Privy Council to hear the case in America; some of them never met, and the conduct of the whole matter was characterized by vast delays, at times deliberately occasioned by one of the parties or the Crown. It appears that the first commission in 1705 found in favour of the Indians, but that upon appeal by the colony most of this decision was reversed by a 1743 commission, whose findings were finally confirmed by the Privy Council in 1772.[112]

Despite the unfortunate lack of detail about the findings of the Privy Council, it may at least be pointed out that the very decision to hear the case by means of Royal Commission is evidence that the Indians were regarded as having legal standing as an entity separate from the jurisdiction of the colony.[113] It also appears that although the colonial parties denied Mohegan title to the land in

---

[112] Smith, *Appeals to the Privy Council*, 426, 435, 442 though cf Youngblood Henderson, "Unraveling the Riddle of Aboriginal Title," 97–99, who seems to imply a different outcome. Smith's account of the case is very detailed but accords far greater space to the arguments of the colonial council (who is quoted extensively in the notes) than to those of the Mohegans. On the other hand, Youngblood Henderson's account is difficult to reconcile with that of Smith; certainly, Youngblood Henderson's claim that Commissioner Horfmanden in 1743 spoke for the majority of the commissioners is contradicted by Horfmanden's own letter to the Board of Trade in which he mentions his dissent "at the time the three Commissioners [who were the majority] delivered their opinion in Court, upon which the Judgement was founded" (Horfmanden to Lords of Trade, October 4, 1744, in O'Callaghan & Fernow, ed. *New York Colonial Documents*, vol. 4, 257). Until the proceedings of the case (in the Columbia University Law Library, the Connecticut Archives, and elsewhere) can be examined, the details of the findings and especially of those of the Privy Council remain unclear.

[113] Cf Smith, *Appeals to the Privy Council*, 415, 442. If the Indians had been perceived as being subject to colonial jurisdiction, the case would have been heard in the colonial courts.

question, their arguments were based almost entirely on the claim that this title had been extinguished, not that it had not existed.[114] Whether the colonists sincerely believed this or not, it demonstrates that such arguments were regarded as essential for their success on an official level. It is most likely that the Privy Council decision turned on the alleged validity of the deeds of transfer rather than on the basic existence of Mohegan rights to their land.

The legal acceptance in Britain of the independence or semi-independence of the Indians is contradicted by the terms used in the Board of Trade memorial from 1697, mentioned earlier. There the Five Nations were referred to as "the King of England's subjects" and it was claimed that they were "united to, or depended on" New York (although they did not even live within that colony).[115] The context of the memorial, however, was that of the struggle with the French for Indian allies, and the intention of the document was clearly to show that the Five Nations were allies of the British, although the French had continually tried to subvert them. Later in the memorial, reference is made to the renewal of the Indians' "dependence or Covenant Chain," the latter phrase being one frequently used in later years to mean alliance. It would thus seem that in reality the Board was concerned to show British suzerainty, rather than sovereignty, over the Indians of that region.

The Royal Proclamation of 1763 (quoted from in Chapter 2 above) stated the position after the area west of the colonies had been ceded to the British by the French. As a consequence of this cession, sovereignty was claimed over the territory, but the Indians were referred to as "Nations [...] with whom We are connected" and they were not to be "disturbed in the Possession of such Parts of Our Dominions and Territories as, not having been ceded to or purchased by Us, are reserved to them."[116] In other words, the Indians continued to be regarded in some measure as a distinct people who were in possession of the land on which they lived until their title was lawfully extinguished by the Crown.[117]

---

[114] See, for example, Smith, *Appeals to the Privy Council*, notes 109, 133, 134, 140.

[115] Memorial of the Right of the British Crown over the New York Indians, 1697, in O'Callaghan & Fernow, ed. *New York Colonial Documents*, vol. 5, 75.

[116] See Chapter 2, 39 above, and note 30. Although the proclamation in that chapter was regarded primarily in the light of a 'policy statement', it also had the force of a statute.

[117] On the legal recognition of Indian rights in the proclamation, see, for example, Cumming & Mickenberg, ed. *Native Rights in Canada*, 30–31 and passim.

Thus it would seem that British legal opinion in the course of the eighteenth century upheld the distinction between conquest and cession on the one hand and inheritance on the other as the means of acquiring inhabited territory, but added that of occupation of "new found and uninhabited country."[118] The significance attached to this new category arises mainly from the possibilities this opened up for the transfer of common law to some of the colonies.

If Blackstone, the only British authority who seems to have addressed the question directly, can be taken to represent the general legal opinion of his day, the American colonies continued to be regarded as being held through conquest or cession, although, through Mansfield's judgement of 1774, it was divorced from its crusading origins. Paradoxically, the authority who is clearest on this point has also contributed to the confusion subsequently surrounding the issue; later authors have held that Blackstone's reference to "desert and uncultivated" land included territory inhabited by hunters and gatherers who (mostly) did not cultivate the land.[119] As shown above, Blackstone's use of the word "uninhabited" later when clearly referring to the same category of colonies proves that he really did mean "empty" land. Blackstone's use of "cultivated/uncultivated" as synonymous with "inhabited/uninhabited" points to the huge influence of the line of thinking noted in connection with Locke and Vattel,[120] but there is nothing to indicate that Blackstone had adopted the position of Vattel – that the colonies in America had been established by occupying land which the Indians did not need. As far as Blackstone was concerned, the Indians had been conquered or had ceded their land to the British.

It has also been suggested that by the mid-eighteenth century British legal opinion recognized Indian possession of the land. This points to the view that the customary property rights of the Indians continued after conquest or cession, an idea which is opposed to Coke's statement on the immediate abrogation of "infidel" laws. Lord Mansfield's firm rejection of this part of Coke's judgement brought common law into line both with prevailing legal views and

---

[118] McNeil, *Common Law Aboriginal Title*, 114–15, who says that "these general rules were well settled before the end of the eighteenth century." McNeil confirms that these categories were considered in connection with the question of which laws applied.

[119] Cf Reynolds, *Aboriginal Sovereignty*, 91.

[120] Cf also the mention in passing of "lands uncultivated and possessed by barbarians" in Pen[n] v. Lord Baltimore, 1750 (quoted in McNeil, *Common Law Aboriginal Title*, 239). The equation between uncultivated land and that inhabited by indigenous peoples were to become of great significance later but in this case it was clearly not regarded as disqualifying the Indians from "possessing" their land.

with colonial practices of purchasing land from the Indians. The continuation of Indian ownership of the land was thus reconcilable with the general doctrine of conquest, which presumed that the laws of the conquered continued until changed by the conqueror.[121]

The indication that even Indians closely connected with the colonies were regarded as autonomous groups may to some extent have been a product of the line of thinking, developing in the seventeenth century and very strongly represented in Vattel, that the two peoples could live as autonomous groups in the vast regions of North America. Although there is little actual evidence of the thinking of Vattel in the legal material which has been cited here, British colonization in America followed quite closely the practice outlined by Vattel; rather than being completely dispossessed all at once, the Indians were gradually "confined within narrower bounds" as British agricultural settlement slowly moved west. The assumption that the settlers had a right based on natural law to share "unused" land with the original inhabitants may also be seen as part of this practice. The influence of this theory, together with the actual situation in North America, which necessitated a great deal of respect for the Indians, may well have contributed to the shaping of the legal view of Indian rights.

While the doctrine of conquest continued to be in force in British law for longer than in the law of nations, again no doubt because of the importance of precedent in common law, it is thus tempting to see a convergence between the two bodies of law in the course of the century, towards a stance which at least to some degree recognized the rights of indigenous people to their land based on natural-law precepts of universal application.

This is supported by the point made by Frederika Hackshaw – that by the mid-eighteenth century it was being explicitly recognized by British courts that international law formed part of the common law. Furthermore, the law of nature, seen to be the foundation of international law, enjoyed an equally strong place in English law; this meant that the "inherent natural law concepts of equality, justice and fairness," to borrow a phrase from Hackshaw, were recognized as guiding principles in English no less than in international law.[122]

---

[121] Cf McNeil, *Common Law Aboriginal Title*, 171–74.

[122] Fredericka Hackshaw, "Nineteenth Century Notions of Aboriginal Title and their Influence on the Interpretation of the Treaty of Waitangi," in *Waitangi, Maori and Pakeha Perspectives on the Treaty of Waitangi*, ed. I.A. Kawharu (Auckland: Oxford UP, 1981): 94–95. Cf, for example, John Locke, *Essays on the Law of Nature*, ed. W. von Leiden (c. 1660; Oxford: Clarendon, 1970), and Blackstone, *Commentaries on the*

These principles were also closely connected with the development of the theory of natural rights which was so influential in the eighteenth century.[123] Thus natural-law rights, which some scholars regard as having been of little value in relation to indigenous peoples at the time,[124] were in fact of great significance during this period. The general acceptance of the rights of indigenous peoples during the greater part of the eighteenth century accorded with the belief that man had certain fundamental rights.

Nineteenth-century developments

By the turn of the century, important changes were taking place in legal perceptions of the way in which the land of indigenous peoples could be acquired and of the rights these peoples had to their land. The outcome was that it became accepted by many jurists that such land was acquirable through discovery and occupation, as in the case of uninhabited land; by further developing this equation with *terra nullius*, the land in some cases came to be seen as legally uninhabited, the inhabitants being deprived of all territorial rights. This remarkable development was brought about by several factors.

One source for the development of the doctrine of *terra nullius* as applicable to the land of hunters and gatherers was the law that developed in the USA. As pointed out above, the rule took shape, in the course of the early eighteenth century, that when unoccupied land was settled by the British, the settlers automatically brought common law with them. To the American colonists, this was highly attractive, because common law would afford protection against what was increasingly seen as the unreasonable rule to which they were subjected under the royal prerogative. For this reason, American essayists were receptive to the idea that the colonies should be seen as settled rather than conquered, and the issues underlying the revolution in this way contributed to questioning the traditional view of the modalities by which the colonies had been acquired.[125]

Laws of England, vol. 1, 39–43 (Of the Nature of Laws in General). See also, for example, Duncan Forbes, "Natural Law and the Scottish Enlightenment" in *The Origins and Nature of the Scottish Enlightenment*, ed. Roy Hutcheson Campbell & Andrew S. Skinner (Edinburgh: John Donald, 1982): 186–205, on discussions of natural law by the Scottish philosophers and jurists.

123 McHugh, *The Maori Magna Carta*, 378.

124 See, for example, Lester, *Inuit Territorial Rights*, 8.

125 Cf McHugh, *The Maori Magna Carta*, 42.

After the Revolution, the question cropped up again in cases concerned with the original title of the Indians. In the case of Johnson v. M'Intosh from 1823, Chief Justice Marshall, in the course of his wide-ranging reasons for judgement, discussed the legal origins of the British colonies in America and the position of the Indians. Marshall attached great significance to the act of discovery. In accordance with the accepted view, Marshall saw this as an action that gave the discovering nation the right to deal with the inhabitants to the exclusion of all other nations; however, he also believed that this rather than conquest was the foundation of English, and in turn North American, title to the country.

> They [the Indians] were admitted to be the rightful occupants of the soil, with a legal as well as just claim to retain possession of it, and to use it according to their own discretion; but their rights to complete sovereignty [...] were necessarily diminished, and their power to dispose of the soil at their own will, to whomsoever they please, was denied by the original fundamental principle, that discovery gave exclusive title to those who made it.[126]

Marshall recognized the rights to the land of the original inhabitants but perceived them to exist as a "burden" on the underlying title of the Crown/State; he characterized the Indians as "domestic dependent nations" who retained power over their own affairs, but not over their foreign relations. Nevertheless, the rights of the Indians recognized by Marshall were qualified by the belief that the Crown had acquired absolute title by discovery.

Creating a coherent and comprehensive doctrine on these issues was not an easy matter, as is revealed by the inconsistencies apparent in the decisions of the Marshall court. Thus, although clearly convinced that the colonies had been acquired by discovery, Marshall also included the notion that America was held through conquest, no doubt because of the clear evidence that this was the view previously held:

> The British government [...] asserted a title to all the lands occupied by Indians [...] It asserted also a limited sovereignty over them . [...] These claims have been maintained and established [...] by the sword.[127]

Having recognized this, Marshall then felt compelled to uphold this point:

---

[126] Johnson and Graham's Lessee v. William M'Intosh, 1823, *Wheaton United States Supreme Court Reports* 8 (1823): 574. See also 592.

[127] Johnson v. M'Intosh, 588.

> However extravagant the pretension of converting the discovery of a country into a conquest may appear; if the principle has been asserted in the first instance and afterwards sustained; if a country has been acquired and held under it; if the property of the great mass of the community originated in it, it becomes the law of the land and cannot be questioned.[128]

These words were echoed by Kent in his *Commentaries on American Law*[129] in a discussion which also incorporated Vattel's treatment of the subject. Similarly, in 1831, in the first of the Cherokee cases, judge Johnson referred to "the principle, that discovery gave the right of dominion over the country discovered."[130] The theory which these judges put forward is best explained as exemplifying the transition from the predominant theory of conquest of the early period to the doctrine of discovery and occupation of the nineteenth century in relation to the colonization of indigenous land.[131]

Later in the century, statements became more blunt. Blackstone was pronounced to have been wrong in his statement on the acquisition of the American colonies, in the following terms:

> Sir William Blackstone considered the British colonies in North America as ceded or conquered countries [....] But this was an error. The claim of England to the soil was made by her in virtue of discovery, not conquest or cession. The aborigines were considered but as mere occupants, not sovereign pro-

---

[128] Johnson v. M'Intosh, 591. In Samuel A.Worcester v. the State of Georgia, 1823, *Peters United States Supreme Court Reports* 6 (January term, 1832): 543, Marshall maintained a similarly confused view of the rights of discovery and conquest. The decisions of the Marshall court have been instrumental in laying down American law concerning the rights of the Indians; dealing with complex and politically sensitive issues, the decisions attempted to find a middle course between the rights of the State and those of the Indians and have therefore given rise to a great variety of interpretations. For discussion, particularly of the discovery/conquest problematic in Johnson v. M'Intosh, see, for example, Howard R. Berman, "The Concept of Aboriginal Rights in the Early Legal History of the United States," *Buffalo Law Review* 27 (1978): 642–50; Nell Jessup Newton, "At the Whim of the Sovereign, Aboriginal Title Reconsidered," *Hastings Law Journal* 31 (July 1980): 1222–25, or Youngblood Henderson, "Unravelling the Riddle of Aboriginal Title," 90–93. These scholars tend to focus on Marshall's emphasis on discovery because they see this as giving scope under modern law for arguing in favour of Indian self-determination.

[129] James Kent, *Commentaries on American Law*(1826–30; New York: Da Capo, 1971), vol. 3: 310.

[130] The Cherokee Nation v. The State of Georgia, 1831, *Peters United States Supreme Court Reports* 5 (January term, 1831): 21.

[131] Lester, *Inuit Territorial Rights*, 7–11 and 17, supports this interpretation.

> prietors; and the argument for the justice of taking possession and driving out the natives was rested upon the ground that a few wandering hordes of savages had no right to the exclusive possession and enjoyment of the vast and fertile regions which were opened for the improvement and progress of civilized man by the discovery of the New World.[132]

The commentator goes on to refer approvingly to Marshall's pronouncements on discovery; then he quotes Blackstone's statement on colonies acquired by occupation, to which the laws of England automatically applied, concluding that "This expresses accurately and fully the well-settled and repeatedly recognized doctrine of the American courts upon the subject of the extension of the English common law and statutes to this country." Although the writer was thus concerned with the question of the application of common law rather than with the title of the Indians, the passage illustrates with great clarity the development within that field. It also shows the increasingly derogatory attitude towards the idea of Indian title, a trend which was continued by the American courts departing from or reinterpreting the Marshall decision.

Thus, through a process of retrospective rationalization, these jurists and legal commentators contributed to the rewriting of the history of contact between colonizers and indigenous people in North America in the light of contemporary interpretations of that history.

Another source for the application of the doctrine of *terra nullius* to land inhabited by indigenous peoples is the development of the legal view on the acquisition of Australia. This question was referred to in a number of cases in the course of the nineteenth century, albeit never in connection with a land claim by Aboriginal people, an issue which was not brought to the courts until the late twentieth century.

In the case of Rex v. Murrell (1836), a murder case involving Aborigines only, defence for the accused attempted to deny the jurisdiction of the court over Aborigines by claiming that the original inhabitants had their own laws (which in theory the British ought to obey, since they had come to live among them). Furthermore, it was argued that since British law offered Aborigines no protection they were not bound by it. In the course of pleading, the mode of colonization of Australia was discussed at some length:

---

[132] Blackstone, *Commentaries on the Laws of England*, vol. 1, 93–94, note 23. The editor, William Draper Lewis, quotes from the comments by George Sharswood in an earlier edition of Blackstone (Philadelphia PA: J.B. Lippincott, 1878).

> This country was not originally desert, or peopled from the mother country, having had a population far more numerous than those that have since arrived from the mother country. Neither can it be called a conquered country, as Great Britain was never at war with the natives, nor a ceded country either; it, in fact, comes within neither of these, but was a country having a population which had manners and customs of their own, and we have come to reside among them.[133]

Judge Burton replied to this that

> although it might be granted that on the first taking possession of the Colony, the aborigines were entitled to be recognised as free and independent, yet they were not in such a position with regard to strength as to be considered free and independent tribes. They had no sovereignty.[134]

He furthermore maintained that "the colony was to be regarded as unappropriated territory taken into the King's possession."[135] Three years previously, the same judge had stated that "the wandering tribes of its natives, living without certain habitation and without laws were never in the situation of a conquered people" and that New South Wales should therefore be seen as having been uninhabited country.[136]

In this way, the early decisions dealing with the issue came to see New South Wales as having been in a situation similar to that of uninhabited land at the arrival of the first settlers. Although the land was inhabited, the people were not strong enough or organized in ways sufficiently like the European to be considered "free and independent" people who had to be conquered. Therefore the colony was seen as having been acquired through discovery and settlement.

In a case from 1847 in which it was held that the feudal system of land tenure had been transferred to New South Wales at first settlement, it was stated in support of this view that at "the moment of its settlement the colonists

---

[133] Rex v. Jack Congo Murrell, 1834, *Legge Supreme Court Cases, New South Wales, 1825–1862* 1 (1896): 72.

[134] Rex v. Murrell, 72

[135] As reported by Barry Bridges, "The Extension of English Law to the Aborigines for Offences Committed Inter Se, 1829–1842," *Journal of the Royal Australian Historical Society* 59 (1973): 265. Bridges relies on the Supreme Court Papers in the New South Wales State Archives; this part of the judgement is not reported in *Legge Supreme Court Cases*. Cf also Reynolds, *Aboriginal Sovereignty*, 46, 52.

[136] Macdonald v. Levy, 1833, quoted in McNeil, *Common Law Aboriginal Title*, 121. Even earlier cases had laid down the same principle, see also below, 232–33, and note 161.

brought the common law of England with them"; this was based on the well-known doctrine of "a newly-discovered country, settled by British subjects."[137] Obviously, then, from the point of view both of the condition of the inhabitants and of the constitutional status of the colony, the country was to be regarded as having been acquired by settlement.

There are several indications, however, that the matter was not perceived as undebatable; thus council for the defence in the Murrell case, who obviously thought it worth arguing the issue, displayed in the course of his argument a clear understanding of the traditional categories of colonies, and suggested that New South Wales did not belong to any of them. Similarly, the argument that British jurisdiction did not extend to Aborigines indicated uncertainty about their status in relation to the colony.[138] This point was further discussed in another murder case involving Aborigines only, in 1842 in Melbourne. In this case (which was later cancelled due to lack of evidence), judge Willis, in disagreement with the judgement in the Murrell case, expressed strong doubts about the applicability of British law to Aborigines.[139]

In his reasons for judgement, Willis argued that the main question was whether the sovereignty claimed by the British wholly extinguished the sovereignty of the Aboriginal people or whether it merely reduced them to "dependent nations" (as laid down by Chief Justice Marshall, also referred to by Willis) who still retained their own laws and customs. He rejected the notion that the whole of New South Wales was acquired by occupation, because it was inhabited at the time; but nor did he think that it was gained by conquest or cession – so, like counsel in Rex v. Murrell, he found that it was a special case. Willis followed Vattel in claiming that parts of the country were gained by occupation because they were not used by the Aborigines; but this did not give

---

[137] Attorney-General v. Brown, 1847, *Legge Supreme Court Cases, New South Wales, 1825–1862* 1 (1862): 318.

[138] This uncertainty is further indicated by the fact that it was not until 1837 that the Aborigines were finally and formally pronounced to be British subjects; Glenelg to Bourke, July 26, 1837 in Frederick Watson, ed. *Historical Records of Australia* (Sydney: Government Printer, 1914–1925), vol. 19: 48.

[139] Chief Justice Dowling in a letter to Governor Gipps in 1842 also mentioned the fact that at the time of his arrival in 1828 the general opinion had been that the court had no jurisdiction in cases involving Aborigines only; enclosure in despatch from Gipps to Stanley, January 24, 1842, *Parliamentary Papers* 8 (1844): 145.

the British sovereignty over Aborigines in those parts of the country not inhabited by settlers.[140]

Willis's arguments were rejected by the other judges in New South Wales, who considered the matter of jurisdiction to have been decided in Rex v. Murrell, and, following their statement, also by the Secretary of State.[141] Nevertheless, Willis's opinion shows that the method of acquiring the colony as well as the status of the Aborigines remained topics of debate among some jurists.[142] However, in the course of the century it became conclusively established that New South Wales had been acquired by occupation. In the Privy Council case Cooper v. Stuart (1889), the judges distinguished between a colony acquired by conquest or cession and

> a Colony which consisted of a tract of territory practically unoccupied, without settled inhabitants or settled law, at the time when it was peacefully annexed to the British dominions. The colony of New South Wales belongs to the latter case.[143]

Largely based on judicial re-interpretation of the situation prevailing in 1788 and of the attitude of the Crown at the time, it was decided that for legal purposes New South Wales should be regarded as having been *terra nullius* at the time when it was settled by the British. Although, as shown by Henry Reynolds, knowledge of Aboriginal society steadily increased throughout the nineteenth century, the British legal system chose to maintain what by then had become a legal fiction.[144]

By extension, the same doctrine was applied to New Zealand, despite very different circumstances. The British government in the early part of the nineteenth century recognized Maori sovereignty and solemnly negotiated a treaty of cession in 1840. Nevertheless, by the end of the century the courts arrived at

---

[140] Case of Bonjon, Reasons for Judgement; enclosure in despatch from Gipps to Stanley, January 24, 1842, *Parliamentary Papers* 8 (1844): 148–155.

[141] Case of Bonjon, 156.

[142] Cf the examples discussed by Reynolds, *Aboriginal Sovereignty*, 40–41, 62–72.

[143] Cooper v. Stuart, 1889, *Law Reports, Appeal Cases, House of Lords and Privy Council*, 14 (1889): 291. The same opinion, albeit modified, was expressed in M'Hugh v. Robertson by the Supreme Court of Victoria in 1885, "The Imperial Parliament was not thinking of them [the Aborigines]. From the first the English have occupied Australia as if it were an uninhabited and desert country": *Victoria Law Reports* 40 (1885): 431. See also cases cited in McNeil, *Common Law Aboriginal Title*, ch. 4, note 55.

[144] Reynolds, *Aboriginal Sovereignty*, ch. 2.

the conclusion that the treaty was invalid and that the country was acquired by occupation. The classic example of this interpretation is the case of Wi Parata v. Bishop of Wellington (1877), in which judge Prendergast stated:

> On the foundation of this colony the aborigines were found without any kind of civil government, or any settled system of law . […] The Maori tribes were incapable of performing the duties, and therefore of assuming the rights, of a civilized community [...] so far as that instrument [the Treaty of Waitangi] purports to cede the sovereignty [...] it must be regarded as a simple nullity. No body politic existed capable of making cession of sovereignty, nor could the thing itself exist.[145]

It is clear from these examples that the factor determining how a colony was acquired – by conquest or cession or by occupation – was no longer primarily whether the inhabitants cultivated the land but, rather, whether they had "settled laws" and were organized along political and social lines recognizable by the British. This was summed up by the jurist Henry Jenkyns in *British Rule and Jurisdiction beyond the Seas* (1902):

> The colonies differ according as they have been acquired by settlement or by conquest or cession . […] The distinction appears to depend upon whether at the time of the acquisition of any territory there existed on that territory a civilized society with civil institutions of laws, whether there in fact existed anything which would be called a *lex loci.*[146]

As in case law, the 'Blackstonian' division of colonies into two groups remained, but the basis upon which they were ascribed to one or the other had changed, emphasizing the degree of similarity between the colonized society and Britain. Paul McHugh claims that the designation of a colony as "settled" (or acquired by occupation) only had consequences for the system of law in operation in the colony and did not have any relevance for the way in which the rights of the indigenous peoples were perceived.[147] As shown above, this was no doubt true for the initial development of the notion of colonies of settlement in the eighteenth century and may be the correct analysis for the situation in New Zealand with which McHugh deals in his book. However, there is little

---

[145] Wi Parata v. Bishop of Wellington and the Attorney-General, 1877, *New Zealand Jurist* 3 (1877): 77–78. On this case, see McHugh, *The Maori Magna Carta*, 113–17.

[146] Henry Jenkyns, *British Rule and Jurisdiction beyond the Seas* (Oxford: Clarendon, 1902): 4–5.

[147] McHugh, *The Maori Magna Carta*, 42–44.

doubt that in Australia the designation of the original state of the colony as similar to that of *terra nullius* had ominous consequences for the rights of the inhabitants to their land.[148]

M.F. Lindley, in his book *The Acquisition and Government of Backward Territory in International Law* (1928), also finds that "a doctrine which denies that International Law recognizes any rights in primitive peoples to the territory they inhabit" is mainly a recent development (that is, from the nineteenth century), whereas in earlier times such lands were regarded as belonging to the people inhabiting them and as acquirable only through conquest.[149] It is important to stress this point, because many scholars have seen it as a principle which was settled, at the latest, by the early eighteenth century; especially Australian scholars have adopted this view.[150]

Thus, for example, the Australian jurist Alex Castles maintains that "by the beginning of the eighteenth century" the courts had laid down that "a 'settled'

---

[148] See esp. Milirrpum and Others v. Nabalco Pty. Ltd. and The Commonwealth of Australia, 1971, *Federal Law Reports* 17 (1971): 141–294. This was not changed until the High Court in 1992 specifically refuted that the country had been *terra nullius* in 1788 (see Eddie Mabo and others v. The State of Queensland, *Australian Law Reports*107 (1992): 1ff..

[149] M.F. Lindley, *The Acquisition and Government of Backward Territories in International Law being a Treatise on the Law and Practice Relating to Colonial Expansion* (London: Longmans, Green, 1926): 12–20. See also, based on Lindley, Elizabeth Evatt, "The Acquisition of Territory in Australia and New Zealand," in *Grotian Society Papers 1968: Studies in the History of the Law of Nations*, ed. Charles Henry Alexandrowicz (The Hague: Martinus Nijhoff, 1970): 16–45. Cf McHugh's comment that this development was due to the influence of a "narrow, unrepresentative group of English publicists on international law" writing under the influence of John Austin, *The Maori Magna Carta*, 113–14.

[150] See, for example, James Simsarian, "The Acquisition of Legal Title to Terra Nullius," *Political Science Quarterly* 53 (1938): 111–28; Robert F. Berkhofer, Jr., *The White Man's Indian: Images of the American Indian from Columbus to the Present* (New York: Alfred A. Knopf, 1978): 120; McNeil, *Common Law Aboriginal Title*, ch. 4; Ernest Scott, "Taking Possession of Australia – The Doctrine of 'Terra Nullius' (No-Man's Land)," *Journal and Proceedings of the Royal Australian Historical Society* 26.1 (1940): 1; R. Else–Mitchell, "Territorial Conquest – Phillip and Afterwards," *The Victorian Historical Journal* 46.3 (August 1975): 437; A.G.L. Shaw, "British Policy Towards the Australian Aborigines, 1830–1850," *Australian Historical Studies* 25 (1992–1993): 266; Alan Atkinson, "The First Plans for Governing New South Wales, 1786–87," *Australian Historical Studies* 24 (1990–1991): 29; Richard Broome, *Aboriginal Australians: Black Response to White Dominance* (Sydney: Allen & Unwin, 1982): 26.

colony was a territory, which at the time of its occupation by the British, was uninhabited or inhabited by a primitive people whose laws and customs were considered in applicable to a civilised race."[151] As his source for this position, Castles refers to "Case 15 – Anonymous," which, however, as shown above, makes no reference to inhabited country in relation to a "settled colony."

Similarly, Alan Frost maintains that by the middle of the eighteenth century it was common practice to consider the land of non-agriculturists as *terra nullius*.[152] Frost mentions the controversies surrounding the Falkland Islands and Nootka Sound as evidence that land was claimed as *terra nullius* by discovery and possession. However, the Falklands were in fact truly uninhabited when the European nations began to shown an interest in the area in the 1760s and therefore cannot be used as evidence that inhabited land was regarded as *terra nullius* at this time.[153] As shown in Chapter 3, the British mentioned "the consent of the natives" as a prerequisite for acquiring land at Nootka Sound.[154] In any case, as pointed out above, the action of "discovery and taking possession" was only of significance as against other European nations, it was not perceived to have any implication vis-à-vis the indigenous inhabitants of a territory.

Furthermore, Frost finds evidence in the journals of Cook and Banks that they explored the coast of New South Wales on the basis of this premise, and feels able to conclude that "To Cook (and to Banks and their contemporaries) eastern New Holland was *terra nullius*."[155] There is, however, little evidence to support the view that any legal notions influenced the observations made by

---

[151] Alex C. Castles, "The Reception and Status of English Law in Australia," *Adelaide Law Review* 2 (1963–66): 2. See also Castles, *An Introduction to Australian Legal History*, 14–15.

[152] Alan Frost, *Botany Bay Mirages: Illusions of Australia's Convict Beginnings* (Melbourne: Oxford UP, 1995): 177–79. This chapter is very similar to an earlier article, "New South Wales as Terra Nullius, the British Denial of Aboriginal Land Rights," *Historical Studies* 19 (1980—81): 446–52. Frost's work on *terra nullius* is frequently cited: for example, Richard Broome, "The Struggle for Australia, Aboriginal-European Warfare, 1770–1930" in *Australia: Two Centuries of War & Peace*, ed. Michael McKernan & Margaret Browne (Canberra: Australian War Memorial and Allen & Unwin, 1988): 92; Bain Attwood, "Aborigines and Academic Historians, Some Recent Encounters," *Australian Historical Studies* 24 (1990–1991): 130.

[153] See, for example, Ian John Strange, *The Falkland Islands* (London: David & Charles, 1983).

[154] See Chapter 3 above, 102.

[155] Frost, *Botany Bay Mirages*, 185.

Cook and Banks about the Aborigines nor, as has been shown above, that land inhabited by hunters and gatherers was viewed in the way indicated by Frost at the time of Cook's voyage.

In this fashion, these scholars have contributed to the notion that land inhabited by indigenous peoples was during the eighteenth century customarily seen as *terra nullius* which could be acquired by occupation. As a consequence of this belief, it has been maintained that New South Wales was from the very beginning firmly regarded as *terra nullius*. While there is no doubt that the legal basis of British settlement there came to be seen in this light, as shown from the development of cases in the nineteenth century touching on this issue, there is no evidence that this was the common view at the time it was decided to establish the colony. In his recent study of Aboriginal sovereignty, Henry Reynolds similarly concludes that late-eighteenth-century legal theories did not preclude the recognition of Aboriginal possession of and sovereignty over their territory, but that this changed in the course of the following century.[156]

There is little doubt that this development in legal thinking was connected with the change in basic legal concepts which took place at the turn of the century. At this time, traditional ideas about natural law began to be replaced by a theory that laws were simply laid down by the sovereign and should be regarded as separate from any considerations of morality. This turn towards positivism, which in Britain is particularly associated with the writings of John Austin, directly affected the view of indigenous societies. It was claimed that such societies (Austin especially refers to the "savage and independent societies" of both New Holland and North America) had no settled system of law because they did not have a sovereign ruler (as seen by Europeans).[157] The implication of this was that indigenous peoples did not have sovereignty over their land; nor could they have any legally defined property rights because of their lack of a system of law. Ultimately, such societies were regarded as not belonging to the "family of nations" to which international law belonged. By thus defining indigenous societies as legally non-existent, the way was opened for regarding their land as acquirable through mere occupation like uninhabited territory.[158]

---

[156] Reynolds, *Aboriginal Sovereignty*, ch. 3.

[157] John Austin, *The Province of Jurisprudence Determined and the Uses of the Study of Jurisprudence*, intro. H.L.A. Hart (1832 & 1863; London: Weidenfeld & Nicolson, 1968): 209; cf Reynolds, *Aboriginal Sovereignty*, 46.

[158] Hackshaw, "Nineteenth Century Notions of Aboriginal Title," 100–101.

Changing legal doctrines

The legal view concerning the acquisition of territory inhabited by indigenous peoples may thus be seen to have undergone a dramatic development in the period from the sixteenth to the nineteenth century. Opinion in Britain maintained rather longer than international law that such territory was acquired by conquest, a view which was originally based on assumptions about Christian rights over infidels but which, even after that view became outmoded, was sustained by the power of precedent. In varying degrees, both international law and English law recognized the existence of indigenous title to the land, either as something that could be extinguished by force or (increasingly) as something that had to be respected. Eighteenth-century perceptions of natural law may be seen to have exerted a considerable influence in this as well as in other areas of the law.

This fits in quite well with official policy and attitudes to indigenous peoples in the eighteenth century, as outlined in previous chapters. It was seen in connection with the Indians in North America that government policy was generally one of recognizing Indian rights to their land and that attempts were made to alleviate Indian discontent when their rights were violated. It was suggested that not only expedience but also a sense of legal and moral obligation were the cause of this policy. This can be traced to a concept of justice based on the entitlement of all mankind to certain fundamental rights as prescribed by the law of nature, which may be presumed to have been a common underlying assumption among ministers and officials at the time.

Policy in other areas, as outlined in Chapter 3, confirmed the view that the rights of indigenous peoples were generally accepted even in the 1780s; this is supported by Lindley, who surveys state practice and reaches a similar conclusion.[159] Thus it is clear that up to the end of the eighteenth century, both government action and legal opinion acknowledged that indigenous peoples were in possession of the land on which they lived and that the land had to be acquired by conquest or cession, the latter by far the more common method throughout the century.

In the late eighteenth century, however, legal views about acquisition of indigenous land began to change. It gradually came to be maintained that such land could be equated with uninhabited land because the inhabitants did not have "systems of law" or "political institutions" recognizable as such by European colonizers. The impact of this was to deny that indigenous peoples

---

[159] Lindley, *The Acquisition and Government of Backward Territories*, 24–44.

should be regarded as having sovereignty over their land, which could therefore be acquired simply through discovery and occupation. The further implication was in some cases also the questioning of the existence of indigenous property-rights. Several causes for this development may be traced, some of which have already been mentioned. The revolutionary spirit in the American colonies was seen to support a view which regarded settlement rather than conquest as the way in which the colonies were acquired, because of its constitutional implications. It may also be suggested that the urge to create order in the somewhat chaotic body of law governing acquisition of territory may have encouraged the legal profession in both Britain and America to establish a doctrine which would make a number of disparate cases similar.

Even more important was the transition from natural law to positivism in legal thinking. This had a significant impact on the theoretical view of indigenous societies. In general, it would have had a profound impact on the perception of obligations of the moral–legal nature mentioned above. Thus, the application of positivism to jurisprudence had serious implications both for the way in which the British understood their own legal principles and for the way in which they came to regard the rights of indigenous peoples.

The development of legal principles regarding the status of the colony of New South Wales has a central place in the application of the doctrine of *terra nullius* to indigenous land. It was seen that in the course of the nineteenth century the opinion developed that this colony was acquired by settlement – debated at first by some, but eventually established as the orthodox view of the British legal system. The novel situation constituted by this colony, whose original inhabitants were unlike others hitherto encountered, may well have contributed to this development; on the other hand, changing perceptions of legal principles may also have shaped the way in which this situation was interpreted.

This legal development corresponds very well to the evolution in official attitude which was observed earlier. The initial view that the country was so sparsely inhabited as to be practically uninhabited no doubt attributed to the creation of the myth of *terra nullius*; likewise, the lack of any attempts to negotiate with the inhabitants for cession of land and the fundamental misunderstandings about the way of life of the Aboriginal people must have created the firm impression that these people had no "settled system of law." On the other hand, the legal debate which took place, with its rejection of the established categories of colonies in the case of New South Wales, must increasingly have encouraged official views of Aborigines as lacking any rights to the land. The outcome was that the original belief that New South Wales was largely uninhabited, based on a misunderstanding of the actual situation, was retained as a legal fiction to fit a doctrine whose function it was to legitimize British colonization.

The legal view that New South Wales was acquired by settlement was well-known in the Colonial Office. In 1822, when James Stephen as legal counsel to the government reported on a case from New South Wales, he accepted the view that the colony had been "acquired neither by conquest nor cession, but by the mere occupation of a desert or uninhabited land."[160] In 1840 Stephen seems to have changed his mind when he noted in a memorandum that "It is an important and unsuspected fact that these Tribes had proprietary rights in the Soil."[161] Yet this does not suggest a permanent shift in official attitude towards Aboriginal title to the land; in 1844, for example, the Secretary of State, Lord Stanley, wrote: "It is impossible to admit, on the part of a population thus situated, any rights in the soil which should be permitted to interfere with the subjugation by Europeans of the vast wilderness over which they are scattered."[162]

Thus official and legal views on the original inhabitants of New South Wales went hand in hand to create a situation in that colony which deviated sharply from the traditional way of dealing with indigenous peoples in the eighteenth century. The official recognition of Xhosa title to the land east of the boundary of the Cape Colony may seem to preclude the suggestion that this was a general development. However, it is significant that the Xhosa were pastoralists, hence had a different relationship to the land (especially one that could be observed more easily by Europeans) than hunters and gatherers. On the other hand, there was little indication of official acknowledgement of San ownership of their land, a situation more comparable to that in New South Wales. Thus the gradual development of the view that the land inhabited by hunters and gatherers could be regarded as ownerless may

---

[160] Vincent Todd Harlow & Frederick Madden, ed. *British Colonial Developments 1774–1834, Select Documents* (Oxford: Clarendon, 1953): 161. Cf Reynolds, *Aboriginal Sovereignty*, 110, who quotes from a legal opinion from 1819 to the same effect.

[161] Memo on Fowler to Russell, August 1, 1840, CO 13/16: 57; cf Henry Reynolds, *The Law of the Land* (Ringwood, Victoria: Penguin Australia, 1987): ch. 4 and 5, on official attitudes in connection with the establishment of South Australia.

[162] Kenneth Norman Bell & William Parker Morrell, ed. *Select Documents on British Colonial Policy 1830–1860* (Oxford: Clarendon, 1928): 572–73.

further support the suggestion, made at the end of Chapter 3, that the British government was beginning to differentiate between the indigenous peoples encountered, depending on their way of life and means of subsistence.

☙

6 Intellectual Developments

THE EUROPEAN DISCOVERY of the existence of the American continents had a profound impact on intellectual ideas. The re-opening of the Near East by the crusades as well as the exploration of and trade with the rest of Asia had certainly provided new food for thought in Europe; nevertheless, the societies encountered were often comparable to those of Europe in terms of social and political organization. In contrast to this, the encounter with the peoples of America (as well as those of sub-Saharan Africa and, somewhat later, of the Pacific) brought Europeans into contact with ways of life almost beyond comprehension.

The meeting with groups of people so radically different from Europeans in life-style and outlook necessitated a fundamental revision in Europe of the philosophical approach to the history of mankind. Based on the available material, often aided by a great deal of conjecture, men of learning set about adjusting, revising and eventually re-thinking theories about man's origins and social and cultural development; more particularly, the conflict between "savagery" and "civilization" became a recurrent theme in intellectual writing.

The number of works, spanning the period from the sixteenth to the nineteenth centuries, which illustrate these developments is very large, as is the amount of present-day, scholarly writing which discusses them. Obviously, an exhaustive discussion of all this material cannot be attempted here. Rather, the intention of the present chapter is to survey the general development which took place in European thinking about indigenous peoples during this period, with a particular focus on the assumptions underlying the works of the eighteenth and nineteenth centuries. Such assumptions must necessarily have formed an important part of the general context within which official attitudes and policy were formed. While the connection is more intangible than with legal theory, the influence may perhaps have been more profound.

Monster or man

Descriptions of indigenous groups were transmitted to Europe through explorers' journals, travel accounts, and the letters and accounts written by missionaries and settlers, and were further popularized in Europe by enterprising publishers and summarized by interested essayists. The amount of this material constantly increased in the period from the sixteenth to the nineteenth centuries and was accompanied by a similar growth in the exhibition of artefacts and natural objects in private museums. Occasionally, exhibition of specimens of mankind kidnapped from the newly discovered areas (especially in the royal courts of Europe) further encouraged interest.

It is useful to bear in mind, however, as Margaret Hodgen points out, that information about these 'new' peoples spread slowly; at the beginning of the expansionist period, beliefs about distant, exotic people were still largely based on medieval assumptions and many of the compilers of ethnographic and geographic works continued to rely on ancient and medieval sources, confining their descriptions to the peoples of Asia and northern Africa and to ancient tribes, mythical peoples and monsters, all mixed up and treated with equal credulity.[1]

The so-called monstrous races occupied a large place in the medieval imagination; they included giants, pygmies, amazons, wild men, cannibals, people with their eyes in their chests, faces like dogs and many other imaginative characteristics, and they were faithfully reported to exist by authors through the centuries, such as Isidore, Bishop of Seville (7th century), Bartholomaeus Anglicus, a Franciscan friar (13th century), and Sir John Mandeville (14th century), the work of the latter being reprinted ten times in the late seventeenth and early eighteenth century alone.[2]

The monstrous races were usually found in Africa or Asia, the places furthest from Europe, though even the Arabs, as Muhammedans, were often depicted as monstrous despite the close contact which existed with them.

---

[1] Margaret Trabue Hodgen, *Early Anthropology in the Sixteenth and Seventeenth Centuries* (Philadelphia: U of Pennsylvania P, 1964): ch. 4, esp. 148.

[2] Peter James Marshall & Glyndwr Williams, *The Great Map of Mankind: British Perceptions of the World in the Age of Enlightenment* (London: Dent, 1982): 8.

Indeed, one may wonder with Hodgen how and why this preoccupation with the monstrous and fabulous flourished to such an extent when it is probable that quite a lot of fairly accurate information about Africa and Asia was available to Europeans through the reports of traders, missionaries, pilgrims, and crusaders.[3] Whatever the reason, it is clear that this tradition was alive and well at the time Columbus sailed west; in his reports he felt called upon to say that he had not (yet) seen any signs of monstrosity. Others, however, were able to confirm that the "new world" had its share of strange creatures, while cannibalism, of course, became a widely reported characteristic of the Indians in both North and South America.[4]

St Augustine, drawing on the monogenetic tradition of the Christian church, had early made a categorical pronouncement on the distinction between the monstrous and the ordinary races of men. If such monsters existed, he said, "they are either no men, or if they be men, they are the progeny of Adam."[5]

The monogenetic doctrine of the Bible similarly played a significant role in geographical discussions. In the Middle Ages, the shape of the earth had not been fully determined; but it was often suggested that it was round and divided into climatic zones, with an impenetrable zone of fire at the equator. Based on this assumption, it was commonly accepted that there could be no men on the other side because they could not stem from the same Adamic origins as the people of the known world. To suggest that mankind could have polygenetic origins was heresy and continued to be unacceptable to generations of Europeans, as is shown by the reception of Isaac de Peyrere's book *Praeadamitae* as late as 1656. The suggestion that there might have existed men before Adam was so vigorously rejected that Peyrere was forced to withdraw the book and retire to a monastery.[6]

The Great Chain of Being, which was the main way of systematizing the natural world from the days of Aristotle to the beginning of the nineteenth century, was consistent with the idea of monogenism. Like other living organisms, mankind had a stable and unchanging position on a scale of existence and

---

[3] Hodgen, *Early Anthropology*, ch. 3.

[4] Cf the discussion of European fascination with cannibalism in Anthony Robin Pagden, *The Fall of Natural Man: the American Indian and the Origins of Comparative Ethnology* (Cambridge: Cambridge UP, 1986): 80–89.

[5] Quoted in Hodgen, *Early Anthropology*, 53.

[6] Cornelius John Jaenen, *Friend and Foe: Aspects of French-Amerindian Cultural Contact in the Sixteenth and Seventeenth Centuries* (New York: McClelland & Stewart, 1976): 21; cf Michael Banton, *Racial Theories* (Cambridge: Cambridge UP, 1987): 1.

was securely delimited from the lower forms of being by the ability to reason (and from the higher forms of spiritual beings by the lack of superior intelligence).[7]

The theory of biblical monogenism was thus extremely influential in explaining human relations and developments in medieval and Renaissance thinking, and it played an important part in the intellectual struggle to come to terms with the peoples of the newly discovered parts of the world. Throughout the sixteenth and seventeenth centuries, the Bible still represented an indispensable source of information for queries about the nature of mankind, and one of the major challenges posed by the encounter with the peoples of America was to incorporate them within its framework.

The Spanish were among the first to try to deal with the theoretical problems caused by the discovery of the Indians. They conducted several theological debates and enquiries not only into the legal but also into the moral and philosophical questions arising from that discovery. The discussions early focused on the status of the Indian, to some extent caused by the institutionalization of the slave-like conditions of the *encomienda* system. Slavery, hitherto based on captives from, for example, the Black Sea area and then replaced by the Portuguese supply of slaves from Africa, was accepted as legitimate; few had any scruples about the trade. Even the Dominicans, who spoke against enslaving the Indians, saw nothing wrong in having black slaves. The difference between African and Indian slaves, as explained by Pagden, was that whereas the African slave trade was the legal and moral responsibility of the Portuguese, Indian slavery was the concern of the Spanish themselves. Thus it was up to the Spanish to ascertain that it was legally and morally justifiable to enslave the Indians, and this was not so easily done as might be expected.[8]

The subjection of the Indians, initially justified by reference to the papal command to convert them, was soon denounced by concerned missionaries for its cruelty, both in America and in Spain. Prompted by such reports, the Pope in 1537 issued the bull *Sublimis Deus*, in which the right of the Indians to justice and humane treatment was established. It was stated that "the Indians are truly

---

[7] Arthur O. Lovejoy, *The Great Chain of Being: A Study of the History of an Idea* (1936; Cambridge MA & London: Harvard UP, 1978). Cf Nancy Stepan, *The Idea of Race in Science: Great Britain 1800–1960* (London: Macmillan, 1982): 6–9, and Henry Reynolds, *Frontier* (Sydney & Boston MA: Allen & Unwin, 1987): 109–111, both of whom point out the adaptability of the Great Chain to ideas of polygenism later on.

[8] Pagden, *The Fall of Natural Man*, 32.

men and that they are not only capable of understanding the catholic faith but, according to our information, desire exceedingly to receive it." Their enslavement was prohibited and it was ordered that neither their property nor their lives should be taken away.[9]

Despite such clear pronouncements, the bull did not put an end either to the enslavement of the Indians or to the attempt to prove the moral justice of this. For a short period of time, Aristotle's notion of natural slavery provided such a theoretical justification. The main proponent in Spain of this idea that barbarians had less reason than civilized men and were therefore naturally meant to serve their superiors was the court chronicler, Juan Gines de Sepúlveda.

In his thesis *Democrates Secundus* (1544), Sepúlveda maintained that the Indians were vastly inferior to the Spanish – in fact, not much different from animals – and underpinned this assertion with a highly negative description of the Indians (although he had never been in America). He further maintained that if the Indians would not voluntarily submit to their natural masters it would be just and reasonable for their own good to use force to subdue and convert them.[10]

Although Sepúlveda was encouraged by many of those who had a personal interest in the colonies, his work was denied publication by the Council of the Indies, which found it too inflammatory. Submitted to the judgement of a number of learned men, most of them pupils of Francisco de Vitoria, the thesis was pronounced unsound. The reason for this, according to Pagden, was the doctrines Sepúlveda laid down as the fact that his style and method did not conform to the standards required by theologians.[11] While the Salamanca School did not accept the Aristotelian notion of natural slavery,[12] nevertheless, in

---

[9] Quoted in Lewis Hanke, *All Mankind is One: A Study of the Disputation between Bartholome de Las Casas and Juan Gines de Sepulveda in 1550 on the Intelligence and Religious Capacity of the American Indians* (DeKalb: Northern Illinois UP, 1974): 21.

[10] Pagden, *The Fall of Natural Man*, 115–18, and Lewis Hanke, *Aristotle and the American Indian: A Study in Race Prejudice in the Modern World* (Bloomington: Indiana UP, 1959): ch. 5–6.

[11] Pagden, *The Fall of Natural Man*, 110–14.

[12] Vitoria, in fact, denied that Aristotle proposed such a thing as outright slavery for those who were "not over-strong mentally," Francisco de Victoria, *De Indis et de Iure Belli Relectiones, being parts of Relectiones Theologiae XII*, tr. John Pauley Bate, ed. Herbert Francis Wright, intro. Ernest Nys (1557; Washington DC: Carnegie Institute, 1917): 128.

Pagden's view, there was not a great distance between their views and those proposed by Sepúlveda.

Basically, he claims, the Salamanca School had reinterpreted the idea of innate inferiority to mean that the Indians were like children (or the Spanish peasantry) – they had a potential for rational deliberation, but it was as yet undeveloped. Thus they needed guidance and instruction to develop their potential, and the relationship between them and their masters would be like that between children and their fathers. Yet, as Pagden also admits, the recognition by the Salamanca theologians of the basic humanity of the Indian undermined the idea of animal-like inferiority; furthermore, their insistence that the Indians had to agree to their subjection and that Spanish rule had to be to the advantage of the Indians is somewhat contradictory to the essence of Sepúlveda's ideas, especially as he rejected the idea that the Indians could ever become like civilized Europeans.[13]

In any case, Sepúlveda's thesis triggered off the most famous of the Spanish debates on the nature of the Indians, the 1550 Council of Valladolid, probably at least in part prompted by Bartolomé de Las Casas, who was outraged by Sepúlveda's ideas. In 1549, the Council of the Indies pointed out to the king that the justness of the conquests made in the New World and the treatment of the Indians were in doubt. All new conquests were suspended in 1550 until it could be decided whether "it is lawful for the King of Spain to wage war on the Indians before preaching the faith to them in order to subject them to his rule so that afterwards they may be more easily instructed in the faith."[14]

In this debate, Las Casas countered the claims of Sepúlveda by arguing at great length for the humanity of the Indians and pointing to their social and political organization, their material culture, their highly developed "mechanical" skills – all in all, firmly claiming for them that "the Indians like all other men are in full possession of a rational soul" and thus, far from being "natural slaves," were ready (and even eager) to be converted to Christianity through peaceful means. This in turn would make them good and obedient citizens of the Spanish empire, of which Las Casas was by no means an enemy.[15]

---

[13] Pagden, *The Fall of Natural Man*, especially 93–106.

[14] Hanke, *All Mankind is One*, 66–67.

[15] Las Casas, quoted in Pagden, *The Fall of Natural Man*, 135–137; cf Hanke, *All Mankind is One*, ch. 3.

Although the formal question was apparently never fully decided on by the jurors,[16] the central issues of the debate are interesting because they illustrate the basic concern among the learned of sixteenth-century Spain about the humanity of the Indians. Ultimately, the implication was that if they were fully human with souls to convert and save, they would be entitled to humane and just treatment, whereas if they were little better than beasts, then force could be used with less scruple.

After this early period, the human character of the Indians was usually accepted, although, as Marshall and Williams point out, most Spanish writers adopted a view of the Indian as inferior to themselves (determined perhaps by the role as slaves which the Indians continued to play).[17] However, the acceptance of the Indian among the ranks of mankind brought with it other fundamental questions of a theological nature. One of the most insistent issues debated by European scholars during subsequent centuries was how they came to be in America, apparently so completely cut off from the centre of human occupation where the creation of man was supposed to have taken place.

The dispersion of the peoples of the known world had long been a matter for scholarly consideration; the point of departure was usually the Flood, after which it was believed that Noah and his three sons travelled into the world and peopled it according to various traditions. Thus it was commonly claimed that the Africans were descended from Ham, who had been cursed by Noah for being naked, an explanation which was easily extended further south as more of the African coast was explored.

The discovery of the Indians demanded a further development of the attempt to incorporate other peoples within the framework established by the Book of Genesis. Some suggested that they, too, were descendants of Ham who, according to some versions, were not satisfied with remaining in Africa and travelled widely. Other theories about the Indians were also suggested, especially, according to Harry Porter, after the Africans began to appear in America as slaves, thus setting off their blackness (and their bonded position) and different status from that of the Indians. Some suggested that the Indians were descended from the ten Lost Tribes of the Israelites who, after the destruction of Jerusalem, had been deported to another country. Others thought it most likely that the Indians were descended from Shem, another of Noah's

---

[16] Hanke, *All Mankind is One*, 113–114.

[17] Marshall & Williams, *The Great Map of Mankind*, 26.

sons.[18] Some discovered similarities with Jewish culture, such as circumcision and language, to support these ideas, which were widespread in the seventeenth century.

Others traced the relatedness to Europeans, variously claiming that Indians were descended from Scandinavians, Romans or (more complicated, while closer to the truth) from various Asiatic peoples. The issue continued to occupy the minds of the learned; by the eighteenth century the link with, or at least through, Asia was generally accepted as the correct explanation, as in the widely read and extremely influential description of the Americas by Father Lafitau (*Les Mœurs des Sauvages Ameriquains*).[19] As Nancy Stepan points out, there was an implication of equality (at least theoretical) in the pervasive presupposition of monogenism in the early expansionist phase;[20] this was usually taken to mean that with the 'right' kind of instruction (i.e., Christian) the Indian could take up his proper position among the other descendants of Adam.

Enslavement affected this perception, as was seen in connection with Spanish attitudes towards the Indians, although after the early doubts about their human status had been settled, there were few suggestions that the Indian or even the African was inherently, *racially* inferior to Europeans.[21] From the very beginning of encounters with the Africans, their appearance had preoccupied European minds. Although the strength of the sun was often suggested as the explanation for the blackness of their skins, it was also frequently maintained by the late sixteenth century that it was caused by the curse of Ham. Sometimes the legend was expanded to trace the ancestry of monsters as well as of ancient barbaric peoples such as the Tartars to Ham as well, thus further strengthening the connection between the descendants of Ham and

---

[18] Harry C. Porter, *The Inconstant Savage: England and the North American Indian 1500–1660* (London: Duckworth, 1979): 93–96.

[19] Joseph François Lafitau, *Les Mœurs des Sauvages Ameriqains Compareé aux Mœurs des premiers Temps* (Paris: Saugrain l'aîné; C.E. Hocherau, 1724): see, for example, a passage quoted in Ronald Lindley Meek, *Social Science and the Ignoble Savage* (Cambridge: Cambridge UP, 1976): 60–61.

[20] Stepan, *The Idea of Race in Science*, 1.

[21] See, for example, Philip D. Curtin, *The Image of Africa: British Ideas and Action 1780–1850* (London: Macmillan, 1965): 36. The term 'race' was indeed used in the eighteenth century, but with a different and less pervasive meaning. It may be, as Banton suggests, that before 1800 'race' was used in the sense of 'lineage' ("a group [...] connected by common descent or origin"), but that it was only in the nineteenth century that 'race' came to be used in the sense of 'type' ("one of a limited number of permanent forms"), Banton, *Racial Theories*, xi and ch. 1–2.

abnormality.[22] Perceptions of the Africans were also influenced by the tradition which linked black and evil in European culture (death, magic, Hell, etc).[23]

Even though David Brion Davis suggests that European feelings of superiority towards the Africans did not only stem from the institutionalization of slavery, and Anthony Barker maintains that the image of the African as "a wild, untutored cousin" differed only minimally from that of the rest of the "uncivilized" world, it can hardly be doubted that the development of African slavery did little to improve the image of the African in the European imagination.[24] It is also often suggested that not only the Africans themselves caused this response, but also their land, which, as opposed to that of the Indians, was unpleasant, even unhealthy, to Europeans. Thus Marshall and Williams maintain that a more negative tone was generally used to describe Africans than that adopted with other peoples, and that descriptions of them and their way of life were fewer and more limited in scope.[25] By the end of the seventeenth century, when the slave trade was a profitable business, it is probable that the African was clearly distinguished from other "savages" by his function as well as his appearance. This is supported by the fact that in European philosophical writing Indians were far more frequently referred to than Africans.[26]

The impact of this development on the attitudes towards other "black" peoples such as the Aboriginals of Australia is also difficult to assess. Certainly the only detailed description of them available from the seventeenth century, that of the adventurer William Dampier, which was based on the most fleeting of contacts, would suggest that prejudices which did not come into play in connection with the initial descriptions of Indians readily presented themselves in this case: they were described as "the miserablest people in the world [...] they all of them have the most unpleasant looks and the worst features of any

---

[22] Porter, *The Inconstant Savage*, 93–94.

[23] Cf David Brion Davis, *The Problem of Slavery in Western Culture* (Ithaca NY: Cornell UP, 1966): 447–453.

[24] Brion Davis, *The Problem of Slavery in Western Culture*, 281; Anthony J. Barker, *The African Link: British Attitudes to the Negro in the Era of the Atlantic Slave Trade 1550–1807* (London: Frank Cass, 1978): 120, 200.

[25] Marshall & Williams, *The Great Map of Mankind*, ch. 8.

[26] Cf Curtin, *The Image of Africa*, 36, who suggests that a difference existed between depictions of individuals and of Africans as a group, the former being far more favourable than the latter.

people that I ever saw, tho I have seen a great variety of savages," a description which was left uncontradicted until Cook's voyages a century later.[27]

In the eighteenth century, the growing interest in the scientific study of the natural world exerted considerable influence on perceptions of the interrelationship between different groups of mankind. Linné's system of classification of the natural world extended the hierarchical division of the Great Chain to man when it introduced the notion that the human species could be divided into varieties based on colour and behavioural characteristics. While the European always came out on top, some naturalists placed the other types on the same level; others graded them, invariably placing the African at the bottom, sometimes together with various mythical "men." The study of the great apes attracted considerable attention, many scholars being convinced of their close connection with human beings and some even arguing for relatedness with, for example, the Khoikhoi, the people often regarded as the lowest in the "scale of humanity."[28]

The hierarchical ordering of groups of people and even the search for a link between man and primate were not necessarily contrary to monogenism, which remained the prevailing belief throughout the century. However, the ideas which grew out of this development obviously opened the way for thoughts about different human origins, and a small but influential section of European scholarship was outspokenly polygenetic, with dangerous implications for human equality.[29]

Other areas of 'scientific' study also gained increasing interest from the end of the sixteenth century and encouraged the development of new fields such as geography, which was often seen as an integral part of history; this development influenced thought about other peoples. The Frenchman Jean Bodin is an example of this tendency; while he generally accepted the orthodox religious view of monogenism, he concentrated on trying to explain contemporary

---

[27] William Dampier, *A new Voyage around the World: Describing particularly the Isthmus of America, several Coasts and Islands in the West Indies, the Isles of Cape Verd, the Passage by Terra Del Fuego, the South Sea Coasts of Chili, Peru and Mexico; the Isle of Guam, on the Ladrones, Mindanao, and other Phillipine and East India Islands near Cambodia, China, Formosa, Luconia, Celebes, &c., New Holland, Hellena, their Soil, Rivers, Harbours, Plants, Fruits, Animals, and Inhabitants: their Customs, Religion, Government, Trade, &c.* (London: James Knapton, 1697–1709). Quoted in, for example, Marshall & Williams, *The Great Map of Mankind*, 40.

[28] Curtin, *The Image of Africa*, 31–38, Stepan, *The Idea of Science in Race*, 6–9.

[29] See below, 272–73.

cultural diversity from considerations of environment and climate. Thus he believed that climatic differences between the north and the south contributed to differences in national character and, in turn, the social and political organization of various peoples:

> And even as they which live at the extremities of the Poles, are Flegmatike, and at the South melancholie; even so they which are thirtie degrees on this side of the Pole, are cholerike; and then drawing towards the South, more sanguin and melancholike.[30]

The idea of the influence of climate on the way of life of peoples continued to be developed until, in the eighteenth century, Montesquieu formulated the theory that government became more despotic the warmer the temperature, and the influential French naturalist Buffon hypothesized that the harshness of the American environment was the cause of the savage nature of the Indian.[31]

Comparing different worlds

As Hodgen points out, emphasis on similarities (and differences) became increasingly noticeable in scholarly works;[32] this was already to be seen in connection with the debate about the origin of the Indians, which was largely based on comparisons with the customs or language of other peoples to prove the connection. Comparisons were frequently used in accounts of indigenous peoples to help the reader envisage unfamiliar customs or characteristic; authors, perhaps more concerned with their own society, often incorporated remarks on the way of life of these peoples in order implicitly – or explicitly – to show the benefits or shortcomings of European life. A survey of some of the best-known writers of the period under consideration will show the frequency of such tendencies.

The French lawyer Michel de Montaigne is an early example of this tradition. His collection of essays, written in the late sixteenth century and widely

[30] Jean Bodin, *Les Six Livre de la République* (Lyon, 1576). Quoted in James Sydney Slotkin, *Readings in Early Anthropology* (London: Methuen, 1965): 71. Cf Hodgen, *Early Anthropology*, 276–280.

[31] Baron de Montesquieu, *Esprit des Lois*, 2 vols. (Geneva, 1748); Comte de Buffon, *L'Histoire Naturelle*, 36 vols. (Paris, 1749–1788). Quoted in Marshall & Williams, *The Great Map of Mankind*, 213 & 216 respectively.

[32] Hodgen, *Early Anthropology*, 296.

read in Britain after they were translated in 1603,[33] deals with almost all conceivable topics, among them being the nature of the inhabitants of America. In the essay "Of the Caniballes" Montaigne described the way of life of the Indians as governed by "a genuitie so pure and simple," and as

> a nation [...] that hath no kinde of traffike, no knowledge of Letters, no intelligence of numbers no name of magistrate, nor of politike superioritie; no use of service, of riches or of povertie; no contracts, no successions, but common, no apparell but naturall, no manuring of lands no use of wine, corne, or mettle. The very words that import lying, falshood, treason, dissimulation, covetousnes, envie, detraction, and pardon, were never heard of amongst them.[34]

This country of "perfection" had no crippled or ill people, an abundance of food which could be acquired without much labour, and a population who lived without superfluous luxuries but also without want. The characteristic with which Montaigne was most impressed was their bravery; even when faced with death and the certainty of being eaten by their enemies, they would never flinch or beg for mercy. They would fight only for the honour of winning, not to gain land or to subdue others

> for to this day they yet enjoy that naturall ubertie and fruitfulness, which without labouring toyle, doth in such plenteous abundance furnish them with all necessary things, that they need not enlarge their limits. They are yet in that happy estate, as they desire no more, than what their naturall necessities direct them.[35]

There is no doubt that this society, governed by the laws of nature, compared favourably for Montaigne with that of his own country. This comes out most clearly perhaps in his discussion of cannibalism, of which he said:

> I thinke there is more barbarisme in eating men alive, than to feed upon them being dead [as the Indians do]; to mangle by tortures and torments a body full of lively sense, to roast him in peeces, to make dogges and swine to gnaw and teare him in mammockes[36]

---

[33] Michel de Montaigne, *The Essays of Montaigne done into English anno 1603 by John Florio*, intro. George Saintsbury (*Les Essais*, 1580; tr. 1603; New York: AMS, 1967): ix. See also Peter Burke, *Montaigne* (Oxford: Oxford UP, 1981): 69.

[34] Montaigne, *The Essays of Montaigne*, 222.

[35] *The Essays of Montaigne*, 227.

[36] *The Essays of Montaigne*, 226.

– which, as Montaigne pointed out, was still happening in Europe, even "under pretence of pietie and religion." To Montaigne, then, the Indians represented an unspoilt, original way of life, the antithesis of European life, where natural ability was corrupted by artificial devices and ingenuity. Obviously one of the main purposes of the essay was to bring out this discrepancy through comparison with a people whose virtue lay in their perceived simplicity.

In spite of Montaigne's favourable attitude towards the Indians, his essay to a certain extent confirms the point, made by several scholars, that this kind of treatment of indigenous society was very often of an ethnocentric nature; the negative description of the Indians (what they did not have, rather than what they did have) shows that the understanding of the Indian way of life was based on European cultural notions.[37] Many writers, however, were much more obviously ethnocentric than Montaigne.

Comparisons with indigenous peoples were further developed in a generalized manner as philosophers in Europe moved from specific concerns about their origin or their disconcerting habits to attempts to generate comprehensive theories about the development of man and the organization of human society. Gradually the tradition was established that indigenous peoples could be used to exemplify the way of life of Europeans in an earlier phase of existence, a function formerly performed by ancient peoples. As Hodgen points out, indigenous society was seen as basically static and could therefore be used as "a form of documentation" of the original way of life of man.[38]

Again, the use to which this exemplary material was put depended on the view of the author. This is shown very clearly in the works of two of the most frequently cited seventeenth-century British political philosophers. In *Leviathan* (1651), Thomas Hobbes used the American Indians to illustrate the original nature of mankind, which he perceived to be a state of constant warfare and danger when man lived without any kind of government and was guided only by his own passions in an essentially irrational manner. As a consequence of perpetual fear and hostility, man would have no opportunity to improve his existence through invention and labour:

---

[37] Cf Hodgen, *Early Anthropology*, 193–201, and Bernard Sheehan, *Savagism and Civility: Indians and Englishmen in Colonial Virginia* (Cambridge: Cambridge UP, 1980): 26–29.

[38] Hodgen, *Early Anthropology*, 332–33; cf Marshall & Williams, *The Great Map of Mankind*, 191.

> there is no place for Industry; because the fruit thereof is uncertain: and consequently no Culture of the Earth; no Navigation [...] No Instruments of moving [...] no account of Time; no Arts; no Letters; no Society; and which is worst of all, continuall feare, and danger of violent death; And the life of man, solitary, poore, nasty, brutish, and short.[39]

This condition represented for Hobbes the fundamental characteristics of man which would predominate unless some form of power existed to control them. Hobbes exemplified this situation by pointing to the Indians:

> there are many places, where they live so now. For the savage people in many places of *America*, except the government of small Families, the concord whereof dependeth on naturall lust, have no government at all; and live at this day in that brutish manner as I said before.[40]

Another example of the original condition Hobbes found in the state of civil war. Although the human state of nature was thus not necessarily a historical phenomenon, the creation of a political "common-wealth" with the power to punish transgressions, such as had occurred in England, would in most cases replace this original state of being, which would then become a past stage in human development.[41]

John Locke, whose statement that "In the beginning all the world was America" has become as famous as Hobbes's description, held a somewhat less negative view of Indian society.[42] The state of nature, which Locke perceived the Indians to be living in, was characterized as "a *State of Perfect Freedom* [and] a *State* also *of Equality*" where man is governed by the law of nature and has the power to punish everyone else according to it.[43] The basis of Indian

---

[39] Thomas Hobbes, *Leviathan or the Matter, Forme & Power of a Commonwealth, Ecclesiasticall and Civill*, ed. A.R. Waller (1651; Cambridge: Cambridge UP, 1904): 84.

[40] Hobbes, *Leviathan*, 85.

[41] Hobbes, *Leviathan*, 115–119. See also Marc F. Plattner, *Rousseau's State of Nature: An Interpretation of the Discourse on Inequality* (Dekalb: Northern Illinois UP, 1971): 71. It is not within the scope of this chapter to discuss the complex social and political theories of the authors quoted; the aim is to give examples of the way in which these theoreticians described indigenous peoples in their works.

[42] Locke, *Two Treatises of Government*, ed. Peter Laslett (1690; Cambridge: Cambridge UP, 1970): 319. The phrase occurs in the discussion of the origin of money; the inland parts of America are given as an example of a place where money had no value.

[43] Locke, *Two Treatises of Government*, 287. On the many different conceptions of the phenomenon of the state of nature during the seventeenth and eighteenth centuries,

existence was thus all mankind's original state of being. As shown in the discussion of his concept of property in the previous chapter, Locke did not regret the passing of the state of nature. Government as it was found in Europe arose because of the need to protect the property acquired by "Industrious" man, who had thereby gained a great many advantages if compared to the Indians.[44]

In the following century, Hume, too, did not agree with Hobbes's characterization of human existence in the "state of nature." In his *Treatise of Human Nature* (1739), Hume discussed the source of government; unlike Hobbes, Hume did not believe that government was a requisite for peaceful coexistence in a given society. In his view, men in an early state of existence would have little to steal from each other or quarrel about and would therefore be able to live peaceably together without government; the American Indian is used as an instance of this condition: "This we find verified in the *American* tribes, where men live in concord and amity among themselves without any established government."[45] Only when disagreements with other groups arose would it be necessary to find a chief who could lead them in war; this in Hume's opinion was the original cause of the establishment of governmental institutions.[46] Like others before him, Hume referred to the Indians simply as an example, and it is not easy to detect what his attitude towards them might be, though elsewhere this was more clearly shown.[47]

There is no doubt that the best-known use of the image of indigenous people in the eighteenth century is to be found in the works of the French philosopher Jean–Jacques Rousseau. In his essay "Discourse on the Origin and Foundation of Inequality among Mankind" (1755), Rousseau propounded the theory that the source of inequality lay in the society made by man rather than in the nature of man himself.[48] To support this claim, Rousseau postulated an original state

---

see Arthur O. Lovejoy, *Essays in the History of Ideas* (1948; Westport CT: Greenwood, 1978): 15 ("The Supposed Primitivism of Rousseau").

[44] Cf Marshall & Williams, *The Great Map of Mankind*, 192.

[45] David Hume, *A Treatise of Human Nature*, ed. Lewis Amherst Selby–Bigge (1739–40; Oxford: Clarendon, 1968): 540.

[46] Cf Frederik Vinding Kruse, *Hume's Philosophy in his Principal Work "A Treatise of Human Nature" and in his Essays*, tr. P.T. Federspiel (London: Oxford UP, 1939): 52–55.

[47] See below, 275.

[48] Adam Smith's review of the "Discourse on Inequality" in "A Letter to the Authors of the *Edinburgh Review*" from 1755 (J. Ralph Lindgren, ed. *The Early Writings of Adam Smith* [New York: Augustus M. Kelley, 1967]: 23–28) illustrates the significance

of nature where such a condition did not exist. Although he at times uses the example of indigenous peoples, particularly the Caribs and the "Hottentots,"[49] to illustrate this state, it becomes clear that it is a hypothetical picture of man in his very earliest stages of development, where neither speech nor any form of social interaction had yet come into being.[50]

However, Rousseau found a place for known indigenous peoples in the intermediate state which he perceived to exist between this original mode of being and that of "civil society." As man became a moral and social being, the need for government by law began to develop. At this stage,

> a just mean [had been reached] between the indolence of the primitive state and the petulant activity of egoism [which] must have been the happiest and most durable epoch [...] The example of savages, most of whom have been found in this condition, seems to confirm that mankind was formed ever to remain in it, that this condition is the real youth of the world, and that all ulterior improvements have been so many steps, in appearance towards the perfection of individuals, but in fact towards the decrepitness of the species.[51]

In this condition, man had developed feelings of mutual affection and respect, and even hostility, though this was moderated by the lack of property or the urge to subject the labour of others to one's own ends. Thus Rousseau perceived men at this stage as living in a state of harmony and perfect equality. While Rousseau's view in this respect is quite close to that of Locke, whom he refers to with approval, he is strongly opposed to Hobbes's idea that man is naturally evil ("But above all things let us beware of concluding with Hobbes, that man, as having no idea of goodness, must be naturally bad").[52]

---

which was attributed to this essay in Britain. Later in the century, Lord Monboddo paid tribute to Rousseau in his *Of the Origin and Progress of Language* (Edinburgh: J. Balfour, 1774–92), vol. 1: iii.

[49] Jean–Jacques Rousseau, *The Social Contract and Discourse on the Origin and Foundation of Inequality among Mankind*, tr. Henry J. Tozer/anon., ed. & intro. Lester G. Crocker (*Du Contrat Social*, 1762, tr. nineteenth century/*Discours sur l'Origine et les Fondements de l'Inégalité parmi les Hommes*, 1755, tr. 1761; New York: Washington Square Press, 1976): 206 & 186 respectively.

[50] Whether Rousseau really saw this original state of nature as hypothetical or merely represented it to be so in order to avoid accusations of heresy, has – like many other aspects of Rousseau's theory – been a matter of considerable discussion among scholars; see, for example, Plattner, *Rousseau's State of Nature*, 19–25.

[51] Rousseau, *The Social Contract*, 220.

[52] *The Social Contract*, 200. In other respects, however, Rousseau agrees with Hobbes, cf Plattner, *Rousseau's State of Nature*, 65.

While Rousseau concedes that man in the original, animal-like state of nature would not have known "what it is to be good," he draws the opposite conclusion to Hobbes from his proposition: namely, that man would therefore not have the capacity for being evil either.[53] This "natural goodness of heart" was somewhat modified in the next stage of development but was not finally subdued until the effects of greed and ambition were felt by "civilized" man.[54]

The picture that Rousseau created of contemporary indigenous peoples as representing the golden age of human development has been seen as the ultimate illustration of the tradition of the Noble Savage, though some scholars question this by pointing to the fact that Rousseau's realism prevented him, in fact, from depicting this existence in the truly idyllic fashion commonly associated with the Noble Savage myth.[55] Strictly speaking, as Arthur Lovejoy points out, the happiness of this intermediate stage was not even the product of man's natural existence but of his slow progress away from it; Rousseau was thus not celebrating the primitivism of "savage man" but the particular level of his human development.[56]

Rousseau's discussion of the further development of human society, dramatically altered by the invention of "metallurgy and agriculture," shows a profound disillusionment with his own times, in which the few ruled over the many. It would be logical to assume on this basis, as has indeed been done many times since the appearance of the essay, that Rousseau was advocating a return to the earlier state of happiness.[57] However, Rousseau himself denies this course; the human mind constantly changes and there is really no way back: "Savage man and civilized man differ so much at the bottom of their hearts and in their inclinations, that what constitutes the supreme happiness of the one

---

[53] "it is neither the development of the understanding, nor the curb of the law, but the calmness of their passions and their ignorance of vice that hinder them from doing ill"; *The Social Contract*, 201. Cf. Plattner, *Rousseau's State of Nature*, 80–81.

[54] *The Social Contract*, 219, 224.

[55] Hoxie Neal Fairchild, *The Noble Savage: A Study in Romantic Naturalism* (New York: Russell & Russell, 1961): 126–27, and Lovejoy, *Essays in the History of Ideas*, 14–31 ("The Supposed Primitivism of Rousseau"). Lovejoy also strongly objects to the frequent claim that it was the original state of nature which Rousseau regarded as the ideal state.

[56] Lovejoy, *Essays in the History of Ideas*, 30–31.

[57] See, for example, Voltaire's caustic comments as quoted in Lester Crocker's introduction to Rousseau, *The Social Contract*, ix–x.

would reduce the other to despair."[58] It is stated even more clearly in note i), in which Rousseau poses the question of whether the conclusion to his reasoning is that "man [must] go back to living in the forest with the bear." His reply is that for those "whose passions have irretrievably destroyed their original simplicity" (including himself and obviously the rest of "civilized" mankind) this would be neither possible nor desirable; instead, the attempt should be made to improve society according to the divine and regal commandments to which man has subjected himself.[59]

The thought that indigenous people could be used as an example of the earliest way of life of mankind also found wide application in Britain in the second half of the century. Perhaps the best examples of this are found among the Scottish philosophers who elaborated the so-called "four stage theory."[60] Among these writers, the way of life of indigenous people was used in a more specific way than had been customary among earlier authors; as Ronald Meek points out, the central feature of the "stadial" theory is that peoples are grouped specifically according to their mode of subsistence rather than generally according to their customs or other aspects of their way of life.[61]

In the words of Adam Smith, one of the first British writers to formulate this thesis,[62] "There are four distinct states which mankind pass thro:– 1st, the Age of Hunters; 2dly, the Age of Shepherds; 3dly, the Age of Agriculture; and 4thly, the Age of Commerce."[63] Later it appears that the American Indians are seen by Smith as an example of the first stage, though, interestingly, he recognizes the fact that the Indians seemingly provide an exception to his categorization because "tho they have no conception of flocks and herds, have nevertheless some notion of agriculture." Smith solves this problem by deprecating the

---

[58] Rousseau, *The Social Contract*, 244.

[59] *The Social Contract*, 253–254.

[60] For a discussion of their precursors in this field, see Meek, *Social Science and the Ignoble Savage*, ch. 1.

[61] Meek, *Social Science and the Ignoble Savage*, 6.

[62] See Meek, *Social Science and the Ignoble Savage*, ch. 3 for simultaneous developments in France (among others by Turgot) and ch. 4 for his detailed argument that Smith was in fact *the* first in Britain to state the essence of the four stages theory.

[63] Adam Smith, *Lectures on Jurisprudence*, ed. Ronald Lindley Meek, David Daiches Rafael & Peter Gonville Stein (vol. 5 of *The Glasgow Edition of the Works and Correspondence of Adam Smith*, 6 vols., general editor Dugald Stewart) (1762–63, 1766; Oxford: Clarendon, 1978): 14.

Indian form of cultivation: "Their women plant a few stalks of Indian corn at the back of their huts. But this can hardly be called agriculture."[64]

Once the stages of development had been established, they could be used to explain the differences existing between various peoples. Smith, for example, applied it to the existence of notions of property:

> It is easy to see that in these severall ages of society, the laws and regulations with regard to property must be very different.- In Tartary, where as we said the support of the inhabitants consists in herds and flocks, *theft* is punished with immediate death; in North America, again where the age of hunters subsists, theft is not much regarded. As there is almost no property amongst them, the only injury that can be done is the depriving them of their game.[65]

Similarly, the Scottish philosopher and judge Lord Kames used the stage theory to explain the differences in societal organization found in different parts of the world:

> The life of a fisher or hunter is averse to society, except among the members of single families. The shepherd life promotes larger societies, if that can be called a society, which hath scarce any other than a local connection. But the true spirit of society [...]was not known until agriculture was invented.[66]

Later in the century, John Millar, professor of law at Glasgow University, developed this theory into a comprehensive philosophy of history; in the introduction to the third edition (first published in 1779) of the *Origin of the Distinction of Ranks*, Millar established the general framework of his discussion. He first notes that a great many circumstances combine to produce the situation in which a people must form its existence (such as "the fertility or barrenness of the soil, the nature of its productions [...] the number of individuals collected together [...] their proficiency in arts [etc.])."[67] Secondly, however, he notes that there is

> in man a disposition and capacity for improving his condition, by the exertion of which, he is carried on from one degree of advancement to another; and the

64 Adam Smith, *Lectures on Jurisprudence*, 15.

65 *Lectures on Jurisprudence*, 16.

66 Lord Kames, *Historical Law Tracts* (Edinburgh: A. Kincaid, 1758), quoted in Meek, *Social Science and the Ignoble Savage*, 103.

67 John Millar, *The Origin of the Distinction of Ranks*, reproduced from the third edition (London: John Murray, 1779), in William C. Lehmann, ed. *John Millar of Glasgow* (Cambridge: Cambridge UP, 1960): 175.

> similarity of his wants, as well as of the faculties by which those wants are supplied, has every where produced a remarkable uniformity in the several steps of his progression.[68]

In other words, mankind everywhere goes through the same stages of development prompted by the desire to ease the conditions of life; man's perceptions and intellectual capacity correspond to the stage of development he has reached. Thus, of the first level, Millar says:

> a nation of savages, who feel the want of almost every thing requisite for the support of life, must have their attention directed to a small number of objects, to the acquisition of food and clothing, or the procuring shelter from the inclemencies of the weather; and their ideas and feeling, in conformity to their situation, must, of course, be narrow and contracted.[69]

Only as man reaches the further stages of agriculture and commerce are such general notions as property and the "rights of mankind" recognized, in turn leading to "a more complex form of government." Millar touches briefly on other explanations commonly offered for the differences between nations, such as climatic theories or the significance of influential individuals, but to his mind they do not present a challenge to the explanatory force of the stage theory. The main part of his work then applies the pattern of stadial development to the evolution of social organization and authority in human society.

The German philosopher Johann Gottfried von Herder, in his *Reflections on the Philosophy of the History of Mankind*, written towards the end of the century, challenged the stage theory. Noting the common use of this theory, Herder pointed to the basic difficulty of defining the modes of subsistence on which it was based, since these varied from one region to another ("The farmers of Whidoh are as unlike those of Japan as the merchants of England are to those of China").[70] Perhaps more importantly, Herder also rejected the idea that, for example, the need to procure more food was the force underlying human development, as claimed by some writers.[71]

---

[68] Millar, *The Origin of the Distinction of Ranks*, 176.

[69] *The Origin of the Distinction of Ranks*, 176.

[70] Frederick M. Barnard, ed. *J.G. Herder on Social and Political Culture* (Cambridge: Cambridge UP, 1969): 302 (book 8, ch. iii).

[71] Johann Gottfried von Herder, *Reflections on the Philosophy of the History of Mankind*, tr. T.O. Churchill, abridged & intro. Frank E. Manuel (*Ideen zur Philosophie der Geschichte der Menscheit*, 1784; tr. 1800; Chicago: U Chicago P, 1968): 50 (book 8, ch. iii).

In Herder's view, climate and "genetic power" combined with tradition to create the national characteristics of individual peoples; the "genius" of these peoples is the key to understanding the history of the world.[72] From his numerous examples of the way of life of indigenous peoples from all over the world, Herder concluded that these peoples learned everything from nature, the forests, the sea and the animals around them, and that they lived sufficient and happy lives in this manner:

> The islanders, whom Nature feeds with vegetable productions, particularly the salubrious breadfruit, and clothes in a delightful climate with the rind of trees, lead a tranquil happy life. [...] Where the climate was less temperate, men were necessitated to live more hardly, and with less simplicity. The New Hollander pursues his opossum and kanguroo, shoots birds, catches fish, and eats yams: he has united as many ways of life as his rude convenience required, till he had rounded them as it were into a circle, in which he could live happily after his fashion [....] [in America] [...] most nations have been hunters in a nobler form. What does a North or South American require, to fit him for the way of life, to which he is destined? He knows the beasts of his chase, their abodes, manners, and artifices, and arms himself against them with strength, address, and exercise.[73]

To Herder, cultural diversity, or pluralism, is one of the concepts central to an understanding of the nature of human society. Each people – and each age – develops at its own pace and according to its own cultural pattern, its own myths and inner forces.[74] Yet Herder could not rid himself entirely of the fundamental notion underlying the stage theory, that somehow the development of mankind was connected with a progression from hunting through herding to agriculture.[75] After his discussion of hunters and fishermen he continues:

> But man went incomparably farther, when he attracted animals about him, and finally brought them under his yoke. The immense difference between neighbouring nations, living with or without these auxiliaries to their powers, is evident.[76]

---

[72] *Reflections on the Philosophy of the History of Mankind*, 3–49 (books 7 & 8).

[73] *Reflections on the Philosophy of the History of Mankind*, 51–52 (book 8, ch. iii).

[74] Cf Isaiah Berlin, *Vico and Herder: Two Studies in the History of Ideas* (New York: Vintage, 1977): 154–55, 190–92 (and passim).

[75] Cf Meek's discussion, *Social Science and the Ignoble Savage*, 192–98.

[76] *Reflections on the Philosophy of the History of Mankind*, 53–54 (book 8, ch. iii).

Herder attributes great importance to this development; he believes, for example, that if the American Indians had had domesticated animals, especially horses and dogs, when the Europeans arrived on their shores they would have been able to fight on an equal footing with the invaders.

Lastly, he discusses the impact of agriculture:

> Generally speaking, no mode of life has effected so much alteration in the minds of men, as agriculture, combined with the enclosure of land. While it produced arts and trades, villages and towns, and, in consequence, government and laws; it necessarily paved the way for that frightful despotism, which from confining every man to his field, gradually proceeded to prescribe to him, what alone he should do on it , what alone he should be.[77]

Recognizing the value of this mode of life in producing "civil society," Herder is nevertheless conscious of the great evils which have attended it in the form of subjugation of men to dependence and near-slavery. Herder, in this fashion, produces a synthesis by combining features of Rousseau's writings with the stage theory, but his conclusion that the equal worth of other ways of life should be recognized leaves both of them far behind.[78] This element of Herder's work will be further discussed below.

Irrespective of the specific role which the stage theory played in the development of the socio-economic sciences,[79] there is thus no doubt about its extensive general influence on European philosophical perceptions about mankind in the second half of the eighteenth century.[80] As such, it may be seen as the culmination of the tendency, illustrated in this section, to use the growing knowledge of other peoples comparatively, in order to clarify the process of human development with which the thinkers of the eighteenth century were so preoccupied. This urge is aptly summed up in a statement made by Edmund Burke to William Robertson in 1777 upon the publication of the latter's book about North America:

> I have always thought with you, that we possess at this time very great advantages towards the knowledge of human Nature. We need no longer go to

---

[77] *Reflections on the Philosophy of the History of Mankind*, 57 (book 8, ch. iii).

[78] "let justice be done to other ways of life, which [...] have been destined, equally with agriculture, to contribute to the education of mankind"; *Reflections on the Philosophy of the History of Mankind*, 57 (book 8, ch. iii).

[79] See Meek, *Social Science and the Ignoble Savage*, ch. 6.

[80] See, for example, Meek, *Social Science and the Ignoble Savage*, passim, for numerous examples of the use of this theory during this period.

> History to trace it in all its stages and periods [....] now the Great Map of Mankind is unrolld at once; and there is no state or Gradation of barbarism, and no mode of refinement which we have not at the same instant under our View. The very different Civility of Europe and of China; The barbarism of Persia and Abyssinia. The erratick manners of Tartary, and of arabia [sic]. The Savage State of North America, and of New Zealand.[81]

'Noble' or 'ignoble' savage?

Discussions of the image of indigenous peoples in this eighteenth-century cartography of mankind have customarily focused on the distinction between the 'noble' and 'ignoble'" representations of 'savages' which have emerged from the European works. While attempts have been made to show the predominance of one or the other at particular times, scholars commonly agree that the two have coexisted ever since the earliest European explorations of the world outside Europe.[82]

The myth of the Noble Savage, drawing variously on the ancient notion of a 'golden age' or on medieval ideas that somewhere far away an earthly paradise could be located, was given nourishment from the very first writings on America; thus Columbus was convinced he had found heaven on earth in the Caribbean islands. A tradition was created which pictured Indians (and other indigenous peoples) as living in innocence and perfect harmony. Nakedness, inactivity and lack of any kind of social or political organization or property characterized people in this state, in accordance with with the original condition of man before the Fall.[83]

The image of the Noble Savage was prominent in France, where writers often idealized the equality and freedom perceived to exist among the Indians (though missionaries saw their religious views as needing amendment).[84]

---

[81] George H. Guttridge, *The Correspondence of Edmund Burke, July 1774–June 1778*, vol. 3 in *The Correspondence of Edmund Burke*, 10 vols., ed. Thomas W. Copeland et al. (Cambridge: Cambridge UP, 1961): 351.

[82] Cf Marshall & Williams, *The Great Map of Mankind*, 191–97; Hugh Honour, *The New Golden Land: European Images of America from the Discoveries to the Present Time* (London: Allen Lane the Penguin Press, 1976): 118–37, and Reynolds, *Frontier*, 108.

[83] See, for example, Fairchild, *The Noble Savage*, ch. 1, and Sheehan, *Savagism and Civility*, ch. 1.

[84] Jaenen, *Friend and Foe*, 28–34.

While the formulation of the idea of the *bon sauvage* may initially have been undertaken by the religiously orthodox, it gradually passed to those critical of the established order and the general conditions of French society; they used the perceived primitivism of the unspoilt and noble Indians to point up the failings and decay of that society. Thus it is probably no coincidence that two of the most widely acclaimed proponents of this tradition, Montaigne and Rousseau, were both Frenchmen.

However, the idea of the Noble Savage was also very well known and widely applied in Britain, particularly in imaginative literature. The first use of the term itself in English has been traced to John Dryden's play *The Conquest of Granada* (1664);[85] the many examples provided by Hoxie Neal Fairchild show that as a literary device this figure became increasingly popular and was, at least by the beginning of the eighteenth century, commonly used either to voice a nostalgic longing for an idealized past or, more frankly, to criticize contemporary society, as in the essays of Addison and Steele, and the writings of Defoe and Swift.[86] Bernard Smith and others have also shown the significance of art in propagating the image of the Noble Savage.[87]

Towards the end of the century, the reverence for nature and the simple life associated with the Romantic movement contributed to idealization of a close relative of the Noble Savage, the "child of nature."[88] The exploration of the Pacific in the second half of the century sped this development by bringing new material about the ideal of "savage" life to the attention of Europeans;[89] Hawkesworth in his edition of Cook's first voyage exemplifies this attitude. Although far from idealizing the New Zealanders (whose customs of canni-

---

[85] Fairchild, *The Noble Savage*, 29.

[86] *The Noble Savage*, passim. See also Marshall & Williams, *The Great Map of Mankind*, 196.

[87] Bernard Smith, *European Vision and the South Pacific 1768—1850: A Study in the History of Art and Ideas* (Oxford: Clarendon, 1960); see also, for example, Honour, *The New Golden Land.*

[88] See Fairchild, *The Noble Savage*, ch. 10 and passim.

[89] See especially Smith, *European Vision and the South Pacific*. Cf. Glyndwr Williams, who points out that this view became modified as knowledge about life in the islands expanded; "Seamen and Philosophers in the South Seas in the Age of Captain Cook," *The Mariner's Mirror* 65 (1979): 3–22.

balism horrified him) or the Aborigines, he gave a highly positive description of the inhabitants of Tahiti, referring to them constantly as "our friends."[90]

A similar impression is created by George Keate in his *Account of the Pelew Islands* (1788), in which the story is recounted of the shipwreck of a British ship in the Palau Islands. Although Keate is at times critical of indigenous peoples, he also presents a rosy picture of the harmonious and uncorrupted islanders; for example, the chief is described in the following terms:

> the excellent man, who ruled over these sons of Nature, [...] in every part of his conduct, shewed himself firm, noble, gracious, and benevolent; there was a dignity in all his deportment, a gentleness in all his manners, and a warmth and sensibility about his heart, that won the love of all who approached him.[91]

The reverse of this image, the so-called ignoble savage, can also be traced back to medieval notions; myths of wild men and the previously mentioned monstrous beings had formed a fertile soil for reports of indigenous peoples living hard and dangerous lives in an unattractive environment – little better, in fact, than beasts. Confronted with a life-style wholly different from that of Europe, many writers fell back on ethnocentric condemnation of what they did not understand; the perceived lack of religion, sexual morality, government or social order, combined with subsistence, often by hunting and gathering rather than by agriculture, made these peoples represent the very opposite of what for a European constituted human existence.

Elaborating on this idea, Bernard Sheehan suggests that during the sixteenth and seventeenth centuries the understanding of the American Indians was formed by an inherent struggle between "savagism" and "civility" in the European mind. The way of life of the Indians was seen as representative of all the dangers of violence, chaos and bestiality that lurked beneath the surface of the Christian order in Europe; the encounter – real or imagined – with eaters of

---

[90] John Hawkesworth, *An Account of the Voyages Undertaken by Order of His Present Majesty for making Discoveries in the Southern Hemisphere and successively performed by Commodore Byron, Captain Wallis, Captain Carteret, and Captain Cook drawn up from the Journals which were kept by the several Commanders and from the Papers of Joseph Banks, Esq.* (London: W. Strahan & T. Cadell, 1773): vol. 2.

[91] George Keate, *Account of the Pelew Islands* (London, 1788) quoted in Smith, European Vision and the South Pacific, 97. Cf the passage from J. Stockdale, *The Voyage of Governor Phillip to Botany Bay* (London, 1789), quoted in Robert Dixon, *The Course of Empire: Neo-Classical Culture in New South Wales 1788–1860* (Melbourne & Oxford: Oxford UP, 1986): 9.

human flesh proved the connection of these people with the devil and confirmed the belief that they represented the very antithesis of human life. In Sheehan's view, a preconceived image of savageness was applied to the Indians to set them apart from the Europeans and to underline the distance which Europeans had put between themselves and the primeval state of nature.[92]

Sheehan's rather rigid interpretation of the Indian image drawn by Englishmen in the seventeenth century is vigorously opposed by Karen Kupperman, who emphasizes the similarities between Indian and European society at a time when belief in supernatural forces, witchcraft and natural medicine was still current in Europe.[93] She suggests that on the basis of the reports written by visitors to America, many of whom attempted to give faithful accounts of Indian life, Europeans attempted to incorporate the Indians in their understanding of the world rather than to set them apart from it. The Indians were fitted into a framework based on social distinctions between rich and poor, most of the Indians conveniently finding a place among the lower classes in Europe.[94]

The great diversity of the accounts of America affords evidence supporting both Sheehan's position and Kupperman's, and in fact emphasized the point that there was indeed no settled view of how the Indians should be understood, either in relation to themselves or to the Europeans. This is further underlined by the simultaneous existence of a tradition depicting the Indians as noble.

The image of the 'ignoble' savage continued to be invoked by authors referring to America, as the examples quoted above have shown. The effect was to show the achievements of European 'civilization' by comparing it with what was perceived as less advanced societies. As Bernard Smith also points out, it even increased on the cusp of the nineteenth century, when indigenous people, especially the Pacific Islanders, came to be criticized for what was perceived as their heathenism and sinful life-style. After the turn of the century, depictions of indigenous peoples as 'noble savages' gradually disappeared, except in the even further sentimentalized version of "the last of his race."[95]

---

[92] Sheehan, *Savagism and Civility*, intro., ch. 2. See also Hodgen, *Early Anthropology*, 361.

[93] Karen Ordahl Kupperman, *Settling with the Indians: The Meeting of English and Indian Cultures in America 1580–1640* (Totowa NJ: Rowman & Littlefield, 1980): 114–18.

[94] Kupperman, *Settling with the Indians*, ch. 6.

[95] Smith, *European Vision and the South Pacific*, 106–109, 128–19.

It is certainly true, however, that for much of the eighteenth century and even before, the idea of the Noble Savage existed side by side in the European mind with that of the 'ignoble' one, and that a discussion of them reveals a great deal about the workings of that mind.[96] It is, however, worth pointing out that the significance of the noble/ignoble imagery can be overemphasized. There is little doubt that the primary function of these images was to comment on European society and it may therefore be suggested that it was comparison that was the real concern. Although this was probably always the case, the significance of comparison becomes very clear in the eighteenth century and is, as mentioned, particularly well illustrated by the development of the stage theory, in which a general concept of 'savage' life (really neither 'noble' or 'ignoble') was systematically used to illustrate the development of mankind, basically with the purpose of enlarging on the latest – European – stage.

Observation and description

The kind of use to which the stage theorists put the accumulated knowledge about indigenous peoples points to a further predominant characteristic of the treatment of these peoples in eighteenth-century intellectual works. Fundamentally, many of these works show a readiness to accept the common humanity of 'savage' and 'civilized' peoples and an openness towards describing other forms of life, often with a conspicuous lack of condemnation (though rarely in a completely unbiased manner).

There are notable early examples of this tendency. Montaigne is well known for his relativistic attitude to other peoples' customs and values, be it French peasants, other Europeans, or Brazilian Indians;[97] thus, in the essay quoted above, he makes the following observation about the Indians:

> there is nothing in that nation, that is either barbarous or savage, unlesse men call that barbarisme which is not common to them. As indeed, we have no other ayme of truth and reason, than the example and Idea of the opinions and customs of the countrie we live in.[98]

---

[96] Cf Honour, *The New Golden Land*, 119–20; Marshall & Williams, *The Great Map of Mankind*, 201, 212

[97] Burke, *Montaigne*, 44–51.

[98] Montaigne, *The Essays of Montaigne*, 221.

Locke, in his *Essay Concerning Human Understanding*, reveals the same kind of thinking; endeavouring to prove that there are no "innate principles" of either a moral or practical nature in man, he arrives at the conclusion that man anywhere in the world has the ability to learn anything (because of God's benevolence). Thus he comments:

> Had you or I been born at the Bay of *Soldania*, possibly our Thoughts, and Notions, had not exceeded those brutish ones of the *Hotentots* that inhabit there: and had the *Virginia* King *Apochancana*, been educated in *England*, he had, perhaps, been as knowing a Divine, and as good a Mathematician, as any in it. The difference between him, and a more improved *English*-man, lying barely in this, That the exercise of his Faculties was bounded within the Ways, Modes, and Notions of his own Country.[99]

Both Montaigne and Locke thus recognized that the outlook and behaviour of a people is shaped by their customs and traditions and that basically all belong to the human species, endowed with equal abilities and possibilities.

This understanding gained further ground during the following century. The spirit of empirical investigation, a central feature of the Enlightenment, contributed to creating an atmosphere of rational enquiry that encouraged many authors to approach the study of other peoples in an open-minded fashion. This was expressed both in relativistic approaches to other cultures similar to the ones just quoted, and in a striking preference for detailed description of other peoples. These tendencies can be found in varying degrees both in accounts of the newly discovered parts of the world and in philosophical works such as those cited earlier. A few examples of each category may illustrate this point.

In 1731, Peter Kolb's account of the Khoikhoi peoples (*Present State of the Cape of Good-Hope*) was translated into English from the German original (1719). Kolb had set himself the goal of writing a balanced account of the Khoikhoi in order to reverse the extremely negative view of the "Hottentot" which existed in Europe. In his fourth chapter, he specifically rejected the current judgement of the Khoikhoi, referring to it as "Excesses of the Imagination, which have made a very wretched People more wretched in *Europe* than they are at home."[100] He proceeded to note their ability to learn languages, their

---

[99] John Locke, *An Essay Concerning Human Understanding*, ed. Peter H. Nidditch (1690; Oxford: Clarendon, 1975): 92.

[100] Peter Kolb, *Present State of the Cape of Good Hope*, tr. Guido Medley, intro. W. Peter Carstens (*Caput Bonae Spei Hodiernum*, 1719; tr. 1731; New York: Johnson Reprint, 1968), vol. 1: 37.

talent for cultivation and for functioning as servants, their loyalty and their honesty. Although, on the debit side, he finds "laziness" and "filthiness," Kolb, overall, finds much to praise in their way of life.[101] While this characterization is openly devoted to the rehabilitation of the Khoikhoi in the eyes of the Europeans, the rest of the work presents a fairly neutral description of Khoikhoi life, including their form of government, their religion, the economic foundations of their life, and their social customs. In the account of a funeral rite which was described as involving the urinating of old men on other members of the community, Kolb makes the following comment

> Strange! The different Notions different Nations entertain of the same Thing! The Force, the Witchcraft of Custom! To be piss'd on in *Europe* is a Token of the highest Contempt: To be piss'd on in the *Hottentot* Countries is a Token of the highest Honour.[102]

As Mary Louise Pratt points out, Kolb throughout his account maintains that even though the Khoikhoi may have customs which are revolting or shocking to the European, they nevertheless have a right to be considered just as human as the Europeans; they cannot be distinguished as some other form of being that can be discriminated against or enslaved.[103]

One of the numerous accounts of the American Indians, *An Account of the European Settlements in America* (1758), attributed to William Burke, is in many respects similar to Kolb's work. The description of the Indians, though by no means idealized, is marked by a desire to present a balanced view. Thus, on the one hand, the lives of the Indians are characterized as "hardy, poor, and squalid," their "only occupations are hunting and war," and their condition is aggravated by the influence of alcohol among them; on the other hand, many of their characteristics are praised – for example, "nothing is more edifying than their behaviour in their public councils and assemblies."[104] Many more examples of both points of view are to be found in the long, detailed account of their way of life and their customs.

---

[101] See also Kolb, *Present State of the Cape of Good Hope*, vol. 1, ch. 29 ("A Review of the Vices and Virtues of the Hottentots").

[102] Kolb, *Present State of the Cape of Good Hope*, vol. 1, 316.

[103] Mary Louise Pratt, *Imperial Eyes: Travel Writing and Transculturation* (London & New York: Routledge, 1992): 44.

[104] William Burke, *An Account of the European Settlements in America*, 2 vols. (1758; New York: Research Reprints, 1970): 168, 169, 170.

Having described in excruciating detail the custom of torturing prisoners to death, the author concludes his account of the Indians by remarking that this shows, "in the strongest light, to what an inconceivable degree of barbarity the passions of men let loose will carry them"; yet the great determination with which the victim would bear this torment, which the author recognized as an important part of the ritual, led him also to comment that "the constancy of the sufferers in this terrible scene shows the wonderful power of an early institution, and a ferocious thirst of glory, which makes men imitate and exceed what philosophy, or even religion can effect."[105]

James Adair, who for many years lived as a trader in North America, in 1775 published an account of the American Indians which is mostly dedicated to showing that they were descendant of the Jews; the account is generally favourable towards the Indian way of life yet also makes note of the "fickle, wild, and cruel tempers" of the Indians.[106] Adair opens with observations about the universality of the human character; remarking that the Indians prefer their own skin colour to any other and even attempt to heighten it, Adair reflects that it is a common characteristic for different peoples to find their own appearance the standard measure of normality and beauty. This prompts him to make the following point:

> If a deformed son of burning Africa, was to paint the devil, he would not do it in black colours [....] his devil would represent one of a different nation or people. But was he to draw an agreeable picture, – according to the African taste, he would daub it all over with sooty black. All the Indians are so strongly attached to, and prejudiced in favour of, their own colour, that they think as meanly of the whites, as we possibly can do of them.[107]

Again, although there is clearly a large amount of ethnocentric prejudice here, nevertheless the passage exemplifies an awareness of the fact that the European is after all not so very much different from the rest of mankind; all are human beings with a similar propensity for judging one other.

---

[105] Burke, *An Account of the European Settlements in America*, 199–200.

[106] James Adair, *The History of the American Indians particularly those Nations adjoining to the Mississippi, East and West Florida, Georgia, South and North Carolina and Virginia, etc. containing an Account of their Origin, Language, manners, Religious and Civil Customs, Laws, Form of Government, Punishments, Conduct in War and Domestic Life, their Habits, Diet, Agriculture, Manufactures, Diseases, and Method of Cure and other Particulars* (London: Edward & Charles Dilly, 1775): 9.

[107] Adair, *The History of the American Indians*, 1.

William Robertson wrote another widely read account of America; the first eight books were published in 1777, the last two posthumously in 1793. The long section devoted to the description of the Indians (Book Four) presents a rather negative view of these people as feeble, inactive and in certain ways living like animals. However, it is clear that the main aim of Robertson's description is not to denigrate the Indians but, rather, to investigate the development of mankind in all its phases. Robertson is clearly influenced by the ideas of the stage theorists; noting the importance of the study of "man in all those various situations in which he has been placed," he specifically states that it is necessary to "follow him in his progress through the different stages of society, as he gradually advances from the infant state of civil life towards its maturity and decline."[108]

Robertson laments the lack of reliable information on the Indians and points out that "to discover their ["uncivilized nations'"] true character under this rude form, and to select the features by which they are distinguished, requires an observer possessed of no less impartiality than discernment."[109] Like Adair, he is aware that man tends to judge other peoples by his own standards and consequently that "polished nations" are "apt to view rude nations with peculiar scorn, and, in the pride of superiority, will hardly allow either their occupations, their feelings, or their pleasures, to be worthy of men."[110] Robertson views with equal distrust the accounts written by the Spaniards, by philosophers (who indulge in speculation rather than sticking to facts), and by travellers and other visitors to America. In conclusion, he states his view of how one should proceed in the difficult matter of portraying "savages":

> Without indulging conjecture [...] we must study with equal care to avoid the extremes of extravagant admiration, or of supercilious contempt for those manners which we describe.[111]

Although – seen with modern eyes – Robertson hardly manages to live up to his own standards, his is a clear statement of the eighteenth-century perception of the ideal of scientific study whose purpose was to broaden knowledge in a particular field rather than to subject it to moral evaluation.

---

[108] William Robertson, *The History of America* (1777 & 1793; London: A. Strahan, T. Cadell Junior & W. Davies, 1800), vol. 2: 50.

[109] Robertson, *The History of America*, vol. 2, 53.

[110] *The History of America*, vol. 2, 54.

[111] *The History of America*, vol. 2, 59.

One of the most renowned of the eighteenth-century travellers and explorers was James Cook; his journals, and to a certain extent that of Joseph Banks from the first of Cook's voyages, epitomize the point being made here. The journals show very clearly the importance attributed to careful observation and detailed description of every aspect of the encounter with other peoples (as with the flora and fauna of their countries); Cook himself acknowledged that it was "my duty as well as my inclination to insert in this Journal every and the least knowledge I may obtain of a people who for many centuries has been shut up from almost every other part of the world."[112]

Cook occasionally volunteers his opinion of a particular custom or of a people. The Tahitian custom of killing babies born of the religious society, the *Arioi*, Cook denounces as "inhuman and contrary to the first principals [sic] of human nature"; the Aboriginal people, on the other hand, he describes in a well-known passage as being

> in reality [...] far more happier than we Europeans; being wholy unacquainted with not only the superfluous but the necessary Conveniences so much sought after in Europe, they are happy in not knowing the use of them.[113]

---

[112] J.C. Beaglehole, ed. *The Journals of Captain James Cook on his Voyages of Discovery*; part 1: *The Voyage of the Endeavour 1768–1771* (Cambridge: Cambridge UP, 1955): 134. Cook had been encouraged in this attitude by the president of the Royal Society, who, in a series of "Hints," had given very specific instructions about the kind of information desired and the form in which it should be represented. In the "Hints," Cook is also admonished to show due regard for the peoples he meets and to respect their unquestionable right to their lands and to peaceful treatment; it is suggested, furthermore, that only with the "voluntary consent" of the inhabitants could Europeans ever settle among them (Beaglehole, ed. *The Voyage of the Endeavour*, 514–19).

[113] Beaglehole, ed. *The Voyage of the Endeavour*, 399. There is a similar, though by no means identical, passage in Joseph Banks's journal, J.C. Beaglehole, ed. *The Endeavour Journal of Joseph Banks 1768–1771* (Sydney: Trustees of the Public Library of New South Wales in association with Angus & Robertson, 1963), vol. 2: 130. Beaglehole considers Cook's "panegyric" to be wholly out of line with the captain's personality and his usual style (he refers to it as "nonsense"), but Williams has shown that while Cook may have been somewhat influenced by Banks, his view of the Aborigines was simply reflecting the general influence of ideas common at this time; J.C. Beaglehole, ed. *The Life of James Cook* (London: A. & C. Black, 1974): 251–52, and Glyndwr Williams, "'Far more happier than we Europeans': Reactions to the Australian Aborigines on Cook's Voyage" in *Through White Eyes*, ed. Susan Janson & Stuart Macintyre (Sydney: Allen & Unwin, 1990): 58–61.

Yet by far the greater part of Cook's account is characterized by a remarkable degree of objectivity in the description of the peoples met with.[114] Thus the account of New Zealand cannibalism is practically free of any emotionally inspired commentary,[115] and when Cook's seamanship prompts him to state that the Aboriginal boats are "as mean as can be conceived," he immediately balances this with the observation that "they do very well for the purpose they apply them to, better than if they were larger."[116] Even when Cook witnessed a ceremony based on human sacrifice, which he condemned and tried to persuade the Tahitian chief to desist from, he retains his sense of relativism, noting at the end of the dispute that "we left him with as great a contempt of our customs as we could possibly have of theirs."[117]

Joseph Banks's journal is somewhat more prone to subjective commentary but is nevertheless characterized by the same spirit of detailed enquiry as that of Cook.[118] Glyndwr Williams makes an interesting comparison between the descriptions of the Aboriginal peoples by Cook and Banks, and that written a little less than a century earlier by William Dampier. The whole point of Dampier's description of the physical appearance of these people clinched his conclusion that "They all of them have the most unpleasant Looks and the worst Features of any People that ever I saw, tho I have seen a great variety of Savages." Although, as Williams shows, both Banks and Cook had Dampier in the back of their minds when they wrote about the Aborigines (Banks probably more so than Cook), they distanced themselves from his description through their careful and detached observation.[119]

---

[114] Cf Alan Frost's characterization of Cook (and Banks) as "percipient, tolerant of racial and cultural difference, and empathetic to a remarkable degree"; Frost, *Botany Bay Mirages: Illusions of Australia's Convict Beginnings* (Carlton, Victoria: Melbourne UP, 1995): 188. See also, by the same author, "A Strange Illumination of the Heart," *Meanjin Quarterly* 29 (1970): 446–52, and Marshall & Williams, *The Great Map of Mankind*, 273.

[115] Marshall & Williams, *The Great Map of Mankind*, 282.

[116] *The Great Map of Mankind*, 397.

[117] J.C. Beaglehole, ed. *The Journals of Captain James Cook on his Voyages of Discovery*; part 3: *The Voyage of the Resolution and Discovery 1776–1780* (Cambridge: Cambridge UP, 1967): 206. For a discussion of the development of Cook's attitude to, and knowledge of, the Pacific islanders in the course of his three voyages, see Williams, "Seamen and Philosophers in the South Seas," 10–21.

[118] Beaglehole, ed. *The Endeavour Journal of Joseph Bank*, vol. 1–2.

[119] Williams, "'Far more Happier than we Europeans'," 52–54. Cf Smith, *European Vision and the South Pacific*, 125–27.

Johann Reinhold Forster, who participated in Cook's second voyage, after the return of the *Resolution*, wrote *Observations made during a Voyage around the World* (1778) – this is not a journal like Cook or Banks's books but a systematic treatise on various topics of natural science such as geography and biology. By far the largest section of the work is concerned with the "human species." Like Robertson, Forster regrets the tendency among writers to give insufficiently researched, subjective accounts of various peoples around the globe; as for his own role, he states that "I collected facts, and now communicate them to the impartial and learned world, with a few inferences, as an imperfect essay."[120]

Indeed, Forster's work is filled to the brim with what he considered observable facts, such as the various varieties or "races" encountered in the South Seas and their characteristics, their "progress [...] from the Savage State towards Civilization," the impact on this of climate, the habits, organization and religion of the inhabitants. Once again, the overwhelming impression is a fondness of detail, even to the extent of fastidiousness. Thus, for example, having described the New Caledonians as being "of a swarthy colour; their hair [...] crisped, but not very woolly," Forster feels compelled to add an explanatory footnote:

> As some of my readers, not having seen a variety of nations, may think the distinction between crisped and woolly hair, either improper or insufficient, I must beg leave to observe that the woolly hair of Negroes, is not only frizzled and crisped, but likewise that each hair is found to bee extremely thin, and proceeding from a root or bulb, remarkably smaller than that observed in other human hair[121]

And so on for another fourteen lines.

John Barrow's account of Southern Africa, written at the very end of the century during the governorship of the Earl of Macartney, has many of the same characteristics as mentioned above, particularly that of extremely detailed description of the peoples he met, set out in a language of neutral observation. Occasionally, however, he becomes more passionate, as when describing the plight of the Khoikhoi or the fear of a group of San during a commando

---

[120] Johann Reinhold Forster, *Observations made during a Voyage round the World on Physical Geography, Natural History, and Ethic Philosophy* (London: G. Robinson, 1778): 213.

[121] Forster, *Observations made during a Voyage round the World*, 239.

attack in which he participated.[122] Like Kolb, Barrow was concerned to correct the generally held view of the Khoikhoi:

> Low as they are sunk in the scale of humanity, their character seems to have been very much traduced and misrepresented. It is true there is nothing prepossessing in the appearance of a Hottentot, but infinitely less so in the many ridiculous and false relations by which the public have been abused.[123]

In his description of the Xhosa men, he comes close to idealization:

> The men [...] were the finest figures I ever beheld: they were tall, robust, and muscular; their habits of life had induced a firmness of carriage, and an open manly manner, which, added to the good nature that overspread their features, shewed them at once to be equally unconscious of fear, suspicion, and treachery.[124]

Although on occasion Barrow thus openly indulged in subjective comments on the peoples he observed, the general impression remains one of dispassionate observation. Pratt characterizes Barrow's writing as "a strange, highly attenuated kind of narrative that seems to do everything possible to minimize the human presence" but given the object of Barrow's travels – to examine the country and its people – he set about doing it in a way entirely characteristic of eighteenth-century observation, which does not mean that the human inhabitants are relegated to a secondary position but, rather, that information had to be ordered in a particular way.[125]

It is by no means my intention here to suggest that eighteenth-century accounts of indigenous peoples were generally objective or free of value judgements; as has been seen, statements to the opposite effect are frequently encountered. Rather, an attempt has been made to show that authors of such accounts were very often guided by a desire to give as much information as possible about the variety of mankind under observation and that they often believed they were presenting an unbiased view of man which, whether true or

---

[122] John Barrow, *Travels into the Interior of Southern Africa, in the years 1797 and 1798* 2 vols. (London: T. Cadell Junior & W. Davies, 1801–1804): 144–45 & 272–73 respectively.

[123] Barrow, *Travels into the Interior of Southern Africa*, 151.

[124] *Travels into the Interior of Southern Africa*, 169.

[125] Pratt, *Imperial Eyes*, 59.

not, at least reflected the ideal of the time.[126] The frequent demands for yet more meticulous studies of other peoples, especially in the second half of the century, is also evidence that this was a common concern in the period.[127] It is also apparent that many of these writers were guided by an attitude which tended to admit the equality, at least theoretically, of different cultures. This did not so much mean that they personally believed other cultures to be of the same value as their own, as that they saw that, to the members of another culture, that culture would seem as valuable as European culture to a European.[128]

Among the philosophical or academic works projecting the indigenous image, the tendency to open-mindedness is often also clear. Again, examples may be found among the Scottish thinkers, dominant as they were in the British intellectual world of the eighteenth century. Their development of the four-stage theory was in itself based on the assumption that all peoples had passed through the stages preceding the one they occupied – even the most highly developed society had at one time subsisted on hunting and gathering and had lived in a "savage" manner. While the life of the American Indian could appear brutal and primitive, it was only an example of what the British, for example, had once been. Again, John Millar provides an eloquent illustration of this view:

> When we survey the present state of the globe, we find that, in many parts of it the inhabitants are so destitute of culture, as to appear little above the condition of brute animals; and even when we peruse the remote history of polished nations, we have seldom any difficulty in tracing them to a state of the same rudeness and barbarism.[129]

In the earlier edition (1773) of his work, Millar had stated this even more categorically: "Man is every where the same; and we must necessarily conclude, that the untutored Indian and the civilized European have acted upon the

---

[126] Cf comments made by Curtin, *Images of Africa*, 206–11. Curtin sees this as an expression of "universal curiosity," which he finds very well illustrated by Mungo Park's account of Africa.

[127] See, for example, Smith, *European Vision and the South Pacific*, 99–102.

[128] Cf George Ward Stocking Jr.'s comments on the emergence of French anthropology around 1800; Stocking, *Race, Culture, and Evolution: Essays in the History of Anthropology* (Chicago & London: U of Chicago P, 1982): 28–29.

[129] Millar, "The Origin of the Distinction of Ranks," 175–76.

same principles."[130] Although the stage theorists constructed a very hierarchical and eurocentric picture of human development, they basically recognized the common human source of this development.

It is therefore also quite logical that the stage theorists, who certainly did not idealize "savage" life, rarely condemned it. Although Millar is quite eloquent on the "shocking barbarity" of people in the earliest stage, he maintains that the mode of life of such peoples is suited to the conditions under which they live; and of course, "how poor and wretched soever the aspect of human nature in this early state, it contains the seeds of improvement."[131]

The ultimate example of eighteenth-century tolerance of other cultures is to be found in the writings of Herder. Basing his argument on a profound belief in the concept of *Humanität* (variously translated as human essence, humanity, or human mutuality) as the source of everything that distinguishes man from the animals, Herder is unequivocal on the equal worth of all mankind:

> [man's] human essence – *Humanität* – [....] is potentially realizable. And this is true of a New Zealand cannibal no less than of a Fénélon, of a wretched gypsy no less than of a Newton, for all are creatures of one and the same species.[132]

Herder points out repeatedly that the European way of life does not constitute the measuring rod for what is good or desirable; any attempt to impose uniformity on mankind is also evil.[133] For example, on the European mode of subsistence he has the following to say:

> Land is cultivated in our manner by the smallest portion of the inhabitants of the Earth, and Nature, herself, has pointed out to the rest their different modes of living [....] If Nature has any where attained her end, she has attained it everywhere. The practical understanding of man was intended, to blossom

[130] John Millar, *Observations Concerning the Distinction of Ranks in Society* (1771; London: J. Murray, 1773): iii.

[131] Millar, "The Origin of the Distinction of Ranks," 198. Cf Meek, *Social Science and the Ignoble Savage*, 172–73, who also finds a measure of relativism in Millar's ideas.

[132] Barnard, *Herder on Social and Political Culture*, 266 (book 4, ch. iv).

[133] Cf Berlin, *Vico and Herder*, 176–78.

> and bear fruit in all its varieties: and hence such a diversified Earth was ordained for so diversified a species.[134]

To Herder, it is important to try to acquire a feeling for other cultures, to understand the essence of other peoples' experience.[135] This is very well illustrated by his introductory remarks to his discussion of the peoples of Africa, in which he admonishes the reader to remember that even as the European commonly denigrates the black man, so the latter may hold himself infinitely above the white man and see himself as the original being living in blessed circumstances of climate and environment.[136]

The belief in human diversity which Herder stresses throughout his work also prompted him to denounce myths of human monsters – myths which, as he points out, tended to disappear upon closer examination of the matter ("when we have a more exact account of the ouran-kubub, and orang-guhu, the tailed savages of the woods in Borneo, Sumatra, and the Nicobar islands will vanish").[137] Herder attacks the notion that some peoples were more closely related to the apes than others; he just as emphatically rejects the idea that different races can be distinguished on the basis of origin or physical characteristics, concluding that "all are at last but shades of the same great picture, extending through all ages, and over all parts of the Earth."[138]

While the relativism of Herder's ideas was unparalleled in his own time, the ability to recognize the common humanity of diverse people or the potential worth of different ways of living was not uncommon in the eighteenth century, as has been seen in the preceding pages. However, as the eighteenth century turned into the nineteenth, the approach of Europeans to other cultures gradually changed in significant ways.

---

[134] Herder, *Reflections on the Philosophy of the History of Mankind*, 57–58 (book 8, ch. iii). See also 71 (book 8, ch. v), where Herder strikes at the notion that "all the inhabitants of the World must be Europeans to live happily."

[135] Berlin, *Vico and Herder*, 186.

[136] Johann Gottfried Herder, *Ideen zur Philosophie der Geschichte der Menschheit*, ed. Martin Bollacher (1784; Frankfurt am Main: Deutsche Klassiker Verlag, 1989): 228 (book 6, ch. iv). These reflections have been omitted from the Chicago abridgement.

[137] Herder, *Reflections on the Philosophy of the History of Mankind*, 5 (book 7, ch. i).

[138] *Reflections on the Philosophy of the History of Mankind*, 7 (book, 7, ch. i).

Into the nineteenth century: race and humanitarianism

Herder's discussion of races reflects the growing significance attributed to this concept towards the end of the eighteenth century. As mentioned earlier, although monogenism remained the dominant view, polygenetic thoughts were voiced by some scholars; one of them was the British physician Charles White, who, in a book published in 1799, argued that the African belonged to a separate species. Edward Long had followed the same line of thinking in his *History of Jamaica* (1774), which was written to support the institution of slavery in the West Indies.[139]

Polygenesis, however, never became the dominant view in Britain; even though some authors continued this tradition, most influential writers on the biological developments of mankind in the late eighteenth and early nineteenth century followed the German scientist Blumenbach, generally rejecting the idea of separate origins for different groups of people and insisting that all of them were distanced by a wide gap from the primates. At the same time, the idea of a chain of being was also discarded because its rigid concept of natural history was found increasingly insufficient and unsatisfactory; the possibility of incorporating the idea of several human species within its hierarchical system also prompted Blumenbach and others to reject it.[140] Vestiges of this tradition remained, though, in the prevailing view that the varieties of man were fixed forms whose characteristics remained unaltered over time; this belief did not change until the work of Darwin, after mid-century, gave prominence to the idea of natural selection as the cause of biological evolution.[141]

Although the common origin of different peoples was generally recognized, however, this did not preclude differentiation between different categories or "races" of human beings within the species, nor the erection of hierarchical systems on that basis. In fact, the upsurge of concern with race which occurred in the early decades of the nineteenth century may well have been due to the

---

[139] Charles White, *An Account of the regular Gradation in Man, and in different Animals and Vegetables; and from the former to the latter* (London, 1799); Edward Long, *The History of Jamaica or a general Survey of the antient and modern State of the Island, with reflections on its Situation, Settlements, Inhabitants, Climate, Products, Commerce, Laws and Government, etc.*, 3 vols. (London, 1774); see Stepan, *The Idea of Race in Science*, 8 and Curtin, *The Image of Africa*, 45–47.

[140] Johann Friederich Blumenbach – for example, *De Generis Humani Varietate Nativa* (Göttingen: A. Vandenhoeck, 1775); see also Stepan, *The Idea of Race in Science*, 9–12, 29–35, and Curtin, *The Image of Africa*, 229–31.

[141] Stepan, *The Idea of Race in Science*, 3.

urge to counter the attraction of polygenist ideas.[142] Where environmental and cultural features had earlier been seen as explanatory of group characteristics and behaviour (and physical ones mainly as indications of biological connections), physical traits began to be seen as important outward signs of yet more significant mental differences of intelligence and ability which could be attributed to the "race" as a whole. Theories of racial difference inevitably concluded that the racial traits of the Europeans made them superior to other races. Such claims received scientific backing because much of the debate about race took place within the field of such sciences as anatomy and biology.[143]

Among race theorists, attention was early devoted to finding a system for establishing racial differences. As early as the 1770s, the Dutchman Pieter Camper had developed a method for measuring the facial angle in order to show the degree of relatedness to the apes; later, attempts were made to establish other forms of craniometry which would show the relationship between observable features of the skull and mental abilities. One popular method in the early part of the nineteenth century was that of phrenology, in Britain most ardently applied by George Combe; in phrenology, measurements of the head were compared with behaviour and on the basis of numerous observations generalizations were made about the correlation between the functions of the brain and particular racial types.[144]

Thus, after the late eighteenth century, race came to be seen as increasingly crucial in explaining the diversity of human culture and society encountered around the globe, pointing ahead to the racial determinism that characterized much British thinking and action throughout the nineteenth century.[145] A passage from a work (1822) by the British surgeon William Lawrence, deeply involved in the debate about race, may serve as an example of the prevalent attitude of scholars who, although energetically maintaining the monogenist tradition, believed in racial differentiation with its implications of inferiority

---

[142] *The Idea of Race in Science*, 30.

[143] Cf Stocking, *Race, Culture and Evolution*, 29–31.

[144] Pieter Camper, *Über den natürlichen Untershied der Gesichtszüge*, (Berlin, 1792); George Combe, *Elements of Phrenology* (Edinburgh: John Anderson Jun., 1824). See Stepan, *The Idea of Race in Science*, 8–28. See, for example, Reynolds, *Frontier*, 113–14, and Andrew Bank, "Liberals and their Enemies, Racial Ideology at the Cape of Good Hope 1820–1850" (unpublished doctoral dissertation, Cambridge University, 1995): ch. 7, on the extension of phrenology to colonial society.

[145] Michael Biddiss, *Images of Race* (Leicester: Leicester UP, 1979): 12–13. Cf Stepan, *The Idea of Race in Science*, ch. 2, Curtin, *The Image of Africa*, 364.

and superiority. The passage also indicates the revival of interest in the link between man and ape, spurred by renewed study of the primates. Lawrence noted that

> the mind of the Negro and the Hottentot, of the Chalmuck and the Carib, is inferior to that of the European and also their organisation is less perfect [...] In all particulars [...] the Negro structure approximates unequivocally to that of the monkey. It not only differs from the Caucasian model; but is distinguished from it in two respects; the intellectual characters are reduced, the animal features enlarged and exaggerated.[146]

There had been examples in the course of the eighteenth century of the belief that colour or other physical traits were indications of innate characteristics; thus Hume had stated in 1754 that

> I am apt to suspect the Negroes, and in general all the other species of men (for there are four or five different kinds) to be naturally inferior to the whites. There never was a civilized nation of any other complexion than white, nor even any individual eminent in action or speculation. No ingenious manufactures amongst them, no arts, no sciences.[147]

It is characteristic that Hume should concentrate on the cultural differences between the two groups as evidence for the inferiority of one, whereas Lawrence emphasizes innate physical traits as the distinguishing features. Although the ultimate point of both passages is the same, Lawrence's statement is also much more uncompromising, stating a fact rather than suggesting a possibility. This surely reflects the fact that in the mid-eighteenth century, racial theories were still relatively undeveloped, whereas by the beginning of the nineteenth century they were becoming the orthodox way of regarding these matters.[148]

The development of theories of racial difference perceptibly changed the way of understanding the varieties of mankind and the attempts to come to terms with the explosion of knowledge about the world. Other developments at the turn of the century, however, also affected the way in which indigenous peoples were regarded. Foremost among these was no doubt the movement

---

146 William Lawrence, *Lectures on Physiology, Zoology, and the Natural History of Man, delivered at the Royal College of Surgeons* (London, 1822), quoted in Stepan, *The Idea of Race in Science*, 15.

147 David Hume, *Essays Moral, Political, and Literary*, ed. T.H. Green & T.H. Grose (1742–77; London: Longmans, Green, 1898?), vol. 1: 252 (note to Essay 21, "Of National Character").

148 Cf Michael Banton, *The Idea of Race* (Boulder CO: Westview, 1977): 18; ch. 3.

eventually leading to the abolition of slavery. The beginning of the campaign in Britain is marked by the Somerset case (1772), in which slavery was declared repugnant to the laws of England; this event was followed by an outburst of writing on the moral injustice of human bondage, countered by other writers defending the system. After a prolonged political struggle, further complicated by the outbreak of the war with France, the slave trade was abolished by Parliament in 1807, and slavery in the British colonies finally in 1833.[149]

For the purposes of this study, the forces behind the movement are of greater significance than the events themselves. In his influential work, David Brion Davis has traced some of the factors that contributed to creating a climate of hostility towards slavery. Some of the roots of the abolition movement identified by Brion Davis have already been mentioned in other contexts in this and the previous chapter; thus he suggests that the tradition of the Noble Savage during the eighteenth century had an impact on the way in which Europeans perceived the Africans who were forced into slavery, transforming them into "children of nature."[150] More generally, he suggests that European philosophers writing on political theory were increasingly confronted with the dilemma posed by slavery to Enlightenment ideas of natural rights, and perhaps especially to doctrines of utility. In the economic theory of Adam Smith, slavery was represented as a monopolistic phenomenon which disrupted the natural interaction of economic factors. Moreover, slavery was an inefficient form of labour because, having no hope of any kind of material reward, the slaves were deprived of any incentive to work hard.[151]

These trends, which contributed to creating opposition to slavery, were strongly supported by religious and moral sentiments. The Quakers, both in Britain and in America, were among the first to denounce slavery, and provided early writings against it. The enslavement of fellow human beings accorded ill with Quaker belief in the equality of all men and their chances of

---

[149] See Reginald Coupland, *The British Anti-Slavery Movement* (London: T. Butterworth, 1933), for a classic description of the events leading to the abolition of slavery in the British Empire.

[150] Brion Davis, *The Problem of Slavery in Western Culture*, 472–82, and "What the Abolitionists were up against" (reprinted from Brion Davis, *The Problem of Slavery in the Age of Revolution 1770–1823* [Ithaca NY & London:, 1975]), in *The Antislavery Debate*, ed. Thomas Bender (Berkeley & Oxford: U of California P, 1992): 24.

[151] Adam Smith, *An Inquiry into the Nature and Causes of the Wealth of Nations* (London: W. Strahan & T. Cadell; 1776). See Brion Davis, *The Problem of Slavery in Western Culture*, ch. 13–14.

seeking the path of salvation, and involvement in slavery came to be seen as a threat to the Quaker cause. By the 1750s, the Quakers had begun to take measures against members who were actively engaged in the slave trade and in 1783 they established a committee to work for abolition.[152]

Within the Anglican church, the development of beliefs in the natural goodness of man and his sense of morality rather than his inherent depravity and fall from grace created a tradition of benevolence which was an important source of the desire to do good and relieve suffering which came to characterize devout Christians.[153] However, in apparent contradiction to this, it took the moral indignation of evangelical revivalists to harness Anglicanism to the abolitionist cause. The evangelicals reacted against the increasing secularization of Christian beliefs and in general against what they saw to be the relaxation of moral norms; they urged the need for every person to struggle against sin, both within the individual and in the world at large. Unfailing belief in salvation by Christ, together with virtuous living, inspired by unselfishness and a high sense of moral duty, became the Evangelicals' weapon against sin. In a sense, they thus combined the ideas of sin and benevolence, rather than creating an opposition between them.[154]

Their belief that all men had been created by God in His image made it clear to the Evangelicals that slavery was an offence against the Divine will, as well as a great evil in itself and in the last decades of the century a number of Evangelicals joined the struggle against it with considerable force. Known as the Clapham sect because many of them lived in Clapham (and intermarried to an amazing extent), such men as William Wilberforce, James Stephen Sr., Henry Thornton, Charles Grant, Granville Sharp and later Thomas Fowell Buxton had all undergone personal experiences of religious revelation and were filled with a sense of inner obligation to struggle against the slave system. With Wilberforce and Buxton in Parliament and with their close connections

---

[152] Brion Davis, *The Problem of Slavery in Western Culture*, ch. 10, and "Quaker Ethic and the Antislavery International," in Bender, *The Anti-Slavery Debate*, 31–34.

[153] Brion Davis, *The Problem of Slavery in Western Culture*, ch. 11. Cf Norman Hampson, *The Enlightenment: An Evaluation of its Assumptions, Attitudes, and Values* (1968; Harmondsworth: Penguin, 1990): 79–84.

[154] Brion Davis, *The Problem of Slavery in Western Culture*, ch.12. Cf Elizabeth Jay, *The Evangelical and Oxford Movements* (Cambridge: Cambridge UP, 1983): 1–20, and Kenneth Hylson–Smith, *Evangelicals in the Church of England* (Edinburgh: T. & T. Clark, 1988): parts 1 and 2.

with important politicians, the Clapham sect undoubtedly played an important role in the abolitionist movement.

Enlightenment ideas thus converged with religious sentiments and humanitarian aspirations to create a pervasive incentive for anti-slavery agitation. Yet scholarly debate in recent decades has shown that other factors also have to be taken into consideration. Ultimately, the antislavery movement was based on, and contributed to, the support of governmental power. The struggle for abolition was not a revolutionary or destabilizing movement which questioned prevailing values but, rather, built on existing principles of authority and social organization. Furthermore, at a time which was marked by the emergence of industrialization and the replacement of mercantilist by capitalist theories of economy, factors that transformed the structure of British society, antislavery combined old-fashioned paternalism with utilitarian ideas of benefit and common interest and thus contributed to preserving and adapting fundamental principles in a period of great change.[155]

The image of the African presented in abolitionist literature confirms the view that the Humanitarians saw the issues solely from within their own frame of reference. William Wilberforce's tract *An Appeal to the Religion, Justice, and Humanity of the Inhabitants of the British Empire in behalf of the Negro Slaves in the West Indies* (1823) may serve as an example. While the slaves are described as being completely depraved in every way, Wilberforce attributes this unequivocally to their inhuman treatment and rejects the claim that the basic reason for their debased character is that they are "creatures of an inferior nature."[156] Evidence of their real character Wilberforce finds in the reports from Africa, which, he claims, depict them in a generally positive light. Thus the Africans, "when prompted by any adequate motives, would work diligently and perseveringly both in agricultural and manufacturing labours" – in fact, "there never was any uncivilized people of whose dispositions we have received a more amiable character."[157] The best proof that Wilberforce can summon of the good character of the Africans, however, is their capacity for transformation; in Sierra Leone, he says, it has been shown that

---

[155] Bender, *The Anti-Slavery Debate*. No attempt is made here to go into the scholarly debate of the authors in this volume in any depth but, rather, to deduct what seems relevant in the present context.

[156] William Wilberforce, *An Appeal to the Religion, Justice, and Humanity of the Inhabitants of the British Empire, in Behalf of the Negro Slave in the West Indies* (London: J. Hatchard, 1823): 32.

[157] Wilberforce, *An Appeal*, 49, 46.

> the poor African barbarians, just rescued from the holds of slave-ships, are capable, not merely of being civilized, but of soon enjoying, with advantage, the rights and institutions of British freemen.[158]

Their willingness to become christianized, the children's aptitude for learning, their gratitude for everything done for them – all this shows the Africans to be worthy recipients of the efforts of the abolitionists.[159] It is clear that the image of the Africans presented here is shaped entirely by the social and political factors mentioned above; the Christian faith and British culture are the standards against which they are measured, even to the extent of showing that they naturally conform to the social ideal of the diligent worker.[160] Wilberforce did not accept ideas about different racial origin, but the quotations clearly show that he perceived the Africans as inferior, basically because of their way of life and his expectation that they would be uplifted through christianization.

Besides abolitionism, evangelicalism and other forms of religious revival found a natural outlet in missionary activity; missionary societies sprouted in the years immediately before and after the turn of the century (such as the Church Missionary Society, 1799; the London Missionary Society, 1795; the British and Foreign Bible Society, 1804), and part of their activity was soon turned towards extending knowledge of Christianity in the colonies and joining the older societies (for example, the Society for the Propagation of the Gospel in Foreign Parts) in attempting to convert the indigenous peoples thus encountered. Missions soon flourished in all the colonies. The impressions formed by the missionaries were transmitted to the societies in Britain and, through their representations, came to play an important role in forming British opinion about indigenous peoples, as was illustrated in the case of the Cape Colony. The missionary view of their prospective converts is therefore significant for understanding the development of the image of indigenous people in Britain.

John Philip, the superintendent of missions at the Cape, provides an easily accessible illustration of this view. In his *Researches in South Africa*, Philip presented a picture of the Khoikhoi and the San which was clearly informed by a great deal of understanding and affection for them; as in the case of Wilberforce, Philip attributed any "degradation of the Hottentot character" to the

---

[158] Wilberforce, *An Appeal*, 47.

[159] *An Appeal*, 48.

[160] Cf Marshall & Williams, ed. *The Great Map of Mankind*, 250–51.

cruelty of the colonists towards them.[161] However, Philip allowed no doubt that the way of life of the Khoikhoi, for instance, was the basic obstruction to their moral "improvement," the acknowledged goal of the missionary endeavour, which involved changing their religious notions as well as their social interaction and their working habits:

> One of the first steps in attempting the elevation of a savage people, in connexion with religious and moral instruction, is, to endeavour to impart to them a relish for the decencies and comforts of life. Little can be done towards their general improvement, till you can get them to exchange their straw cabins for decent houses. Their miserable reed-huts are unfavourable to health and morals [....] These huts are as unfavourable to industry, as they are to health [...] While they live in these huts, habits of cleanliness can never be acquired [...] These habitations are also unfavourable to decency.[162]

In this way, Philip selected one element of Khoikhoi life and showed how it presented an obstruction to their being christianized. Thus, although Philip commiserated with the Khoikhoi situation and believed in their essential humanity and good nature, he was wholly convinced that their whole way of life needed to be changed. As the goal was to turn them into Christians, the European, especially the Briton, became the standard against which the Khoikhoi were measured; inevitably, the Europeans assumed a position of superiority in relation to the indigenous people.

Some missionaries presented a much more hostile picture of the natural state of the indigenous people with whom they were confronted. Thus Johannes Kicherer, also of the London Missionary Society, described the habits of the San in the following terms:

> Their huts are formed by digging a hole in the earth about three feet deep, and then making a roof of reeds, which is however insufficient to keep off the rains. Here they lie close together like pigs in a sty. They are extremely lazy, so that nothing will rouse them to action, but excessive hunger.[163]

---

[161] John Philip, *Researches in South Africa: Illustrating the Civil, Moral and Religious Condition of the Native Tribes* (1828; New York: Negro UP, 1969), vol. 1: 57.

[162] Philip, *Researches in South Africa*, vol. 1, 209–12.

[163] Johannes Kicherer, "The Rev. Mr. Kicherer's Narrative of his Mission to the Hottentots," *Transactions of the Missionary Society* 2.1 (1804): 6, quoted in Nigel Penn, "The Northern Cape Frontier Zone 1700–c.1815" (unpublished doctoral dissertation, Cape Town University, 1995): 420.

Kicherer is much less convinced of the basic equality of humankind; finding that the San lack "domestic happiness," affection for their children, and care for the elderly members of the group, Kicherer comments that "In some few instances, however, you meet with a spark of natural affection, which places them on a level with the brute creation."[164]

In New South Wales, the Reverend Cartwright, entrusted by Governor Macquarie with the conduct of the "civilizing mission" to the Aboriginal people, in 1819 made the following description of the Aboriginal character: "Buried as is the intellect of these Savages in Augean filth, we may yet find Gems of the first Magnitude and brilliance." He mentions their "roving habits," which make them "accustomed to wander about in companies," and generally considers them an "abject, wretched race." In line with the general missionary view, his plan for "civilizing" them included "their improvement in the knowledge of our useful Arts, as well as in the knowledge and practice of our most holy religion."[165]

The goal of transforming the indigenous peoples in this twofold way was clearly expressed by the London Missionary Society. In a representation to the British government, the treasurer of the society referred to

> the necessary connexion existing between the communication of the Christian Religion and the promotion of the moral and social wellbeing of mankind, and this even in reference to barbarous and uncivilized tribes.[166]

The Society was in no doubt about the earthly advantage of this process to colonial ventures:

> To raise uncivilized and wandering hordes, which formerly subsisted by the chase or by plunder, to the condition of settled laborers and cultivators of the soil, to lead them to increase the sum of productive labor and to become consumers of the commodities of other countries, to convert such as were a terror to the inhabitants of an extended frontier into defenders of that frontier against

---

[164] Penn, *The Northern Cape Frontier Zone*, 421.

[165] Cartwright to Macquarie, December 6, 1819, in Frederick Watson, ed. *Historical Records of Australia* (Sydney: Government Printer, 1914–1925), vol. 10: 264.

[166] Memorial by the London Missionary Society, January 22, 1827 in George McCall Theal, ed. *Records of the Cape Colony* (Cape Town: Government of the Cape Colony, 1897–1905), vol. 30: 121.

> the inroads of remoter barbarians cannot, your Memorialists presume, but be regarded as highly important and beneficial results.[167]

In other words, the humanitarian and religious concern to protect the indigenous peoples by christianizing them and teaching them to live like Europeans would assist the running of the colonies by assimilating them and making them governable. Conversely, many missionaries were favourably inclined towards colonial expansion, as this would bring more "heathens" into this position.

Thus, whether individual missionaries were positive or negative towards the "natural" characteristics of indigenous peoples, missionary activity was inherently based on the premise that indigenous organization and customs had to be changed; the people had, as it were, to be "saved" from their own culture.[168] Everything the missionaries said and wrote implicitly carried this message: the superiority of the Christian religion and of Western culture was openly asserted; consequently the indigenous people were inferior, "poor," "wretched" and to be pitied until they could be changed.[169]

To some missionaries such as Kitcherer, the racial ideas outlined above held an attractive explanatory force, though all missionaries would of course have been monogenists.[170] To some adherents of the theories of racially determined differences, missionary endeavours would have seemed laudable humanitarian efforts. Rather than being mutually exclusive, both phenomena had the effect of making indigenous peoples look "backward" and they complemented each

---

[167] Memorial by the London Missionary Society, January 22, 1827 in Theal, ed. *Records of the Cape Colony*, vol. 30, 121.

[168] Although early Cape missionaries such as Van der Kemp may have constituted an exception to this rule with their very egalitarian ideas, cf Andrew Bank, "Liberals and their Enemies: Racial Ideology at the Cape of Good Hope, 1820–1850" (unpublished doctoral dissertation, Cambridge University, 1995): 68–71. See also Timothy Keegan, *Colonial South Africa and the Origins of the Racial Order* (Cape Town & London: David Philip, 1996): ch. 4, for a detailed discussion of the aims of missionary activity.

[169] Cf Smith, *European Vision and the South Pacific*, 105–109; Smith points out that the missionaries "detested noble savagery and the sentimentalism associated with it" and greatly contributed to the demise of this image; see also Smith, ch. 11.

[170] Bank argues that the humanitarian drive for assimilation was based on egalitarian views of human nature intrinsically opposed to the idea of innate racial differences; this does not, however, rule out occasional leanings towards racial ideas among missionaries. Nor does it necessarily contradict the claim that humanitarianism fostered belief in European superiority, as Bank seems to agree, in "Liberals and their Enemies," ch. 2, esp. 88–89, 92–96. Bank goes into considerable detail about the inherent contradictions in what he terms "humanitarian liberalism."

other in creating a myth of European superiority which, in those not inspired by pious notions of Christian charity, easily led to a contemptuous and even hostile attitude towards such peoples.

Many of the works written during the transitional period (which covered several decades on both sides of the century) in varying degrees showed traits from the earlier eighteenth century and at the same time pointed towards future tendencies. An interesting example of the development of depictions of indigenous peoples may be found in the two volumes on New South Wales written by the judge-advocate David Collins. In the first volume, there were many descriptions of the Aborigines and attempts to come to terms with them, including a long appendix containing an account of their customs. Although Collins occasionally remarked on customs or characteristics which he found disgusting, in general his comments show a noticeable degree of tolerance towards the Aborigines. Thus, in June 1791, he noted with obvious satisfaction "the establishment of that familiar intercourse which now subsisted between us and the natives." He described an incident in which of some of the convicts

> who were so unthinking, or so depraved, as wantonly to destroy a canoe belonging to a fine young man, a native, who had left it at some little distance from the settlement, and as he hoped out of the way of observation while he went with some fish to the huts.[171]

Collins went on to describe the anger of the Aborigine, "Bal-loo-der-ry," and noted that, notwithstanding the punishment of the convicts, the consequence had been an interruption in the friendship with them and a stop to all commerce. Collins's final comment was a rhetorical question "How much greater claim to the appellation of savages had the wretches who were the cause of this, than the native who was the sufferer?"[172]

The tenor of this passage should be compared with that of the second volume, written by Collins in 1800 or 1801 after his return to Britain, on the basis of information supplied from the colony. Collins's remarks on the Aborigines now take a quite different turn:

---

[171] David Collins, *An Account of the English Colony in New South Wales with Remarks on the Dispositions, Customs, Manners, etc. of the native Inhabitants of that Country* (1798–1802; Sydney & London: A.H. & A.W. Reed for the Royal Historical Society, 1975), vol. 1: 137.

[172] Collins, *An Account of the English Colony in New South Wales*, vol.1, 139. Cf also the passage quoted in ch. 3 above, 109.

> The savage inhabitants of the country, instead of losing any part of their native ferocity of manners by an intercourse with the Europeans among whom they dwelt, seemed rather to delight in exhibiting themselves as monsters of the greatest cruelty, devoid of reason, and guided solely by the impulse of the worst passions.[173]

In another context, Collins stated that "It was distressing to observe, that every endeavour to civilise these people proved fruitless"; noting the increasing frequency of attacks on the settlers, in which the latter were sometimes killed:

> Could it have been foreseen, that this was their natural temper, it would have been wiser to have kept them at a distance and in fear, which might have been effected without so much of the severity [which had later been used].[174]

The attitude of Collins had clearly changed dramatically. Rather than sympathizing with the Aborigines and being curious about them, he now condemns them; rather than delighting in "friendly intercourse" with them, he laments that they have not been "civilised." On this basis, he repudiates the former policy of trying to "conciliate" them, and is now in favour of "expelling" them.

Perhaps part of the reason for this change may be found in the fact that Collins was no longer relying on his own observations but on those of others, perhaps always more hostile to the Aborigines, communicated to him by letter. It may also be a reflection of the change of policy pursued in New South Wales as described in Chapter 3. Nevertheless, the change of attitude between the two volumes provides a very good illustration of the changing image of indigenous peoples which took place around the turn of the century and which has been outlined in the preceding pages.

Changing intellectual perceptions

The very broad ground traversed in this chapter has shown how intellectual ideas in Europe about indigenous peoples developed from the earliest interaction with them until the early nineteenth century. In this long span of time, the first couple of centuries were first and foremost marked by the attempt to come to terms with the existence of fundamentally different ways of life. Questions concerning the nature and origins of human existence in the "new world" were answered primarily within the universe of the Bible, although as time

---

[173] *An Account of the English Colony in New South Wales*, vol. 2, 9.

[174] *An Account of the English Colony in New South Wales*, vol. 2, 25–26.

went on attempts were increasingly made to explore the possible explanations beyond the rather rigid framework established by religion. As the eighteenth century progressed, the study of man as an object of natural science gradually produced (and was formed by) a wealth of new disciplines such as anatomy, physical anthropology and biology.

Simultaneously, the large number of descriptions, especially of Indians, some negative, others positive, provided abundant material for philosophical speculation about the social and political development of human society. Depending on the theoretical approach of the author, the image of the indigenous people was often either idealistic or denigrating. As pointed out earlier, however, in most of these cases the function of the indigenous people was primarily to illustrate a point that had very little to do with them as such.

There is no doubt that the contradictory images and conclusions produced in these works had an impact on the way indigenous peoples were seen by later observers. It has been argued above, though, that other aspects of the European approach to indigenous communities should also be taken into account. The amassing of detailed information to be found in accounts of indigenous peoples, the generally dispassionate tone used in conveying it, and statements revealing the authors' awareness of other cultures represent common elements in the eighteenth-century way of dealing with this encounter. Irrespective of the personal opinion of the author towards the people he was describing (and some writers were exceedingly negative), the overall impression of the accounts is that description of these peoples was more important than emotional evaluation of them. Those philosophical works which did more than just refer in passing to, for example, the Indians frequently leave the same impression.

Around the turn of the century, this began to change. In the manner of what was to become anthropology, more precise methods of describing other peoples were demanded and slowly developed. Yet the accounts made by religiously inspired humanitarians also became increasingly influential; these writers tended to add a new tone of morality as they described indigenous peoples from the point of view of the changes desired rather than the way they actually were. Assumptions about unchallengeable primacy inherent in Christianity were transferred to the whole way of life of Europeans and were supported by the simultaneous development of theories of race which sought scientific proof for the view that the "Caucasian race" was innately superior to other "races." As the early years of the nineteenth century passed, this markedly ethnocentric view resulted in a change in the intellectual perception of indigenous peoples, which was now increasingly based on a negative evaluation of their way of life, although the aim for many, their conversion to Christianity, was perceived as a benevolent gesture.

This development is connected with some of the general tendencies characterizing intellectual thought in this period. For much of the eighteenth century, thinkers strove to liberate themselves from the limitations imposed by religious orthodoxy and attempted to replace traditional methods of investigation with empirical observation. "Rational enquiry" is the keyword for much of the activity of such people and led directly to the creation of "the sciences." Although the Romantic movement towards the end of the century reacted against the excessive demand for "rationality," the growth of (and admiration for) scientific work continued in the nineteenth century. In the process, this work acquired a greater degree of confidence as methods and results became more firmly established. The emerging intellectual confidence was strengthened by the moral revival of Christianity, which confirmed basic social values. It may thus be suggested that eighteenth century "enquiry" grew into nineteenth-century "conviction" and that this transition was also visible in the transformation of perceptions of indigenous peoples.

It is notoriously difficult to show connections between political decisions and current attitudes; it is tempting, though, to see a connection between the official attitude to the Indians in North America in the mid-eighteenth century and the intellectual approach towards the study of these peoples. It may be suggested that the official policy, marked as it was by a recognition of the rights of the Indians, was linked to the general attitude of open-mindedness towards other peoples that has been seen to characterize much of the eighteenth century.

It is also noteworthy that the decades on either side of the turn of the century, where policy is often inconsistent and on a changing course from that of the previous period, should coincide with a period of transition in which new theories and views about indigenous peoples were becoming prevalent. The increasingly hierarchical ideas about indigenous peoples which were becoming common from the late eighteenth century can be connected with the tendency to allow for a more summary way of dealing with indigenous peoples. This is nowhere better illustrated than in the case of New South Wales.

It is less difficult to show the impact of current ideas on official attitudes towards the end of the period covered in this study. James Stephen and Lord Glenelg were both born into the Clapham Sect; others showed clear signs of sympathy with Evangelical ideas; Buxton, the champion of abolition, became the chairman of the Committee on Aborigines; and missionary advice was frequently admitted by officials. Thus it is clear that at this time the contemporary ideals of Evangelicalism and humanitarianism were represented among those who formulated policy; their attitudes were indisputably influenced by these ideals and their policy was at least to some extent shaped by them. Up to a certain point this is reflected in directives given in connection with New South Wales, but the impression remains that of the colonies discussed here, this development was particularly felt at the Cape. The interaction between missionary interests and official policies in that case is clearly documented.

Conversely, government reactions to the peoples and the circumstances they encountered in the colonies may very well have confirmed current ideas and reinforced changing ones. On a more general level, the extension of the Empire would certainly have had this impact by bringing new peoples within the purview of the intellectual classes.

Conclusion

FROM THE AVAILABLE MATERIAL, it is clear that throughout most of the second half of the eighteenth century government attitudes in London towards indigenous peoples in the colonies were marked by a desire to establish friendly relations; instructions to "conciliate their affections" or words to the same effect were issued in almost every instance of contact, and the obtaining of "their consent" to settlements was common procedure.

The case of the North American colonies, so well documented, shows beyond reasonable doubt that at least in the period 1760–75 such instructions were backed by measures designed to secure this aim. Attempts were made to halt settler expansion by negotiating a boundary between Indians and colonists and plans were drawn up to regulate the trade that had been causing considerable trouble. Although other considerations such as expenditure and the desire to maintain control over the settlers were also important factors in formulating this policy and although it is equally clear that most of the measures failed, there is sufficient evidence to show that respect for Indian military power and concern about their "just complaints" were crucial in shaping policy.

Examples from the final decades of the century show that this policy had become established precedent in the conduct of colonial affairs. Even if the mistaken notion that New South Wales was practically uninhabited or the fact that the Cape Colony was obtained by conquest from another colonizing power meant that no provision was made for obtaining permission to settle, early instructions show the same concern for securing the friendship of the original inhabitants.

Yet when developments during the first couple of decades of settlement in the two latter colonies are examined, it becomes clear that a change was taking place in official attitudes towards this area of policy. In both cases there is, right from the beginning, a marked decrease in references to the indigenous inhabitants as compared to the North American colonies before the Revolution. It is also striking that the government in London tended much less to interfere with the policy laid down in the two colonies; rather, Secretaries of State were by and large content to accept the line pursued by the governors. Most strikingly in contrast with the North American policy, the government on several occasions approved of retaliatory measures against the "depredations and hostile incursions" of the indigenous peoples. Although the government also approved of fighting against the Indians in Pontiac's war, the repercussions of that war in hastening the issuing of the Royal Proclamation were not mirrored in either of the other colonies. Finally, missionary involvement, although present in North America, became much more influential in New South Wales and especially in the Cape Colony. During the early decades of the nineteenth century, the government in London came to accept a dual policy towards the indigenous peoples – on the one hand, applying force to break resistance; on the other, reliance on missionary endeavours to support assimilation.

Several factors contributed to this development. While both the period of official involvement in Indian policy in North America and the early years of British rule in New South Wales and the Cape were marked by wars with France, there was a significant difference between them. In both the Seven Years War and the War of Independence, the Indians played an important role as allies; by contrast, the Napoleonic Wars involved neither Aborigines nor the original inhabitants at the Cape (except in the most indirect of ways). Consequently, whereas it was necessary for British military success to be alert to Indian issues, this did not apply in the latter case and no doubt served to lessen interest in such affairs.

As pointed out in Chapter 1, the administrative apparatus for ruling the colonies underwent considerable change in the second half of the eighteenth century. Whether arrangements were beneficial or not, the existence in the middle decades of the century of several bodies concerned with the government of the colonies was evidence of, and ensured lively interest in, such important issues as relations with the Indians. In contrast to this, the lack of any department or even section devoted to colonial affairs by the turn of the century testifies to a low mark of interest in these affairs at that time. Although the long secretaryship of Bathurst gradually brought improvements, it was not until the mid-1820s that an efficient bureaucracy came into being.

One effect of both these factors was a heavy reliance on the policy-making of the governors in both New South Wales and the Cape Colony. In respect of the American colonies, the British government had at a critical point decided to remove policy-making from the governors, whose position in any case had been hampered by the assemblies, and had inserted superintendents who were to report directly to London. On the other hand, the governors in New South Wales and at the Cape generally had autocratic powers. This, as Bayly points out, was a consequence of the authoritarian rule which existed in Britain at this time as well as of the particular circumstances surrounding the establishment of these two colonies.[1] Having furnished their representatives with broad powers, it was only natural that the government should to a large extent rely on their assessment of the colonial situation.

Although factors such as these provide some explanation for the identifiable change in official attitude, it is suggested that further understanding of the development which took place may be achieved by seeing it against the intellectual and legal background of the period. The Enlightenment preoccupation with natural law and natural rights provided an obvious basis for the development of official acceptance of indigenous rights to their land and, in general, for the concern with just treatment of these peoples. The intellectual interest in non-Europeans and the relativistic attitudes towards their cultures which can be seen in a considerable number of works evinces a general climate of open-mindedness, which influenced official thinking in the direction of seeing indigenous peoples like other foreign nations with whom arrangements for coexistence had to be made. While there is definitely no wish to idealize either official or other attitudes towards indigenous peoples (the image of the "ignoble savage" would in any case prevent that), there is a striking difference between the way they were perceived and treated during the greater part of of the eighteenth century and the stance that developed later, which is traceable to the very nature of Enlightenment views about the world.

The growth of notions of British superiority developing out of racial theories and Evangelical sentiments transformed the basis for the approach to other peoples. Curiosity and an inclination to show tolerance were displaced by moral certainty about the unrivalled position of Christian culture and the desirability of making everyone else part of it. While ethnocentrism and the urge to christianize the "heathen" had been present since the earliest encounters, both phenomena reached unprecedented heights in the nineteenth century. Assimilation was the aim of missionaries and gradually became that of the

[1] C.A.Bayly, *Imperial Meridian: The British Empire and the World 1780–1830* (London: Longman, 1989): 193–95.

government. Given the hierarchical structure of British society, there was no contradiction between a sense of superiority and attempts at conversion. The dual policy of force and assimilation was a consistent result of the intellectual ideas that developed from the late eighteenth century onwards.

The influence of missionary views on official attitudes reached a climax in the 1830s, when humanitarian and Evangelical sentiments held sway among the majority of ministers in the Colonial Office. The policy adopted and the views expressed confirm the direction attitudes were taking. Even though some of the language used at this time was very similar to that used in the 1760s and 1770s, concerned as it was with justice and rights, the outspoken aim of conversion and "civilization" was different from that of peaceful coexistence in the earlier period. Although the use of force receded during the decade, the assumptions of superiority remained, no matter how much they were veiled in humanitarian language.

The legal development which replaced concepts of natural rights with positivistic theories, diminishing the legal standing of indigenous peoples and thereby undermining their territorial ownership, fits very neatly into the pattern outlined here. Clearly, inherent notions of European superiority would have cemented the perception of legal views which defined the law of nations as applying only to "civilized" states. Official attitudes to legal issues may not always have corresponded to those developed by the legal profession but in the case of New South Wales the two supplemented each other in causing the application of the doctrine of *terra nullius* to inhabited land.

The tendency to distinguish between different groups of indigenous peoples was a natural outcome of the intellectual changes around the turn of the century; even though scales of gradation had been applied earlier on, racial hierarchies established inherent differences between various "races" which shows beyond doubt that not all peoples were alike. The confrontation with increasing numbers of peoples with very different ways of life contributed to this development. It became a common belief that Aborigines and Khoisan constituted the lowest levels of human existence, whereas American Indians and Xhosa were more "advanced." Notions of this kind were instrumental in the formation of the legal view mentioned above; they also help explain the low level of official interest in the Aboriginal and Khoikhoi peoples, for example; similar ideas were expressed later on by Lord Glenelg in connection with New Zealand.[2]

[2] Memorandum by Glenelg, December 15, 1837, CO 209/2: 412.

It has frequently been argued that British policy towards indigenous peoples was motivated more by expedience and pragmatism than by anything else. Concern with Indian affairs in America was caused solely by their military power and their position as trading partners; the Aboriginal people and the Khoisan had far less of this "bargaining power," so were almost completely disregarded. The Xhosa were in a somewhat similar position to the North American Indians, and for that reason elicited a more active response. There is no denying that these features played a significant role in shaping policy, as has indeed been mentioned at various points in this study, though perhaps such factors had more of an impact on colonial governments than on the government in London. However, the argument presented here is that this is insufficient to explain the development that can be discerned in official attitudes. The pragmatic interpretation would be based on the assumption that attitudes remained constant (and presumably negative) even if policy did not; yet the official documents show that there was a clear change in attitude towards indigenous peoples in this period. Views current in the upper echelons of society had not a little to do with this change.

Appendix

Secretaries of State and Presidents of the Board of Trade with responsibility for the colonies: Year of accession

	Secretary of State for the Southern Department		President of the Board of Trade
1747	John Russell, Duke of Bedford		
		1748	George Montague–Dunk, Earl of Halifax
1751	Robert Darcy, Earl of Holdernesse		
1754	Sir Thomas Robinson		
1755	Henry Fox		
1756	William Pitt the Elder		
1761	Charles Wyndham, Earl of Egremont	1761	Samuel Sandys, Lord Sandys
1763	Earl of Halifax	1763	Charles Townshend
		1763	William Petty, Earl of Shelburne
		1763	Wills Hill, Earl of Hillsborough
1765	Henry Seymour Conway	1765	William Legge, Earl of Dartmouth
1766	Duke of Richmond and Lennox	1766	Earl of Hillsborough
1766	Earl of Shelburne	1766	Robert Nugent, Viscount Clare
			Secretary of State for the Colonies
1768	Thomas Thynne, Viscount Weymouth	1768	Earl of Hillsborough
1770	William H. Nassau de Zuylestein, Earl of Rochford		
		1772	Earl of Dartmouth
1775	Viscount Weymouth	1775	Lord George Sackville–Germain
1779	Earl of Hillsborough (to March 1782)		
		1782	Welbore Ellis (to March 1782)

Secretary of State for the Home Department		Under-Secretary of State for the Home Department	
1782	Earl of Shelburne	1782	Evan Nepean
1782	Thomas Townshend	1782	Thomas Orde
		1782	Henry Strachey
1783	Lord North	1783	Hon. George Augustus North
1783	Earl Temple		
1783	Lord Sydney		
		1784	Hon. John Thomas Townshend
1789	William Wyndham Grenville	1789	Scrope.Bernard
1791	Henry Dundas		
1794	Duke of Portland	1794	Hon. Thomas Broderick
		1796	Charles Greville
		1798	William Wickham
1801	Lord Pelham	1801	Edward Finch–Hatton

Permanent Under-Secretary	
1782	John Bell
1782	Evan Nepean
1791	John King

Secretary of State for War		Under-Secretary of State for War	
1794	Henry Dundas	1794	Evan Nepean
		1795	William Huskisson

Secretary of State for War and the Colonies		Under-secretary of State for War and the Colonies	
1801	Robert Hobart, Lord Hobart	1801	John Sullivan
1804	John Jeffreys Pratt, Earl Camden	1804	Edward Cooke
1805	Robert Stewart, Viscount Castlereagh		
1806	William Windham	1806	George Shee
1807	Viscount Castlereagh	1807	Edward Cooke
1809	Robert Banks Jenkinson, Earl of Liverpool	1809	Charles Jenkinson
		1810	Robert Peel
1812	Henry Bathurst, Earl of Bathurst	1812	Henry Goulburn
		1821	R.J. Wilmot
1827	Frederick John Robinson, Viscount Goderich	1827	Edward Geoffrey Smith–Stanley, Lord Stanley
1827	William Huskisson		
1828	Sir George Murray	1828	Francis Leveson–Gower (Francis Egerton)
		1828	Horace Twiss
1830	Viscount Goderich	1830	Viscount Howick
1833	Lord Stanley	1833	J.G. Shaw Lefevre
1834	Thomas Spring Rice	1834	George Grey

1834 Duke of Wellington
1834 George Hamilton–Gordon, Earl of Aberdeen
1835 Charles Grant, Baron Glenelg
1839 C.H. Phipps, Marquess of Normanby
1839 Lord John Russell

1835 Hon. John Stuart Wortley
1835 William Ewart Gladstone
1835 George Grey
1839 Henry Labouchere
1839 R.V. Smith

PERMANENT UNDER-SECRETARY

1825 R.W. Hay
1836 James Stephen
1848 Herman Merivale

SOURCES

Sainty, John Christopher. *Home Office Officials 1782-1870* (London: Athlone, 1975).

——. *Colonial Office Officials: Officials of the Secretary of State for War 1794–1801, of the Secretary of State for War and Colonies 1801–1854, and of the Secretary of State for Colonies 1854–1870* (London: Institute of Historical Research, 1976).

Smith, Hubert Llewellyn. *The Board of Trade* (New York & London: G.P. Putnam's Sons, 1928).

Thomson, Mark Alméras. *The Secretaries of State 1681–1782* (London: Frank Cass, 1968).

Bibliography

Primary Sources

Manuscript Records

A. Public Record Office, London

ABBREVIATIONS

ADM	Records of the Admiralty, Naval Forces, Royal Marines, Coast Guard, and Related Bodies: Admiralty and Ministry of Defence.
CO	Records of the Colonial Office, Commonwealth and Foreign and Commonwealth Office, Empire Marketing Board, and Related Bodies: Colonial Office and Predecessors; Foreign and Colonial Office.
FO	Records created and inherited by the Foreign Office: Foreign Office and Predecessor: Political and Other Departments.
HO	Records created or inherited by the Home Office, Ministry of Home Security, and Related Bodies.
PRO	Domestic Records of the Public Record Office, Gifts, Deposits, Notes, and Transcripts.
T	Records created and inherited by Her Majesty 's Treasury.

Asia

CO 77/26 East Indies, Original Correspondence, Secretary of State, 1788–92.

FO 41/1 General Correspondence, Court of Directors, Chairman and Deputy-Chairman of the East India Company: British Settlements, 1776–97.

PRO 30/8/360 Original Records acquired as gift or on deposit, William Pitt, First Earl of Chatham: Papers, 2. Series: Papers relating to India.

Madagascar

CO 201/8 New South Wales, Original Correspondence, Port Jackson, 1793.

HO 42/10 Domestic Corrspondence: George III, 1784–86.

New South Wales

ADM 1/4152 Correspondence and papers, Secretary of State, 1786–87.

CO 201/1–14 New South Wales, Original Correspondence, Secretary of State and Port Jackson, 1783–98.

13/16 South Australia, Original Correspondence, Secretary of State: Despatches, 1840.

HO 7/1 Criminal Department, Convicts: Minutes of House of Commons Committee respecting Transportation of Convicts to West Coast of Africa, 1785.

28/4 Admiralty Correspondence: Lords of the Admiralty, 1784.

35/1 Treasury Correspondence: Colonial, 1781–90.

42/5-7, 42/10 Domestic Correspondence: George III, Letters and Papers, 1784–86.

100/18 Ireland, Correspondence and Papers: Civil, 1786.

PRO 30/8/342 pt.2 Original Records acquired as gift or on deposit, William Pitt, First Earl of Chatham: Papers, 2. Series: Papers relating to India.

New Zealand

CO 209/2 New Zealand, Original Correspondence, Secretary of State: Despatches, Offices and Individuals, 1836–37.

North America

ADM 1/4156 Correspondence and Papers, Secretary of State, 1791–92.

CO 5/6, 5/23, 5/69, 5/214, 5/225, 5/403, 5/504, 5/1345, 5/1352, 5/1367-1368 Board of Trade and Secretaries of State: America and West Indies, Original Correspondence, 1749–68.

42/32, 42/44 Canada, formerly British North America, Original Correspondence, 1773–83.

323/15–16 Colonies General, Original Correspondence, Board of Trade: Q nos 1–75, 1760–63.

324/17 General Entry Books, Series 1: Commissions, Instructions, Board of Trade Correspondence, 1756–60.

FO 72/17 General Correspondence: Charles Henry Fraser, Alleyne Fitzherbert and Consuls, 1790.

HO 28/61 Admiralty Correspondence: Supplementary.

Southern Africa

CO 49/9–10 Cape of Good Hope Colony, Letters from Secretary of State: Despatches, 1795–1816.

323/46, 323/49 Colonies General, Law Officers' Reports on Colonial Acts, 1829–33.

PRO 30/8/128 Original Records acquired as gift or on deposit, William Pitt, First Earl of Chatham: Papers, 2. Series: Correspondence of William Pitt the Younger.

West Africa

CO 267/20 Sierra Leone, Original Correspondence, Secretary of State: Despatches and Miscellaneous, 1781–84.

HO 7/1 Criminal Department, Convicts: Minutes of House of Commons Committee respecting Transportation of Convicts to West Coast of Africa, 1785.

28/5 Admiralty Correspondence: Lords of the Admiralty, 1784.

35/1 Treasury Correspondence: Colonial, 1781–90.

42/1, 42/6-7 Domestic Correspondence: George III, Letters and Papers, 1782–85.

T 1/641 Treasury: Papers nos 2–215, 1787.

B. South African State Archives, Cape Town Depot

A 1415(74) Accessions. Andrew Barnard, Letters, 1797–1803.

BO 222 First British Occupation 1795–1803. Memorials received, 1796.

GH 1/1, 1/5-7, 1/11, 1/14, 1/17, 1/70, 1/72 Government House, 1800–1911. Despatches received 1806–29.

23/4, 23/8 Government House, 1800–1911. Despatches sent, 1812–28.

Printed Records

Bell, Kenneth Norman, & W.P. Morrell, ed. *Select Documents on British Colonial Policy 1830–1860* (Oxford: Clarendon, 1928).

Boucher, Maurice, & Nigel Penn, ed. *Britain at the Cape 1795–1803* (Houghton: Brenthurst, 1992).

Carter, Carter Edwin, ed. *The Correspondence of General Thomas Gage with the Secretaries of State 1763–75*, 2 vols. (New Haven CT: Yale UP, 1931–33).

Cavendish, Henry. *Debates of the House of Commons in the Year 1774, on the Bill for Making More Effectual Provision for the Government of the Province of Quebec. Drawn up from the notes of Sir Henry Cavendish* (1839; Toronto: Johnson Reprint, 1966).

Frost, Alan. *Botany Bay Mirages: Illusions of Australia's Convict Beginnings* (Carlton, Victoria: Melbourne UP, 1995): 104–105 ("Memorandum of Matters to be brought before Cabinet," *Dixon Add Ms* Q: 522).

Harlow, Vincent Todd, & Frederick Madden, ed. *British Colonial Developments 1774–1834, Select Documents* (Oxford: Clarendon, 1953).

Hewison, Anthony ed. *The Macquarie Decade: Documents illustrating the History of New South Wales 1810–1821* (Melbourne: Cassell Australia, 1972).

Humphreys, R.A. "Lord Shelburne and the Royal Proclamation of 1763," *English Historical Review* 49 (1934): 258–64 ("Mr Pownall's Sketch of a Report," *Shelburne Papers* 49: 333–64).

Journals of the House of Commons 37 (1778–80): 310–15 ("Considerations of the several Acts relating to the Transportation of Offenders to Foreign Parts").

Kingsbury, Susan Myra, ed. *The Records of the Virginia Company of London* 4 vols. (Washington: Government Printing Office, 1906–33).

Martin, Ged. *The Founding of Australia: the Argument about Australia's Origins* (Sydney: Hale & Iremonger, 1978).

Mississippi Valley Historical Review 8 (1921–22): 370–73 ("Hints Relative to the Division of the Conquered and Newly Acquired Countries in America").

Moodie, Donald, ed. & tr. *The Record, or a Series of Official Papers relative to the Condition and Treatment of the Native Tribes of South Africa*, intro. Anna Smith (1838; Amsterdam & Cape Town: A.A. Balkema, 1960).

O'Callaghan, Edmund Bailey, & Berthold Fernow, ed. *Documents Relative to the Colonial History of the State of New York Procured in Holland, England and France by Romeyn Brodhead* 14 vols. (Albany NY: Weed & Parsons, 1856–83).

Parliamentary Papers, House of Commons 25.339 (1829): 2–8 ("Ordinance of His Honour the Lieutenant Governor in Council, for improving the Condition of the Hottentots and other Free Persons of Colour at the *Cape of Good Hope*, and for consolidating and amending the laws affecting those Persons" [no. 50]).

——. 21.584 (1830): 2–24 ("The *Cape of Good Hope*; Hottentot Population and Missionary Institutions").

——. 19.259 (1831): 3–75 ("Copies of all correspondence between Lieutenant-Governor *Arthur* and His Majesty's Secretary of State for the Colonies, on the Subject of the Military Operations lately carried on against the Aboriginal Inhabitants of *Van Diemen's Land*").

——. 19.261 (1831): 3–19 ("Copies of Instructions given by His Majesty's Secretary of State for the Colonies, for promoting the Moral and Religious Instruction of the Aboriginal Inhabitants of *New Holland* or *Van Diemen's Land*").

——. 39.50 (1831): 46–212 ("Papers relative to the Condition and Treatment of the Native Inhabitants of the *Cape of Good Hope*").

——. 39.252 (1835): 23–142 ("Papers relative to the Condition and Treatment of the Native Inhabitants of the *Cape of Good Hope*").

——. 39.279 (1836): 59–73 ("The *Cape of Good Hope*, Papers Relating the Caffre War and the Death of Hintza").

——. 8 (1844): 143–156 ("Papers relative to the Aborigines in the *Australian Colonies*").

Shortt, Adam, & Arthur G. Doughty, ed. *Documents Relating to the Constitutional History of Canada*, 2 vols. (Ottawa: Historical Documents Publication Board, 1918).

Theal, George McCall, ed. *Records of the Cape Colony*, 36 vols. (London & Cape Town: Government of the Cape Colony, 1897–1905).

Vaughan, Alden T., gen. ed. *Early American Indian Documents: Treaties and Laws 1607–1789*, 18 vols. (Washington DC: U Publications of America, 1979–2001).

Watson, Frederick, ed. *Historical Records of Australia*, 33 vols. (Sydney: Government Printer, 1914–1925).

Legal Cases

Attorney-General v. Brown, 1847. *Legge Supreme Court Cases, New South Wales, 1825–1862* 1 (1896): 312–25.

Case 15 – Anonymous, 1722. *Reports of Cases collected by Peere Williams 1695–1734* 2 (1826): 646.

Calvin's Case, 1608. Coke's Reports, part 7, 1A in *English Law Reports* 77 (1907): 377–411.

Campbell v. Hall, 1774. *All England Law Reports Reprints 1558–1774, revised and annotated* (1968): 252–57.

Cherokee Nation v. The State of Georgia, 1831. *Peters United States Supreme Court Reports* 5 (January term, 1831): 9–69.

Cooper v. Stuart, 1889. *Law Reports, Appeal Cases, House of Lords and Privy Council* 14 (1889): 286–94.

Johnson and Graham's Lessee v. William M'Intosh, 1823. *Wheaton United States Supreme Court Reports* 8 (1823): 543–605.

Mabo v. The State of Queensland (No 2), 1992. *Australian Law Reports* 107 (1992): 1; *Commonwealth Law Reports* 175 (1992): 1.

Milirrpum and Others v. Nabalco Pty. Ltd. and The Commonwealth of Australia, 1971. *Federal Law Reports* 17 (1971): 141–294.

M'Hugh v. Robertson, 1885. *Victoria Law Reports* 40 (1885): 422–31.

Samuel A.Worcester v. The State of Georgia, 1823. *Peters United States Supreme Court Reports* 6 (January term, 1832): 515–97.

Rex v. Jack Congo Murrell, 1836. *Legge Supreme Court Cases, New South Wales, 1825–1862* 1 (1896): 72–73.

Wi Parata v. Bishop of Wellington and the Attorney-General, 1877. *New Zealand Jurist* 3 (1877): 72–83.

Contemporary Works

Adair, James. *The History of the American Indians particularly those Nations adjoining to the Mississippi, East and West Florida, Geogia, South and North Carolina and Virginia, etc. containing an Account of their Origin, Language, Manners, Religious and Civil Customs, Laws, Form of Government, Punishments, Conduct in War and Domestic Life, their Habits, Diet, Agriculture, Manufactures, Diseases, and Method of Cure and other Particulars* (London: Edward & Charles Dilly, 1775).

Anon. *Journal of a Voyage round the World in His Majesty's Ship Endeavour in the Years 1768, 1769, 1770 and 1771, undertaken in pursuit of natural Knowledge at the Desire of the Royal Society* (London: T. Beckett and P.A. De Hondt, 1771).

Austin, John. *The Province of Jurisprudence Determined and the Uses of the Study of Jurisprudence,* intro. H.L.A. Hart (1832 & 1863; London: Weidenfeld & Nicolson, 1968).

Barrow, John. *An Account of Travels into the Interior of Southern Africa, in the years 1797 and 1798*, 2 vols. (London: T. Cadell Junior & W. Davies, 1801–1804).

Blackstone, William. *Commentaries on the Laws of England in four Books*, 4 vols., ed. William Draper Lewis (1765–69; Philadelphia PA: Rees Welsh, 1902).

Blumenbach, Johann Friederich. *De Generis Humani Varietate Nativa* (Göttingen: A. Vandenhoeck, 1775).

Bodin, Jean. *Les Six Livre de la République* (Lyon, 1576).

Buffon, Comte de. *L'Histoire Naturelle*, 36 vols. (Paris, 1749–1788).

Burke, William. *An Account of the European Settlements in America (revised by Edmund Burke)*, 2 vols. (1758; New York: Research Reprints, 1970).

Camper, Pieter. *Über den natürlichen Untershied der Gesichtszüge* (Berlin, 1792).

Collins, David. *An Account of the English Colony in New South Wales with Remarks on the Dispositions, Customs, Manners, etc. of the Native Inhabitants of that Country* 2 vols. (1798–1802; Sydney & London: A.H. & A.W. Reed for the Royal Australian Historical Society, 1975).

Combe, George. *Elements of Phrenology* (Edinburgh: John Anderson Jun., 1824).

Dampier, William. *A new Voyage around the World: Describing particularly the Isthmus of America, several Coasts and Islands in the West Indies, the Isles of Cape Verd, the Passage by Terra Del Fuego, the South Sea Coasts of Chili, Peru and Mexico; the Isle of Guam, on the Ladrones, Mindanao, and other Phillipine and East India Islands near Cambodia, China, Formosa Luconia, Celebes, &c., New Holland, Hellena, their Soil, Rivers, harbours, Plants, Fruits, Animals, and Inhabitants: their Customs, Religion, Government, Trade, &c.* (London: James Knapton, 1697–1709).

Forster, Johann Reinhold. *Observations made during a Voyage round the World on Physical Geography, Natural History, and Ethic Philosophy* (London: G. Robinson, 1778).

Gentili, Alberico. *De Iure Belli Libri Tres* 2 vols., tr. John C. Rolfe, ed. James Scott Brown, intro. Coleman Philipson (1612; Oxford: Clarendon & London: Humphrey Milford, 1933).

Grotius, Hugo. *De Jure Belli ac Pacis Libri Tres, in quibus Jus Naturae & Gentium, item Juris Publici praecipua explicantur: Editio Nova cum Annotatis Auctoris, ex postrema ejus ante Obitum cura multo nunc Auctior*, 2 vols., tr. Francis W. Kelsey, ed. & intro. James Scott Brown (1646; Washington DC: Carnegie Institute & Oxford: Clarendon & London: Humphrey Milford, 1913–25).

Guttridge, George H., ed. *The Correspondence of Edmund Burke, July 1774–June 1778;* vol. 3 in *The Correspondence of Edmund Burke*, 10 vols., ed. Thomas W. Copeland et al. (Cambridge: Cambridge UP, 1961).

Hawkesworth, John. *An Account of the Voyages undertaken by the Order of His Present Majesty for making Discoveries in the Southern Hemisphere and successively performed by Commodore Byron, Captain Wallis, Captain Carteret, and Captain Cook drawn up from the Journals which were kept by the several Commanders and from the Papers of Joseph Banks, Esq.*, 3 vols. (London: W. Strahan & T. Cadell, 1773).

Herder, Johann Gottfried von. *Ideen zur Philosophie der Geschichte der Menscheit*, ed. Martin Bollacher (1784; Frankfurt am Main: Deutsche Klassiker Verlag, 1989).

——. *Reflections on the Philosophy of the History of Mankind,* tr. T.O. Churchill, abridged & intro. Frank E. Manuel (*Ideen zur Philosophie der Geschichte der Menscheit*, 1784; tr. 1800; Chicago: U of Chicago P, 1968).

Hobbes, Thomas. *Leviathan or the Matter, Forme & Power of a Commonwealth, Ecclesiasticall and Civill*, ed. A.R. Waller (1651; Cambridge: Cambridge UP, 1904).

Hume, David. *Essays Moral, Political, and Literary*, 2 vols., ed. T.H. Green & T.H. Grose (1742–77; London: Longmans, Green, 1898?).

——.*A Treatise of Human Nature*, ed. Lewis Amherst Sellby–Bigge (1739–40; Oxford: Clarendon, 1967).

Jenkyns, Henry. *British Rule and Jurisdiction beyond the Seas* (Oxford: Clarendon, 1902).

Kames, Lord. *Historical Law Tracts* (Edinburgh: A. Kincaid, 1758).

Keate, George. *Account of the Pelew Islands* (London, 1788).

Kent, James. *Commentaries on American Law*, 4 vols. (1826–30; New York: Da Capo, 1971).

Kicherer, Johannes. "The Rev. Mr. Kicherer's Narrative of his Mission to the Hottentots," *Transactions of the Missionary Society* 2.1 (1804).

Kolb, Peter. *Present State of the Cape of Good Hope*, 2 vols., tr. Guido Medley, intro. W. Peter Carstens (*Caput Bonae Spei Hodiernum*, 1719; tr. 1731; New York: Johnson Reprint, 1968).

Knox, William. *Justice and Policy of the late Act of Parliament* (London, 1774).

Lafitau, Joseph François, Compagnie de Jesus. *Les Mœurs des Sauvages Ameriquains Compareés aux Mœurs des premiers Temps* (Paris: Saugrain l'aîné; C.E. Hochereau, 1724).

Lawrence, William. *Lectures on Physiology, Zoology, and the Natural History of Man, delivered at the Royal College of Surgeons* (London, 1822).

Lindgren, J. Ralph, ed. *The Early Writings of Adam Smith* (New York: Augustus M. Kelly, 1967).

Locke, John. *An Essay Concerning Human Understanding*, ed. Peter H. Nidditch (1690; Oxford: Clarendon, 1975).

——. *Essays on the Law of Nature*, ed. W. von Leiden (1676; Oxford: Clarendon, 1970).

——. *Two Treatises of Government*, ed. & intro. Peter Laslett (1690; Cambridge: Cambridge UP, 1970).

Long, Edward. *The History of Jamaica or a general Survey of the antient and modern State of the Island, with reflections on its Situation, Settlements, Inhabitants, Climate, Products, Commerce, Laws and Government, etc.*, 3 vols. (London, 1774).

Millar, John. *Observations concerning the Distinction of Ranks in Society* (1771; London: J. Murray, 1773).

Millar, John. "The Origin of the Distinction of Ranks" reproduced from the third edition, (London: John Murray, 1779) in *John Millar of Glasgow 1735–1801; His Life and Thought and his Contributions to Sociological Analysis,* ed. W.C. Lehmann (Cambridge: Cambridge UP, 1960): 165–322.

Monboddo, Lord. *Of the Origin and Progress of Language*, 6 vols. (Edinburgh: J. Balfour, 1774–1792).

Montesquieu, Baron de. *Esprit des Lois*, 2 vols. (Geneva, 1748).

Montaigne, Michel de. *The Essays of Montaigne done into English anno 1603 by John Florio*, intro. George Saintsbury (*Les Essais*, 1580; tr. 1603; New York: AMS, 1967).

Philip, John. *Researches in South Africa: Illustrating the Civil, Moral and Religious Condition of the Native Tribes*, 2 vols. (1828; New York: Negro UP, 1969).

Pufendorf, Samuel von. *De Jure Naturae et Gentium Libri Octo*, tr. Charles Henry & William Abbott Oldfather, ed. James Scott Brown, intro. Walter Simons (1688; tr. 1710 & 1717 (Basil Kennett); Oxford: Clarendon & London: Humphrey Milford, 1934).

Purchas, Samuel. *Hakluytus Posthumus or Purchas His Pilgrimes, Contayning a History of the World in Sea Voyages and Lande Travells by Englishmen and others*, 20 vols. (1625; New York: AMS, 1965).

Robertson, William. *The History of America* (1777 & 1793; London: A. Strahan, T. Cadell Junior & W. Davies, 1800).

Rousseau, Jean–Jacques. *The Social Contract and Discourse on the Origin and Foundation of Inequality among Mankind,* tr. Henry J. Tozer/anon., ed. & intro. Lester G. Crocker (*Du Contrat Social*, 1762, tr. nineteenth century/ *Discours sur l'Origine et les Fondements de l'Inégalité parmi les Hommes*, 1755, tr. 1761; New York: Washington Square Press Pocket Books, 1976).

Smith, Adam. *Lectures on Jurisprudence*, ed. Ronald Lindley Meek, David Daiches Rafael & Peter Gonville Stein; vol. 5 of the *Glasgow Edition of the Works and Correspondence of Adam Smith*, 6 vols., gen. ed. Dugald Stewart (1762–63, 1766; Oxford: Clarendon, 1978).

Smith, Adam. *An Inquiry into the Nature and Causes of the Wealth of Nations* (London: W. Strahan & T. Cadell; 1776).

Stockdale, J. *The Voyage of Governor Phillip to Botany Bay* (London, 1789).

Vattel, Emerich de. *The Law of Nations or the Principles of Natural Law, applied to the Conduct and to the Affairs of Nations and of Sovereigns* 3 vols., tr. Charles G. Fenwick, ed. James Scott Brown, intro. Albert de Lapradelle (*Le Droit de Gens, ou Principes de la Loi Naturelle, appliqués a la Conduite et aux Affaires des nations et de Souverain*, 1758; tr. 1759; Washington DC: Carnegie Institute, 1916).

White, Charles. *An Account of the regular Gradation in Man, and in different Animals and Vegetables; and from the former to the latter* (London, 1799).

Victoria, Francisco de. *De Indis et de Iure Belli Relectiones, being part of Relectiones Theologiae*, tr. John Pauley Bate, ed. Herbert Francis Wrigth, intro. Ernest Nys (1696; Washington DC: Carnegie Institute, 1917).

Wilberforce, William. *An Appeal to the Religion, Justice, and Humanity of the Inhabitants of the British Empire, in Behalf of the Negro Slave in the West Indies* (London: J. Hatchard, 1823).

Wolff, Christian. *Jus Gentium, Methodo Scientifica Pertractum*, 2 vols., tr. Joseph H. Drake, ed. James Scott Brown, intro. Otfried Nippold (1764; Oxford & London: Clarendon, 1934).

Secondary Sources

Alden, John Richard. "The Albany Congress and the Creation of the Indian Superintendencies," *Mississippi Valley Historical Review* 27 (1940–41): 139–210.

——. *John Stuart and the Southern Colonial Frontier: A Study of Indian Relations, War, Trade and Land Problems in the Southern Wilderness 1754–1775* (1944; New York: Gordian, 1966).

Allen, Robert S. *A History of the British Indian Department in North America (1755–1830)* (Manuscript Report 109; Ottawa: Department of Indian Affairs and Northern Development, 1971).

Alvord, Clarence Walworth. *The Mississippi Valley in British Politics: A Study of the Trade, Land Speculation, and Experiments in Imperialism culminating in the American Revolution*, 2 vols. (1917; New York: Russell & Russell, 1959).

Armstrong, James C., & Nigel A. Worden. " The Slaves, 1652–1834," in *The Shaping of South African Society, 1652–1840*, ed. Elphick & Giliomee, 109–83.

Atkinson, Alan. "The First Plans for Governing New South Wales 1786–1787," *Australian Historical Studies* 24 (1990–91): 22–40.

Attwood, Bain. "Aborigines and Academic Historians: Some Recent Encounters," *Australian Historical Studies* 24 (1990–91): 123–35.

Bailyn, Bernard, & Philip D. Morgan, ed. *Strangers within the Realm: Cultural Margins of the First British Empire* (Chapel Hill & London: U of North Carolina P, 1991).

Bank, Andrew. "Liberals and their Enemies: Racial Ideology at the Cape of Good Hope, 1820-1850" (unpublished doctoral dissertation, Cambridge University, 1995).

Banton, Michael. *The Idea of Race* (Boulder CO: Westview, 1977).

——. *Racial Theories* (Cambridge: Cambridge UP, 1987).

Barker, Anthony J. *The African Link: British Attitudes to the Negro in the Era of the Atlantic Slave Trade 1550–1807* (London: Frank Cass, 1978).

Barnard, Frederick M., ed. *J.G. Herder on Social and Political Culture* (Cambridge: Cambridge UP, 1969).

Bartlett, Richard H. *Native Title in Australia* (Chatswood, NSW: Butterworths, 2000).

Basye, A.H. *The Lords Commissioners of Trade and Plantations, commonly known as the Board of Trade 1748–1782* (New Haven CT: Yale UP, 1925).

——."The Secretary of State for the Colonies," *American Historical Review* 28 (1923): 13–23.

Bayly, C.A. *Imperial Meridian: The British Empire and the World 1780–1830* (London: Longman, 1989).

Beaglehole, J.C. "The Colonial Office, 1782–1854," *Historical Studies Australia and New Zealand* 1 (1940–41): 170–89.

——. *The Life of James Cook* (London: A & C Black, 1974).

——, ed. *The Endeavour Journal of Joseph Banks 1768–1771*, 2 vols. (Sydney: Trustees of the Public Library of New South Wales in association with Angus & Robertson, 1963).

——, ed. *The Journals of Captain James Cook on his Voyages of Discovery*, 3 vols. (Cambridge: Cambridge UP, 1955–67).

Bender, Thomas, ed. *The Anti-Slavery Debate: Capitalism and Abolitionism as a Problem in Historical Interpretation* (Berkeley & Oxford: U of California P, 1992).

Berkhofer, Robert F., Jr. *The White Man's Indian: Images of the American Indian from Columbus to the Present* (New York: Alfred A. Knopf, 1978).

Berlin, Isiah. *Vico and Herder: Two Studies in the History of Idea* (New York: Vintage, 1977).

Berman, Howard R. "The Concept of Aboriginal Rights in the Early Legal History of the United States," *Buffalo Law Review* 27 (1978): 637–67.

Biddiss, Michael, ed. *Images of Race* (Leicester: Leicester UP, 1979).

Bitterli, Urs. *Cultures in Conflict: Encounters between European and Non-European Cultures 1492–1800* tr. Ritchie Robertson (*Alte Welt – neue Welt: Formen des europäisch–überseeischen Kulturkontakts vom 15. bis zum 18. Jahrhundert*, 1986; Cambridge: Polity, 1989).

Blainey, Geoffrey. "Sydney, 1788," in *Australians, An Historical Library*, part 1: *Australians to 1788,* ed. Derek John Mulvaney & Peter J. White (Broadway, NSW: Fairfax, Symes & Weldon, 1987): 412–43.

Bridges, Barry. "The Extension of English Law to the Aborigines for Offences Committed Inter Se, 1829–1842," *Journal of the Royal Australian Historical Society* 59 (December 1973): 264–69.

Broome, Richard. *Aboriginal Australians, Black Response to White Dominance 1788–1980* (Sydney: Allen & Unwin, 1982).

——. “The Struggle for Australia: Aboriginal–European Warfare, 1770–1930,” in *Australia, Two Centuries of War & Peace,* ed. Michael McKernan & Margaret Browne (Canberra: Australian War Memorial and Allen & Unwin, 1988): 92–120.

Bumsted, J.M., ed. *Interpreting Canada's Past*, 2 vols. (Toronto: Oxford UP, 1986).

Burke, Peter. *Montaigne* (Oxford: Oxford UP, 1981).

Böeseken, Anna Jacoba. *Slaves and Free Blacks at the Cape 1658–1700* (Cape Town: Tafelberg, 1977).

Cain, P.J., & Anthony G. Hopkins. *British Imperialism*, 2 vols. (London & New York: Longmans, 1993).

Carter, Clarence Edwin. “The Office of Commander in Chief: A Phase of Imperial Unity on the Eve of the Revolution,” in *The Era of the American Revolution,* ed. Richard Brandon Morris (1939; Gloucester MA: Peter Smith, 1971): 170–213.

Carter, Paul. *The Road to Botany Bay: An Essay in Spatial History* (London & Boston MA: Faber & Faber, 1987).

Castles, Alex C. *An Introduction to Australian Legal History* (Sydney: Law Book Company, 1971).

——. “The Reception and Status of English Law in Australia,” *Adelaide Law Review* 2 (1963–66): 1–31.

Christie, Ian R. *Myth and Realities in Late Eighteenth Century British Politics* (Berkeley: U of California P, 1970).

Clark, C.M.H. *A History of Australia*, 6 vols. (Carleton, Victoria: Melbourne UP, 1962–99).

Clark, Jonathan C.D. *English Society 1688–1832: Ideology, Social Structure and Political Practice during the Ancient Regime* (Cambridge: Cambridge UP, 1985).

Clarke, Mary Patterson. “The Board of Trade at Work,” *American Historical Review* 17 (1911–12): 17–43.

Cook, W.L. *Floodtide of Empire* (New Haven CT:Yale UP, 1973).

Colley, Linda. *Britons: Forging the Nation 1707–1837* (New Haven CT & London: Yale UP, 1992).

Coupland, Reginald. *The British Anti-Slavery Movement* (London: T. Butterworth, 1933).

Crais, Clifton C. *White Supremacy and Black Resistance in Pre-Industrial South Africa* (Cambridge: Cambridge UP, 1992).

Cumming, Peter A., & Neil H. Mickenberg, ed. *Native Rights in Canada* (Toronto: Indian–Eskimo Association of Canada / General, 1972).

Curtin, Philip D. *The Image of Africa: British Ideas and Action 1780–1850* (London: Macmillan, 1965).

Davis, David Brion. *The Problem of Slavery in Western Culture* (Ithaca NY: Cornell UP, 1966).

Dickerson, Oliver Morton. *American Colonial Government 1696-1765: A Study of the British Board of Trade in its Relation to the American Colonies, Political, Industrial, Administrative* (Cleveland OH: Arthur H. Clarke, 1912).

Dickinson, J.A. "French and British Attitudes to Native Peoples in Colonial North America," *Storia Nordamericana* 4 (1987): 41–45.

Dixon, Robert. *The Course of Empire: Neo-Classical Culture in New South Wales 1788–1860* (Melbourne & Oxford: Oxford UP, 1986).

Duly, Leslie Clement. *British Land Policy at the Cape 1795-1844: A Study of Administrative Procedures in the Empire* (Durham NC: Duke UP, 1968).

Eccles, William John. *The Canadian Frontier 1534–1760* (New York: Holt, Rinehart & Winston, 1969).

Edwards, Isobel Eirlys. *The 1820 Settlers in South Africa: A Study in British Colonial Policy* (London: Longmans, Green, 1934).

Eldershaw, Marjorie Barnard. *Phillip of Australia: An Account of the Settlement at Sydney Cove 1788–1792* (London: George G. Harrap, 1938).

Elphick, Richard. *Khoikhoi and the Founding of White South Africa* (Johannesburg: Ravan, 1985).

——, & V.C. Malherbe, "The Khoisan to 1828," in *The Shaping of South African Society, 1652–1840*, ed. Elphick & Giliomee, 3–65.

——, & Hermann Giliomee, ed. *The Shaping of South African Society, 1652–1840* (Pinelands: Maskew Miller Longman, 1989).

Else–Mitchell, R. "Territorial Conquest – Phillip and Afterwards," *The Victorian Historical Journal* 46.3 (August 1975): 429–46.

Evatt, Elizabeth. "The Acquisition of Territory in Australia and New Zealand," in *Grotian Society Papers*; 1968: *Studies in the History of the Law of Nations*, ed. Charles Henry Alexandrowicz (The Hague: Martinus Nijhoff, 1970): 16–45.

Fairchild, Hoxie Neale. *The Noble Savage: A Study in Romantic Naturalism* (New York: Russell & Russell, 1961).

Forbes, Duncan. "Natural Law and the Scottish Enlightenment," in *The Origins and Nature of the Scottish Enlightenment* ed. Roy Hutcheson Campbell & Andrew Skinner (Edinburgh: John Donald, 1982): 186–205.

Fredrickson, George M. *White Supremacy: A Comparative Study in American and South African History* (New York: Oxford UP, 1981).

Frost, Alan. *Arthur Phillip 1783–1814: His Voyaging* (Melbourne: Oxford UP, 1987).

——. *Botany Bay Mirages: Illusions of Australia's Convict Beginnings* (Carleton, Victoria: Melbourne UP, 1995).

——. *Convicts and Empire: A Naval Question 1776–1811* (Melbourne: Oxford UP, 1980).

——. "A Strange Illumination of the Heart," *Meanjin Quarterly* 29 (1970): 446–52.

——, ed. *Dreams of a Pacific Empire: Sir George Young's Proposal for a Colonization of New South Wales (1784–1785)* (Sydney: Resolution Press, 1980).

Galbraith, John S. *Reluctant Empire: British Policy on the South African Frontier 1834–1854* (Berkeley: U of California P, 1963).

Getty, Ian A.L., & Antoine S. Lussier, ed. *As Long as the Sun Shines and Water Flows: A Reader in Canadian Native Studies* (Vancouver: U of British Columbia P, 1983).

Giliomee, Hermann. "The Eastern Frontier, 1770–1812," in *The Shaping of South African Society, 1652–1840*, ed. Elphick & Giliomee, 421–71.

Gillen, Mollie. "The Botany Bay Decision, 1786: Convicts, not Empire," *English Historical Review* 97 (1982): 740–66.

Glausser, Wayne. "Three Approaches to Locke and the Slave Trade," in *Race, Gender and Rank*, ed. Horowitz, 31–48.

Graham, Gerald Sandford. *British Policy and Canada 1774–1791: A Study in Eighteenth Century Trade Policy* (London: Longmans, 1930).

Gray, John Milner. *A History of the Gambia* (Cambridge: Cambridge UP, 1940).

Hackshaw, Frederika. "Nineteenth Century Notions of Aboriginal Title and their Influence on the Interpretation of the Treaty of Waitangi," in *Waitangi, Maori and Pakeha Perspectives on the Treaty of Waitangi*, ed. I.H. Kawharu (Auckland: Oxford UP, 1989): 92–121.

Hammond, John Lawrence, & Barbara Hammond. *The Village Labourer 1760–1832: A Study in the Government of England before the Reform Bill* (1927; London: Longman, 1978).

Hampson, Norman. *The Enlightenment: An Evaluation of its Assumptions, Attitudes, and Values* (1968; Harmondsworth: Penguin, 1990).

Hanke, Lewis. *Aristotle and the American Indian: A Study in Race Prejudice in the Modern World* (Bloomington: Indiana UP, 1959).

——. *All Mankind is One: A Study of the Disputation between Bartholome de Las Casas and Juan Gines de Sepulveda in 1550 on the Intelligence and Religious Capacity of the American Indians* (Dekalb: Northern Illinois UP, 1974).

Harlow, Vincent Todd. *The Founding of the Second British Empire 1763–1793*, 2 vols. (London: Longmans & New York: Green, 1952–64).

Heydte, Friderich August Freiherr von der. "Discovery, Symbolic Annexation and Virtual Effectiveness in International Law," *American Journal of International Law* 29 (1935): 448–71.

Hodgen, Margaret Trabue. *Early Anthropology in the Sixteenth and Seventeenth Centuries* (Philadelphia: U of Pennsylvania P, 1964).

Honour, Hugh. *The New Golden Land: European Images of America from the Discoveries to the Present Time* (London: Allen Lane the Penguin Press, 1976).

Horowitz, Maryanne Cline, ed. *Race, Gender and Rank: Early Modern Ideas of Humanity* (Rochester NY: U of Rochester P, 1992).

Horton, David, ed. *Encyclopedia of Aboriginal Australia: Aboriginal and Torres Strait Islander History, Society and Culture*, 2 vols. (Canberra: Aboriginal Studies Press, 1994).

Hulme, Peter, & Neil L. Whitehead, ed. *Wild Majesty: Encounters with Caribs from Columbus to the Present Day; An Anthology* (Oxford: Oxford UP, 1992).

Humphreys, R.A. "Lord Shelburne and British Colonial Policy, 1766–1768," *English Historical Review* 50 (1935): 257–77.

——. "Lord Shelburne and the Royal Proclamation of 1763," *English Historical Review* 49 (1934): 241–65.

Hyam, Ronald. "British Imperial Expansion in the late Eighteenth Century," *Historical Journal* 10 (1967): 113–31.

——, & Ged Martin, ed. *Reappraisals in British Imperial History* (London: Macmillan, 1975).

Hylson-Smith, Kenneth. *Evangelicals in the Church of England* (Edinburgh: T & T Clark, 1988).

Jacobs, Wilbur Ripley. "British–Colonial Attitudes and Policies toward the Indian in the American Colonies," in *Attitudes of Colonial Powers Toward the American Indian*, ed. Peckham & Gibson, 81–106.

——. *Dispossessing the American Indian: Indians and Whites on the Colonial Frontier* (New York: Charles Scribner's Sons, 1972).

Jaenen, Cornelius John. *Friend and Foe: Aspects of French-Amerindian Cultural Contact in the Sixteenth and Seventeenth Centuries* (Toronto & New York: McClelland & Stewart, 1976).

——. "The Meeting of the French and the Amerindians in the Seventeenth Century," in *Interpreting Canada's Past*, ed. Bumsted, vol. 1: 27–33.

Jay, Elisabeth. *The Evangelical and Oxford Movements* (Cambridge: Cambridge UP, 1983).

Janson, Susan, & Stuart Macintyre, ed. *Through White Eyes* (Sydney: Allen & Unwin, 1990).

Jennings, Francis. *The Invasion of America: Indians, Colonialism and the Cant of Conquest* (Chapel Hill: U of North Carolina P, 1976).

Jones, Dorothy V. *License for Empire: Colonialism by Treaty in Early America* (Chicago & London: U of Chicago P, 1982).

Juricek, John. "English Territorial Claims in North America under Elizabeth and the Early Stuarts," *Terra Incognita* 7 (1976): 7–22.

Katzen, M.F. "White Settlers and the Origin of a New Society, 1652–1778," in *A History of South Africa to 1870*, ed. Wilson & Thompson, 187–232.

Keegan,Timothy. *Colonial South Africa and the Origins of the Racial Order* (Cape Town & London: David Philip, 1996).

Kennedy, John Harold. *Jesuit and Savage in New France* (New Haven CT: Yale UP, 1950).

King, Jonathan, ed. *In the Beginning ...: The Story of the Creation of Australia from the Original Writings* (Melbourne: Macmillan, 1985).

King, Robert. "Terra Australis: Terra Nullius aut Terra Aboriginum," *Journal of the Royal Australian Historical Society* 72 (1986): 75–91.

Knaplund, Paul. *James Stephen and the British Colonial System 1813–1847* (1953; Westport CT: Greenwood, 1974).

Kociumbas, Jan. *The Oxford History of Australia*, vol. 2: *1770–1860 Possessions* (Oxford & Melbourne: Oxford UP, 1992).

Kupperman, Karen Ordahl. *Settling with the Indians: The Meeting of English and Indian Cultures in America 1580–1640* (Totowa NJ: Rowman & Littlefield, 1980).

Lamar, Howard, & Leonard Thompson. *The Frontier in History: North America and South Africa compared* (New Haven CT: Yale UP, 1981).

Lawson, Philip. *The Imperial Challenge: Quebec and Britain in the Age of the American Revolution* (Montreal & London: McGill–Queen's UP, 1989).

Lebovics, Herman. "The Uses of America in Locke's *Second Treatise of Government*" (1986), in *Race, Gender and Rank*, ed. Horowitz, 49–63.

Lester, Geoffrey S. *Inuit Territorial Rights in the Canadian Northwest Territories: A Survey of the Legal Problems* (Nunavut: Tungavik Federation, 1984).

——. "Primitivism versus Civilization: A Basic Question in the Law of Aboriginal Rights to Land," in *Our Footprints are Everywhere*, ed. Carol Brice–Bennett (Nain: Labrador Inuit Association, 1977): 351–74.

——, & Graham Parker. "Land Rights: the Australian Aborigines have lost a Legal Battle, but ...," *Alberta Law Review* 11 (1973): 189–237.

Lindley, M.F. *The Acquisition and Government of Backward Territories in International Law being a Treatise on the Law and Practice Relating to Colonial Expansion* (London: Longmans, Green, 1926).

Llewellyn Smith, Hubert. *The Board of Trade* (New York & London: G.P. Putnam's Sons, 1928).

Lovejoy, Arthur O. *The Great Chain of Being: A Study of the History of an Idea* (1936; Cambridge MA & London: Harvard UP, 1978).

——. *Essays in the History of Ideas* (1948; Westport CT: Greenwood, 1978).

McFarlane, Anthony. *The British in the Americas 1480–1815* (London: Longman, 1994).

McHugh, Paul. *The Maori Magna Carta: New Zealand Law and the Treaty of Waitangi* (Auckland: Oxford UP, 1991).

Mackay, David L. "Direction and Purpose in British Imperial History, 1783–1801," *Historical Journal* 17.3 (1974): 487–501.

——. "Far-Flung Empire: A Neglected Imperial Outpost at Botany Bay 1788–1801," *Journal of Imperial and Commonwealth History* 9.1 (October 1980): 125–45.

——. *A Place of Exile: The European Settlement of New South Wales* (Oxford & Melbourne: Oxford UP, 1985).

Maclennan, Ben. *A Proper Degree of Terror* (Johannesburg: Ravan, 1986).

Macmillan, William Miller. *Bantu, Boer and Briton: The Making of the South African Native Problem* (London: Faber & Gwyer, 1929).

——. *The Cape Colour Question: A Historical Survey* (London: Faber & Gwyer, 1927).

McNeil, Kent. *Common Law Aboriginal Title* (Oxford: Clarendon, 1989).

Madden, A.F., & Wyndraeth Humphries Morris–Jones, ed. *Australia and Britain, Studies in a Changing Relationship* (London: Frank Cass, 1980).

Manning, Helen Taft. *British Colonial Government after the American Revolution 1782–1820* (New Haven CT:Yale UP & London: Oxford UP, 1933).

Manning, William Ray "The Nootka Sound Controversy," *Annual Report of the American Historical Association* (1904): 283–479.

Marais, Johannes Stephanus. *The Cape Coloured People 1652–1937* (1939; Johannesburg: Witwatersrand UP, 1957).

Marshall, Peter [James]. “Colonial Protest and Imperial Retrenchment: Indian Policy 1764–68,” *American Studies* 5.1 (1971): 1–17.

——. “The Eighteenth Century Empire,” in *British Politics and Society from Walpole to Pitt 1742–1789*, ed. Jeremy Black (Basingstoke: Macmillan, 1990): 177–200.

——. “The First and Second British Empires: A Question of Demarcation,” *History* 49.165 (February 1964): 14–23.

——, & Glyndwr Williams. *The Great Map of Mankind: British Perceptions of the World in the Age of Enlightenment* (London: Dent, 1982).

Martin, Ged. *The Founding of Australia: The Argument about Australia's Origins* (Sydney: Hale & Iremonger, 1978).

Meek, Ronald Lindley. *Social Science and the Ignoble Savage* (Cambridge: Cambridge UP, 1976).

Merrell, James H. “‘The Customes of Our Countrey’: Indians and Colonists in Early America,” in *Strangers within the Realm*, ed. Bailyn & Morgan, 117–56.

Miller, James Rodger. *Skyscrapers Hide the Heavens: A History of Indian–White Relations in Canada* (Toronto & London: Toronto UP, 1989).

Milloy, John S. “The Early Indian Acts: Developmental Strategy and Constitutional Change,” in *As Long as the Sun Shines and the Water Flows*, ed. Getty & Lussier, 56–64.

Morgan, Edmund Sears. *American Slavery, American Freedom: The Ordeal of Colonial Virginia* (New York: W.W. Norton, 1975).

Namier, Lewis B. *England in the Age of the American Revolution* (London: Macmillan, 1930).

——. *The Structure of Politics at the Accession of George III*, 2 vols. (London: Macmillan, 1928).

Newton, Nell Jessup “At the Whim of the Sovereign: Aboriginal Title Reconsidered,” *Hastings Law Journal* 31 (July 1980):1215–85.

Newton–King, Susan. “The Labour Market of the Cape Colony, 1807–1828,” in *Economy and Society in Pre-Industrial South Africa,* ed. Shula Marks & Anthony Attmore (London: Longman, 1980): 171–207.

——, & V.C. Malherbe. *The Khoikhoi Rebellion in the Eastern Cape (1799–1803)* (Communications No. 5; Cape Town: Centre for African Studies, 1981).

Norris, John M. “The Policy of the British Cabinet in the Nootka Crisis,” *English Historical Review* 70 (1955):562–80.

Oldham, W. Hugh, ed. *Britain's Convicts to the Colonies by Wilfried Oldham* (Sydney: Library of Australian History, 1990).

Pagden, Anthony R. *The Fall of Natural Man: the American Indian and the Origins of Comparative Ethnology* (Cambridge: Cambridge UP, 1986).

Parkman, Francis. *The Conspiracy of Pontiac*, 2 vols. (1870; London: Macmillan, 1899).

Parry, J.H., Philip M. Sherlock & Anthony P. Maingot. *A Short History of the West Indies* (Basingstoke: Macmillan Caribbean, 1987).

Peckham, Howard H. *Pontiac and the Indian Uprising* (Princeton NJ: Princeton UP, 1947).

——, & Charles Gibson, ed. *Attitudes of Colonial Powers Toward the American Indian* (Salt Lake City: U of Utah P, 1969)

Peires, J.B. *The House of Phalo: A History of the Xhosa People in the Days of their Independence* (Johannesburg: Ravan, 1981).

Penn, Nigel. "The Northern Cape Frontier Zone 1700–c.1815" (unpublished doctoral dissertation, Cape Town University, 1995).

Plattner, Marc F. *Rousseau's State of Nature: An Interpretation of the Discouse on Inequality* (Dekalb: Northern Illinois UP, 1979).

Porter, Harry C. *The Inconstant Savage: England and the North American Indian 1500–1660* (London: Duckworth, 1979).

Pratt, Mary Louise. *Imperial Eyes: Studies in Travel Writing and Transculturation* (London & New York: Routledge, 1992).

Priestley, L.J. "Communal Native Title and the Common Law: Further Thoughts on the Gove Land Rights Case," *Federal Law Review* 6 (1974): 150–73.

Prucha, Francis Paul. *American Indian Policy in the Formative Years: The Indian Trade and Intercourse Acts 1790–1834* (Cambridge MA: Harvard UP, 1962).

Reese, Trevor Richard. "The Origins of Colonial America and New South Wales: An Essay on British Imperial Policy in the Eighteenth Century," *Australian Journal of Politics and History* 7.2 (November 1961): 186–97.

Reitan, Earl A. *Politics, War and Empire: The Rise of Britain to a World Power* (Arlington Heights IL; Harlan Davidson, 1994).

Reyburn, H.A. "Studies in Cape Frontier History," *The Critic* 3.1 (October 1934): 40–56.

Reynolds, Henry. *Aboriginal Sovereignty: Reflections on Race, State and Nation* (St. Leonards, NSW: Allen & Unwin, 1996).

——. *Frontier* (Sydney & Boston MA: Allen & Unwin, 1987).

——. *The Law of the Land* (Ringwood, Victoria: Penguin Australia, 1987).

——. *The Other Side of the Frontier* (1981; Ringwood, Victoria & Harmondsworth: Penguin, 1982).

Robinson, Ronald, & John Gallagher, with Alice Denny. *Africa and the Victorians: the Official Mind of Imperialism* (London: Macmillan & New York: St Martin's, 1961).

Ross, Andrew. *John Philip (1775–1851): Missions, Race and Politics in South Africa* (Aberdeen: Aberdeen UP, 1986).

Rowley, C.D. *The Destruction of Aboriginal Society* (Ringwood, Victoria: Penguin, 1972).

Sainty, John Christopher. *Colonial Office Officials: Officials of the Secretary of State for War 1794–1801 of the Secretary of State for War and Colonies 1801–1854, and of the Secretary of State for Colonies 1854–1870* (London: Institute of Historical Research, 1976).

——. *Home Office Officials 1782–1870* (London: Athlone, 1975).

Schutte, Gerrit. “Company and Colonists at the Cape, 1625–1795,” in *The Shaping of South African Society, 1652–1840*, ed. Elphick & Giliomee, 283–323.

Schwartz, Bill. “Conquerors of Truth: Reflections on Postcolonial Theory,” in *The Expansion of England: Race, Ethnicity and Cultural History*, ed. Bill Schwartz (London & New York: Routledge, 1996): 9–31.

Scott, Ernest. “Taking Possession of Australia – The Doctrine of ‘Terra Nullius’ (No-Man's Land),” *Journal and Proceedings of the Royal Australian Historical Society* 26.1 (1940): 1–19.

Shaw, A.G.L. “British Policy towards the Australian Aborigines 1830–50,” *Australian Historical Studies* 25 (1992–93): 265–85.

——. *Convicts and the Colonies: A Study of Penal Transportation from Great Britain and Ireland to Australia and other Parts of the British Empire* (London: Faber & Faber, 1966).

——. “London and the Governors: Relations in Eastern Australia 1825–45,” in *Australia and Britain*, ed. Madden & Morris–Jones, 1–20.

——. “James Stephen and Colonial Policy: The Australian Experience,” *Journal of Imperial and Commonwealth History* 20.1 (January 1992): 11–34.

Sheehan, Bernard. *Savagism and Civility: Indians and Englishmen in Colonial Virginia* (Cambridge: Cambridge UP, 1980).

Simsarian, James. “The Acquisition of Legal Title to Terra Nullius,” *Political Science Quarterly* 53.1 (1938): 111–28.

Slattery, Brian. *Ancestral Lands, Alien Laws: Judicial Perspectives on Aboriginal Title* (Saskatchewan: University of Saskatchewan Native Law Centre, 1983).

Slotkin, James Sydney, ed. *Readings in Early Anthropology* (London: Methuen, 1965).

Smith, Bernard. *European Vision and the South Pacific 1768–1850: A Study in the History of Art and Ideas* (Oxford: Clarendon, 1960).

Smith, Joseph Henry. *Appeals to the Privy Council from the American Plantations* (New York: Columbia UP, 1950).

Sosin, Jack Marvin. *English America and the Revolution of 1688: Royal Administration and the Structure of Provincial Government* (Lincoln: U of Nebraska P, 1982).

——. “The Use of the Indians in the War of the American Revolution: A Re-Assessment of Responsibility,” *Canadian Historical Review* 46.2 (June 1965): 101–21.

——. *Whitehall and the Wilderness: The Middle West in British Colonial Policy 1760–1775* (Lincoln: U of Nebraska P, 1961).

Spector, Margaret Marion. *The American Department of the British Government 1768–1782* (1940; New York: Octagon, 1976).

Stanner, W.E.H. *After the Dreaming: Black and White Australians; An Anthropologist’s View* (Sydney: Australian Broadcasting Commission, 1968).

——. “The History of Indifference thus Begins,” *Aboriginal History* 1.1 (1977): 2–26.

Starke, Joseph Gabriel. *An Introduction to International Law* (1947; London: Butterworth, 1963).

Stepan, Nancy. *The Idea of Race in Science: Great Britain 1800–1960* (London: Macmillan, 1982).

Stocking, George Ward, Jr. *Race, Culture and Evolution: Essays in the History of Anthropology* (Chicago & London: U of Chicago P, 1982).

Strange, Ian John. *The Falkland Islands* (London: David & Charles, 1983).

Theal, George McCall. *History of South Africa from 1795 to 1872*, 5 vols. (1888–93; London: Allen & Unwin, 1915–20).

Thomson, Mark Alméras. *The Secretaries of State 1681–1782* (London: Frank Cass, 1968).

Tobias, John L. "Protection, Civilization, Assimilation: An Outline of the History of Canada's Indian Policy," in *As Long as the Sun Shines and Water Flows*, ed. Getty & Lussier, 39–55.

Trelease, Allen W. "Dutch Treatment of the American Indian, with Particular Reference to New Netherland," in *Attitudes of Colonial Powers Toward the American Indian*, ed. Peckham & Gibson, 47–60.

Turner, L.C.F. "The Cape of Good Hope and the Anglo-French Conflict, 1797–1806," *Historical Studies, Australia and New Zealand* 9 (1959–1961): 368–78.

Vaughan, Alden T. *New England Frontier: Puritans and Indians 1620–1675* (Boston MA & Toronto: Little, Brown, 1965).

Vinding Kruse, Frederik. *Hume's Philosophy in his Principal Work "A Treatise of Human Nature" and in his Essays*, tr. P.T. Federspiel (London: Oxford UP, 1939).

Wade, Mason. "The French and the Indians," in *Attitudes of Colonial Powers Toward the American Indian*, ed. Peckham & Gibson, 61–80.

Ward, John Manning. *British Policy in the South Pacific* (Sydney: Australasian Publishing Company, 1948).

Washburn, Wilcomb Edward. *Red Man's Land/White Man's Law* (Norman: U of Oklahoma P, 1995).

Wickwire, Franklin Bacon. *British Subministers and Colonial America 1763–1783* (Princeton NJ: Princeton UP, 1966).

Williams, Glyndwr. "'The common centre of we discoverers': Sir Joseph Banks, Exploration and Empire in the late Eighteenth Century," in *Sir Joseph Banks: A Global Perspective,* ed. R.E.R. Banks et al. (Kew: Royal Botanical Gardens, 1994): 177–91.

——. "'Far more Happier than we Europeans': Reactions to the Australian Aborigines on Cook's voyage," in *Through White Eyes*, ed. Janson & Macintyre, 51–64.

——. "Seamen and Philosophers in the South Seas in the Age of Captain Cook," *The Mariner's Mirror* 65 (1979): 3–22.

Williams, Robert A. Jr. *The American Indian in Western Legal Thought: The Discourses of Conquest* (Oxford & New York: Oxford UP, 1990).

Wilson, Bruce. "The Struggle for Wealth and Power at Fort Niagara 1775–1783," in *Interpreting Canada's Past*, ed. Bumsted, vol. 1: 124–38.

Wilson, Monica. "Co-operation and Conflict: The Eastern Cape Frontier," in Wilson & Thompson, ed. *A History of South Africa to 1870*, 233–71.

——. “The Hunters and Herders,” in Wilson & Thompson, ed. *A History of South Africa to 1870*, 41–74.

——. “The Nguni People,” in Wilson & Thompson, ed. *A History of South Africa to 1870*, 75–131.

——, & Leonard Thompson, ed. *A History of South Africa to 1870* (London: Croom Helm, 1982).

Wise, S.F. “The American Revolution and Indian History,” in *Character and Circumstance: Essays in Honour of Donald Grant Creighton*, ed. John S. Moir (Toronto: Macmillan of Canada, 1970): 182–201.

Young, Douglas MacMurray. *The Colonial Office in the Early Nineteenth Century* (London: Longmans, 1961).

Youngblood Henderson, James. “Unraveling the Riddle of Aboriginal Title,” *American Indian Law Review* 5 (1975): 75–137.